Ghosts in Enlightenment Scotland

SCOTTISH HISTORICAL REVIEW MONOGRAPH SERIES

SCOTTISH HISTORICAL REVIEW MONOGRAPH SECOND SERIES

The Scottish Historical Review Monograph Second Series aims to promote major works of scholarly research covering any aspect or period of Scottish history. The series seeks, in particular, to support the work of early-career scholars active in the discipline. Its volumes are selected in partnership with the Trustees of the *Scottish Historical Review*.

Proposals or queries may be sent directly to the series editor at the address given below; all submissions will receive prompt attention before being sent to expert readers.

Professor Steve Boardman, School of History, Classics and Archaeology, William Robertson Wing, Doorway 4, Teviot Place, University of Edinburgh, EH8 9AG.

Details of volumes in the first series are available from Edinburgh University Press.

Previous volumes in the second series:

1. *The Scots in Australia, 1788–1938*, Benjamin Wilkie (2017)

Ghosts in Enlightenment Scotland

Martha McGill

THE BOYDELL PRESS

First published 2018
The Boydell Press, Woodbridge

ISBN 978-1-78327-362-1

The Boydell Press is an imprint of Boydell & Brewer Ltd
PO Box 9, Woodbridge, Suffolk IP12 3DF, UK
and of Boydell & Brewer Inc.
668 Mt Hope Avenue, Rochester, NY 14620–2731, USA
website: www.boydellandbrewer.com

A catalogue record for this book is available
from the British Library

This publication is printed on acid-free paper

MIX
Paper from
responsible sources
FSC® C013056
FSC
www.fsc.org

Printed and bound in Great Britain by TJ International Ltd, Padstow, Cornwall

To my parents

Contents

Acknowledgements

While writing this book, I have been supported and inspired by numerous colleagues and friends. I am especially grateful for the patience, kindness and expertise of Julian Goodare and Thomas Ahnert, who have offered advice and constructive criticism on innumerable occasions. Colin Kidd and Esther Mijers gave me substantial guidance and encouragement, and I have drawn on stimulating discussions with Adam Fox, Stana Nenadic, Alasdair Raffe, Dòmhnall Uilleam Stiùbhart and Louise Yeoman. I am indebted to Adam Budd for convincing me to embark on this project in the first place, and to Sarah Daw for moral support during the latter phases of writing. I have also received helpful comments from the Scottish Historical Review Trust's anonymous readers.

I gratefully acknowledge the support of the Arts and Humanities Research Council, which funded the bulk of this research, and the Institute for Advanced Studies in the Humanities, Edinburgh, where I was welcomed as a Fellow for part of the writing process. I also owe thanks to staff at Aberdeen University Library, the British Library, Edinburgh City Archives, Edinburgh University Library, Glasgow University Library, the National Library of Scotland and St Andrews University Library.

It is nice, now and then, to be distracted from the dead. On this front, I am particularly thankful to Alice, Boris, Katherine, and the community at the Columcille Centre, Edinburgh. My partner, Matt, has supported and fed me from the earliest phases of this research. Finally, I am grateful to my family for the love and books, and to my parents especially for their advice and encouragement, both for the gestation of this project and for some time previously. This book is dedicated to them.

Abbreviations

AUL	Aberdeen University Library
BL	British Library
DSL	Dictionary of the Scots Language
GUL	Glasgow University Library
NLS	National Library of Scotland
NRS	National Records of Scotland
OED Online	Oxford English Dictionary Online
Oxford DNB	Oxford Dictionary of National Biography
StA	St Andrews University Library
STC	Short Title Catalogue

Introduction

Over the last five hundred years, the figure of the ghost has allegedly died many a death. After the Reformation (1560 in Scotland), Protestant theologians attempted to rout ghosts from their tenuous place within the Christian framework, and in 1597 James VI boasted that a Scotsman would scarcely ever hear word of 'Ghostes and spirites'.[1] Sceptical approaches towards the supernatural flourished during the Enlightenment, such that ghosts were said to have been 'chased from the realities of existence ... before the light of the sun of science'.[2] The nineteenth-century folklorist Walter Gregor blamed industrialisation, declaring that ghosts were scared away by 'the scream of the railway whistle', while the literary scholars Peter Buse and Andrew Stott suggested that twentieth-century western society had replaced ghosts with aliens and conspiracy theories.[3] Nevertheless, the idea of the ghost has – appropriately enough – lingered on post-mortem. Polls have consistently suggested that between 30 and 40 per cent of British adults believe in ghosts, a marked increase from 10 to 20 per cent in the 1950s.[4] Ghosts have retained a prominent position within popular culture, and over the last few decades they have increasingly infiltrated the academic world. Scholars of diverse disciplines are coming to recognise the ways in which ghosts can reflect on societal development.

Scotland has long been characterised as a haunted nation. An 1842 magazine article declared: 'Were we seriously asked what part of Christendom, whether in remoter ages or comparatively modern times, was most troubled with supernatural horrors, we should without doubt or hesitation, answer, "Scotland"'. It went on to explain that when it came to ghosts, the 'best known

1 James VI, *Daemonologie, in Forme of Ane Dialogue*, in James Craigie and Alexander Law (eds), *Minor Prose Works of King James VI and I* (Edinburgh, 1982), bk. 2, ch. 7, 37.

2 J. Mitchell and John Dickie, *The Philosophy of Witchcraft* (Paisley, 1839), 355.

3 Walter Gregor, *Notes on the Folk-Lore of the North-East of Scotland* (London, 1881), 3; Peter Buse and Andrew Stott, 'Introduction: A Future for Haunting', in Peter Buse and Andrew Stott (eds), *Ghosts: Deconstruction, Psychoanalysis, History* (Basingstoke, 1999), 1.

4 Owen Davies, *The Haunted: A Social History of Ghosts* (New York, 2007), 241. See also Paul Cowdell, 'Belief in Ghosts in Post-War England' (University of Hertfordshire Ph.D. thesis, 2011), 1. For a recent poll see BMG Research, 'British Public Reveal Their Beliefs in New Survey', May 2017 (Bostock Marketing Group), http://www.bmgresearch.co.uk/british-public-reveal-beliefs-new-survey, accessed 1 Feb. 2018.

and most widely diffused of all the spectral race', Scotland had more than any other part of Europe, and probably more than half of Europe put together.[5] Admittedly, similar claims have been made for a host of other countries, including England and Wales.[6] Narratives of Scottish exceptionalism should be read with caution. But whether or not Scotland is especially haunted, historical ghosts have occasionally taken on a Scottish tinge, and have been used by Scots to navigate concepts of national identity.

This book is particularly concerned with the period from 1685, when a university professor called George Sinclair published a collection of supernatural stories, to the death of Walter Scott in 1832. I sometimes refer to this period as the 'long eighteenth century', borrowing a term that is generally employed by British historians to refer to the period from the 1688 Revolution to the 1815 Battle of Waterloo, or sometimes the 1832 Reform Act. I also refer to 'Enlightenment Scotland'. The Enlightenment was traditionally located in the period between the 1740s and the 1790s. However, in recent decades the Enlightenment has been stretched at both ends. Scholars now tend to locate the origins of the Enlightenment in the 1670s, and trace its influence up to at least the 1830s.[7]

My focus in this book is not on the Scottish Enlightenment per se, but rather on Scotland during the Enlightenment. Philosophers' discussions of spirits form only a narrow segment of my discussion. The Enlightenment does, however, provide important framing. Academic culture has increasingly rejected simplistic visions of Enlightenment rationality, but there remains a popular perception that the intellectual developments of the eighteenth century overhauled a fantastical pre-modern worldview.[8] It is undeniable that attitudes towards the supernatural evolved significantly in Enlightenment Scotland. Intellectuals increasingly explained mysterious occurrences in natural, rather than supernatural, terms. Witch-hunting came to an end, and much ink was spilled bemoaning the superstitious inclinations of the uneducated. However,

5 'A Sketch of Scotch Diablerie in General', *Fraser's Magazine for Town and Country*, Mar. 1842, 317, 318.

6 Davies, *Haunted*, 1; Richard Holland, *Haunted Wales* (Stroud, 2011), 8.

7 See the discussions in David Allan, 'Enlightenment (1660–1843): General (Including Philosophy)', in Michael Lynch (ed.), *Oxford Companion to Scottish History*, electronic edn (University of Oxford, 2007), http://www.oxfordreference.com/view/10.1093/acref/9780199234820.001.0001/acref-9780199234820-e-74?rskey=qoL62n&result=1#acref-9780199234820-eSub-0040, accessed 1 Feb. 2018; R. H. Campbell and Andrew S. Skinner (eds), *The Origins and Nature of the Scottish Enlightenment* (Edinburgh, 1982); Roger Emerson, 'The Contexts of the Scottish Enlightenment', in Alexander Broadie (ed.), *The Cambridge Companion to the Scottish Enlightenment* (Cambridge, 2003), 9–30; Alexander Broadie, 'The Rise (and Fall?) of the Scottish Enlightenment', in T. M. Devine and Jenny Wormald (eds), *The Oxford Handbook of Modern Scottish History* (Oxford, 2012), 370–85.

8 This perception is built upon older scholarship. Perhaps the most influential proponent of the traditional picture of Enlightenment rationalism is Peter Gay, *The Enlightenment: An Interpretation* (New York, 1966).

I argue that this was also a period when ghosts attained a new cultural prominence. The study of ghosts will not revolutionise our conception of eighteenth-century culture, but it does add nuance, and demonstrates the layers of complexity involved in any process of social change.

The study of the supernatural has only recently found its place within the world of academic history. It has been hindered by the long-standing perception that supernatural beliefs cease to be relevant as societies progress into modernity. Max Weber famously argued that the Reformation inaugurated a gradual 'disenchantment of the world': religion became less dependent on ritual and sacramental magic, which laid the groundwork for subsequent secularisation and rationalisation.[9] There was an important step forward for the historical study of ghosts in 1971: Keith Thomas devoted a chapter to 'Ghosts and Fairies' in his ground-breaking *Religion and the Decline of Magic*. Thomas allowed seventeenth-century English ghosts a significant role in upholding moral standards and social norms. However, he was working in the Weberian tradition, and suggested that ghosts faded away over the eighteenth century, losing their 'social relevance'.[10] Thereafter, Enlightenment ghosts vanished from historians' radars for another few decades. The one significant exception is R. C. Finucane's *Appearances of the Dead: A Cultural History of Ghosts* (1982), later revised as *Ghosts: Appearances of the Dead and Cultural Transformation* (1996). Finucane's work is useful as an introduction to European ghosts from antiquity onwards, but it covers too broad a geographical area and too long a timespan to delve into much detail. Finucane also follows in Thomas's footsteps, arguing that 'apparitions ... no longer played an important part in the serious debates of the articulate' during the Enlightenment. Ghosts were 'victims of eighteenth-century rationality', such that 'the apparition-world went into eclipse'.[11]

According to Buse and Stott, it is in theoretical texts that we can find the twentieth century's most significant engagements with the figure of the ghost. In particular, they highlight the importance of ghosts within psychoanalysis and deconstruction.[12] Jacques Derrida's 1993 *Spectres de Marx* pioneered this approach.[13] Derrida's spectres are 'standard-bearers of deconstructionism',

9 For example, Max Weber, 'Science as a Vocation', in H. H. Gerth and C. Wright Mills (eds), *From Max Weber: Essays in Sociology* (New York, 1946), 139.

10 Keith Thomas, *Religion and the Decline of Magic: Studies in Popular Beliefs in Sixteenth and Seventeenth Century England* (London, 1971), 706, 724.

11 R. C. Finucane, *Ghosts: Appearances of the Dead and Cultural Transformation* (Amherst [N.Y.], 1996), 165–9 (quotations 165 and 169).

12 Buse and Stott, 'Introduction', 5.

13 Jacques Derrida, *Specters of Marx: The State of the Debt, the Work of Mourning, and the New International*, trans. Peggy Kamuf (New York, 1994). See Colin Davis, 'État Présent: Hauntology, Spectres and Phantoms', *French Studies* 59 (2005), 373–9.

breaking down barriers between past and present, life and death, body and spirit.[14] His notion of 'hauntology' holds that the present exists only in relation to the past, and that history is formed through the 'spectral iteration' of texts or ideas, such that modern society is fashioned by the ghosts of the past. Derrida employs the ghost as a metaphorical figure, but his analysis is nonetheless significant for those studying encounters with ghosts. The sociologist Avery F. Gordon builds upon Derrida's work to interpret modern-day ghost-sightings as the haunting of the present by dark, repressed aspects of the past, such as slavery. The historian Shane McCorristine speaks of Derrida as forming part of the essential theoretical framework behind his study of late-eighteenth and nineteenth-century ghost belief: his notion of the ghost as being expressive of 'the haunted nature of modern subjectivity' is decidedly in the Derridean tradition.[15]

Folklorists and literary scholars have also made regular forays into the study of the ghost story.[16] Gillian Bennett is perhaps the folklorist whose work is of most interest to the historian: her *Traditions of Belief: Women and the Supernatural* (1987) offers one of the earliest overviews of changing attitudes towards the ghost from the late seventeenth century. Bennett initially suggested that ghosts lost their purposes from the eighteenth century as part of a process of Weberian disenchantment, but this argument is removed from the 1999 revised edition of the work, *Alas Poor Ghost!: Traditions of Belief in Story and Discourse*.[17] The work of literary scholars has also frequently spilled over into reflections on social history. Stephen Greenblatt's 2001 *Hamlet in Purgatory* focuses on the seventeenth century, analysing how the ghost of Hamlet's father expresses a multitude of fears and longings regarding death that were exacerbated by the Protestant rejection of Purgatory.[18] More recently, Pierre Kapitaniak's *Spectres, Ombres et Fantômes: Discours et Représentations Dramatiques en Angleterre, 1576–1642* (2008) provides a meticulous survey of theatrical ghosts, as well as reflecting on the broader discourses that shaped understandings of apparitions.[19] On the eighteenth century, a particularly important work is Terry Castle's *The Female Thermometer: Eighteenth-Century Culture and the Invention of the Uncanny*. Castle offers a more nuanced evaluation of the disenchantment theme,

14 Owen Davies, 'Introduction', in Owen Davies (ed.), *Ghosts: A Social History*, 5 vols (London, 2010), vol. 1, xv; Buse and Stott, 'Introduction', 10.

15 Avery F. Gordon, *Ghostly Matters: Haunting and the Sociological Imagination* (Minneapolis, 2008); Shane McCorristine, *Spectres of the Self: Thinking About Ghosts and Ghost-Seeing in England, 1750–1920* (Cambridge, 2010), 4, 32.

16 See H. R. E. Davidson and W. M. S. Russell (eds), *The Folklore of Ghosts* (Cambridge, 1981), and the discussion in Peter Marshall, *Beliefs and the Dead in Reformation England* (Oxford, 2002), ch. 6.

17 Gillian Bennett, *Traditions of Belief: Women and the Supernatural* (London, 1987), 175–88. An earlier, but less notable folkloric work is Eric Maple, *The Realm of Ghosts* (London, 1964).

18 Stephen Greenblatt, *Hamlet in Purgatory* (Princeton, 2001), 235–57.

19 Pierre Kapitaniak, *Spectres, Ombres et Fantômes: Discours et Représentations Dramatiques en Angleterre, 1576–1642* (Paris, 2008).

arguing that apparitions gradually passed from the realm of objective reality to that of internal, subjective experience.[20]

Historians, too, have increasingly challenged traditional understandings of disenchantment. Particularly notable critiques have come from Robert Scribner, who argues that magic changed rather than disappearing in the wake of the Reformation, and Alexandra Walsham, who suggests that it is more useful to think in terms of cycles of 'desacralization' and 'resacralization'.[21] This has contributed to a surge of historical studies on various supernatural topics in the twenty-first century.[22] There are now plentiful surveys of English conceptions of ghosts. Peter Marshall, Amanda Jane McKeever and John Newton have discussed how apparitions reflect on attitudes towards death and the afterlife in the sixteenth and seventeenth centuries.[23] Sasha Handley, Jo Bath, John Newton and Frederick Valletta have explored the late-seventeenth-century rehabilitation of the ghost by Protestant authorities.[24] Handley's excellent *Visions of an Unseen World: Ghost Beliefs and Ghost Stories in Eighteenth-Century England* (2007) analyses the manifold functions of ghosts in long-eighteenth-century culture. The aforementioned work of Shane McCorristine traces the evolution of ideas about apparitions in the late eighteenth century and beyond, and Karl Bell analyses ghosts (alongside other magical phenomena) in nineteenth-century urban

20 Terry Castle, *The Female Thermometer: Eighteenth-Century Culture and the Invention of the Uncanny* (Oxford, 1995), ch. 10.

21 Robert W. Scribner, 'The Reformation, Popular Magic, and the "Disenchantment of the World"', *Journal of Interdisciplinary History* 23 (1993), 475–94; Alexandra Walsham, 'The Reformation and "The Disenchantment of the World" Reassessed', *Historical Journal* 51 (2008), 497–528.

22 Setting aside works focusing on Scotland, which are outlined below, a few examples include Alexandra Walsham, *Providence in Early Modern England* (Oxford, 1999); William E. Burns, *An Age of Wonders: Prodigies, Politics, and Providence in England, 1657–1727* (Manchester, 2002); Diane Purkiss, *Troublesome Things: A History of Fairies and Fairy Stories* (London, 2000); Euan Cameron, *Enchanted Europe: Superstition, Reason, and Religion, 1250–1750* (Oxford, 2010); Stuart Clark, *Thinking with Demons: The Idea of Witchcraft in Early Modern Europe* (Oxford, 1997).

23 Marshall, *Beliefs and the Dead*; Peter Marshall, 'Deceptive Appearances: Ghosts and Reformers in Elizabethan and Jacobean England', in Helen Parish and William G. Naphy (eds), *Religion and Superstition in Reformation Europe* (Manchester, 2002), 188–208; Amanda Jane McKeever, 'The Ghost in Early Modern Protestant Culture: Shifting Perceptions of the Afterlife, 1450–1700' (University of Sussex D.Phil. thesis, 2010); John Geoffrey Newton, 'An Examination of Interpretations of Ghosts from the Reformation to the Close of the Seventeenth Century' (Durham University Ph.D. thesis, 2003).

24 Sasha Handley, 'Reclaiming Ghosts in 1690s England', in Kate Cooper and Jeremy Gregory (eds), *Signs, Wonders, Miracles: Representations of Divine Power in the Life of the Church* (Woodbridge, 2005), 345–55; Jo Bath and John Newton, '"Sensible Proof of Spirits": Ghost Belief during the Later Seventeenth Century', *Folklore* 117 (2006), 1–14; Frederick Valletta, *Witchcraft, Magic and Superstition in England, 1640–1670* (Aldershot, 2004), ch. 3.

society.[25] More broadly, Owen Davies and Susan Owens have discussed the social and cultural history of ghosts over a long time-span. Focusing on Europe as a whole, Jean-Claude Schmitt and Nancy Caciola have surveyed medieval ghosts, and P. G. Maxwell-Stuart has looked at evolutions in belief from antiquity to the twentieth century.[26] Many of these works take an interdisciplinary approach. Handley draws upon sociolinguistic theories to analyse narrative patterns within ghost stories; Davies delves into the world of folklore; Owens employs literary and art historical analysis; McCorristine's study is quasi-psychological, building on the work of Terry Castle and (as we have seen) Derrida. Nevertheless, they are first and foremost historical studies, and have demonstrated how ghosts can be used as cultural signifiers despite (or because of) the impact of the Reformation and the Enlightenment.

However, while English ghosts have been thoroughly surveyed, there have yet to be any academic works on Scottish ghost belief. Other supernatural phenomena have fared better. Witchcraft in Scotland has attracted a number of excellent studies, and trial records have been catalogued in the online database *The Survey of Scottish Witchcraft* (2003). Fairies, second sight, the Devil and (to a lesser extent) angels have also received scholarly attention.[27] However, none of these works have given more than a brief nod to ghosts. Studies of witchcraft, moreover, tend to focus primarily on the sixteenth and seventeenth centuries; historians have paid less attention to how supernatural belief evolved as the Enlightenment progressed. There is a useful introductory

[25] Sasha Handley, *Visions of an Unseen World: Ghost Beliefs and Ghost Stories in Eighteenth-Century England* (London, 2007); McCorristine, *Spectres of the Self*; Karl Bell, *The Magical Imagination: Magic and Modernity in Urban England, 1780–1914* (Cambridge, 2012).

[26] Davies, *Haunted*; Susan Owens, *The Ghost: A Cultural History* (London, 2017); Jean-Claude Schmitt, *Ghosts in the Middle Ages: The Living and the Dead in Medieval Society*, trans. Teresa Lavender Fagan (Chicago, 1998); Nancy Caciola, *Afterlives: The Return of the Dead in the Middle Ages* (Ithaca [N.Y.], 2016); P. G. Maxwell-Stuart, *Ghosts: A History of Phantoms, Ghouls and Other Spirits of the Dead* (Stroud, 2006).

[27] Julian Goodare et al., *The Survey of Scottish Witchcraft* (University of Edinburgh, 2003), http://www.shca.ed.ac.uk/witches, accessed 1 Feb. 2018; Brian P. Levack, *Witch-Hunting in Scotland: Law, Politics and Religion* (London, 2008); Julian Goodare (ed.), *The Scottish Witch-Hunt in Context* (Manchester, 2002); Julian Goodare, Lauren Martin and Joyce Miller (eds), *Witchcraft and Belief in Early Modern Scotland* (Basingstoke, 2008); Julian Goodare (ed.), *Scottish Witches and Witch-Hunters* (Basingstoke, 2013); Lizanne Henderson and Edward J. Cowan, *Scottish Fairy Belief: A History* (East Linton, 2001); Emma Wilby, *Cunning Folk and Familiar Spirits: Shamanistic Visionary Traditions in Early Modern British Witchcraft and Magic* (Brighton, 2005); Julian Goodare, 'Between Humans and Angels: Scientific Uses for Fairies in Early Modern Scotland', in Michael Ostling (ed.), *Fairies, Demons and Nature Spirits: 'Small Gods' at the Margins of Christendom* (London, 2018), 169–90; Michael Hunter (ed.), *The Occult Laboratory: Magic, Science, and Second Sight in Late Seventeenth-Century Scotland* (Woodbridge, 2001); Michelle D. Brock, *Satan and the Scots: The Devil in Post-Reformation Scotland, c.1560–1700* (Abingdon, 2016); Martha McGill, 'Angels, Devils, and Discernment in Early Modern Scotland', in Michelle D. Brock, Richard Raiswell and David Winter (eds), *Knowing Demons, Knowing Spirits* (Basingstoke, 2018), 239–63.

analysis in Colin Kidd's 'The Scottish Enlightenment and the Supernatural', which appears in Lizanne Henderson's 2009 edited collection *Fantastical Imaginations* (itself a valuable resource on a range of supernatural topics).[28] A more extensive analysis of supernaturalism during the Enlightenment can be found in Paul Kléber Monod's *Solomon's Secret Arts: The Occult in the Age of Enlightenment* (2013). Monod concentrates primarily on practices such as alchemy, astrology and ritual magic, defining 'occult' as 'a type of thinking, expressed either in writing or in action, that allowed the boundary between the natural and the supernatural to be crossed by the actions of human beings'.[29] The Scottish Enlightenment, he argues, succeeded in stamping out the occult, backed by 'a century of determined Presbyterian denunciation of anything occult as diabolical'. This is in contrast to England, where the second half of the eighteenth century saw a 'remarkable revival' of occult thinking.[30] His conclusions underline the value of considering the English and Scottish cases separately.

Finally, Lizanne Henderson's *Witchcraft and Folk Belief in the Age of Enlightenment: Scotland, 1670–1740* (2016) provides a valuable survey of the survival of beliefs about witchcraft and charming. Henderson writes that 'Even at the height of the Enlightenment ... the workings of the "invisible world" had not yet lost their attractions'. She also warns against overly simplistic models of social stratification, positing that in the eighteenth century the 'mood of suspicion and terror' that drove the witch trials 'continued to linger among many Scots at all levels of society'.[31] My own conclusions place less stress on the persistence of fear about witchcraft. Educated people could very well fear the supernatural in the later eighteenth century, but it usually manifested as a dread of the mysterious, otherworldly forces that might lurk in literal or metaphorical recesses, rather than a suspicion that one's neighbours were dabbling in diabolism. However, in emphasising the cultural value of eighteenth-century ghosts, I am broadly in agreement with Henderson's conclusions about the survival of supernatural belief, at diverse levels of society. This is not to argue that supernatural beliefs should be viewed as quaint relics of a bygone era. Eighteenth-century ghosts often recalled older traditions, but were also dynamic figures. Their value to the historical profession stems, in large part, from their tendency to take on new roles in response to changing cultural contexts.

28 Colin Kidd, 'The Scottish Enlightenment and the Supernatural', in Lizanne Henderson (ed.), *Fantastical Imaginations: The Supernatural in Scottish History and Culture* (Edinburgh, 2009), 91–109.

29 Paul Kléber Monod, *Solomon's Secret Arts: The Occult in the Age of Enlightenment* (New Haven, 2013), 5.

30 Ibid., 227, 340–6.

31 Lizanne Henderson, *Witchcraft and Folk Belief in the Age of Enlightenment: Scotland, 1670–1740* (Basingstoke, 2016), 2, 371.

From the medieval period to the early nineteenth century, a variety of terms were used to refer to ghosts. Probably the most common was the generic 'spirit' (or variations such as 'spreit' or 'spreyt'), which could also apply to angels and demons. 'Apparition' was another vague term that appeared with reasonable frequency. The word 'ghost' was used too, along with its Scots equivalent 'ghaist', and variations including 'gost' and 'ghest'. It was understood more broadly than it is today, however: it could refer to the returning dead, but also to a soul or spirit. 'Giving up the ghost' was a common euphemism for dying, and the Holy Ghost was understood to be a spirit. In 1616, a character of the poet William Drummond's lamented that he was left to wail in the fashion of 'some Heaven-banish'd Ghost': here the term perhaps signifies a demon.[32] In 1707, the minister Robert Wodrow recorded a story of a 'gost' that closely resembled a demon: it took the form of 'ane litle old man about the height of the table, with a fearful ougly face, as if it had been all brunt'. It declared that it had come from Hell, and attacked a set of bibles.[33] The 'demon' interpretation does not seem to have been widely recognised, however. In a work published posthumously in 1692, the minister Thomas Bell wrote: 'a Spirit clashing with the Word, is surely a Ghost and an evil Spirit.' The 1705 edition saw fit to revise this to 'a false and an evil spirit'.[34]

It was also possible to use the term to refer to a monstrous living being. The ballad 'King Henry' (Child 32) presents a 'grisly ghost' – a living woman under a spell, who appears as a huge, hideous creature with teeth like tethering stakes.[35] The poets Alexander Montgomerie and William Dunbar also employed the term in this manner. Around 1580, Montgomerie proclaimed that his flyting opponent, Patrick Hume of Polwart, had been born to an ape and abandoned under a bush, swaddled in pig's skin and smeared with soot. The 'Weird Sisters', coming across him, wondered how the 'gaist had been gotten'. In an equally colourful passage from the late fifteenth or early sixteenth century, Dunbar has an unhappy wife complain of her husband:

32 William Drummond, *Poems: By William Drummond, of Hawthorne-Denne* (Edinburgh, 1616, STC 7255), pt. 1, E3v.

33 Robert Wodrow, *Analecta: Or Materials for a History of Remarkable Providences Mostly Relating to Scotch Ministers and Christians*, ed. Matthew Leishman, 4 vols (Edinburgh, 1842–3), vol. 1, 112–14.

34 Thomas Bell, *Nehemiah the Tirshatha, or, The Character of a Good Commissioner to Which Is Added Grapes in the Wilderness* (Edinburgh, 1692), 25; Thomas Bell, *Grapes in the Wilderness: Or, A Discourse of the Dispensations of God towards His People* (Glasgow, 1705), xxi.

35 Francis James Child, *The English and Scottish Popular Ballads*, 5 vols (Boston, 1882–98), vol. 1 pt. 2, 298–9.

> Bot quhen that glourand gaist grippis me about,
> Than think I hiddowus Mahoune hes me in armes;[36]

Over the seventeenth and eighteenth centuries the anglicised 'ghost' gradually became more common, however, and in the eighteenth and early nineteenth centuries the 'returning dead person' definition seems to have become dominant.

'Bogle' is another noteworthy Scots word. It could signify a ghost, but tended to denote a mischievous spirit of uncertain origin. The term cropped up fairly frequently in the sixteenth century, and survived into the nineteenth. An 1817 article described a bogle who was 'neither fairy, ghost, nor brownie, but appears to have partaken somewhat of the peculiar attributes of all the three', while James Hogg explained:

> A fairy is a spirit sweet,
> The Brownie kind an' just, too;
> A ghaist, row'd in its windin' sheet,
> I own, is nought to trust to:
> ...
> But o' the awsome things complete
> To ruin youthfu' sporting,
> A bogle is the warst to meet,
> When fo'ks gang to the courting.[37]

Rarer terms for ghosts included the English 'bugbear'; variants of 'shadow'; and Latin terms. William Birnie wrote in 1606 of 'Larvae or Lemures, that is, bogils or gaistes', and James VI used 'umbrae mortuorum' to refer to ghosts (the literal translation being 'shades of the dead').[38] An English/Latin vocabulary published in Edinburgh in 1720 included a section on 'created beings', which translated ghosts as 'Umbrae', fairies as 'Lemures', and a vision or phantom as 'Spectrum'.[39] The Latin 'spectrum' and 'phantasma' also spawned the terms 'spectre' and 'phantom'. The former was perhaps in use

36 Alexander Montgomerie and Patrick Hume, 'The Flyting betwixt Montgomery and Polwart', in James Cranstoun (ed.), *The Poems of Alexander Montgomerie* (Edinburgh, 1887), line 291, p. 69; William Dunbar, 'Apon the Midsummer Evin, Mirriest of Nichtis (The Tretis Of The Twa Mariit Wemen and the Wedo)', in Jacqueline Tasioulas (ed.), *The Makars: The Poems of Henryson, Dunbar and Douglas* (Edinburgh, 1999), lines 100–1, p. 550. 'Mahoune' signified the Devil. On the passage from Montgomerie see Jacqueline Simpson, '"The Weird Sisters Wandering": Burlesque Witchery in Montgomerie's Flyting', *Folklore* 106 (1995), 9–20.

37 E., 'Border Sketches No. II', *Edinburgh Magazine and Literary Miscellany*, Oct. 1817, 238; James Hogg, 'The Bogle', *Edinburgh Literary Journal*, Mar. 1831, 171–2.

38 William Birnie, *The Blame of Kirk-Buriall, Tending to Perswade Cemiteriall Civilitie* (Edinburgh, 1606, STC 3089), ch. 12, D; James VI, *Daemonologie*, bk. 3, ch. 1, 39.

39 *A New Vocabulary English and Latin, for the Use of Schools*, 5th edn (Edinburgh, 1720), 2.

from the sixteenth century (James VI employs it in his 1597 *Daemonologie*) and the latter from the fourteenth.[40] However, they became significantly more popular in the late eighteenth and early nineteenth centuries. Their relative rarity at the beginning of this timespan can be seen in an extract from a 1787 poem by James Fordyce:

> At length a voice the solemn silence broke,
> And thus, in hollow tone, the phantom* spoke;

A helpful note clarified that 'phantom' meant an 'apparation'.[41] By the nineteenth century, however, 'phantoms' were a common feature of romantic writing. The terminology for ghosts thus evolved in response to changing cultural contexts. The difficulty of determining the precise nature of a reported apparition can be a challenge for the historian, but as we shall see, it was no less a problem for contemporaries.

For the sake of clarity, this book will generally use the term 'ghost' to refer to a dead person reappearing among the living, even if it was not the term employed by the contemporary describing the event. I will, however, assign different labels to certain sub-categories of ghost. 'Wraith' (or similar terms such as 'wrath', 'wrathys', 'wrethis', 'wrayth', 'wratch') was a Scots word that appeared in Gavin Douglas's 1513 translation of *The Aeneid*. Douglas seems to equate wraiths with ghosts:

> in diverse places
> The wraiths walks of ghaists that are deid,[42]

For James VI, however, the term had a more precise meaning. He explained that a wraith was the spectral appearance of a person either soon before their death, or when 'newlie dead'.[43] I will employ James's definition, as there is a relatively large body of stories on apparitions appearing for a few brief moments at the precise time of death, and it is useful to have a label for them.[44] 'Revenant' and 'poltergeist' are also helpful terms, although anachronistic (both appeared in English in the nineteenth century).[45] Revenants were a subset of ghosts, particularly popular during the medieval period, who returned as walking

40 James VI, *Daemonologie*, preface, xix.

41 James Fordyce, 'The Vision', in *A Collection of Hymns and Sacred Poems* (Aberdeen, 1787), 140.

42 Gavin Douglas, *The Aeneid (1513)*, ed. Gordon Kendal (London, 2011), bk. 10, line 93, p. 517.

43 James VI, *Daemonologie*, bk. 3, ch. 1, 42.

44 See the discussion on pp. 66–8.

45 'Revenant, n. and adj.2', *OED Online* (University of Oxford, June 2015), http://www.oed.com/view/Entry/164711; 'poltergeist, n.', *OED Online* (University of Oxford, June 2015), http://www.oed.com/view/Entry/147029. Both accessed 1 Feb. 2018.

corpses. They were especially common in the Icelandic sagas, where they were known as *draugr*, but they were well attested in England, the Low Countries, northern France and parts of Germany.[46] As we shall see, there were also a few Scottish cases. Revenants had generally lost all vestiges of humanity, and behaved in a violent and cruel manner. Poltergeists – spirits who haunted houses – likewise tended to be malevolent in nature. The direct translation, 'noisy ghosts', reflects the fact that they were generally heard, rather than seen. They did occasionally take visible forms, however. Animal forms were perceived quite frequently, and several poltergeists appeared as naked arms, perhaps in reference to their habits of knocking and throwing things.[47] As we shall see, poltergeists could be interpreted as returning dead people, but were more usually classed as demons.

My use of the term 'supernatural' is also anachronistic. In the period from the Middle Ages to the early nineteenth century, this term had a more precise meaning. As explained by Thomas Aquinas (1225–74), supernatural events were the unmediated actions of God, and could not be explained by any natural laws. Preternatural events were out-of-the-ordinary occurrences that happened by the agency of created beings, or by the agency of nature, as directed by God. God himself was supernatural, whereas other spiritual beings (with the possible exception of angels) were usually consigned to the realms of the preternatural. For theologians, therefore, ghosts were not supernatural beings.[48] In practice, however, the terms 'preternatural' and 'supernatural' did not generally appear in Scottish discussions of ghosts. It could certainly be argued that these labels were debated implicitly, if not explicitly. To interpret a ghost as a message from God, a diabolic trick, or the product of a diseased mind was to define its place on the scale of supernatural, preternatural and natural. Nevertheless, to insist too much on the distinctions between these categories is to assign them an importance that is not justified by their limited use in the source material. I therefore generally use the term 'supernatural' in its modern sense, as a convenient shorthand for a range of phenomena (ghosts included) that transcend the natural order.

Another point that requires justification is my use of the designations of 'popular' and 'elite' culture. Ever since E. P. Thompson's 1966 essay on 'History from Below', there have been ongoing attempts to find the boundaries between

46 N. K. Chadwick, 'Norse Ghosts (A Study in the *Draugr* and the *Haugbúi*)', *Folklore* 57 (1946), 50–65; Ármann Jakobsson, 'The Fearless Vampire Killers: A Note about the Icelandic *Draugr* and Demonic Contamination in *Grettis Saga*', *Folklore* 120 (2009), 307–16; Nancy Caciola, 'Wraiths, Revenants, and Ritual in Medieval Culture', *Past & Present* 152 (1996), 15.

47 Sinclair, *Satans Invisible World Discovered*, 159; Wodrow, *Analecta*, vol. 2, 95.

48 Clark, *Thinking with Demons*, 152–5; Walsham, *Providence*, 230; Lorraine Daston and Katharine Park, *Wonders and the Order of Nature, 1150–1750* (New York, 1998), 121–6; Lorraine Daston, 'Marvelous Facts and Miraculous Evidence in Early Modern Europe', *Critical Inquiry* 18 (1991), 95–100.

those 'above' and those 'below', and the distinctions between 'popular' and 'elite' remain debated among theorists today.[49] This work is not concerned with the knotty question of how, exactly, these terms should be defined. I do work to the premise that there was a 'popular culture' in Enlightenment Scotland. This should not be taken as a given; Holt N. Parker explains that 'nearly all theories of popular culture take it as given that popular culture is a phenomenon dating from, or indeed caused by, the Industrial Revolution'.[50] In Scotland, the industrial revolution is most commonly dated from about the 1780s.[51] Furthermore, many historians reject the terms 'popular' and 'elite' outright, noting that these categories imply a clean social divide that did not and could not exist in practice.

However, there was a meaningful distinction between popular and elite in pre-industrial Scottish society, despite the fact that the boundaries were not clear-cut. R. A. Houston suggests that in the mid-eighteenth century about 5 per cent of Lowland males were lairds and professional men, 20 per cent were craftsmen and tradesmen, 25 per cent tenant farmers, and 50 per cent labourers, cottars or servants. He also estimates an illiteracy level of about 35 per cent for men and 70 per cent for women in the Lowlands. In the Highlands the rates stood at about 55 to 60 per cent for men, or 90 per cent for women.[52] Alexander Webster's pioneering 1755 census placed over half of Scots north of the Tay. In 1750, around 17 per cent of Scots lived in towns with more than 2,500 inhabitants, and while this was high by European averages, it further underlines that the cluster of educated men living and writing in Edinburgh or other large burghs were anomalous in Scottish society as a whole.[53] The vast majority of surviving records of ghosts were made by men who fall into the class of lairds and professionals, as well as being literate and (most usually) based in urban centres. The available evidence is, therefore, skewed. It is

49 E. P. Thompson, 'History from Below', *The Times Literary Supplement* 3345 (1966), 279. The literature on this topic is extensive, but for a few examples of the continuing debate see Bob Scribner, 'Is a History of Popular Culture Possible?', *History of European Ideas* 10 (1989), 175–91; Gerald Strauss, 'The Dilemma of Popular History', *Past & Present* 132 (1991), 130–49; William Beik, 'The Dilemma of Popular History', *Past & Present* 141 (1993), 207–15; Gerald Strauss, 'The Dilemma of Popular History: Reply', *Past & Present* 141 (1993), 215–19; Holt N. Parker, 'Toward a Definition of Popular Culture', *History & Theory* 50 (2011), 147–70.

50 Parker, 'Toward a Definition of Popular Culture', 148.

51 Christopher A. Whatley, *The Industrial Revolution in Scotland* (Cambridge, 1997), 7.

52 R. A. Houston, *Scottish Literacy and the Scottish Identity: Illiteracy and Society in Scotland and Northern England, 1600–1800* (Cambridge, 2002), 56; R. A. Houston, 'Women in the Economy and Society of Scotland, 1500–1800', in R. A. Houston and I. D. Whyte (eds), *Scottish Society, 1500–1800* (Cambridge, 1989), 136.

53 R. E. Tyson, 'Population Patterns to 1770', in Michael Lynch (ed.), *Oxford Companion to Scottish History*, electronic edn (University of Oxford, 2007), http://www.oxfordreference.com/view/10.1093/acref/9780199234820.001.0001/acref-9780199234820-e-238?rskey=I3vw3P&result=1#acref-9780199234820-eSub-0180, accessed 1 Feb. 2018.

important to bear in mind that there was a divide between these educated, socially privileged individuals and the broad swathes of Scottish folk who did not have the leisure hours, financial freedom or education to directly participate in print culture. 'Elite' and 'popular' are convenient labels here, despite lacking precise definitions.

The sources on early modern Scottish ghosts are limited. Besides a few interesting needles that can be found in the haystacks of kirk and court session records, the main sources are those few ghost stories that were published in treatises and pamphlets, or recorded in letters and other manuscripts. Matters improve from the second half of the eighteenth century. As the print market expanded, ghosts increasingly appeared in periodicals, broadsides, chapbooks, plays and collections of poetry. In the nineteenth century, they worked their way into short stories and novels. This period also saw the rapid development of antiquarian studies, resulting in a huge increase in useful material. Many nineteenth-century folklorists claimed to be recording stories from centuries previously, but my approach in this book is to use only material that can be demonstrably traced back to the period in question. Thus, in the absence of supplementary evidence, I use the records of early-nineteenth-century folklorists to reflect on nineteenth-century patterns, not to draw conclusions about earlier parts of the period.

This book makes use of both fictional and non-fictional accounts of ghosts. There are three reasons for this. Firstly, fictional works played an important role in creating and popularising new visions of the ghost. Secondly, the ways in which people thought about fictional ghosts could influence their readings of non-fictional accounts. Thirdly, it is often difficult to disentangle fictional ghosts from their non-fictional counterparts; many accounts straddled both categories. This is not to imply that it is pointless to ask whether a given ghost story was read as a piece of entertainment or a factual account. The question of belief is an important one, and I shall return to it throughout the book. It is, however, a very difficult question to address. It is generally impossible to know how a ghost story was received, and how widely it was credited. The only information available about levels of popular belief is the anecdotal (and often inconsistent) accounts of folklorists. It is also possible to get blinkered by the question of belief, and overlook the ways in which ghosts could be important even when not presented or received as objective realities. Ghosts did not have to be actually patrolling the ramparts of Scottish castles to have a significant cultural presence.

If belief (or the lack thereof) coloured early modern views of ghosts, the same might be said regarding modern historians. Lyndal Roper, writing about reports of witchcraft, points out that 'as a profession used to addressing documents for their reliability, it is hard to know how to interpret documents which we do not believe to be factual'.[54] Roper tackles the problem through a psychoanalytical approach, aiming to get inside the head of those who produced the documents in question. It would be harder to adopt this approach in the case of ghosts, because very few first-hand accounts of ghost sightings survive. Most stories describe ghosts seen by relatives, acquaintances or communities. This renders it difficult to make generalisations about those people who actually saw ghosts (or thought they did). The issue is complicated by the fact that the non-existence of ghosts is probably not as generally accepted nowadays as the non-existence of witches. The historical belief in witches had terrible consequences; ghosts do not carry the same emotional baggage. The edited collection *Early Modern Ghosts* (2002) contains not only a selection of academic essays on the historical value of ghosts, but also an essay by Ian S. Baker on contemporary parapyschological research. Baker concludes that it is very difficult to say whether ghosts do or do not exist.[55] I do not believe in ghosts myself, which inevitably influences my reading of the sources to an extent – but historians must always be bound by their personal perspectives. Furthermore, the lack of first-hand accounts has its advantages: rather than delving into the thorny question of why people saw ghosts, it becomes natural to ask instead why people chose to circulate ghost stories. This book is not concerned with whether or not ghosts were really making appearances, but rather with the ways in which they were used, and how they can reflect on contemporary concerns.

The first chapter of the book provides context, sketching attitudes towards ghosts from the Middle Ages to the late seventeenth century. Medieval ghosts could be understood as demons or as the genuine spirits of the dead. However, after the 1560 Reformation, the demonic interpretation became dominant. Some ghost stories did survive, but witches and the Devil attracted significantly more attention. From the Reformation up to the late seventeenth century, ghosts were sidelined. Subsequent chapters demonstrate the developing importance of ghosts in the long eighteenth century, and are arranged thematically. The second chapter discusses ghosts in religious culture. It is mainly grounded in the late seventeenth and early eighteenth centuries, as this period saw a tentative drive to rehabilitate ghosts as Protestant propagandists. Ghosts were used to 'prove' the reality of the soul and afterlife, revealing how religious priorities had shifted since the Reformation. There were continued attempts to use ghosts to make religious arguments throughout the eighteenth century.

54 Lyndal Roper, 'Witchcraft and Fantasy in Early Modern Germany', *History Workshop* 32 (1991), 21–2.

55 Ian S. Baker, '"Do Ghosts Exist?": A Summary of Parapsychological Research into Apparitional Experiences', in John Newton and Jo Bath (eds), *Early Modern Ghosts* (Durham, 2002), 120.

Ghosts never became orthodox, but from the late seventeenth century, telling ghost stories was intellectually defensible.

The third chapter looks at how perceptions of ghosts changed amid the philosophical and scientific advances of the Enlightenment, particularly in the latter half of the eighteenth century. Most intellectuals continued to accept the possibility of supernatural intervention, but ghosts were increasingly explained in natural terms. They were interpreted as dreams, symptoms of a mental disorder, or superstitions stemming from a poor education. However, this was not a uniform approach. Periodicals featured heated debates on the reality of ghosts. Meanwhile, satirical works promoted melodramatic conceptions of ghosts that became fixed within the popular imagination. The chapter as a whole acknowledges the importance of naturalised visions of ghosts, but cautions against the idea that ghosts melted away under the glare of scepticism.

The fourth chapter considers how ghosts were explored in gothic and romantic writing, chiefly in the late eighteenth and early nineteenth centuries. The emergence of gothic saw the horrifying aspects of the ghost exploited in new ways, offering reflections on death and insanity that were in stark contrast to the visions of the kirk and Enlightenment physicians. Romantic writers also took a fresh approach to ghosts. From Macpherson's *Ossian* poetry to the writing of Walter Scott and James Hogg, ghosts were entangled with notions of Scottishness. This carried across into antiquarian studies; folklorists worked ghosts into the Scottish landscape, and developed a unique conception of the Highland ghost. Ghosts served as symbols of the past, and this gave them power in a society that was negotiating its own history and identity.

The first four chapters are mainly concerned with the ways in which ghosts were used, discussed and explored in educated discourses. The final chapter focuses on popular culture. Using sources including ballads, pamphlets and folklorists' accounts, it investigates perceptions of ghosts among the majority of the population. The chapter examines the ways in which ghost stories engaged with communities' concerns, and allowed traditions to be passed down over generations. Ghosts demonstrated the correct way of approaching death, moralised about love and violence, and subverted social hierarchies. They also allowed people to retain a connection to local landscapes amid the upheaval of urbanisation and industrialisation.

Over the course of the book, ghosts appear in a wide variety of guises. Mouldering corpses lumber at the side of pale, gliding maidens. Friends and relatives pop back to visit from Heaven; criminals bewail the agonies of hellfire; those who died premature deaths wander the hills and woods. Ghosts are servants of God and the Devil, symptoms of mental disorders, spokespeople for past generations, shadows, metaphors. Ghosts never had a fixed identity, but in the long eighteenth century the concept of the ghost further diversified, as ghosts took on a wider array of roles in Scottish society. Intellectuals increasingly explained ghosts away in natural terms, and associated ghost belief with old wives and serving girls. However, ghost stories spread more freely and easily; it became possible to use ghosts as religious propagandists; and the development of gothic and romanticism made ghosts a fashionable subject, and associated them with a certain brand of Scottishness. As the eighteenth century progressed, the kirk lost (in part relinquished) much of its authority over representations of the supernatural, meaning that there was greater scope for individuals to develop their own conceptions of the magical world. Poets toured the tenebrous corners of churchyards, and antiquarians established spectral warriors on Highland hillsides. Philosophers and writers extolled the attractions of supernatural awe. Ghosts inhabited a broader range of imagined worlds, and the boundaries between fantasy and reality sometimes became blurred. I do not wish to overstate levels of belief, which are, at any rate, impossible to assess with any degree of accuracy – but there is cause to question the sceptics' proclamations that ghost belief was gone from polite society. Moreover, even when they were not credited, ghosts were useful. By breaking down the barriers between past and present, living and dead, ghost stories could offer unique commentaries on religion, mortality, history and identity.

1

Medieval and Reformation Ghosts

Most early modern Scots would have agreed that the world was imbued with spirits. However, the nature of these spirits was open to debate. Educated folk commonly erased ghosts from the celestial schema, instead identifying apparitions as angels or (more frequently) as demons. The main biblical justification for ghosts was the Old Testament story of the Witch of Endor (1 Samuel 28:3–25), which focused on the tribulations of King Saul of Israel and Judah. Saul had driven the magicians and mediums from his land, but while preparing to wage war against a host of Philistines, he became afraid. He repaired to a medium who had remained in Endor, and by his request, she raised the deceased prophet Samuel. The tidings were bleak. Saul learned that he was to lose the battle, and that he and his sons were to die – prophecies that were shortly fulfilled. The story suggested that ghosts might appear on earth, but it was not conclusive. The apparition of Samuel was tainted by the association with witchcraft and necromancy, and might be read as a devil in disguise.[1] In the absence of clear biblical guidance, medieval theologians expressed varying views on the orthodoxy of ghosts. Scepticism became more pronounced with the sixteenth-century Protestant Reformation, when ghosts were widely identified as demons. Stories of ghosts circulated in sixteenth- and seventeenth-century Scotland, but were often dogged with disclaimers.

Ghosts in the Middle Ages

There are few records of Scottish ghosts before the eighteenth century. The Europe-wide picture is better documented, however, and offers some contextualisation for the sparse Scottish sources. In early medieval Europe, most clerical figures rejected the idea that dead souls could return to earth. Ghost stories had been common in ancient Greek and Roman culture, and were tinged with paganism in the eyes of the early church fathers. Tertullian (c.160–c.230) and Lactantius (c.250–c.325) dismissed ghosts as a vulgar

1 For a fuller discussion of the Witch of Endor, see Peter Marshall, *Beliefs and the Dead in Reformation England* (Oxford, 2002), 236–40.

superstition. Augustine of Hippo (354–430) allowed only for the 'image' of a dead person to return, as opposed to an actual spirit or soul, and explained that this image was created by angels or demons.[2] Ghost stories remained rare until the ninth century, when the liturgy for the dead developed, and Augustine's teachings on ghosts were forgotten. Records of popular ghost stories multiplied over the eleventh and twelfth centuries, and in the wake of the 'birth of Purgatory' in the late twelfth century, some clerical figures began actively to promote ghost stories as proof of a middle ground for souls.[3] Ghosts were tentatively endorsed by Thomas Aquinas (1225–74), who suggested that 'according to the disposition of Divine Providence separated souls sometimes come forth from their abode and appear to men'.[4]

Medieval ghosts usually looked much as they had when alive. The ghosts of knights sported armour and weapons, while monks wore robes. Sometimes the colours of the ghosts' garments took on particular significance. Many ghosts made their first appearances in black. For their next visitation they dressed in half black, then in half white, and finally all in white: this change represented the progression through Purgatory.[5] Red was also a popular colour for ghosts. The archetypal all-white ghost was less common, although Claude Lecouteux has suggested that there was a tradition of 'white ladies' who appeared to foreshadow deaths.[6] Medieval artwork occasionally depicted ghosts as immaterial phantoms, invisible beings, or souls in animal forms, but more usually they were corporeal, and retained close ties to their dead bodies. If a ghost had died from wounds, they might still be bleeding when it returned.[7] The extreme example of the corporeal ghost was the revenant, or 'living corpse', which chiefly appeared in northern Europe.[8] Revenants rose soon after death,

2 Jean-Claude Schmitt, *Ghosts in the Middle Ages: The Living and the Dead in Medieval Society*, trans. Teresa Lavender Fagan (Chicago, 1998), 17–22.

3 Ibid., 4–5; Jacques Le Goff, *The Birth of Purgatory*, trans. Arthur Goldhammer (Chicago, 1986).

4 Thomas Aquinas, *Summa Theologica*, trans. Fathers of the English Dominican Province, 3 vols (New York, 1947–8), vol. 3, supplement 69.3, 2832.

5 Schmitt, *Ghosts in the Middle Ages*, 204.

6 Claude Lecouteux, *Return of the Dead: Ghosts, Ancestors, and the Transparent Veil of the Pagan Mind*, trans. John E. Graham (Rochester [Vt.], 2009), 119–20.

7 Schmitt, *Ghosts in the Middle Ages*, 196–8, 206.

8 There are detailed discussions of revenants in Nancy Caciola, 'Wraiths, Revenants, and Ritual in Medieval Culture', *Past & Present* 152 (1996), 10–15, and Nancy Caciola, *Afterlives: The Return of the Dead in the Middle Ages* (Ithaca [N.Y.], 2016), pt. 2. See also Jacqueline Simpson, 'Repentant Soul or Walking Corpse? Debatable Apparitions in Medieval England', *Folklore* 114 (2003), 389–402; Andrew Joynes (ed.), *Medieval Ghost Stories: An Anthology of Miracles, Marvels, and Prodigies* (Woodbridge, 2001), pt. 3; Darren Oldridge, *Strange Histories: The Trial of the Pig, the Walking Dead, and Other Matters of Fact from the Medieval and Renaissance Worlds*, 2nd edn (Abingdon, 2018), ch. 4; Winston Black, 'Animated Corpses and Bodies with Power in the Scholastic Age', in Joëlle Rollo-Koster (ed.), *Death in Medieval Europe: Death Scripted and Death Choreographed* (Abingdon, 2017), 71–92.

before the body was decayed, and were often aggressive towards the living. From the thirteenth century, theologians increasingly interpreted revenants as demons.[9]

The dead almost always appeared at night time. Some ghosts liked wild outside spaces, or abandoned houses, but most returned to the houses they had inhabited when alive, or to cemeteries.[10] They appeared most often to their past friends or relatives. With the exception of the bloodthirsty revenants, most ghosts had some positive moral or religious function. They often returned to confess to sins committed during their lifetimes, and atone for them where possible. Some came back to request that more prayers should be said for them, or that some irregularity in their burial should be corrected. Certain people were condemned to wander as ghosts because they had died a violent or untimely death, or died in an unfinished state – unbaptised, in childbirth, or with some important business left unresolved. Others were unable to rest because their sins during life made for an agonisingly long spell in Purgatory.[11] Most of these European patterns seem to have been known in Scotland. The ghost of Gy de Thurno (or de Corvo) demonstrates how stories could travel across borders. After conducting an illicit sexual act (not further elaborated), Gy could not escape Purgatory; he haunted his house until the local friars said enough prayers to speed his passage to Heaven. The story, originally from France, was published in a mid-fourteenth-century Latin tract entitled *Spiritus Guidonis*, which was translated into Middle English as *The Gast of Gy*. In Scotland, William Dunbar (b. c.1460) insulted Walter Kennedy by calling him 'thow spreit of Gy', and David Lindsay (c.1486–1555) noted that he would dress up for the young James V's amusement 'sumtyme lyke the greislie gaist of Gye'.[12]

Stories originating from Scotland presented a fairly broad range of ghosts. In 1547, Lindsay imagined the return of the murdered Cardinal Beaton. He appeared 'rycht suddantlie', in the form of

9 Caciola, *Afterlives*, 185–205; Black, 'Animated Corpses', 71–92.

10 Schmitt, *Ghosts in the Middle Ages*, 172–94.

11 Alexander Murray, *Suicide in the Middle Ages, Vol. 2: The Curse on Self-Murder* (Oxford, 2000), 471–81; Schmitt, *Ghosts in the Middle Ages*, 2–3, 185–94. There are also some useful comments in R. A. Bowyer, 'The Role of the Ghost-Story in Mediaeval Christianity', in Helen Parish (ed.), *Superstition and Magic in Early Modern Europe: A Reader* (London, 2015), 177–92.

12 William Dunbar, 'Schir Johine the Ros, Ane Thing Thair Is Compild (The Flyting of Dumbar and Kennedie)', in Jacqueline Tasioulas (ed.), *The Makars: The Poems of Henryson, Dunbar and Douglas* (Edinburgh, 1999), v. 22, line 172, p. 347; David Lindsay, 'The Dreme', in David Laing (ed.), *The Poetical Works of Sir David Lyndsay*, 3 vols (Edinburgh, 1879), vol. 1, line 16, p. 1. See Keely Fisher, 'The Crying of Ane Play: Robin Hood and Maying in Sixteenth-Century Scotland', in John Pitcher (ed.), *Medieval and Renaissance Drama in England, Vol. 12* (Cranbury, 1999), 44–6; William Henry Schofield, *Mythical Bards and The Life of William Wallace* (Cambridge [Mass.], 1920), 41–3; Caciola, *Afterlives*, 291–6.

Ane woundit man, aboundantlie bledyng,
With vissage paill and with ane deidlye cheir
In rayment reid cloithit full curiouslie,
Of vellvoit, and of satyn crammosie.
With febyll voce, as man opprest with paine,[13]

The unhappy ghost returned to admit a multitude of misdemeanours (Lindsay was using it to comment on ecclesiastical corruption). This ghost adhered to many common medieval patterns, being corporeal, bleeding, clad in red, and determined to confess its sins. However, the notion of luminous silvery apparitions also existed in Scotland, at least by the sixteenth century and probably before. George Buchanan's *Rerum Scoticarum Historia*, published in 1582, told of a cunning plan executed in the mid-ninth century by Kenneth II (Kenneth I by modern historians' reckoning). Kenneth needed the support of his nobles to raise an army. He clothed a young man in fish skins and had him appear to the nobles and exhort them to war, speaking through a tube to amplify his voice. Buchanan explains that 'the sudden flashing of light from the fishes skins, darting about [the nobles'] drowsie eyes and dazling them, drove them into great astonishment', and 'a kind of religious consternation seized upon their minds'. The boy vanished by the means of a secret passage, and the nobles promptly agreed to the war.[14]

The same apparition might be presented in different ways. In the 1440s, Walter Bower wrote of a possible ghost at the second wedding of Alexander III. This wedding took place in 1285, when famine was gripping Scotland. A show was put on, and included a procession that wound its way among the guests. At the rear came a figure that might have been a man or an apparition (*fantasma*). It seemed to glide rather than walk. Then it disappeared. The procession halted, and the music and dancing ceased. The text noted that 'laughter is always mixed with grief, and mourning takes over from extremes of joy'.[15] In his 1527 *Scotorum Historiae a Prima Gentis Origine*, Hector Boece retained the melancholy message of the spectre, but presented it in a different guise. He explained that the plague had killed many Scots in the years prior to the wedding, then noted that when the bridegroom was leading the bride to dance, a dead man with no flesh on his bones was seen bringing up the rear. This

[13] Lindsay, 'The Tragedie of the Cardinall', in *Poetical Works*, vol. 1, lines 17–22, p. 140. 'Cheir' translates as 'look', 'countenance' or 'demeanour'; 'crammosie' translates as 'crimson'.

[14] George Buchanan, *Rerum Scoticarum Historia*, ed. Dana F. Sutton, electronic edn (University of Birmingham, 2009), http://www.philological.bham.ac.uk/scothist, accessed 1 Feb. 2018, bk. v, para. 56.

[15] Nicola Royan and Dauvit Broun, 'Versions of Scottish Nationhood, c.850–1707', in Ian Brown et al. (eds), *The Edinburgh History of Scottish Literature, Vol. 1: From Columba to the Union (until 1707)* (Edinburgh, 2007), 172–3.

ill omen put an end to all celebration.[16] Boece's version of the apparition was reminiscent of the skeletons that populated late medieval artwork, especially within the *Danse Macabre* ('Dance of Death') genre. It presented a more grisly reminder of death than Bower's ambiguous spectre.

Revenants could also be found in Scotland. The chronicler William of Newburgh (1136–98), who was from Yorkshire, recorded a couple of twelfth-century stories.[17] One took place in Berwick, which was then a part of Scotland. It began with the death of a wealthy, sinful man. He persistently rose from his tomb at night and wandered around the town, announced by a cacophony of barking from the local dogs. The terrified townspeople debated their options, and agreed that ten strong young men should dig up the corpse, chop it into pieces, and burn the remains. This was duly done, and the visitations ceased. However, the putrid corpse had infected the air, and a raft of townspeople subsequently died in an outbreak of pestilence. The other story concerns a chaplain who lived near Melrose Abbey, Roxburghshire. He was little inclined to pass his days in prayer, and his fondness for hunting earned him the sobriquet 'Hundeprest', or 'hounds' priest'. After his death he regularly rose from his grave. He visited the monastery, or dawdled by the chamber of his former mistress, making terrible mumbling and groaning noises. She begged for help from one of the priests at the monastery. This priest recruited another of his brethren, as well as a pair of sturdy young men from the area, and the four armed themselves and took up guard at the cemetery one night. Midnight came and went; the grave remained undisturbed. The priest's companions retreated to a nearby house to warm up, leaving him alone. Then the revenant emerged from its tomb. It advanced on the priest, groaning in a dreadful manner. The priest was aghast, but steeled himself, and as the revenant came near he struck it with his battle-axe. The injured creature then made a swift retreat. With the priest in pursuit, it disappeared back into the safety of the tomb. The priests' companions later returned, and at dawn the party opened the tomb and dug up the corpse. The axe wound was found to be fresh. They carried the body beyond the confines of the monastery and burned it. Both of these accounts emphasise the physicality of the revenant, and it is noteworthy that the creatures were defeated by fire and sword, not through prayer.

The northern English *Chronicon de Lanercost* includes two more Scottish cases, this time from the 1290s. One concerned a deceased monk who haunted a knight, Sir Duncan de Insula, near Paisley:

[16] Hector Boethius, *Scotorum Historia*, ed. Dana F. Sutton, electronic edn (University of Birmingham, 2010), http://www.philological.bham.ac.uk/boece, accessed 1 Feb. 2018, bk. 13, para. 84.

[17] William of Newburgh, *Historia Rerum Anglicarum*, ed. Hans Claude Hamilton, 2 vols (London, 1856), vol. 2, 184–90; see also Joynes's retellings in Joynes (ed.), *Medieval Ghost Stories*, 136–9.

> Now there was a certain fellow wearing the garments of holy religion who lived wickedly and died most wretchedly, being bound by sentence of excommunication ... Long after his body had been buried, it vexed many in the same monastery by appearing plainly in the shade of night. This child of darkness proceeded to the house of the said knight in order to disturb the faith of simple persons and terrify them by molesting them in broad daylight, or, more probably, by a secret decree of God, that he might indicate by such token those who were implicated in his misdoing. Having then assumed a bodily shape (whether natural or aerial is uncertain, but it was hideous, gross and tangible) he used to appear at noon-day in the dress of a black monk and settle on the highest parts of the dwellings or store houses ... Also he so savagely felled and battered those who attempted to struggle with him as well-nigh to shatter all their joints.[18]

In the end, the revenant killed the family's heir. The other story was from the historic district of Cunninghame in Ayrshire. It told of how God taught a drunkard to mend his ways by terrifying him with a visitation from 'an exceedingly hideous likeness of a spirit of the air ... with a foul body, ghostly countenance, fiery eyes and of terrific dimensions'.[19] The apparition was identified as the owner of a nearby tavern. He was not obviously dead, but drew on revenant traditions nonetheless; if the 'spirit of the air' conjures up notions of incorporeality, they are swiftly dispelled by the 'foul body' with its burning eyes.

It was recognised, then, that the dead could return in a range of forms. Ways of interpreting apparitions also varied. There was certainly doubt over how far ghost stories ought to be credited. In the prologue to his translation of *The Aeneid* (1513), Gavin Douglas noted that his readers would complain:

> 'All is but ghaists and eldritch fantasies,
> Of brownies and of bogles full this book:
> Out on thir wandering spirits, wow!' thou cries.[20]

He suggested that people would scoff at these 'vain superstitions against our richt belief'.[21] This vision of ghosts as a vulgar superstition would reappear frequently over the following centuries. However, there were other possible approaches. Two can be seen in Blind Harry's *The Actes and Deidis of the Illustre and Vallyeant Campioun Schir William Wallace*, written in the 1470s. First of all, Harry wrote of the ghost of Fawdon. Fawdon was one of sixteen men with

[18] Herbert Maxwell (ed. and trans.), *The Chronicle of Lanercost, 1272–1346* (Glasgow, 1913), 118–19; see Caciola, 'Wraiths, Revenants, and Ritual', 24.

[19] Maxwell, *Chronicle of Lanercost*, 75–6.

[20] Gavin Douglas, *The Aeneid (1513)*, ed. Gordon Kendal (London, 2011), prologue 6, lines 17–19, p. 237. 'Eldritch' tended to mean 'elvish' or 'fairy-like', but could also refer to the supernatural more broadly.

[21] Ibid., line 22, p. 237.

whom Wallace fled from the English, following a battle in which they were vastly outnumbered. After they had gone a little distance Fawdon grew tired, and protested that he was not able to go any further. Angered, Wallace drew his sword and sliced off Fawdon's head. In defence of this brutality the text suggested that Fawdon might have been a traitor, noting that he was strong, they had not gone far, and he was commonly held to be fickle ('of brokill complexioun'). Nevertheless, retribution awaited Wallace. When he and his remaining men reached their stronghold at Gask Hall, Perthshire, they heard the sound of blaring horns. Wallace sent two men to investigate. When they did not return he sent two more. In the fashion of a horror film protagonist, he dispatched his companions in turn until he was alone. He then drew his sword and left the hall himself. Outside he saw Fawdon, holding his own decapitated head. Wallace crossed himself, and Fawdon flung the head at him, which he caught and threw back. His heart 'gretlye agast', Wallace ran away up the stairs and jumped out of a window, making his retreat along a riverbank. Glancing back he thought he saw Fawdon once more, holding a great rafter, having set the hall on fire.[22]

Later in *The Wallace*, Harry presented a very different ghost. An old monk who had lived a good life promised a younger monk that, if God permitted it, he would return after his death to report on the afterlife. God allowed him to keep his word. He appeared from Purgatory, radiating light. The bulk of his time was spent eulogising Wallace, who (as he explained) was shortly to go to Heaven.[23] The spectres of Fawdon and the monk may have both been the apparitions of returning dead people, but their similarities ended there, and Harry interpreted them differently. The monk, come to perform a noble duty by honouring Wallace, had been genuinely allowed to return by God. The malicious Fawdon, on the other hand, was recognised by Wallace as a demon:

> Rycht weill he trowit that was no spreit of man;
> It was sum devill at sic malice began.[24]

Later, Blind Harry speculated on possible explanations for the apparition. He noted that it could be the work of the Devil, and also recalled a notion found in Dante's *Inferno* (1317), that demons could take over the bodies of traitors once their souls had departed:

22 Hary, *The Wallace: Selections*, ed. Anne McKim, electronic edn (Medieval Institute Publications, 2003), http://d.lib.rochester.edu/teams/publication/mckim-the-wallace-selections, accessed 1 Feb. 2018, bk. 4, lines 91–120, lines 174–209 (quotations line 116, line 198). See John Balaban, 'Blind Harry and "The Wallace"', *Chaucer Review* 8 (1974), 248–9 on possible Celtic sources for Fawdon's apparition.

23 Hary, *Wallace*, bk. 12, lines 1238–99.

24 Ibid., bk. 5, lines 199–200. 'Trowit' translates as 'believed'; see McKim's editorial notes.

gif the man endyt in evill entent,
Sum wikkit spreit agayne for him present;[25]

The apparition of Fawdon was in the revenant tradition, with its physicality and violence, and it was common for revenants to be interpreted as demons inhabiting corpses. Again, however, this interpretation was not universal. The violent black-clad monk described above had probably been allowed to wander by God, but as Nancy Caciola concludes, 'there is no question of demonic possession or reanimation by anything other than the creature's own residual life-force'.[26]

Overall, medieval apparitions could appear in a range of different guises and for a variety of reasons. Nevertheless, there were some particularly common patterns in the European sources, and the limited evidence does not suggest that Scotland was markedly different. The typical ghost was corporeal, returned in the clothes it had worn during its lifetime, and retained some link to its dead body. Its appearance made some moral, usually religious, point. There was no guarantee, however, that an apparition would be understood as a returning dead person, despite the fact that this interpretation was theologically defensible by the late Middle Ages. Ghosts could be dismissed as a mere superstition, or interpreted as demons. The figure of the ghost was certainly recognised in medieval Scotland, but this does not mean that ghosts had an unequivocal place within religious culture.

The Reformation

If the correct interpretation of ghosts was ambiguous before the Reformation, it theoretically became clearer thereafter. Protestantism stripped away Purgatory, and for most theologians, this meant that ghosts could not exist. It was generally agreed that it was impossible to leave Hell, and that nobody would ever choose to leave Heaven. In 1569, the Swiss theologian Ludwig Lavater published his *De Spectris, Lemuribus et Magnis Atque Insolitis Fragoribus* (the English edition, *Of Ghostes and Spirites Walking by Nyght*, appeared in 1572). Lavater explained that those who were 'thinking every small motion and noyse to be spirites' and those who were 'fondely perswaded that there are no spirites' were equally in error.[27] However, the idea of dead souls in an intermediary state was a Catholic deception. Most apparitions were the result of trickery, error, or the hallucinogenic fumes of melancholy. Remaining apparitions

25 Ibid., bk. 5, lines 221–2. The point about Dante is from Matthew P. McDiarmid's edition, referenced by McKim, bk. v, 219–24n.
26 Caciola, 'Wraiths, Revenants, and Ritual', 24.
27 Ludwig Lavater, *Of Ghostes and Spirites Walking by Nyght*, trans. Robert Harrison (London, 1572, STC 15320), 16.

were either angels or, more usually, demons. Samuel's appearance to Saul was one example of a diabolic trick.[28] The work was widely read and discussed, and translated into five languages. Lavater probably did more than any other author to establish the new Protestant orthodoxy on ghosts.

Catholic clerics fought back in the face of this challenge. Dense theological works defended the doctrine of Purgatory, often with reference to apparitions.[29] Collections of stories claimed to demonstrate the reality of ghosts. The best known works of this type were the 1586 *Discours et Histoires des Spectres, Visions, et Apparitions des Esprits* by Pierre Le Loyer, and the 1588 *Psichologie, ou Traité de l'Apparition des Esprits* by Noel Taillepied. In fact, there was not much to choose between Lavater's interpretation and those of Le Loyer and Taillepied.[30] All three men discussed various impediments – ignorance, drunkenness, illness, an over-active imagination – that could cause people to see apparitions. Women, children, the elderly and the infirm were thought to be especially susceptible. In addition, all three men asserted that the Devil or demons sometimes pretended to be ghosts. The important difference was that both Le Loyer and Taillepied asserted that sometimes, albeit rarely, apparitions were indeed the returning spirits of the dead. The fact that the three theologians would probably have agreed in most cases did not prevent Protestants from making much of Catholic ignorance and credulity on the subject of apparitions. Catholics acquired an undeserved reputation as the defenders of all ghost stories, no matter how fantastical.[31]

Scotland's Reformation was instigated by the Scottish parliament in 1560. The Catholic Mary Queen of Scots was forced to abdicate seven years later in favour of her one-year-old son, who became James VI. After an unsuccessful attempt to regain her throne she fled to England, where she was kept in custody by Elizabeth I until her execution in 1587. Aside from her abortive resistance, there was little in the way of a Catholic counter-movement, and Scotland's religious scene in the following decades was defined more by disagreements among different Protestant factions than by rivalry between Protestants and Catholics.[32] Nevertheless, there was an effort to stamp out the

[28] Ibid., 74–7.

[29] R. C. Finucane, *Ghosts: Appearances of the Dead and Cultural Transformation* (Amherst [N.Y.], 1996), 97.

[30] Timothy Chesters, *Ghost Stories in Late Renaissance France: Walking by Night* (Oxford, 2011), ch. 2; Amanda Jane McKeever, 'The Ghost in Early Modern Protestant Culture: Shifting Perceptions of the Afterlife, 1450–1700' (University of Sussex D.Phil. thesis, 2010), 117–36.

[31] On the undeserved nature of this reputation see Francis Young, *English Catholics and the Supernatural, 1553–1829* (Farnham, 2013), which argues that 'the post-Reformation Catholic community was not preoccupied with ghosts to a greater extent than anyone else in the population' (79).

[32] See Jenny Wormald's description of the 'remarkable success story' of the new kirk in Jenny Wormald, *Court, Kirk, and Community: Scotland, 1470–1625* (Edinburgh, 1991), 132–39 (quotation 133).

remnants of Catholicism. Public office was restricted to orthodox Protestants, and kirk sessions imposed strict discipline on Scottish parishes.[33] Within this context, the new king became the most important Scottish proponent of the Protestant interpretation of ghosts. James was an erudite ruler: he wrote treatises on kingship, literary theory, and, significantly, demonology. His 1597 *Daemonologie* focused primarily on witchcraft and the wiles of the Devil. However, James also devoted some space to ghosts, under the labels 'spectra' and 'umbrae mortuorum'. His stance was that all such spirits were actually demons or emanations of the Devil. He divided spirits into several categories:

> That kinde of the Devils conversing in the earth, may be divided in foure diffrent kindes, whereby he affrayeth and troubleth the bodies of men ... The first is, where spirites troubles some houses or solitarie places: The second, where spirites followes upon certaine persones, and at divers houres troubles them: The thirde, when they enter within them and possesse them: The fourth is these kinde of spirites that are called vulgarlie the Fayrie.[34]

He added: 'doubtleslie they are in effect, but all one kinde of spirites, who for abusing the more of mankinde, takes on three sundrie shapes, and uses diverse formes of out-ward actiones.' He explained that these demons might take the form of incorporeal spirits, or might choose to borrow a dead body.[35] James, in fact, went further than Lavater. He did not allow for the appearance of angels or good spirits, and asserted that no miracles had been performed since biblical times.[36] Any kind of spectral apparition was demonic by James's definition, just as any kind of magical capability implied a pact with the Devil.

Few other Scottish authors wrote about ghosts before the late seventeenth century. If mentioned, ghosts were usually interpreted according to James's template, and associated with Catholicism. William Birnie, minister of Lanark from 1597, wrote a treatise arguing against kirk burial in 1606. He explained that many Catholic errors stemmed from those of the 'olde Heathen', who 'became

33 Julian Goodare, 'Scotland', in Bob Scribner, Roy Porter and Mikuláš Teich (eds), *The Reformation in National Context* (Cambridge, 1994), 95–110; Michael Lynch, 'Preaching to the Converted? Perspectives on the Scottish Reformation', in A. A. MacDonald, M. Lynch and I. B. Cowan (eds), *The Renaissance in Scotland: Studies in Literature, Religion, History and Culture* (Leiden, 1994), 301–43.

34 James VI, *Daemonologie, in Forme of Ane Dialogue*, in James Craigie and Alexander Law (eds), *Minor Prose Works of King James VI and I* (Edinburgh, 1982), bk. 3, ch. 1, 39–40.

35 Ibid., bk. 3, ch. 1, 40, 41.

36 Ibid., bk. 3, ch. 1, 45. On Protestants and miracles see D. P. Walker, 'The Cessation of Miracles', in Ingrid Merkel and Allen G. Debus (eds), *Hermeticism and the Renaissance: Intellectual History and the Occult in Early Modern Europe* (Washington, 1988), 111–24; Alexandra Walsham, 'Miracles in Post-Reformation England', in Kate Cooper and Jeremy Gregory (eds), *Signs, Wonders, Miracles: Representations of Divine Power in the Life of the Church* (Woodbridge, 2005), 273–306; Jane Shaw, *Miracles in Enlightenment England* (New Haven, 2006); R. M. Burns, *The Great Debate on Miracles: From Joseph Glanvill to David Hume* (London, 1981); Philip M. Soergel, *Miracles and the Protestant Imagination: The Evangelical Wonder Book in Reformation Germany* (New York, 2012).

plunged in infinite errors anent the estate of the dead'. These heathens divided the world into good and bad men, and then subdivided each estate into two categories. The best of the good became gods. The lesser good folk experienced some of the Elysian fields, but were also required to serve mankind as benevolent spirits; they were known as 'Lares', or 'Brunies' (brownies) in Scots. The worst of the bad men were 'assigned the pitte of Pluto for prison'. However,

> the next were the not so bad: who being not Lares, but Larvae or Lemures, that is, bogils or Gaistes, were by the world adjudged to such a purgatoriall pennance, that wandring in a vagarant estate about graves and alrish deserts, they were suspended till their pennance was ended from elisean repose.

These pagan beliefs remained 'in hote tread' among the Catholics.[37] Birnie's picture was based on ancient Roman ideas, revisited during the Renaissance, which presented Lares as the spirits of the good dead and Lemures or Larvae as the spirits of the wicked.[38] In fact, Catholic accounts of ghosts did not generally follow this framework, but Birnie succeeded in underlining the unorthodoxy of ghost belief, and in entangling ghosts with notions of Purgatory. He also linked ghosts to superstitious folk culture, complaining that kirk burial meant that 'Gods seemely sanctuarie ... becommeth in populare opinion thereby the alrishe Innes of bogles and Gaists. So that many for that presumed feare dare not enter alone in the Kirk.'[39]

About a decade later, the Stirling minister Patrick Simson offered an equally critical analysis. He explained that 'visions, dreames and apparitions' constituted one of the three pillars used by Catholics to support Purgatory, and added:

> In end, Purgatorie finding no sure allowance in scripture, nor yet in the writings of ancient fathers began to creepe under the skirts of apparitions of dead men & by dreames, fables, apparitions and foolish inventions it was so strengthened, that the verity of the Gospel was not so much regarded by a foolish bewitched people as the fables confirming Purgatorie.[40]

William Guild, a minister of Aberdeen and theological writer, similarly noted in 1655 and 1656 that 'apparitions of soules' were a Catholic superstition, and added that the visions proceeded 'from the fraud and deceat of the devill'.[41]

37 William Birnie, *The Blame of Kirk-Buriall, Tending to Perswade Cemiteriall Civilitie* (Edinburgh, 1606, STC 3089), ch. 12, C4v–D. 'Alrish' is an alternative form of 'eldritch'.

38 See Armando Maggi, *In the Company of Demons: Unnatural Beings, Love, and Identity in the Italian Renaissance* (Chicago, 2006), 9–12, 94–8, 128–9.

39 Birnie, *Blame of Kirk-Buriall*, ch. 17, E3v.

40 Patrick Simson, *A Short Compend of the Historie of the First Ten Persecutions Moved against Christians Divided into III Centuries*, 3 vols (Edinburgh, 1613–1616, STC 23601), vol. 1, cent. 3, 'A Treatise of Purgatorie and Prayer for the Dead', O3.

41 William Guild, *Anti-Christ Pointed and Painted Out in His True Colours* (Aberdeen, 1655), 164; William Guild, *An Answer to a Popish Pamphlet Called The Touch-Stone of the Reformed Gospell* (Aberdeen, 1656), 223.

The minister Alexander Wedderburn (c.1620–78) offered an unusually sympathetic picture, arguing that God had sent the dead souls of Moses and Elijah from Heaven to Earth for the Transfiguration. However, he added that although God had the power to restore the dead, 'that it is his Will so to do, or that it is now needfull to be done, is that which [Popish writers] can never prove'.[42] Demons, on the other hand, were thought to have free rein to travel as they wished. The Glasgow minister James Durham explained in 1658: 'That there are evill spirits rangeing up and down through the earth is certain, even though hell be their prison properly, yet have they a sort of dominion and abode both in the earth and air.'[43]

Similar scepticism can be seen in poetry. The Bannatyne Manuscript, a sixteenth-century anthology, included an anonymous and undated poem entitled 'Lord Fergus Gaist'. Burlesque in style, it presented an early case of a ghost 'wyne in ane wynden schet', and described a complex ceremony for laying a ghost, involving ten foxes' tails, holy water, snuff, a dog's ear, some blue wool, and other miscellaneous artefacts. The ghost was to be addressed as follows:

> Littill gaist I conjure the
> With lierie & larie
> bayth fra god & sanct marie
> first with ane fisschis mowth
> And syne with ane fowlis towth
> With ten partane tais
> and nyne knokis of windil strais
> With thre heidis of curle doddy[44]

At the end of this speech the sign of the cross should be made, and the ghost would disappear, never to return. The poem mocked Catholic ritual. The ghost itself was associated with a fantastical folkloric world; later in the poem it married the 'Spenzie fle' and fathered 'Orpheus King and Elpha Quene'.[45]

42 Alexander Wedderburn, *Heaven upon Earth, or, The History of the Transfiguration of Jesus Chirst Opened* (Edinburgh, 1703), 157–8.

43 James Durham, *A Commentarie upon the Book of the Revelation* (Edinburgh, 1658), 679.

44 'Lord Fergus Gaist' in George Bannatyne, *The Bannatyne Manuscript*, ed. W. Tod Ritchie, 4 vols (Edinburgh, 1928–34), vol. 2, 304. This poem is also recorded by Walter Scott in Appendix V to *The Minstrelsy of the Scottish Border*. The version in *The Poetical Works of Sir Walter Scott, Bart.*, ed. J. G. Lockhart, 12 vols (Edinburgh, 1833–4), vol. 1, 265–9 has fuller annotations than earlier editions of the Minstrelsy. Scott translates 'lierie and larie' as 'with laying and with lore' and 'ten partane tais' as 'ten crabs' claws'. He also notes that a 'curle doddy' is a small plant found in marshes. The *DSL* defines a 'windil stray' as a 'withered stalk of grass'. 'Wyndil(l) stray n.', *DSL* (Scottish Language Dictionaries, 2004), http://www.dsl.ac.uk/entry/dost/wyndill_stray, accessed 1 Feb. 2018.

45 Scott translated the 'Spenzie fle' as the 'Spanish fly'. Scott, *Poetical Works*, vol. 1, 269.

Another two works, both from the 1580s, similarly placed ghosts in the realm of vulgar superstition. In 'The Legend of the Bischop of St. Androis Lyfe', a lampoon against Archbishop Patrick Adamson, Robert Sempill presented a witch riding out with fairies, nature spirits and dead neighbours:

> Ane carling of the Quene of Phareis,
> That ewill win geir to elphyne careis.
> Through all Braid Abane scho hes bene
> On horsback, on Hallow ewin;
> And ay in seiking, certayne nyghtis,
> As scho sayis, with our sillie wychtis;
> And names out nychtbouris sex or sewin,
> That we belevit had bene in heawin.[46]

Secondly, as part of a flyting with the Catholic Alexander Montgomerie, Patrick Hume of Polwart declared:

> Thy speach but purpose, sporter, is espyed,
> That wrytes of witches, warlocks, wraiths, and wratches;
> But invectives against him well defyed,
> Rob Stevin, thou raves, forgetting whom thou matches.
> Leave boggles, brownies, gyr-carlings and gaists:
> Dastard, thou daffes, that with such divilrie mels.[47]

In these two extracts, ghosts were associated with even more theologically questionable beliefs such as brownies, fairies and ogres (gyr-carlings). There was also a demonic undertone: Sempill linked the ghosts to an old woman who brought evilly obtained goods to fairyland, while Hume used the term 'divilrie'. Ghosts were dismissed as vulgar superstitions and diabolic tricks in the medieval period as well, but these interpretations became more dominant following the Reformation.

Alternative interpretations of apparitions were rare, but not unheard of. One example can be seen in the work of Paracelsian physician and antiquarian Christopher Irvine (c.1620–93). In *Medicina Magnetica: Or, The*

[46] Quoted in Julian Goodare, 'The Cult of the Seely Wights in Scotland', *Folklore* 123 (2012), 206–7. See also David J. Parkinson, '"The Legend of the Bischop of St. Androis Lyfe" and the Survival of Scottish Poetry', *Early Modern Literary Studies* 9 (2003), 5.1–24. 'Carling' is an old woman; 'ewill win geir' is ill-gotten goods; 'elphyne' is the land of the elves. On 'sillie wychtis', or seely wights, see Goodare, 'Cult of the Seely Wights', 198–219.

[47] Alexander Montgomerie and Patrick Hume, 'The Flyting betwixt Montgomery and Polwart', in James Cranstoun (ed.), *The Poems of Alexander Montgomerie* (Edinburgh, 1887), lines 657–662, pp. 81–2. See Jacqueline Simpson, '"The Weird Sisters Wandering": Burlesque Witchery in Montgomerie's Flyting', *Folklore* 106 (1995), 9–20. To 'daf' is to err; 'Rob Stevin' is seemingly a nickname.

Rare and Wonderful Art of Curing by Sympathy (1656), Irvine outlined his theory on vital human spirits, which (he argued) lent a curative power to the flesh and blood of the freshly dead. Those who had died violent deaths were particularly potent. Irvine explained that the soul could still perform some operations after death, whether because it was 'not utterly and absolutely free as long as any vital spirit remaineth any where safe and untoucht' or simply because it could function without the 'instruments of its proper natural heat'. He continued:

> But of what hath been said the cause is plain, why about the Graves of them that *die a violent death* there are apparitions seen: for the *vital heat and natural moisture* being not quite dissolved, the *soul* sticks, and gives sometimes in these *exhallations, impregnated with the spirit, the shape and form of a man:* And the same may be the reason, why sometimes in *Church-yards* such things appear: and from the same head it is, that the slain Corps bleedeth at the presence or touch of the Murderer: for, the *soul* being yet present, doth by the dispensation of Providence, work such things.[48]

Irvine's interpretation recalled the theory of Renaissance magus Cornelius Agrippa, who suggested that ghosts might be understood as natural projections from the dead body.[49] However, it was unusual in Scotland to draw so heavily on physiology in explaining apparitions (as well as the bleeding corpse, which will be discussed further below). Admittedly, Irvine still owned the importance of the 'dispensation of Providence', so his account was not wholly devoid of supernatural elements. It constituted a middle ground between supernatural and rational interpretations of spirits: the apparition remained a dead soul, but it appeared through physiological functions rather than for theological reasons. Irvine's approach is interesting, but it does not really represent an alternative trend in interpreting apparitions. Some Scottish thinkers recalled Ludwig Lavater's argument that melancholy or drunkenness could lead people to see apparitions. James VI, although generally dismissive of this explanation, did suggest that melancholy might be behind werewolf stories.[50] In 1678, George Mackenzie of Rosehaugh argued that 'the fumes of wine or melancholy will represent strange apparitions, and make us think them real'.[51] However, it was not until the eighteenth century that physiological explanations for ghosts appeared frequently. In the late sixteenth and seventeenth centuries, the demonic explanation remained predominant.

48 Christopher Irvine, *Medicina Magnetica: Or, The Rare and Wonderful Art of Curing by Sympathy* (Edinburgh, 1656), 16–17.

49 Marshall, *Beliefs and the Dead*, 249.

50 James VI, *Daemonologie*, bk. 3, ch. 1, 42.

51 George Mackenzie, *The Laws and Customes of Scotland, in Matters Criminal* (Edinburgh, 1678), 98.

Surviving Ghost Stories

Although apparitions were usually depicted as demons or Catholic errors after the Reformation, they did not disappear from educated culture altogether. One well-known story was recorded by two sixteenth-century Scottish historians, the aforementioned George Buchanan and Robert Lindsay of Pitscottie. Both were Protestants. Buchanan served as a tutor to Mary Queen of Scots and James VI, and was Moderator of the kirk's General Assembly in 1567. Robert Lindsay did not hold such influential posts as Buchanan, but he is remembered for producing the first history of Scotland to be written in Scots. His *Historie and Cronicles of Scotland* was completed in the late 1570s or early 1580s, but remained unpublished until 1728. It seems to have been well known all the same; W. W. Scott notes that at least sixteen manuscript versions survive, and that continuations up to 1603 were produced.[52] The apparition story began with James IV and a party of lords at church in Linlithgow, preparing to set out for the Battle of Flodden (9 September 1513). While James was in prayer, another figure entered the church and approached him. Lindsay described his appearance as follows:

> there came a Man clad in a blue Gown in at the Kirk Door, and belted about him in a Roll of Linen Cloth; a Pair of Brotikins on his Feet, to the Great of his Legs, with all other Hose and Clothes conform thereto; but he had nothing on his Head, but syde red yellow Hair behind, and on his Haffits, which wan down to his Shoulders; but his Forehead was bald and bare. He seemed to be a Man of two and fifty Years, with a great Pyke Staff in his Hand.[53]

In Buchanan's version the figure was 'an old man, the hair of his head being red inclining to yellow and hanging down on his shoulders, his forehead sleek thro' baldness, bare-headed, in a long coat of a russet colour, girt with a linen girdle about his loins'.[54] He reached James, and in Lindsay's version he declared, with 'little Reverence or Salutation':

> Sir King, my Mother hath sent me to you, desiring you not to pass, at this Time, where thou art purposed; for, if thou does, thou wilt not fare well in thy Journey, nor none that passeth with thee. Further, she bade thee mell with no Woman, nor use their Counsel, nor let them touch thy Body, nor thou theirs; for, if thou do it, thou wilt be confounded and brought to Shame.

He gave a very similar warning in Buchanan's text. The king hesitated, and according to Lindsay the man then 'vanished away, and could noways be seen

52 W. W. Scott, 'Lindsay, Robert, of Pitscottie (c.1532–c.1586)', *Oxford DNB* (Oxford University Press, 2004), http://www.oxforddnb.com/view/article/16715, accessed 1 Feb. 2018.

53 Robert Lindsay, *The History of Scotland: From 21 February, 1436 to March, 1565* (Edinburgh, 1728), 111. 'Haffits' are temples.

54 Buchanan, *Rerum Scoticarum Historia*, bk. 13, para. 23.

nor comprehended, but vanished away as he had been a Blink of the Sun, or a Whip of the Whirlwind'.[55] James went on to Flodden and was killed.

There has been some speculation that this incident was engineered by nobles as an anti-war stunt – or, perhaps, choreographed by James's disgruntled wife.[56] However, there is really no need to look for rational explanations: the story might well have been devised only after James's death. The mysterious warning, the moralising reflection on James's partiality for mistresses, and the dramatic disappearance were all familiar narrative elements; a story of this sort could circulate regardless of whether or not there happened to be any truth in it. This apparition was not necessarily a returning dead person, but nor was it presented as a demon. Perhaps as a result, Buchanan was cautious about including the story in his history. He noted that one of those present was the poet David Lindsay, 'a man of approved worth and honesty (and a great scholar too)'. He explained that 'if I had not received this story from him as a certain truth, I had omitted it as a romance of the vulgar'.[57] For all Buchanan's hesitancy, the story seems to have been popular. When George Sinclair republished it in his 1685 *Satans Invisible World Discovered*, details had been added or modified. The precise church was specified (St Michael's), and the man was described as 'an Ancient Man ... his Amber coloured Hair hanging down upon his Shoulders, his forehead high, and inclining to Baldness, his Garments of Azure colour, somewhat long, girded about with a Towel, or Table-Napkin, of a Comely and very Reverend Aspect'.[58] The apparition did not mention his mother, and the reference to touching women's bodies was toned down into a recommendation that James should not make use of the 'company' of women. This suggests that the story had circulated and been retold in the hundred years after the deaths of Lindsay and Buchanan.

Buchanan and Lindsay also wrote of an apparition that visited James V in a dream. In 1540, James V had James Hamilton of Finnart executed on a charge of treason. He was subsequently visited by Hamilton's apparition. In Buchanan's words: 'in his sleep [James V] saw James Hamilton running at him with his drawn sword, and that he first cut off his right arm, then his left, and threatned him shortly to come and take away his life, and then disappeared'.[59] The king's two sons died soon afterwards. This story was also given by John Knox in his history of the Scottish Reformation, written in the late 1550s and early 1560s. Knox described a second vision as well, related to the same affair:

[55] Lindsay, *History of Scotland*, 111.

[56] R. L. Mackie, *King James IV of Scotland: A Brief Survey of His Life and Times* (London, 1976), 264–5; Norman Macdougall, *James IV: The Stewart Dynasty in Scotland* (Edinburgh, 2006), 265–6.

[57] Buchanan, *Rerum Scoticarum Historia*, bk. 13, para. 23.

[58] George Sinclair, *Satans Invisible World Discovered* (Edinburgh, 1685), 39.

[59] Buchanan, *Rerum Scoticarum Historia*, bk. 14, para. 47; Lindsay, *History of Scotland*, 167–8.

the justice clerk Thomas Scott of Balwearie appeared moments after his death in the company of devils, and declared to the king: 'O wo to the day that ever I knew thee or thy service; for serving of thee, against God, against his servants, and against Justice, I am adjudged to endlesse torment.'[60] Knox's Protestant credentials are hardly in doubt, but he was seemingly ready to countenance ghost stories when they suited his own purposes – in this case, highlighting the impiety of a Catholic king.

Knox was writing before the publication of Ludwig Lavater's work on ghosts, and all three of these writers pre-dated James VI's *Daemonologie*. Even after the publication of *Daemonologie*, however, ghosts made occasional appearances in print. David Person, who described himself as a gentleman from the Lowlands, produced a 1635 text entitled *Varieties: Or, A Surveigh of Rare and Excellent Matters Necessary and Delectable for All Sorts of Persons*. The text covered a diverse range of subjects, including the nature of the Earth, sun, moon, stars, sea and meteors; battles and duels; laughing and mourning; 'divine Philosophy'; sleep and dreams; death, miracles and prodigies; the Philosopher's Stone; metaphysics; and the numbers three and seven. As part of his discussion of death, Person explained that poets 'affirme that the spirits and Manes of them who want their due burialls, wander here and there in Ghostly apparitions untill their bones be interred'.[61] He added that 'the punishment of the neglect of it may appeare in one of our Northern Countries', and proceeded to tell a story from Lauder. A woman on her deathbed beseeched her husband to bury her in the churchyard, 'which if hee did not, shee threatned that her Ghost would haunt him after her death'. However, there was an outbreak of the plague at the time. The man feared that if he buried her publicly his friends would suspect that she had been infected, and would break off contact with him. He therefore concealed her death, burying her in a corner of his garden. Person explained:

> thereafter, this womans ghost, I say, did so incessantly both haunt and affright, both him, his children, and family, that there was no resting for them at any time; till by the advise of the Clergy she was taken up againe and buried, where she desired to be in her life-time; which being done, both she and they rested.[62]

[60] John Knox, *The History of the Reformation of the Church of Scotland* (London, 1644), bk. 1, 25. On Balwearie's supernatural associations see Julian Goodare, 'The Scottish Witchcraft Panic of 1597', in Julian Goodare (ed.), *The Scottish Witch-Hunt in Context* (Manchester, 2002), 58–9.

[61] 'Manes' was another term for departed spirits in Roman mythology. For a discussion of them see Charles W. King, 'The Roman Manes: The Dead as Gods', in Mu-chou Poo (ed.), *Rethinking Ghosts in World Religions* (Leiden, 2009), 95–114.

[62] David Person, *Varieties: Or, A Surveigh of Rare and Excellent Matters Necessary and Delectable for All Sorts of Persons* (London, 1635, STC 19781), 165.

This was in line with medieval tradition, which held that ghosts might return because of irregularities in their burials. Person's work was a motley collection on all kinds of different topics, but it is nonetheless interesting to note that a ghost story could be presented seriously in a quasi-scientific treatise.

Even ministers sometimes had doubts about how to interpret ghost stories. In 1666, some inhabitants of South Ronaldsay, Orkney, were troubled with dreams and apparitions of four fishermen who had died at sea. The fishermen claimed to have been murdered. After their widows appealed to the local minister, he went with the baillie and the kirk session to inspect the graves, and those who had found the bodies were required to handle them (more on this presently).[63] No evidence of wrongdoing was discovered, but it is interesting that these steps were taken at all. Just over a decade later, in December 1675, the Leith kirk session recorded the following:

> Compeared James Dempster and declared against John Robertson (whose wife died about six weeks ago and being thrice proclaimed upon Janet Trotter was intended to be married this day) that his wife's ghost hath severall tymes appeared to him and commanded him to go to the ministers and session and beg that his marriage might be stopt, averring that the said John had murthered his wife and brybed him with half a crown and promised him some more to hold his peace.[64]

The entry went on to explain that 'the business being criminall the session referred it to the baillies'. Both the kirk session and the baillies were apparently prepared to take ghosts seriously.

Finally, it is worth noting the sentence cast on five prisoners convicted of treason for their part in the Battle of Bothwell Bridge (22 June 1679). The battle was waged between Covenanters and the Episcopalian government. In the previous month, a group of militant Covenanters had murdered Archbishop James Sharp, who was held responsible for persecution of Presbyterians. The five prisoners were not involved, but were declared accessories because they expressed sympathy towards the murderers. In November 1679, the judges sentenced the men to execution, and declared that they should be 'hanged up in chains in Magus-moor, to expiate and appease the Archbishop's ghost, who was there murdered'.[65] The judges may not have been referring to a literal ghost, but their sentence indicates the survival of the medieval notion that those who had died a violent, untimely death would be condemned to wander until they had been avenged. Although the demonic interpretation of ghosts had become prevalent, traditional beliefs lingered on.

[63] J. B. Craven, *Church Life in South Ronaldshay and Burray in the Seventeenth Century* (Kirkwall, 1911), 53.

[64] David Robertson (ed.), *South Leith Records, Compiled from the Parish Registers for the Years 1588 to 1700* (Edinburgh, 1911), 133. 'Compeared' is 'appeared'.

[65] John Lauder (ed.), *The Decisions of the Lords of Council and Session, from June 6th, 1678, to July 30th, 1712*, 2 vols (Edinburgh, 1759–61), vol. 1, 62–3.

Popular Belief and the Dead Body

If ghost traditions endured among educated folk, they were likely to be even more persistent among the large part of the population that was not wont to consult theological treatises. Importantly, there were plenty of continuities in religious experience before and after the Reformation. Churches were stripped of their Catholic decorations, and services of their ritual elements. Kirk sessions endeavoured to impose strict standards of piety and sexual morality, and educational provision gradually improved, in line with the reformers' aim that everybody should be able to read a copy of the newly-available vernacular Bible. However, these changes were more pronounced in some areas than others. The big towns were the real centres of Protestantism.[66] Even so, Michael Lynch argues that popular Protestantism enjoyed only gradual growth in most of Scotland's towns.[67] Change came even more slowly in rural areas. It took time to train new ministers, and there was a shortage of appropriately skilled candidates. In the early 1590s some four hundred parishes were left unfilled.[68] In many parishes, 'readers' were appointed instead of ministers. Readers could deliver prayers but not preach or administer the sacraments. The reader would frequently be the same individual as had delivered services before the Reformation, making for a certain continuity of experience.[69]

The *Gàidhealtachd*, or Gaelic-speaking area of Scotland, was particularly neglected. Reading material was very limited compared to Lowland Scotland: the Book of Common Order was translated in 1567, but into classical rather than vernacular Gaelic, and there was no Gaelic Bible. A Gaelic catechism was not published until 1653, and a Gaelic psalter not until 1659. Ministers often had to oversee several different parishes, sometimes over large geographical areas.[70] Under these circumstances, the kirk had little power to start educating people about the unorthodox elements of their belief systems. Julian Goodare argues that 'the church had at best a missionary character up to the nineteenth century, leaving the lively pattern of folk-belief largely undisturbed'.[71] Certainly, when the minister Robert Kirk (1644–92) and the writer Martin Martin (d. 1718) began investigating popular culture in the *Gàidhealtachd*, they found plenty of surviving traditions that the kirk would have associated with Catholicism or paganism. Communities from the western isles threw ale into the sea as a tribute to the sea god Shony, or honoured Saint Finbarr with a wooden effigy,

66 Goodare, 'Scotland', 95–110; Lynch, 'Preaching to the Converted?', 301–43.

67 Lynch, 'Preaching to the Converted?', 323.

68 Ibid., 308–9, 302.

69 John McCallum, *Reforming the Scottish Parish: The Reformation in Fife, 1560–1640* (Aldershot, 2010), 87.

70 Geoffrey Parker, 'Success and Failure during the First Century of the Reformation', *Past & Present* 136 (1992), 61; Goodare, 'Scotland', 101.

71 Goodare, 'Scotland', 101.

attired in a shirt.[72] Even in the Lowlands, the kirk was required to wage an ongoing war against practices such as guising, Yule celebrations, May plays and midsummer bonfires.[73] Pilgrimages to healing wells also continued, as did belief in magical charms and amulets. When the Aberdeen synod requested in 1659 that all its ministers should speak against 'heathenish customes in cutting of thee heades of beasts, and carieing off them from one lairds lands to another', it was expressing just the sort of complaint against 'abominable, heathenish superstition' that had been cropping up regularly in kirk session records all over the country.[74]

One significant area in which popular belief persisted regardless of Reformation teachings was death. After the Reformation, the kirk began to strip away many of the ceremonies and rituals associated with death. *The First Book of Discipline* (1560) stated:

> For avoiding of all inconveniences we judge it best, that neither singing nor reading be at burial. For albeit things sung and read may admonish some of the living to prepare themselves for death, yet shall some superstitious think that singing and reading of the living may profite the dead. And therefore we think it most expedient, that the dead be conveyed to the place of buriall with some honest company of the kirk, without either singing or reading; yea without all kind of ceremony heretofore used, other than that the dead be committed to the grave, with such gravity and sobriety, as those that be present may seeme to feare the judgements of God, and to hate sinne which is the cause of death.[75]

The age of elaborate funeral services was, at least in theory, past.[76] The kirk also tried to clamp down on boisterous lykewakes, or parties held while watching over the corpse before its burial.[77] The dead were more cut off from the living than they had been under Catholic theology. As there was no more Purgatory, the living could no longer assist their departed relatives with prayers or masses. Furthermore, although the 1560 Confession of Faith declared that bodies would rise again at the Last Judgement, the kirk played down their

72 Martin Martin, *A Description of the Western Isles of Scotland* (London, 1703), 29–30, 92; see also 17, 49, 85–6, 110–13, 117–19, 242, 277–8, 300–35; Robert Kirk, 'Robert Kirk's *The Secret Commonwealth* and his "A Short Treatise of the Scotish-Irish Charms and Spells"', in Michael Hunter (ed.), *The Occult Laboratory: Magic, Science, and Second Sight in Late Seventeenth-Century Scotland* (Woodbridge, 2001), 77–117.

73 Lynch, 'Preaching to the Converted?', 323–6; see also Ronald Hutton, *The Stations of the Sun: A History of the Ritual Year in Britain* (Oxford, 1996).

74 John Stuart (ed.), *Selections from the Records of the Kirk Session, Presbytery, and Synod of Aberdeen* (Aberdeen, 1846), xxxv; Charles Donald Bentinck, *Dornoch Cathedral and Parish* (Inverness, 1926), 262.

75 James K. Cameron (ed.), *The First Book of Discipline* (Edinburgh, 1972), 200.

76 See Gordon Raeburn, 'The Long Reformation of the Dead in Scotland' (Durham University Ph.D. thesis, 2012).

77 Anne Gordon, *Candie for the Foundling* (Edinburgh, 1992), 508.

importance.[78] In 1628, religious writer Zacharie Boyd demanded of his readers: 'Is it not your greatest desire to flitte from this bodie which is but a Booth, a shoppe, or Tabernacle of clay.' The kirk rejected the idea that bodies should be buried in consecrated ground; as Boyd explained, 'God will never inquire of a mans Soule where was thy bodie buried'.[79] There were also attempts to put an end to burial within churches, and headstones were viewed with some suspicion. In 1646, the Leith Session refused to allow Christian Robertson to set 'ane hewen stone' at the head of her husband's grave, noting that if they allowed it, 'everie ane wold strive to have the lyke favor'.[80]

However, the kirk's message about the impotency of the dead body was at odds with folk belief. In the absence of substantial source material on popular ghost stories from this period, ideas about the supernatural power of the corpse merit examination.[81] First of all, a dead body was thought to bleed in the presence of its murderer, as Christopher Irvine explained above. This phenomenon was known as 'cruentation', or sometimes by the Scots term, 'bierricht'. George Buchanan offered an early (although historically unsubstantiated) reference to this belief. He wrote that after the murder of King Duff (d. 966/7), the assassins carried the body carefully so that no blood could appear, 'because there is an opinion, received from our ancestors, which as yet obtains among the vulgar, that blood will issue from a dead body many days after the party was murdered, if the murder[er] be present, as if the fact had been but newly committed'.[82] Cruentation cropped up in a diverse range of sources. In versions of the ballad 'Young Hunting' (Child 68), a dead man's wounds bled when his murderer approached, and James VI explained in *Daemonologie* that a dead body handled by the murderer would 'gush out of bloud, as if the blud wer crying to the heaven for revenge'.[83]

78 Arthur C. Cochrane (ed.), 'The Scottish Confession of Faith, 1560', in *Reformed Confessions of the Sixteenth Century* (Philadelphia, 1966), 184.

79 Zacharie Boyd, *The Last Battell of the Soule in Death* (Edinburgh, 1628, STC 3446a.5), 84, 1046.

80 On burial see Gordon, *Candie for the Foundling*, 483; Andrew Spicer, '"Defyle Not Christ's Kirk with Your Carrion": Burial and the Development of Burial Aisles in Post-Reformation Scotland', in Bruce Gordon and Peter Marshall (eds), *The Place of the Dead: Death and Remembrance in Late Medieval and Early Modern Europe* (Cambridge, 2000), 149–69. Session quotation from Robertson, *South Leith Records*, 71. This rule, however, increasingly slipped by the wayside, and by the eighteenth century the session was regularly granting permission for headstones (71–2). Equally, the rule about church burial was not always upheld; see Spicer, '"Defyle Not Christ's Kirk"', 149–69.

81 On the potent corpse see also Owen Davies and Francesca Matteoni, *Executing Magic in the Modern Era: Criminal Bodies and the Gallows in Popular Medicine*, electronic edn (Palgrave Macmillan, 2017), https://doi.org/10.1007/978-3-319-59519-1, accessed 1 Feb. 2018; Richard Sugg, *Mummies, Cannibals, and Vampires: The History of Corpse Medicine from the Renaissance to the Victorians* (Abingdon, 2011); Sarah Tarlow, *Ritual, Belief and the Dead in Early Modern Britain and Ireland* (Cambridge, 2011), ch. 5.

82 Buchanan, *Rerum Scoticarum Historia*, bk. 6, para. 21.

83 James VI, *Daemonologie*, bk. 3, ch. 1, 56.

Cruentation was also used as evidence in criminal trials. In 1644, a couple from Shetland, Marioun and Swene Peebles, were made to handle the bodies of fishermen whom they had allegedly drowned. The bodies bled, 'to the great admiration of the beholders – and revelation of the judgement of the Almytie'.[84] As we have seen, the baillies and kirk session of South Ronaldsay compelled suspected murderers to handle the corpses.[85] In 1688, a Scottish defence counsel objected to the use of the bleeding corpse as evidence in court. Philip Standsfield of Newmilns, Ayrshire, was accused of murdering his father, and a surgeon swore that after being touched by Standsfield, the corpse began 'darting out blood through the linnen, from the left side of the neck'.[86]

Dead bodies were also used for magical ends. A dead hand might be placed in a man's path as part of a spell to kill him; a belt that had been put on a dead child was thought to have healing properties, as was water that had been used to wash human bones; and dead flesh was hung above the doors of stables to harm cattle or other animals.[87] The corpses of young men who had died premature deaths were thought to be particularly potent.[88] When the corpse was ascribed supernatural power, it was no great leap to envisage that it might be able to rise again, in the fashion of medieval revenants. In 1641, the synod of Fife condemned the traditions of carrying the dead about the kirkyard before burial, and of burying unbaptised children separately.[89] Both of these practices were believed to prevent the dead from returning. In 1643, the Aberdeen council had to prohibit the use of mort bells, or bells rung while the body was carried to the graveyard and sometimes left at the grave itself. Several folklorists have

[84] Robert Pitcairn (ed.), *Criminal Trials in Scotland, 1488–1624*, 4 vols (Edinburgh, 1833), vol. 3, 194.

[85] Lizanne Henderson, 'The Survival of Witchcraft Prosecutions and Witch Belief in South-West Scotland', *Scottish Historical Review* 85 (2006), 57–8. Henderson also includes other examples of the bleeding corpse being used as evidence.

[86] Thomas Jones Howell and William Cobbett, *A Complete Collection of State Trials and Proceedings for High Treason and Other Crimes and Misdemeanors from the Earliest Period to the Year 1783*, 21 vols (London, 1816), vol. 11, 1402–3.

[87] Julian Goodare et al., *The Survey of Scottish Witchcraft* (University of Edinburgh, 2003), http://www.shca.ed.ac.uk/witches, accessed 1 Feb. 2018. The specific cases referred to are John Smith, Katherine Wilson and Neill John, 1623–30; John Philip, 1631; Isobell Strauthaquhin, 1597; Johnne Brughe, Margaret Kinard and Katherine Mitchell, 1642–3. However, many other examples can be found, for example by searching for 'bone' or 'flesh' used as a ritual object. Unless otherwise specified, all subsequent references to witch trials are taken from the *Survey of Scottish Witchcraft*.

[88] See, for example, the case of Janet Wishart (tried in 1597); she was said to have dismembered the corpse of a recently hanged man. Edward J. Cowan, 'Witch Persecution and Folk Belief in Lowland Scotland: The Devil's Decade', in Julian Goodare, Lauren Martin and Joyce Miller (eds), *Witchcraft and Belief in Early Modern Scotland* (Basingstoke, 2008), 79; Julian Goodare, 'Scottish Witchcraft in its European Context', in Julian Goodare, Lauren Martin and Joyce Miller (eds), *Witchcraft and Belief in Early Modern Scotland* (Basingstoke, 2008), 49n82.

[89] Andrew Edgar, *Old Church Life in Scotland: Lectures on Kirk-Session and Presbytery Records* (Paisley, 1886), 253.

posited that their original purpose was to frighten away evil spirits.[90] The kirk session of Pencaitland reprimanded a woman in 1651 for putting an iron nail between the corpse and its winding sheet, to prevent the spirit from returning (iron was thought to be a deterrent for ghosts).[91] The aforementioned ghost stories recorded by Person and the kirk sessions of South Ronaldsay and Leith also indicate the survival of ghost belief. Surveying the English patterns, Peter Marshall has argued that 'the emotional claims and cultural leverage exercised by dead ancestors could prove peculiarly intractable to the dictates of Protestant orthodoxy, and even encourage some of the self-proclaimed defenders of that orthodoxy to muffle the distinctive tones of their divinity'.[92] Similarly in Scotland, the Reformation does not seem to have precipitated a dramatic shift in how ghosts were understood. Although kirk sessions made efforts to clamp down on illegitimate practices, local clergy were probably not over-zealous when it came to policing their parishioners' conceptions of the dead.

Witches and Poltergeists

The proper interpretation of apparitions was also negotiated through discussions of witches and haunted houses. The Scottish Witchcraft Act was passed in 1563, making witchcraft a capital offence. It was not overturned until 1736. In the interim, at least 3,837 people were accused of witchcraft, of whom about 84 per cent were women. There were particularly marked periods of persecution in 1590–1, 1597, 1628–30, 1649 and 1661–2. Execution rates are difficult to establish, as few cases record the sentence passed, but may have been in the region of two thirds.[93] As such, Scotland experienced relatively severe witch-hunting, executing as many as ten times more witches per head of the population than England, and five times the European average.[94] Scholars focusing on England have argued that ghosts, having been reinterpreted as demonic, were absorbed into witchcraft discourses in the sixteenth and seventeenth centuries.[95]

90 Ibid., 257–8; Gordon, *Candie for the Foundling*, 496.

91 Lizanne Henderson and Edward J. Cowan, *Scottish Fairy Belief: A History* (East Linton, 2001), 88.

92 Marshall, *Beliefs and the Dead*, ch. 6 (quotation 234).

93 Julian Goodare et al., 'Introduction to Scottish Witchcraft', *The Survey of Scottish Witchcraft* (University of Edinburgh, 2003), http://www.shca.ed.ac.uk/research/witches/introduction.html, accessed 1 Feb. 2018.

94 James Sharpe, 'Witch-Hunting and Witch Historiography: Some Anglo-Scottish Comparisons', in Julian Goodare (ed.), *The Scottish Witch-Hunt in Context* (Manchester, 2002), 182; Julian Goodare, 'Witchcraft in Scotland', in Brian P. Levack (ed.), *The Oxford Handbook of Witchcraft in Early Modern Europe and Colonial America* (Oxford, 2013), 302.

95 Gillian Bennett, 'Ghost and Witch in the Sixteenth and Seventeenth Centuries', *Folklore* 97 (1986), 9, 3; McKeever, 'Ghost in Early Modern Protestant Culture', 136–46.

Certainly, witches and ghosts became closely associated in Scotland – although it could be argued that witch beliefs complemented ghost traditions, rather than replacing them. Popular belief in the potency of the corpse was reinforced by stories of how witches used dead body parts. Furthermore, witches were thought to have dealings with ghosts. Jonet Reid (tried in 1643) was able to advise a man called Robert Sinclair on how to rid himself of 'apparitiounes of his ffirst wyiff, which wexit him and disquietit him verie much'.[96] Margaret Lang (tried in 1697) was a sort of medium who could contact people's dead relatives. Bessie Dunlop (tried in 1576), Alison Pearson (tried in 1588) and Elspeth Reoch (tried in 1616) all had spectral advisers who were said to be dead men (Thom Reid, William Symsone and Johne Stewart respectively).[97] Ghosts and witches also attended the same parties. Margaret Bell (tried in 1649) met the Devil in a quarry; he was accompanied by a group of people who had died of the plague. Andro Man (tried in 1597–8) claimed to have encountered the ghosts of James IV and the prophet Thomas the Rhymer at a fairy gathering. However, even when apparitions were described as returning dead people, they frequently still carried demonic connotations. This can be seen in the case of the ghostly advisers who visited Bessie, Alison and Elspeth. Thom Reid urged Bessie to renounce Christianity, while William Symsone was interpreted as an 'evil spirit' and Johne Stewart as a 'devell' by the interrogators.[98]

Witches could also become apparitions themselves. Margaret Hutchison (tried in 1661) was said to have appeared several times in a house in apparition form, and finally to have suffocated a baby there. Other witches appeared as animals: in the same year, Beatrix Leslie was accused of taking the form of an apparition cat to attack some neighbours with whom she had quarrelled. James VI discussed the idea of witches appearing as beasts. He denied that there was any actual physical transformation, but posited that the Devil could make witches appear in different guises.[99] George Mackenzie presented a similar interpretation in 1678:

> if we consider the strange tricks of Juglers, and the strange apparitions that *Kercher* and others relate from natural causes, we may believe that the Devil may make a woman appear to be a beast, *& è contra*, by either abusing the sense of the beholders, or altering the Medium, by inclosing them in the skin of the beast represented, or by inclosing them in a body of air, shap'd like that which he would have them represent,[100]

96 G. F. Black, *County Folklore III: Examples of Printed Folklore Concerning the Orkney and Shetland Islands*, ed. Northcote W. Thomas (London, 1903), 101.

97 Henderson and Cowan, *Scottish Fairy Belief*, 60; Emma Wilby, *Cunning Folk and Familiar Spirits: Shamanistic Visionary Traditions in Early Modern British Witchcraft and Magic* (Brighton, 2005), 18, 56.

98 Wilby, *Cunning Folk and Familiar Spirits*, 91.

99 James VI, *Daemonologie*, bk. 2, ch. 4, 28.

100 Mackenzie, *Laws and Customes of Scotland*, 100.

In this context, ghosts were more at risk of being simply absorbed into witchcraft discourses. In the medieval period, this type of apparition might be interpreted as a ghost, as souls were known to appear in animal forms.[101] In the wake of the Reformation it was much more likely to be explained in demonic terms.

The argument about ghost and witch discourses blending together has also been applied to poltergeists, a relatively common supernatural bugbear. Poltergeists ranged from being minor irritants to dangerous adversaries who could beat children black and blue, or set houses on fire. They might tear clothes, throw items around, make mysterious noises, put pins in food, or attempt to ruin bibles. P. G. Maxwell-Stuart argues that poltergeists were generally thought of as spirits of the dead in the medieval period, and again in the eighteenth century. In between, they were primarily seen as spirits conjured up by witches.[102] Sixteenth- and seventeenth-century Scottish poltergeists were, indeed, often thought to be the servants of witches. James VI explained that witches had the power to 'make spirites either to follow and trouble persones, or haunt certaine houses, and affraie oftentimes the inhabitantes'.[103] In 1644, the Presbytery of Strathbogie suspected witchcraft in the case of 'clodding and fearfull trouble' experienced by a household.[104] The most common means of ending the haunting of a house was not by talking with the offending spirit and performing some service for it, but rather through a sort of exorcism, conducted by ministers through prayer and Scripture readings. In 1670, the minister William Annand noted that 'if our houses be haunted, by evil spirits', the proper way to be delivered was through 'courage, and faith ... and a goodly life, fasting, prayer'.[105] Even John Knox was said to have dispossessed an evil spirit from a house in this fashion.[106]

The best-known poltergeist from this period haunted a house in Glenluce, Galloway, for a few years from 1654. Robert Baillie, Professor of Divinity at Glasgow, wrote in 1661 that the case was 'notourlie known'. It was also described as famous by Robert Kirk in the mid-1670s, and was discussed at length by the Glasgow philosopher George Sinclair, both in his *Hydrostaticks* (1672) and *Satans Invisible World Discovered* (1685).[107] The unfortunate house

101 For a (somewhat ambiguous) Scottish example see Maxwell, *Chronicle of Lanercost*, 4–5.

102 P. G. Maxwell-Stuart, *Poltergeists: A History of Violent Ghostly Phenomena* (Stroud, 2011), 96, 132.

103 James VI, *Daemonologie*, bk. 2, ch. 5, 33.

104 John Stuart (ed.), *Extracts from the Presbytery Book of Strathbogie, A.D. 1631–1654* (Aberdeen, 1843), 50–1.

105 William Annand, *Pater Noster, Our Father, or, The Lord's Prayer Explained the Sense Thereof and Duties Therein from Scripture, History, and Fathers* (Edinburgh, 1670), 449.

106 John Livingstone, *Memorable Characteristics, and Remarkable Passages of Divine Providence*, in W. K. Tweedie (ed.), *Select Biographies*, 2 vols (Edinburgh, 1845), vol. 1, 295.

107 Michael Hunter, 'Introduction', in Hunter, *Occult Laboratory*, 16; George Sinclair, *The Hydrostaticks, or, The Weight, Force, and Pressure of Fluid Bodies, Made Evident by Physical, and Sensible Experiments* (Edinburgh, 1672), 239–47; Sinclair, *Satans Invisible World Discovered*, 56–67.

was occupied by the family of a weaver – John Campbell in Baillie's version, Gilbert Campbell in Sinclair's. In Baillie's version the poltergeist threw stones, set fire to the house, and cut the webs in the looms, but without ever doing serious harm. Many ministers came to pray and fast in the house, and one had long conversations with the offender. A beggar often lodged in the house, but was subsequently hanged at Dumfries for atheism. Around the time of his death the poltergeist became subdued, but later resumed its agitations. Baillie noted that it had been quiet for the past year, however. He clarified his own interpretation of this story with the closing observation that 'there is much witcherie up and downe our land'.[108] Sinclair's version of the story was similar, but placed the blame more squarely at the door of the blasphemous beggar. The disturbances began after the family refused him alms. He threatened to hurt them, and was later hanged. This would have been a recognisable witchcraft pattern for early modern folk: beggars were often suspected of turning to dark arts if their requests were refused.[109]

Other cases were not linked to witchcraft, but still implied the agency of demons. A story set down in 1659 concerned a man and his son, both ministers, who lived in Edinburgh. Their house was 'extraordinarily troubled with noises'. Locks flew open, and their clothes were regularly strewn about. Once they awoke to find their bed linen spread across the table, along with used napkins and cups containing traces of liquor. The persistent noises subsided to a 'gentle knocking' when the family prayed, but escalated again as soon as they stopped. They never heard a voice or saw an apparition. However, one night a maid took to bed half a cannonball, kept for breaking coals. She told a fellow servant that 'if the Devil troubled them that Night, she would brain him'. When she was awoken by the usual strange noises she threw the cannonball, which vanished, never to be seen again. The diabolic nature of the poltergeist was strongly implied. Another case recorded in 1659 concerned a gentleman called Johnston, who lived in Dumfries. His house had been haunted for some fifty or sixty years. He had heard drums and trumpets before the outbreak of the last war (Oliver Cromwell's invasion of Scotland, which began in 1650), and some English soldiers quartering in the house had been beaten by the poltergeist.[110] This poltergeist was more

[108] Robert Baillie, *Letters and Journals of Robert Baillie, A. M.*, ed. David Laing, 3 vols (Edinburgh, 1841–2), vol. 3, 436.

[109] On this pattern in England especially see Alan Macfarlane, *Witchcraft in Tudor and Stuart England: A Regional and Comparative Study* (London, 1970), 172–6, 196–8, 206; Keith Thomas, *Religion and the Decline of Magic: Studies in Popular Beliefs in Sixteenth and Seventeenth Century England* (London, 1971), ch. 17; Robin Briggs, *Witches and Neighbours: The Social and Cultural Context of European Witchcraft*, 2nd edn (Oxford, 2002), 118–23.

[110] Richard Baxter, *The Certainty of the Worlds of Spirits, and Consequently, of the Immortality of Souls of the Malice and Misery of the Devils and the Damned* (London, 1691), 82–92.

ambiguous – prophetic, and apparently a Scottish nationalist. However, the violence suggests that it, too, was demonic in nature.

Poltergeists, in summary, were usually identified as demons. However, the medieval association between poltergeists and the spirits of the dead had not completely disappeared, especially within popular culture. When the Earl of Huntly died in 1562, reports circulated afterwards of disturbances in his house. Strange noises were heard, and people fell mysteriously ill. This led one of the men of his house to fear that 'the brute wald pas through the cuntrey that the erle of Huntley wer risen againe'.[111] It is possible that Huntly was more likely to be associated with this kind of quasi-demonic activity because he was a Catholic and had died as an enemy of the state (his body was convicted of treason in 1563), but there was no explicit suggestion that demons were involved.[112] In *The Secret Commonwealth*, written in the early 1690s, Robert Kirk noted:

> [The Mountain People] affirm those Creatures that move invisibly in a House, and cast huge <great> Stones ... to be Souls that have not atteaned their Rest, thorough a vehement desyre of revealing a murther or notable injury don or receav'd, or a Treasure that was forgot in their Lyftime on Earth, which when disclos'd to a Conjuror alon the Ghost quite removes.[113]

George Sinclair told a story, apparently from 1635, of a hanged man who was not pardoned despite a miraculous resurrection; he went on to haunt his own house.[114]

Overall, some strands of witch belief could reinforce a belief in the returning dead, and stories of cooperation between witches and ghosts allowed ghosts a distinct identity. However, apparitions became closely associated with witchcraft, and the demonic interpretation of ghosts and poltergeists was dominant among educated folk. If ghost beliefs were not completely eclipsed by witch discourses, they were certainly overshadowed.

Special Providences

After the Reformation demonised apparitions, the place of ghosts in Scottish society did not undergo any significant changes until the late seventeenth century. However, there was (arguably) a gradual change in perceptions of the

[111] Richard Bannatyne, *Memorials of Transactions in Scotland, 1569–1573*, ed. Robert Pitcairn (Edinburgh, 1836), 336–8 (quotation 337).

[112] See Allan White, 'Gordon, George, Fourth Earl of Huntly (1513–1562)', *Oxford DNB* (Oxford University Press, 2004), http://www.oxforddnb.com/view/article/11034, accessed 1 Feb. 2018.

[113] Kirk, 'Robert Kirk's *The Secret Commonwealth*', 85. Hunter's use of angle brackets for '<great>' indicates that the word was inserted above the line in the original.

[114] Sinclair, *Satans Invisible World Discovered*, 127.

supernatural, which may have had some impact on apparition beliefs. Both general and special providence became increasingly fashionable concepts in the late sixteenth and seventeenth centuries. General providence was God's overarching plan for the universe, as drawn up at the Creation. In England, religious groups increasingly made use of the concept of God's providence in the late sixteenth and early seventeenth centuries. George Hakewill painted a picture of the English church and society as having been blessed and upheld by God throughout history. Thomas Beard's 1597 *Theatre of Gods Judgements* demystified the historical process, taking past events as a clear revelation of God's purpose.[115] In Scotland, John Knox likewise initiated a form of history-writing that sought to unravel God's will, using providence as a propaganda tool.[116]

Special providences, by most authors' definitions, were God's spontaneous acts of intervention in the universe.[117] A wide range of events could fall under the heading, from monstrous births to showers of blood, from a minister finding a spider in his porridge to the apparition of a battle in the sky.[118] The Renfrewshire minister Ninian Campbell explained in 1635 that 'by his speciall providence' God had 'an extreame fatherly regard to us'; without it, Campbell wrote, 'one hair cannot fall out of our head, one cubit cannot be added to our stature ... a little sparrow cannot fall to the ground'.[119] The Covenanting movement swept Scotland in the 1630s, demanding a Presbyterian kirk free from monarchical interference. The Covenanters placed emphasis on introspection and a spiritual conversion experience. Spiritual journals blossomed within this religious climate, and provided a vehicle for Covenanters to explore marks of God's favour. James Mitchell of Dykes in Ardrossan, reflecting on the period from the 1620s to the 1640s, cited 'many singular instances of Divine Providence', including

> that my two years accounts crop 1643 and 1644 with my lord Montgomerie are fitted and subscribed without any debat or contest betwixt his Lordship and me, which I did readily expect in some particulars as anent the six baggage horse ... and fourteen bolls meal of indrink in the girnil.[120]

115 Ronald J. VanderMolen, 'Providence as Mystery, Providence as Revelation: Puritan and Anglican Modifications of John Calvin's Doctrine of Providence', *Church History* 47 (1978), 27–47.

116 Richard Kyle, 'John Knox's Concept of Divine Providence and Its Influence on His Thought', *Albion* 18 (1986), 395–410. See also the essays in Roger Mason (ed.), *John Knox and the British Reformations* (Aldershot, 1998).

117 Alexandra Walsham, *Providence in Early Modern England* (Oxford, 1999), 12.

118 Ibid., 20.

119 Ninian Campbell, *A Treatise upon Death* (Edinburgh, 1635, STC 4533), sec. 'The assertion, It is appointed, &c', [C4v]. The reference to sparrows follows Matthew 10:29.

120 James Mitchell, *Memoirs of the Life of James Mitchell of Dykes, in the Parish of Ardrossan* (Glasgow, 1759), 69–72, 70. 'Fourteen bolls meal of indrink' meant 'fourteen bolls of meal short'; a girnil was a barrel or chest.

Mitchell's account of divine intervention might be rather mundane, but more dramatic stories also appeared. Covenanting ministers were said to prophesy and heal the sick. One, John Welch, even raised a dead man through his prayers.[121]

With the 1660 Restoration, Episcopacy was re-established in Scotland. Around a quarter of ministers refused to conform to the new religious settlement.[122] In the following decades the government alternated between clamping down on the rebellious Presbyterians and granting indulgences, which allowed evicted ministers to return to their parishes if they agreed to keep the peace. Presbyterianism was not officially reinstated until 1690, after James VII was deposed in favour of his daughter Mary and her husband William of Orange. Within this context there was a particular motivation for the deposed Presbyterians to look for proofs of God's favour. Visionaries reported encouraging encounters with Christ, and ministers collated accounts of providences.[123] Notable collections include John Livingstone's *Memorable Characteristics, and Remarkable Passages of Divine Providence, Exemplified in the Lives of Some of the Most Eminent Ministers and Professors in the Church of Scotland* (written in 1668); Robert Fleming's *The Fulfilling of the Scripture, or, An Essay Shewing the Exact Accomplishment of the Word of God in his Works of Providence, Performed & to be Performed* (1669); and Robert Law's *Memorialls: Or, The Memorable Things that Fell Out Within this Island of Brittain from 1638 to 1684*. Special providences became such an ingrained feature of Presbyterian religious culture that individuals continued to gather them even after Presbyterianism had been reinstated. The minister Robert Wodrow began recording providences in 1701 and continued until his death in 1734, while the radical Patrick Walker amassed stories of Covenanting ministers in the late 1720s and early 1730s (they were eventually published together as *Six Saints of the Covenant* in 1901).[124]

For all their interest in special providences, most Presbyterians took James VI's view on ghosts (Wodrow, as we shall see, was an exception). Robert Fleming spoke of how wicked spirits appeared frequently, but described 'apparitions of the dead ... delivered out of purgatory' as a 'blind superstition'.[125] The Presbyterian minister Robert Blair (1593–1666) stayed in an allegedly haunted room and saw an apparition, but refused to be frightened

[121] Margo Todd, *The Culture of Protestantism in Early Modern Scotland* (New Haven, 2002), 394–9 (Welch on 397). See also Louise Yeoman, '"Away with the Fairies"', in Lizanne Henderson (ed.), *Fantastical Imaginations: The Supernatural in Scottish History and Culture* (Edinburgh, 2009), 29–46.

[122] Stewart J. Brown, 'Religion and Society to c.1900', in T. M. Devine and Jenny Wormald (eds), *The Oxford Handbook of Modern Scottish History* (Oxford, 2012), 84.

[123] On visionaries see Yeoman, '"Away with the Fairies"'.

[124] Wodrow is discussed at length on pp. 59–64.

[125] Robert Fleming, *The Fulfilling of the Scripture, in Three Parts*, reprint of 1681 3rd edn, 2 vols (Glasgow, 1801), vol. 2, 57, 238.

by it. He explained that the affair was God teaching him to pray fervently, and demonstrating through the apparition's impotency 'that devils were chained with chains of darkness, reserved to the judgment of the last day'.[126] However, stories of special providences often featured apparitions. The minister Alexander Stirling saw a group singing a psalm, accompanied by a white horse with a blood-red saddle; the whole party subsequently vanished. Archibald Gillespie saw two pointed clouds attacking a woman in the sky until her dress tore and blood rained down, and Robert Law recounted a tale of an apparition in the form of 'a man sett on a whyt horse ... with his eyes lyke flammes of fyre'.[127] Visionaries also told of encounters with angels. In 1661, Grizell Love met golden-haired angels bearing harps, with eyes sparkling like diamonds. In the 1680s, the ten-year-old daughter of Donald McGreger was visited by angels in the form of beautiful children, who 'had sometimes white feathers in there hands like wings'.[128] Apparitions were no longer automatically identified as emanations of the Devil.[129]

In addition, stories of ghostly armies enacting airborne fights were popular: at least a dozen separate accounts survive from the late seventeenth and early eighteenth centuries. Sometimes these apparitions foreshadowed genuine battles. At other times they followed them, a sort of spectral echo. While the soldiers were not necessarily ghosts, there was a link to the dead. Ghostly battles in the air were popular in Greek and Roman times. They were associated with notions of souls battling on their way to the land of the dead, and were perhaps related to medieval tales of the 'Wild Hunt'.[130] Years of warfare encouraged the re-emergence of stories of this sort, and they circulated more easily as the printing industry developed. Frederick Valletta notes that there was a surge of English stories about ghostly battles after the civil wars, and argues that this was linked to a contemporary fear that the ghosts of soldiers were returning, having not had proper burials.[131] The Scottish ministers collecting and publishing stories of ghostly battles may not have been presenting them as accounts of the returning dead, but the stories were nonetheless related to ghost beliefs, and might have been read as such by sections of their audience.

126 Robert Blair, *The Life of Mr. Robert Blair*, ed. T. M'Crie (Edinburgh, 1848), 8.

127 Patrick Walker, *Six Saints of the Covenant*, ed. David Hay Fleming, 2 vols (London, 1901), vol. 1, 35; Robert Wodrow, *The Correspondence of the Rev. Robert Wodrow*, ed. Thomas M'Crie, 3 vols (Edinburgh, 1842–3), vol. 1, 561–2; Robert Law, *Memorialls: Or the Memorable Things That Fell out Within This Island of Brittain from 1638 to 1684*, ed. Charles Kirkpatrick Sharpe (Edinburgh, 1818), 162.

128 Martha McGill, 'Angels, Devils, and Discernment in Early Modern Scotland', in Michelle D. Brock, Richard Raiswell and David Winter (eds), *Knowing Demons, Knowing Spirits* (Basingstoke, 2018), 239–63.

129 On the incorporation of English ghosts into a providential framework, see Marshall, *Beliefs and the Dead*, 252.

130 Lavater, *Of Ghostes and Spirites*, 81; Schmitt, *Ghosts in the Middle Ages*, 93–122.

131 Frederick Valletta, *Witchcraft, Magic and Superstition in England, 1640–1670* (Aldershot, 2004), 81–2.

The interest in special providences hinted at the possibility that ghosts, too, might be transformed into divine messengers.

Conclusion

In medieval Scotland, the dead could return to make moral or religious points, or because some residual life-force lingered in the corpse. At least in theory, this changed after the Reformation, in line with broader European patterns. James VI was one of the most powerful critics of ghosts, and theologians generally fell into step with him, redefining ghosts as demons (that may or may not have been summoned by witches). However, it is important not to over-simplify this picture. Ghosts might be viewed sceptically before the Reformation as well: recall Gavin Douglas's concern that people would scorn the 'vayn superstitionys aganyst our richt beleve'. It is probable that many Catholics did not believe in ghosts, and that many Protestants continued to do so in spite of James's arguments. Ghost stories still cropped up in the work of educated men, or in kirk session records. James was probably over-optimistic when he declared: 'For as we know, moe Ghostes and spirites were seene, nor tongue can tell, in the time of blinde *Papistrie* in these Countries, where now by the contrarie, a man shall scarcely all his time here once of such things.'[132]

There was no sustained effort to educate people regarding the unorthodoxy of ghosts. The kirk was hampered by the difficulty of ensuring suitable religious provision throughout the country. Gaelic-speaking areas were particularly neglected. Although kirk sessions did criticise and punish superstitious practices, there is little evidence that they triumphed; plenty of 'heathenish' charming was still going on by the eighteenth and nineteenth centuries.[133] The notion of the supernatural power of the corpse also survived, reinforcing medieval revenant beliefs. The witch-hunts were an area where popular and elite culture met, and it does seem that the demonic notion of ghosts had some impact there. Apparitions were frequently classed as witches rather than as ghosts, and poltergeists were usually associated with witches and demons rather than with dead people. However, several aspects of the witch discourse complemented traditional ghost belief. Accounts of witches and their practices often emphasised the potency of the corpse. Witches also had dealings with the spirits of dead people. The ghost probably did retain a distinct identity,

132 James VI, *Daemonologie*, bk. 3, ch. 7, 37.

133 Numerous accounts of superstitious practices can be found in the Statistical Accounts of 1791–9 and 1834–45. *The Statistical Accounts of Scotland, 1791–1845* (University of Glasgow, University of Edinburgh), http://stataccscot.edina.ac.uk, accessed 1 Feb. 2018. See also Lizanne Henderson, *Witchcraft and Folk Belief in the Age of Enlightenment: Scotland, 1670–1740* (Basingstoke, 2016).

insofar as any supernatural being can be called distinct given the intertwined nature of folk beliefs. Witchcraft became a focal point for investigations into the supernatural, but ghosts lingered on, and stand as a reminder that we should hesitate to view the Scottish Reformation as an unmitigated success story.

It is also possible that the climate became gradually more amenable to ghosts as time went by. In the mid-seventeenth century, the Covenanters' emphasis on communion with divine forces, combined with the surge of accounts of special providences coming from war-stricken England, reinvigorated the idea that God made direct interventions in the world. Accounts of apparitions circulated more freely. This laid the groundwork for the late-seventeenth- and eighteenth-century trend towards reclaiming ghosts as religious servants, which will be explored in the next chapter. But in closing, it is worth reiterating that although ghost beliefs were not wiped out, surviving stories from this period are few and far between. In the medieval period ghosts did not have an uncontested place within religious culture, and matters worsened after the Reformation. Ghosts were a familiar concept, but they were not the dominant supernatural tradition that they would later become.

2

Evangelising Ghosts

In 1659, John Maitland, second Earl and later first Duke of Lauderdale (1616–82), sent a handful of supernatural stories to the English theologian Richard Baxter.[1] These stories covered cases of demonic possession, haunted houses and attempted exorcisms. Keen to avoid accusations of credulity, Lauderdale devoted some of his space to mocking Catholic fraudulence. He described travelling to see a group of demonically possessed nuns, only to find them 'nothing but wanton Wenches singing baudy Songs in *French*'. An Antwerp exorcism sought to relieve a gaggle of burping Dutch girls; Lauderdale quipped that 'if those were Devils, they were windy Devils', and suggested that the women were possessed with no more than 'a Mornings Draught of too new Beer'. However, Lauderdale also presented some 'authentically attested' accounts. They included two stories of poltergeists discussed in the previous chapter: the Edinburgh poltergeist who clattered around a minister's house, and the Dumfries poltergeist who assaulted English soldiers.[2] Lauderdale told these stories with spirit and humour. However, he thought of them as more than mere curiosities. His declaration at the beginning of the letter hints at the deeper significance of the accounts: 'It is sad that the Sadducean, or rather Atheistical denying of Spirits, or their Apparitions should so far prevail; and sadder, that the clear Testimonies of so many Ancient and Modern Authors should not convince them.'

References to Sadducism and atheism appear frequently in the supernatural literature of the late seventeenth century. According to the Bible, Sadducees believed that 'there is no resurrection, neither angel, nor spirit'.[3] For James VI, Sadducees were those who fell into the error of 'denying of spirits'.[4] The term 'atheism' could be employed in the modern sense, to mean denial of a deity. However, it was frequently used more broadly, to reference philosophical outlooks that devalued the importance of spiritual entities, the

1 Richard Baxter, *The Certainty of the Worlds of Spirits, and Consequently, of the Immortality of Souls of the Malice and Misery of the Devils and the Damned* (London, 1691), 82–92.

2 See p. 42.

3 Acts 23:8, King James Version.

4 James VI, *Daemonologie, in Forme of Ane Dialogue*, in James Craigie and Alexander Law (eds), *Minor Prose Works of King James VI and I* (Edinburgh, 1982), preface, xix.

afterlife, divine providence and miracles.[5] Lauderdale was reluctant to allow that his poltergeists could stem the tide of unbelief. Atheists, he wrote, 'are not to be convinced by Stories'.[6] Other writers were more optimistic. Although Lauderdale requested that his stories should not be published, Richard Baxter included them in *The Certainty of the Worlds of Spirits* (1691), a work that was written 'for the Conviction of Sadduces and Infidels'.[7] Some Scottish authors, most notably the natural philosopher George Sinclair (d. 1696) and minister Robert Wodrow (1679–1734), embarked on similar projects. In their work, ghosts were incorporated into the Protestant schema, tasked with demonstrating the reality of the soul and afterlife. This trend belonged primarily to the late seventeenth and early eighteenth centuries. The evangelising ghost nonetheless made sporadic reappearances over the course of the eighteenth century, sometimes delivering moral messages, sometimes engaging with theological debates.

'That prevailing Spirit of Atheism and Infidelity'[8]

The notion that society was battling a rising tide of atheism was spurred by the philosophical developments of the late seventeenth century. The controversial work of René Descartes (1596–1650) became dominant within universities in most Protestant countries, including Scotland.[9] Descartes argued for a mechanistic universe, created by God but left to function according to simple mathematical laws. Many of his opponents were uncomfortable with the notion of a God who did not directly govern on a day-to-day basis. Descartes

5 Michael Hunter and David Wootton, 'Introduction', in Michael Hunter and David Wootton (eds), *Atheism from the Reformation to the Enlightenment* (Oxford, 1992), 2. See also Michael Hunter, 'The Problem of "Atheism" in Early Modern England', *Transactions of the Royal Historical Society* 35 (1985), 135–57; David Wootton, 'New Histories of Atheism', in Michael Hunter and David Wootton (eds), *Atheism from the Reformation to the Enlightenment* (Oxford, 1992), 13–54; Nigel Smith, 'The Charge of Atheism and the Language of Radical Speculation, 1640–1660', in Michael Hunter and David Wootton (eds), *Atheism from the Reformation to the Enlightenment* (Oxford, 1992), 131–58.

6 In Baxter, *Certainty of the Worlds of Spirits*, 88.

7 Ibid., title page.

8 Alexander Telfair, *A True Relation of an Apparition, Expressions and Actings, of a Spirit* (Edinburgh, 1696), 3.

9 Jonathan I. Israel, *Radical Enlightenment: Philosophy and the Making of Modernity, 1650–1750* (Oxford, 2001), 23–42; Michael Wasser, 'The Mechanical World-View and the Decline of Witch-Beliefs in Scotland', in Julian Goodare, Lauren Martin and Joyce Miller (eds), *Witchcraft and Belief in Early Modern Scotland* (Basingstoke, 2008), 216; Christine M. Shepherd, 'Philosophy and Science in the Arts Curriculum of the Scottish Universities in the 17th Century' (University of Edinburgh Ph.D. thesis, 1975), esp. 61–165; Alasdair Raffe, 'Intellectual Change before the Enlightenment: Scotland, the Netherlands and the Reception of Cartesian Thought, 1650–1700', *Scottish Historical Review* 94 (2015), 27, 45–6.

was also criticised for emphasising scientific observation rather than Scripture as a means of explaining the universe, while his dualistic system of mind and matter was thought to undervalue spiritual entities.[10] Even more contentious than Descartes was Baruch Spinoza (1632–77). Spinoza argued that everything was composed of a single substance. God did not alter the universe; he *was* the universe. No event could transcend the laws of nature, as God and nature were indistinguishable. Miracles were therefore impossible. Spinoza also rejected the existence of demons.[11] His ideas were lambasted from all sides. In 1697, the St Andrews regent John Loudon described Spinoza colourfully, but not untypically, as a 'prodigious monster … the leader of this generation of atheists'.[12]

Similarly controversial ideas emerged from England. Both Thomas Hobbes (1588–1679) and John Locke (1632–1704) were criticised for placing a dangerous emphasis on the role of reason, rather than revelation, within religion. Although neither went so far as Spinoza in denying the existence of miracles, both suggested that testimony should be taken with caution.[13] There was also a handful of English figures commonly termed deists. There has been much debate over how this term should be defined, and to what extent it is possible to speak of a 'deist movement' when the men associated with it were few in number and diverse in their ideas.[14] However, the thinkers associated with deism generally held that religion should be subject to the dictates of reason. Charles Blount, John Toland, Thomas Woolston and Matthew Tindal were among those late-seventeenth- and early-eighteenth-century figures who argued for a natural religion, emphasising reason at the expense of revelation.[15]

The extent to which these philosophers posed a genuine threat to late-seventeenth- and early-eighteenth-century religious culture is debatable. Jonathan I. Israel underlines the importance of the rise of secularisation and rationalisation. He argues that 'In England a veritable sea-change had taken place by the early eighteenth century', and quotes Keith Thomas: 'The triumph of the mechanical philosophy meant the end of the animistic conception of the universe which had constituted the basic rationale for magical thinking.'[16] However, the monster of atheism was part myth. S. J. Barnett argues that the

10 Israel, *Radical Enlightenment*, 28.

11 Ibid., 603.

12 '…monstrum prodigiosum *Spinoza* Atheorum hujus aevi Antesignanus…' John Loudon, *Theses Philosophicae* (Edinburgh, 1697), 1.

13 See Patricia Springborg, 'Hobbes on Religion', in Tom Sorell (ed.), *The Cambridge Companion to Hobbes* (Cambridge, 1996), 346–80; Nicholas Wolterstorff, 'Locke's Philosophy of Religion', in Vere Chappell (ed.), *The Cambridge Companion to Locke* (Cambridge, 1994), 172–98.

14 S. J. Barnett, *The Enlightenment and Religion: The Myths of Modernity* (Manchester, 2003).

15 See Jeffrey R. Wigelsworth, *Deism in Enlightenment England: Theology, Politics, and Newtonian Public Science* (Manchester, 2009).

16 Israel, *Radical Enlightenment*, 7; Keith Thomas, *Religion and the Decline of Magic: Studies in Popular Beliefs in Sixteenth and Seventeenth Century England* (London, 1971), 664.

deist challenge was much exaggerated, and could never really endanger the church. Even Israel concedes that the foremost thinkers of the late seventeenth and early eighteenth centuries tried to fit scientific and mathematical developments into a Christian framework, with emphasis on the authority of Scripture (he excepts Spinoza from this picture, and also – disputably – Pierre Bayle).[17] The reality of miracles, providence, the soul and the afterlife was still beyond question for the vast majority of philosophers. Nevertheless, however flimsy the evidence may have been, there was a popular perception that the core tenets of Christianity were under threat. Within this context, some authors began to look for new ways to defend religious values.

Rehabilitating Ghosts

Several historians have argued that England saw a 'conscious and sustained reintegration of ghosts into Protestant theology' in the late seventeenth century.[18] Multiple works were produced collating 'true' stories about ghosts (usually alongside other creatures, such as witches). Henry More's 1652 *An Antidote Against Atheisme* was the first of this genre. It was followed by a host of similar works, most famously by Joseph Glanvill (*Sadducismus Triumphatus*, 1681), Richard Bovet (*Pandaemonium*, 1684), and Richard Baxter (*The Certainty of the Worlds of Spirits*, 1691). John Aubrey collected folklore, while Samuel Wesley co-edited *The Athenian Mercury* (1691–7), which devoted itself to 'curious questions' and frequently reported and discussed ghost stories.[19] This rehabilitation of ghosts owed something to a mid-seventeenth-century rise of Neoplatonism. Henry More and Joseph Glanvill were prominent within this movement. The Cambridge Platonists, as they became known, were more doctrinally flexible than strict Calvinists.[20] Furthermore, within the context of the Scientific Revolution, supernatural phenomena were considered an interesting subject for investigation: as Sasha Handley outlines, attested accounts might be used to explore the value of empirical analysis.[21] However, most authors explained that their primary motive was to refute atheists. Ghosts could confirm the existence of an afterlife, and also demonstrate providential justice, punishing crimes and righting wrongs from beyond the grave.[22]

17 Barnett, *Enlightenment and Religion*, 11–129; Israel, *Radical Enlightenment*, 15.

18 Sasha Handley, 'Reclaiming Ghosts in 1690s England', in Kate Cooper and Jeremy Gregory (eds), *Signs, Wonders, Miracles: Representations of Divine Power in the Life of the Church* (Woodbridge, 2005), 355.

19 See Handley, 'Reclaiming Ghosts', 345–55.

20 Sasha Handley, *Visions of an Unseen World: Ghost Beliefs and Ghost Stories in Eighteenth-Century England* (London, 2007), 29; Bath and Newton, '"Sensible Proof of Spirits"', 7.

21 Handley, *Visions of an Unseen World*, 35.

22 Peter Marshall, *Beliefs and the Dead in Reformation England* (Oxford, 2002), 232–64, 261; Thomas, *Religion and the Decline of Magic*, 701–35.

In Scotland the religious context was different. Presbyterians utilised divine providences as a propaganda tool. However, ghosts were a step too far for most. Belief in unorthodox supernatural forces was associated with 'enthusiasm', or religious excesses bordering on superstition. In the 1690s, which Handley identifies as the key decade in the English rehabilitation of ghosts, the Presbyterians were newly restored to power and had to tread carefully.[23] Frequently accused by Episcopalians of enthusiastical tendencies, Presbyterian churchmen emphasised their sobriety: 'We are no wayes led by enthusiastick impulses without the word but walk only by the word, and reject all impulses either contrare to, or beside it, yea not warranted by it.'[24] In 1684–5, Jonet Fraser of Dumfries garnered some renown for her dramatic visions of angels, swords and blood-caked bibles. Although her visions served the Presbyterian cause, they fell foul of the authorities after Presbyterianism was reinstated; in 1691, Fraser was compelled to confess to her presbytery that she had 'pretended to prophecying and seeing of visions and that she had sinned greatly in being deluded by Satan'.[25] Alasdair Raffe writes that the period from 1690 to 1730 witnessed 'growing ecclesiological and theological rigidity among Presbyterians', partly in response to Episcopalian and Anglican opposition. This period is also associated with a more 'reasonable' approach to religion. Michael Heyd takes as representative the 1707 declaration of the Presbyterian minister James Hog: 'Visions, voices and Dreams, are no bottom on which we may build, and we ought to cease from regard to them.'[26]

However, the fear of atheism was also prominent in Scotland. As Heyd demonstrates, enthusiasm and atheism were often thought to be two sides of the same coin.[27] The 1689 General Assembly declared that 'there hath been in some a dreadful atheistical boldness against God'. The following decade saw the criminalisation of blasphemy, with the result that Edinburgh student Thomas Aikenhead was hanged in 1697. Persecution continued in the early eighteenth century: John Simson, professor of divinity at Glasgow, was investigated for

23 Handley, 'Reclaiming Ghosts', 345–55.

24 See Michael Heyd, *Be Sober and Reasonable: The Critique of Enthusiasm in the Seventeenth and Early Eighteenth Centuries* (Leiden, 1995), 15–23. The quotation is an answer to George Hickes's 1680 *The Spirit of Popery*, and is cited in Alasdair Raffe, *The Culture of Controversy: Religious Arguments in Scotland, 1660–1714* (Woodbridge, 2012), 138.

25 Louise Yeoman, '"Away with the Fairies"', in Lizanne Henderson (ed.), *Fantastical Imaginations: The Supernatural in Scottish History and Culture* (Edinburgh, 2009), 40.

26 Alasdair Raffe, 'Presbyterianism, Secularization, and Scottish Politics after the Revolution of 1688–1690', *Historical Journal* 53 (2010), 335; Heyd, *Be Sober and Reasonable*, 175–6.

27 Heyd, *Be Sober and Reasonable*, 168; M. A. Stewart, 'Religion and Rational Theology', in Alexander Broadie (ed.), *The Cambridge Companion to the Scottish Enlightenment* (Cambridge, 2003), 33–4; Colin Kidd, 'The Scottish Enlightenment and the Supernatural', in Lizanne Henderson (ed.), *Fantastical Imaginations: The Supernatural in Scottish History and Culture* (Edinburgh, 2009), 96.

allegedly disseminating heterodox ideas, and suspended in 1729.[28] In 1696, the minister Alexander Telfair published an account of a demonic haunting, framed as an attack on 'that prevailing Spirit of Atheism and Infidelity in our time'. George Mackenzie's 1708 *Synopsis Apocalyptica* used miracles and prophecy to refute 'Atheists and Antiscripturists'.[29] It was within this context that some scholars began to revisit unorthodox supernatural stories. Lizanne Henderson suggests that 'the Kirk, which had been attacking popular culture ever since 1560, now embraced and exploited the very superstitions that both church and state authorities had been seriously attempting to destroy'.[30] It is questionable that the kirk as a whole entered into this endeavour, but there were select individuals who took a fresh interest in elements of folklore, including ghosts. Chief among them were George Sinclair and Robert Wodrow, who gathered stories in the late seventeenth and early eighteenth centuries respectively.

Sinclair was from the Lothians, and was most likely educated at St Andrews. He moved to Glasgow in 1655 and was appointed as a professor of philosophy, but refused to submit to episcopacy and was forced to resign in 1667. He then found employment as an engineer in coal-mines, and was responsible for developing new techniques in draining and measurement with barometers. In 1692, he rejoined the University of Glasgow, becoming professor of mathematics and experimental philosophy.[31] Sinclair first demonstrated his dual interest in natural philosophy and the supernatural in his 1672 *Hydrostaticks*, a work of theoretical and practical physics that included a description of the demon of Glenluce.[32] *Satans Invisible World Discovered* followed in 1685. It included thirty-nine stories, of which twenty-one or twenty-two were of Scottish origin (one cannot be determined). Sinclair noted that he had taken some stories from Glanvill and More, while the rest were 'purchased from Persons of eminent honesty and Faith'.[33] Witches, ghosts, poltergeists, demonic possession and magical charms all made appearances.

28 General Assembly quoted in Gordon Donaldson, *The Faith of the Scots* (London, 1990), 104. See Michael F. Graham, *The Blasphemies of Thomas Aikenhead: Boundaries of Belief on the Eve of the Enlightenment* (Edinburgh, 2008); Anne Skoczylas, *Mr Simson's Knotty Case: Divinity, Politics, and Due Process in Early Eighteenth-Century Scotland* (Montreal, 2001).

29 Telfair, *True Relation of an Apparition*, 3; George Mackenzie, 'An Essay on the Revelation of St. John', in *Synopsis Apocalyptica: Or, A Short Plain Explication and Application of Daniel's Prophecy and of St. John's Revelation* (Edinburgh, 1708), dedication, i.

30 Lizanne Henderson, *Witchcraft and Folk Belief in the Age of Enlightenment: Scotland, 1670–1740* (Basingstoke, 2016), 12–13.

31 John Anderson, 'Sinclair, George (d. 1696?)', *Oxford DNB* (Oxford University Press, 2009), http://www.oxforddnb.com/view/article/25615, accessed 1 Feb. 2018.

32 George Sinclair, *The Hydrostaticks, or, The Weight, Force, and Pressure of Fluid Bodies, Made Evident by Physical, and Sensible Experiments* (Edinburgh, 1672), 238–47.

33 George Sinclair, *Satans Invisible World Discovered* (Edinburgh, 1685), Av.

In part this work reflects Sinclair's continued investigations into the workings of the world. He took the supernatural to be a subject of scientific interest. *Satans Invisible World Discovered* was dedicated to George Seton, fourth Earl of Winton, because of the latter's interest in coal-mining. Sinclair proclaimed to him:

> Your Experimental Skill in improving *your Coal*, for making of *Salt*, is praise worthie. Your defending of the *Salt-pans* against the imperious Waves of the raging Sea, from the N.E, is singular. Your renting of *Rocks*, for clearing of Passages into Your *Harbours*, which none of *your Predecessors* were able to do, is stupendious.[34]

However, Sinclair also had a more specific aim within *Satans Invisible World Discovered*. The work was presented as 'A choice Collection of Modern Relations, proving evidently against the *Saducees* and *Atheists* of this present Age, that there are *Devils, Spirits, Witches*, and *Apparitions*'.[35] Expanding on this idea in the preface, Sinclair enquired: 'what can be the reason of so much Atheism in the World?' He then explained that

> there are a monstruous rable of men, who following the *Hobbesian* and *Spinosian* Principles, slight Religion, and undervalue the Scripture, because there is such an express mention of Spirits and Angels in it, which their thick and plumbeous capacities cannot conceive. Whereupon they think, that all contained in the Universe comes under the notion of things matterial, and bodies only; and consequently, no GOD, no Devil, no Spirit, no Witch.[36]

As this passage indicates, Sinclair's primary concern was with philosophies that placed too much stress on material, rather than spiritual, entities. He was eager not to be seen as narrow-minded, insisting: 'Let no man mistake me, for its not my design to discourage any man that teaches or learns new *Philosophy*.' However, he added that 'there ought to be layed down some sure principles, as a foundation upon which *Students* may walk surely, which for their *evidence* and *certainty*, may never be called in *question*'.[37] Although he mentioned Hobbes and Spinoza, Sinclair believed that the main threat to these 'sure principles' was Descartes. He acknowledged that Cartesians did not assert that there was no God, but objected that they 'seem to prove so much'.[38] As noted above, Cartesianism had become the dominant philosophy taught in Scottish universities – Sinclair's natural milieu, although he had left his post at Glasgow. Sinclair was not alone in regretting the prominence of Cartesianism. Robert Forbes, regent at Marischal College and King's College, Aberdeen, produced a 1680 thesis that discussed the 'deceitful Cartesian novelty and heterodoxy of

34 Ibid., dedication, [*7].
35 Ibid., title page.
36 Ibid., A4v.
37 Ibid., [A7].
38 Ibid., [A5].

this insolent age'. Forbes explained that 'to philosophise freely is permissible, beautiful and worthy of a Christian man: nonetheless, it is truly miserable and grievous to come up with arguments against many, if not all, the opinions received in the Reformed Church'.[39] Sinclair's position was not generally representative, but nor was it indefensible by contemporary standards.

The extent to which Sinclair had a studied philosophical stance is, however, debatable. The remainder of his preface was dedicated to an exposé of fifty-four unorthodox beliefs supposedly maintained by Cartesians.[40] Among many other things, Sinclair dismissed Cartesian methodology, arguing that Cartesians placed too much emphasis on reason and the power of philosophy as the 'infallible Interpreter of the Scripture'. He saw the methodology of doubt as sacrilegious. He complained about the belief that humans 'can will all things which God can will'. He rejected the notion of animals as automata, and decried the idea that 'the first Chaos, was able of it self, to produce all things material', such that 'God did not creat all things for Man'. However, these points were not original thinking on Sinclair's part; most of them were copied directly from the chapter headings of Petrus van Mastricht's 1677 *Novitatum Cartesianarum Gangraena*. Many did not actually refer to the beliefs of Descartes at all, but to radical Dutch followers of his, or to other thinkers altogether.[41] Descartes was a straw man; Sinclair's actual engagement with his ideas remained limited.

This is further demonstrated by the fact that the preface's manifold objections to Cartesianism were barely addressed by the material included in *Satans Invisible World Discovered*. The most relevant points from the preface were those about spirits and the afterlife. Regarding the nature of spirits, Sinclair objected to Cartesian dualism, noting that according to the Cartesians 'GOD cannot properly be called a Spirit; because (say they) a Spirit, to speak properly, denotes some corporeal thing'. He was concerned about the place of the Holy Spirit, also complaining that Descartes did not distinguish between the three components of the Trinity. In fact, Descartes carefully avoided addressing the nature of the Trinity, although it is true that there was a corporeal element to his notion of 'spirit': he saw man as a spirit and God as a spiritual substance.[42] *Satans Invisible World Discovered* did showcase incorporeal spirits. Corporeal apparitions were also included, however. Moreover, Sinclair drew heavily

39 Giovanni Gellera, 'The Philosophy of Robert Forbes: A Scottish Scholastic Response to Cartesianism', *Journal of Scottish Philosophy* 11 (2013), 206.

40 They can be found in Sinclair, *Satans Invisible World Discovered*, [A5]–[A6v]. Sinclair actually stated that he gave fifty-six reasons, but two – 38 and 39 – are missing. There is some useful discussion in Wasser, 'Mechanical World-View', 210–18.

41 Raffe, 'Intellectual Change before the Enlightenment', 38–9. I am grateful to Dr Raffe for discussion of this subject.

42 Stephen Menn, *Descartes and Augustine* (Cambridge, 2002), 348; Deborah Brown, 'The Sixth Meditation: Descartes and the Embodied Self', in David Cunning (ed.), *The Cambridge Companion to Descartes'* Meditations (Cambridge, 2014), 247; M. Glouberman, *Descartes: The Probable and the Certain* (Amsterdam, 1986), 102.

on the work of Joseph Glanvill, who argued more explicitly than Descartes that spirits were corporeal.[43] Sinclair further complained that Cartesians did not believe that death was the separation of the soul and body, nor that the Resurrection was their reunion, and also that they did not see the righteous passing immediately to Heaven nor the wicked to Hell. This was not something Descartes addressed explicitly, although Cartesian dualism already maintained a separation between soul and body, and he does not seem to have believed in the resurrection of the body upon the Last Judgement.[44] *Satans Invisible World Discovered* demonstrated a separation between soul and body after death (as we shall see). However, it was not explicit about whether apparitions came from Heaven, Hell or some intermediate state. Overall, although the preface ostensibly situated the work within a broader philosophical debate, Sinclair made little attempt to engage with precise metaphysical questions through the material included in *Satans Invisible World Discovered*. His position, quite simply, was that it was dangerous to doubt the reality of spirits. *Satans Invisible World Discovered* aimed to empirically demonstrate their existence.

Even on the topic of spirits, it is difficult to determine Sinclair's exact thinking. Sinclair interpreted apparitions demonically to greater degree than most of his English counterparts. He explained that Glanvill believed that it was the true ghost of Samuel who appeared to Saul. However, he argued that it was much more probable that the apparition was actually the Devil imitating Samuel, pointing out that Samuel 'pretends himself to be disquieted and brought up by *Sauls* instigation, and the Witches Art, which is most false, impious, and absurd to imagine concerning those blessed souls who are returned to their God'.[45] Even more noteworthy is Sinclair's evaluation of the story of Isabel Heriot.[46] Isabel was servant to a minister in Ormiston – probably Sinclair's brother, John.[47] In the winter of 1680 she became ill, and around the time of her death her face turned black. Soon after her burial her apparition was seen, black-faced and wearing the white robes in which she was buried. When confronted, the apparition explained that the Devil had charged her to destroy the minister. Sinclair resolved that Isabel was most likely a witch. He continued: 'But what could her *Apparition* be? It behoved, either to be her reall Body informed and acted by the Devil (for her soul could not be brought back) or only the Devil taking upon him her shape and form, acting and imitating her to the life, which is more probable.'[48] Here Sinclair seemed to be taking the traditional Protestant line: dead souls could not return, and ghosts were tricks of the Devil. Isabel's case was the only one Sinclair evaluated so

43 Euan Cameron, *Enchanted Europe: Superstition, Reason, and Religion, 1250–1750* (Oxford, 2010), 278.

44 Stephen Gaukroger, *Descartes: An Intellectual Biography* (Oxford, 1997), 199.

45 Sinclair, *Satans Invisible World Discovered*, A4–A4v.

46 Ibid., 144–54.

47 Hew Scott, *Fasti Ecclesiae Scoticanae*, new edn, 7 vols (Edinburgh, 1915–28), vol. 1, 340.

48 Sinclair, *Satans Invisible World Discovered*, 153.

explicitly, but he also presented other apparitions who seemed to be diabolic, judging by their unnatural and malevolent behaviour. In a story from Silesia, the apparition of a dead apothecary's servant returned and touched a maid. He left a visible mark, and she fell ill. His body was then dug up and found to be 'putrified with *purulent Matter* flowing from it'.[49]

However, Sinclair also told stories in which ghosts were presented as the genuine spirits of dead people. Most were taken from Glanvill. Major George Sydenham returned to Captain William Dyke to confirm the reality of God and the immortality of the soul; Edward Avon visited his son-in-law Thomas Goddard to reveal a murder he had committed; Mistress Breton appeared to a servant to ensure that land was given to the poor; and the ghost of Sir George Villiers materialised with warnings about his son's forthcoming murder. In a story from John Webster, a woman returned bearing five large wounds, and revealed that her lover had arranged her murder.[50] Sinclair also told a Scottish story, from Edinburgh, of a dead woman called Helen Brown who returned to her philandering husband. She reproached him for courting another woman so soon after her death, and invited him to join her. He became ill and was buried within a month after her death.[51] Sinclair's approach seems to have been that dead souls could return provided they were on godly business, righting wrongs or upholding Christian values. Malevolent figures like Isabel Heriot remained the work of the Devil.

Compared to the medieval period, there was no dramatic overhaul in the presentation of ghosts. Medieval ghosts might return because they had died in an unfinished state (rather than to complete a specific mission), whereas Sinclair's ghosts all had useful purposes.[52] However, medieval ghosts often returned with moral or religious purposes as well. Sinclair's story of the ghost of Helen Brown echoes the folkloric tradition that contact with the dead could harm the living.[53] The story from Webster recalls medieval themes of wounded ghosts, and seems inconsistent with Sinclair's insistence on the separation of soul and body after death. Mistress Breton could not rest until her land had been given to the poor, reminiscent of the Catholic notion that salvation came through good deeds (rather than faith alone). None of Sinclair's ghosts were tailored to make a specifically Protestant message. Instead, a subset of traditional stories was revisited. *Satans Invisible World Discovered*, overall, has its limitations as a piece of scholarship. Its philosophy is unoriginal, as are its ghosts. Nevertheless, the work is a significant one. The idea of using ghosts

49 Ibid., 132–4, 191–2.

50 Ibid., 40–5, 102–8, 128–131, 120–2, 19–22; Glanvill, *Saducismus Triumphatus*, 219–24, 209–15, 238–42, 225–7; John Webster, *The Displaying of Supposed Witchcraft* (London, 1677), 298–300.

51 Sinclair, *Satans Invisible World Discovered*, postscript, [¶¶6–8].

52 Alexander Murray, *Suicide in the Middle Ages, Vol. 2: The Curse on Self-Murder* (Oxford, 2000), 480.

53 See pp. 38, 161.

to defend against dangerous ideas would have been laughable to Scottish Protestant theologians a century previously. Sinclair proposed a new role for ghosts within Protestant society.

Sixteen years after the publication of *Satans Invisible World Discovered*, the minister Robert Wodrow began his collection of 'remarkable providences'. Wodrow was born in Glasgow in 1679, and elected to the parish of Eastwood in 1703. He was fiercely devoted to the Presbyterian cause throughout his lifetime, and is best known for his record of Presbyterian persecution, *The History of the Sufferings of the Church of Scotland*, published in two volumes in 1721 and 1722.[54] He was a conservative minister; in the words of Richard Sher, he and his fellow 'old-school Calvinists' did their best to 'keep the kirk on the straight and narrow path of their forefathers'.[55] However, he was also the most prolific of the Scottish providentialists. When he died in 1734 his *Analecta: Or Materials for a History of Remarkable Providences* was still little more than a collection of notes, but it was an extensive collection: the Maitland Club's published version spans four volumes. In addition to the traditional demons, prodigies and benevolent acts of God, Wodrow covered topics such as angels, second sight and ghosts.

As in the case of Sinclair, Wodrow's work can in part be explained as scientific and geographic investigation. Wodrow initially wrote that he wished to collect providences to satisfy his 'curiosity and Athenian spirit'.[56] In letters to his correspondents, requests for providences were interspersed with extensive questions about plants, shells and other aspects of nature. For Wodrow, providences were a way to understand how the world worked. He wrote, for example, about how providence regulated the heat levels of human armpits and the temperature of a hen while laying eggs.[57] He was an empiricist, collecting information about the natural world in order to theorise; he once wrote to a contact: 'I think we have not as yet a sufficient stock of experiments & tryalls to build our hypotheses on.'[58] Like Sinclair, however, there was an extra

54 For more on Wodrow's life see Louise Yeoman, 'Wodrow, Robert (1679–1734)', *Oxford DNB* (Oxford University Press, 2004), http://www.oxforddnb.com/view/article/29819, accessed 1 Feb. 2018.

55 Richard B. Sher, *Church and University in the Scottish Enlightenment: The Moderate Literati of Edinburgh* (Edinburgh, 1985), 45.

56 Robert Wodrow, *Early Letters of Robert Wodrow, 1698–1709*, ed. L. W. Sharp (Edinburgh, 1937), 285. An 'Athenian spirit' implied that one was always eager for news. See L. W. Sharp, 'Introduction', in L. W. Sharp (ed.), *Early Letters of Robert Wodrow* (Edinburgh, 1937), xxvii.

57 Robert Wodrow, *Analecta: Or Materials for a History of Remarkable Providences Mostly Relating to Scotch Ministers and Christians*, ed. Matthew Leishman, 4 vols (Edinburgh, 1842–3), vol. 2, 372–3; vol. 3, 310. On Wodrow's scientific interests see Roger Emerson, 'Did the Scottish Enlightenment Emerge in an English Cultural Province?', *Lumen: Selected Proceedings from the Canadian Society for Eighteenth-Century Studies* 14 (1995), 8–13.

58 Quoted in Charles W. J. Withers, *Geography, Science and National Identity: Scotland Since 1520* (Cambridge, 2001), 86.

motivation behind his investigations into the supernatural. In 1717, Wodrow explained that he was seeking to confirm 'the great foundations of our holy religion'. Many young people were 'grossly ignorant and unconcerned'. Men and women were not reading and praying every morning as they used to; the ministry was undervalued, and was viewed by many with a 'spirit of jealousy'; communion services were less popular than they had once been, and were prompting fewer conversions. Even among the faithful, he noted 'a good deal of damp, sinking, and distress'.[59] He saw remarkable providences as a means of encouraging Christian feeling. He also noted his desire to show that 'in poor Scotland, the Lord, since the Reformation, hath manifested himself, and the secret of his covenant, to his servants and people, as much as any where since the primitive times'.[60]

While Sinclair's preface suggests that his work was targeted at a well-educated audience with knowledge of philosophical trends, Wodrow seems to have been more interested in using stories of the supernatural to appeal to his parishioners. Both men, however, were addressing the perceived decline of religious feeling. Sinclair was imitating English works, but Wodrow's collection was very much in the Presbyterian providentialist tradition, although his definition of a providence was unusually broad. He drew from a wider range of sources than Sinclair, and included significantly more material from Scotland. He cited many other ministers as his informants, and also recorded stories from his parishioners. In all, at least twenty different individuals communicated accounts of ghost-like apparitions to Wodrow, and if we include their named sources, the number goes up to around forty-five. Of those, if we allow only apparitions that were definitely identified as returning dead people, we can count eight informants (some of whom gave Wodrow more than one story), with an additional ten or so as their sources. Most were ministers, although the list also includes a servant, a pious lady, and the judge James Erskine, Lord Grange, a keen demonologist who opposed the repeal of the Witchcraft Act.[61] In addition to these named sources, Wodrow describes several ghost stories as coming 'from several hands' or 'from two or three people'. Overall, his work suggests that ghost stories were still in broad circulation.

Like Sinclair, Wodrow did not reject the idea of demonic apparitions. He was a firm believer in witchcraft, and told stories of the Devil appearing in different guises to trick men. One apparition took the form of a small, ugly man. He declared that he had come from Hell, warned the nation to repent, and threw a shelf of bibles to the floor.[62] In another story, a gentleman was

59 Robert Wodrow, *The Correspondence of the Rev. Robert Wodrow*, ed. Thomas M'Crie, 3 vols (Edinburgh, 1842), vol. 2, 244; vol. 1, 46–59.

60 Ibid., vol. 2, 244.

61 See Ian Bostridge, 'Witchcraft Repealed', in Jonathan Barry, Marianne Hester and Gary Roberts (eds), *Witchcraft in Early Modern Europe: Studies in Culture and Belief* (Cambridge, 1996), 321–32.

62 Wodrow, *Analecta*, vol. 1, 112–14. On the man from Hell see p. 8, above.

keen to marry a young woman, but she died before the match could take place. A mysterious old man offered the gentleman three pills, which he said would restore the lady to life. The gentleman accepted the offer, administered the pills, and married the newly revived lady. However, when a pious friend met with the lady, he instantly recognised her as a devil. This friend convinced the gentleman to perform an exorcism, which swiftly reduced the lady to a half-rotten corpse.[63] Stories like this recalled the threat of diabolic impostures. However, Wodrow also presented apparitions in a positive light. He told several stories of mysterious figures who appeared in the nick of time to help good Christians by paying their debts, donating food to their families, or rescuing them from perilous situations. Other apparitions played beautiful music and sang psalms.[64] In the medieval period, these figures might have been interpreted as saints, but for Wodrow they were angels. In another of his accounts, a dying woman was visited by the apparition of a beautiful young child. The two were seen surrounded in a glowing halo, and Wodrow declared it 'a plain instance of the Ministry of Angells'.[65]

Furthermore, Wodrow often presented ghosts as returning dead people, rather than as emanations of the Devil. Some returned to reveal murders. The minister Gilbert Rule, Principal of Edinburgh University from 1690 to 1701, was obliged to stay in a haunted room. He was visited by the ghost of a tradesman, who explained that he had been murdered, and led Rule to the location of his buried bones. The next day Rule gathered together the local people and told the story, accompanying it with a sermon. An elderly man broke down and confessed to the crime.[66] Wodrow also presented some purposeless ghosts, including two young boys who haunted a room because they had been sold as slaves during their lifetimes.[67] However, the most common pattern was for ghosts to return to old friends or family members in order to confirm the reality of the afterlife. In 1729, Wodrow recorded 'a very strange account', explaining that he had been told it by several people 'as what is really belived at Edinburgh, though the persons concerned decline to speak of it, and it's keeped very closs'. Acknowledging the account's 'strangeness' while similarly underlining its credibility was a common strategy of Wodrow's when introducing his more theologically questionable providences. In this particular story, a girl sprained her arm in a dance at an Edinburgh Assembly, and then entered a decline. When she was drawing close to death her brother came to entertain her with music and dancing. This brother was 'a youth about seventeen, very rackish, and loose in principles, at best a Deist'. The girl objected that she wished to remain in a serious frame of mind. Wodrow continued:

63 Ibid., vol. 1, 351–2.
64 Ibid., vol. 1, 53–4, 57, 222; vol. 2, 180–1, 307, 322; vol. 3, 89.
65 Ibid., vol. 2, 142–4.
66 Ibid., vol. 4, 87–90.
67 Ibid., vol. 4, 91.

> He insisted that she was roving, and should be diverted; and told her he did not belive ther was any thing after death to fear, and wished she might not belive any thing she sau not, and make herself easy. She answered, She did belive she had an immortall soul; that ther was a heaven and a hell. His words I do not repeat, being horrid, but ended with that:– 'Girl, when thou dyes, if ther be any thing in those dreams, come back and tell me! I belive none of that preistcraft!' When she died, it's confidently said she appeared to him. What passed is not told; but this is certain, the youth came running, like one distempered, to my Lord, his father, his room, in his shirt, as I am told, all in sweat, and told what passed.[68]

The fashionable, rakish young man with the lax religious principles was the kind of character Wodrow was keen to reform, and the story offers a clear example of how ghosts could be utilised to that end. When a ghost made regular visits to Archibald Pitcairne, who was rumoured to be an atheist, Wodrow explained that the episodes were 'vouchsafments of Providence' and 'methods of conviction'.[69]

Wodrow's ghosts, like Sinclair's, were relatively vague in their religious teachings. Consider the case of John Middleton, first Earl of Middleton (c.1608–74), and James Wood, the Laird of Balbegno. This story offers an interesting example of how Wodrow's interpretation of apparitions differed from that of most Presbyterian providentialists. Middleton and Balbegno made a pact that whoever died first should return to report on the afterlife. Balbegno was killed in battle in 1651, and reportedly appeared to Middleton while the latter was imprisoned in the Tower of London. He told Middleton 'of many things to come, of his oun delivery out of prison; of the King's Restauration, and that he should be in favour with him, and in the highest trust in the kingdome'.[70] This story was also recorded by Robert Law in his *Memorialls*. Law explained that it was the Devil in Balbegno's likeness who visited Middleton.[71] While Law would probably have judged all ghosts to be diabolic, he had particular reason to dismiss this one. Middleton was an Episcopalian, and the ghost seemingly held similar sympathies. Law, on the other hand, was a strict Presbyterian, and was deposed after the 1660 Restoration. He was almost certainly writing before the 1689 reinstatement of Presbyterianism, and would naturally be hostile towards an Episcopalian ghost.[72] In Wodrow's version, there was no suggestion that the ghost was actually a devil. Wodrow was writing in 1702, and thus from a position of comparative security. Nevertheless, it is interesting that he

68 Ibid., vol. 4, 45–6.

69 Ibid., vol. 3, 520–2. On Pitcairne see pp. 86–8.

70 Wodrow, *Analecta*, vol. 1, 34–6.

71 Robert Law, *Memorialls: Or the Memorable Things That Fell out Within This Island of Brittain from 1638 to 1684*, ed. Charles Kirkpatrick Sharpe (Edinburgh, 1818), 162.

72 Law's work covered the period up to 1684. Vaughan T. Wells writes that Law died around 1686. Vaughan T. Wells, 'Law, Robert (d. c.1686)', *Oxford DNB* (Oxford University Press, 2004), http://www.oxforddnb.com/view/article/16152, accessed 1 Feb. 2018.

would present an Episcopalian ghost in a reasonably favourable light. Tensions between Presbyterians and Episcopalians had by no means disappeared after 1689, with debates about toleration dominating the religious scene in the run-up to the 1707 union with England.[73] Many of Wodrow's other providences emphasised God's favours for loyal Presbyterian ministers. However, his ghosts did not concern themselves with the wrangling between Presbyterians and Episcopalians, instead delivering more general religious messages.

Just as Episcopalianism remained an important concern while Wodrow was working, Catholicism had not disappeared as a threat to the kirk. In 1685, the Catholic James VII ascended to the Scottish throne. James attempted to introduce limited toleration for Catholics, and was deposed four years later in favour of the Protestant William and Mary of Orange. Jacobite support for James and his descendants ensured that the possibility of a revolution and a Catholic monarch lingered on for much of the eighteenth century. Nevertheless, in Wodrow's collection as in Sinclair's, ghosts were not fully purged of their medieval elements. One particularly interesting story is preserved among Wodrow's manuscripts. Originally from London, the story was communicated to Wodrow in a letter by Scottish Presbyterian minister James Cowan around 1707.[74] It concerned a lady called Mary Turberville, who was visited by the ghost of her deceased landlady. The figure was hideous, clad in black, and gave off a 'Noysom smell'. She was also violent; when Mary ventured to speak to her she swore that if Mary had not spoken first 'I would have torn you, & thrown you down Stairs'. She revealed that she had broken a promise to her late husband by not donating money to the poor. Mary found and donated this money, after which the ghost reappeared in shining white, with a 'pleasent beautifull and Smileing Countenance'. She answered some questions of Mary's, and soon afterwards was carried away to Heaven by a beautiful young child.

The pattern of ghosts changing from black to white clothing was relatively common in the medieval period, and represented the progression of the soul through Purgatory.[75] Furthermore, the landlady's ghost asserted that after her death she had gone neither to Heaven nor to Hell, but was 'under great horror'. Despite these none-too-subtle references to Purgatory, this story seems to have circulated widely. Cowan claimed that it had evoked great interest in many Scottish gentlemen. This assertion is supported by the fact that James Garden, Episcopalian professor of theology at Aberdeen, wrote to John Aubrey about the story in 1695. Garden specifically mentioned the ghost's changing from

73 See Ryan K. Frace, 'Religious Toleration in the Wake of Revolution: Scotland on the Eve of Enlightenment (1688–1710s)', *History* 93 (2008), 355–75; Karin Bowie, *Scottish Public Opinion and the Anglo-Scottish Union, 1699–1707* (Woodbridge, 2007); Jeffrey Stephen, *Scottish Presbyterians and the Act of Union 1707* (Edinburgh, 2007).

74 James Cowan to Robert Wodrow, [1707]: NLS, Wod.Fol.XXVIII 4846, fols 222v–223.

75 See p. 18.

black to white, and asked whether it was true.[76] The persistence of Catholic themes has been played down within the English historiography. Handley writes that Protestant authorities stripped ghost stories of their 'popish associations', and Owen Davies argues that in post-Reformation England, the symbolism of ghosts changing from black to white clothing 'was obviously rendered redundant'.[77] However, the process of reclaiming ghost stories, at least in Scotland, was not quite this streamlined; medieval remnants lingered within the corpus. This reaffirms the idea that the stories were not targeted at those of the wrong Christian persuasion, but rather at those whose philosophies might lead them to doubt basic religious tenets altogether. It was only in the late seventeenth century that ghosts were revisited in a serious way by Presbyterian ministers because it was only then that atheism had emerged, not necessarily as a more important concern than Episcopalianism or Catholicism, but at least as a significant rival.

Considering the case of England, Jo Bath and John Newton argue that by the end of the seventeenth century, the demonic interpretation was 'only used rarely and sparingly'.[78] Instead, ghosts were commonly identified as returning dead people. There is little evidence that this was the case in Scotland, where the religious context required greater theological exactness. The Quaker John Robertson noted in 1694 that 'the Presbyterians believe that any such apparitions [of the returning dead] are but Devils assuming the body, or the shape of the dead'.[79] William Cheyn's 1720 *The Great Danger and Vanity or Folly of Atheism Discovered* offered a series of defences against atheism, framed as a dialogue between an atheist and a believer. The atheist dismissed the idea that testimonies about ghosts could prove the reality of spirits. He noted that people also claimed to have seen outlandish entities such as 'water-wraths', creatures whose appearance or cries foreshadowed deaths near the bodies of water they inhabited; 'elf-bulls', which impregnated cows; and fairies. Cheyn, writing partly as himself and partly in the guise of the believer, acknowledged that many of these things 'may appear meerly like Old Wives Fables', and confessed some doubt as to whether or not ghosts existed.[80] He did, however, underline that evil spirits appeared on Earth to cause mischief, and haunted houses in a 'fearfull and terrifying manner'. By evil spirits he meant demons: he clarified

76 James Garden, 'James Garden's Letters to John Aubrey', in Michael Hunter (ed.), *The Occult Laboratory: Magic, Science, and Second Sight in Late Seventeenth-Century Scotland* (Woodbridge, 2001), 158.

77 Handley, 'Reclaiming Ghosts', 354; Owen Davies, *The Haunted: A Social History of Ghosts* (New York, 2007), 22.

78 Jo Bath and John Newton, '"Sensible Proof of Spirits": Ghost Belief during the Later Seventeenth Century', *Folklore* 117 (2006), 3–4 (quotation 4).

79 John Robertson, *Rusticus Ad Clericum, or, The Plow-Man Rebuking the Priest in Answer to Verus Patroclus* ([Aberdeen?], 1694), 89.

80 William Cheyn, *The Great Danger and Vanity or Folly of Atheism Discovered in a Dialogue between an Atheist and a Believer* (Edinburgh, 1720), 151–2.

that they were fallen angels.[81] For Cheyn and others, demons still furnished a surer proof against atheism than ghosts. Nevertheless, the accounts preserved by Wodrow and Sinclair indicate both that ghost stories were in circulation, and that some educated people were prepared to take them seriously.

Second Sight, Wraiths and Resurrections

Ghosts and ministering angels were not the only supernatural beings to be reclaimed in the late seventeenth and early eighteenth centuries. Robert Kirk (1644–92), the Episcopalian minister of Aberfoyle, wrote about his parishioners' fairy beliefs in *The Secret Commonwealth* (1692). He gave fairies a theological explanation and significance, placing them within the Christian framework. He explained that they were 'of a midle nature betwixt man and Angell', and argued that they served as proof of the world of spirits.[82] However, when Lizanne Henderson and Edward J. Cowan take Kirk's *Secret Commonwealth* to mark the 'reinstatement of fairy belief', they are probably overstating the case.[83] Kirk was an exceptional figure. For most authors, fairies remained in the domain of superstition, and Wodrow and Sinclair avoided them.

The Highland phenomenon of second sight garnered more interest. Second sight was a gift that allowed people to see into the future. In 1678, the English natural philosopher Robert Boyle enquired about second sight during an interview with George MacKenzie, Lord Tarbat. Boyle was looking for ways to prove the reality of the supernatural in the face of declining witch beliefs. The Welsh polymath Edward Lhuyd, and the Englishmen Samuel Pepys and John Aubrey, subsequently took an interest.[84] There were also several Scotsmen who investigated and wrote on the topic. Both Kirk and Wodrow recorded second sight beliefs. Martin Martin (d. 1718), a native of Skye, wrote about second sight in his 1703 *A Description of the Western Isles of Scotland*, while Dean of the Isles John Fraser (1647–1702) explored the subject in *Deuteroskopia, or A Brief Discourse Concerning the Second Sight* (1707).

81 Ibid., 119, 120–1, 125–6.

82 Robert Kirk, 'Robert Kirk's *The Secret Commonwealth* and his "A Short Treatise of the Scotish-Irish Charms and Spells"', in Hunter, *Occult Laboratory*, 79, 96. On Kirk see also Julian Goodare, 'Between Humans and Angels: Scientific Uses for Fairies in Early Modern Scotland', in Michael Ostling (ed.), *Fairies, Demons and Nature Spirits: 'Small Gods' at the Margins of Christendom* (London, 2018), 169–90; Lizanne Henderson, 'The (Super)natural Worlds of Robert Kirk: Fairies, Beasts, Landscapes and Lychnobious Liminalities', *Bottle Imp* 20 (2006), 1–4.

83 Lizanne Henderson and Edward J. Cowan, *Scottish Fairy Belief: A History* (East Linton, 2001), ch. 6 (quotation from the chapter title).

84 Michael Hunter, 'Introduction', in Hunter, *Occult Laboratory*, 8–9.

Second sighted people saw apparitions presaging oncoming events, most commonly marriages, deaths and battles. The usual way to predict death was to see a vision of an individual dressed in a shroud or other death-garments, or carried by a spectral funeral procession. These apparitions appeared before death, but were otherwise similar to ghosts.[85] Their nature was debated. As early as 1623, the poet William Drummond of Hawthornden (1585–1649) declared:

> it hath beene ever and of all held as infallible and most certaine, that [the soul] often (either by outward inspiration, or some secret motion in it selfe) is augure of its owne Misfortunes, and hath Shadowes of approching dangers presented unto it before they fall forth. Hence so many strange apparitions and signes, true Visions, uncouth heavinesse, and causelesse uncomfortable languishings:[86]

Kirk linked second sight apparitions to fairies, but it was more common to interpret them as divine or diabolic.[87] Sinclair declared that 'it is not improbable but that such preternatural knowledge comes first by a compact with the Devil'. John Fraser toyed with the idea that either angels or demons might be responsible for second sight apparitions.[88] Wodrow turned premonitions into a gift from God. His stories of predicting the future revolved around pious ladies and gentlemen, rather than the Highland peasants associated with second sight. A lady who had a prophetic dream was 'of great piety and good sense, and noe visionary'; a man who had a premonition of a fire was 'of very considerable sense and learning, and of an excellent and fair character, not to be imposed on by fancy and vapours'.[89] Wodrow even asked a friend if he could send him cases of second sighted men who were 'piouse and treuly Religiouse' and 'free from all suspicion of a Compact with Satan'.[90] In the case of second sight we again see the survival of old ideas that apparitions were linked to demons, but also an attempt to transform these apparitions into something godly.

The Lowland equivalent of second sight apparitions was the wraith (often termed a 'fetch' in English and Irish folklore). James VI defined a wraith as the spectral appearance of a person either soon before their death, or when 'newlie dead'. In practice, this generally meant at the precise moment of death.

85 This was not just a Scottish phenomenon; Lavater discusses these funeral processions as well. Ludwig Lavater, *Of Ghostes and Spirites Walking by Nyght*, trans. Robert Harrison (London, 1572, STC 15320), 79.

86 William Drummond, *Flowres of Sion* ([Edinburgh], 1623, STC 7247), 45.

87 Kirk, 'Robert Kirk's *The Secret Commonwealth*', 79–80.

88 Sinclair, *Satans Invisible World Discovered*, 215–16; John Fraser, 'John Fraser's *Deuteroskopia*', in Hunter, *Occult Laboratory*, 199–201.

89 Wodrow, *Analecta*, vol. 1, 281; vol. 4, 105. This reference to 'vapours' meant the hallucinogenic fumes of melancholy.

90 Questionnaire reproduced in Hunter, *Occult Laboratory*, 207.

Unsurprisingly, James argued that wraiths were actually the Devil.[91] Robert Kirk explained that there were various possible interpretations of wraiths. According to some second sighted people, 'what the Low-countrey-Scot calls a Wreath ... is only exuvious fumes of the Man approaching death, exhal'd and congeald into a various likeness ... and are neither Souls nor Counterfeiting Spirits'. Others held that wraiths were 'a numerous people by themselves'.[92] Sinclair seemingly had more patience for wraiths than for second sight, as he included a story of one. A man appeared to a close friend and looked at him with a 'ghaistly and Pale countenance'. His friend, clearly knowledgeable in the ways of ghosts, addressed him: 'what art thou? Art thou my dear Friend Thomas Coltheart? ... Art thou dead my friend? Tell me, if thou hast any commission to me from Almighty God, tell it me and it shall be welcome?' The apparition shook his hand at his friend three times, and vanished. He was later established to have died at that moment.[93]

Sinclair's story conveniently illustrates both the similarities and differences between wraiths and ghosts. In terms of appearance they were indistinguishable, but wraiths did not tend to fulfil useful purposes or deliver religious messages. Furthermore, they were even more guilty than ghosts of perpetuating unorthodox folkloric traditions. In 1711, the husband of Lady Teviot of Cromarty appeared to her at the moment of his death, his face 'black and oily' – possibly a reference to discolouration after death, but perhaps a reflection of the aforementioned medieval notion that the dead appeared black before they had passed through Purgatory.[94] Wraiths also demonstrate the importance that early modern society attached to the moment of death. In the Middle Ages there was a common belief that a dying person's state of mind for the second prior to death determined whether they were bound for salvation or damnation – a belief that was unorthodox by both Catholic and Protestant theology. Philippe Ariès argues that this belief was 'more or less abandoned' within educated circles after the sixteenth century.[95] However, wraiths demonstrate the enduring importance of the final moment within the popular imagination.[96]

Moreover, the wraith did not depict an appropriate Christian attitude towards death. It was a poignant figure, and suggested that the dying person's

91 James VI, *Daemonologie*, bk. 3, ch. 1, 42.

92 Kirk, 'Robert Kirk's *The Secret Commonwealth*', 83.

93 Sinclair, *Satans Invisible World Discovered*, postscript, [¶¶4v–6]. See also Relation 16, 120–2, and Relation 29, 187–91.

94 William Fraser, *The Earls of Cromartie, Their Kindred, Country and Correspondence*, 2 vols (Edinburgh, 1876), vol. 1, ccvi–ccvii. Fraser explains that he is quoting a manuscript then in the Cromartie repositories at Tarbat House and signed by Robert Keith, whom Fraser believes to be the historian and bishop (1681–1757).

95 Philippe Ariès, *The Hour of Our Death*, trans. Helen Weaver (Oxford, 1981), 298.

96 See also Richard Wunderli and Gerald Broce, 'The Final Moment before Death in Early Modern England', *Sixteenth Century Journal* 20 (1989), 259–75.

last thoughts were of earthly friends or family members, rather than the world beyond. James Cowan passed a wraith story on to Wodrow around 1707.[97] It concerned the minister James Short, and dated from about ten years previously, when Short was doing his trials in the Presbytery of Earlston. He was lying in bed awake at about five o' clock in the morning when he saw the apparition of John Scrimzeor, a good friend and fellow trainee minister. Short had seen Scrimzeor in a 'sickly condition' in Edinburgh a few days previously. Scrimzeor approached the bed, looked at Short, and turned away. He then departed, leaving Short 'a trembling and sweating for a considerable time'. When he got up Short travelled to Edinburgh and made enquiries, only to find that Scrimzeor had died at the precise time he had seen the apparition. Scrimzeor was described as having a 'heavy, mournfull-like countenance' – hardly suggesting the joy a good Christian should feel about proceeding to Heaven. Like ghosts, these apparitions were reclaimed and turned into messages from God, but they were not thoroughly purged of unorthodox elements.

Resurrection stories also presented the return of the dead. Admittedly, stories of post-mortem revivals were not necessarily supernatural. Deficiencies in early modern medical knowledge resulted in cases of people being buried alive. This was a recognised theme in folklore, and Scotland had its own version of a folk-tale, found throughout Europe, in which a grave-robber awakens a recently-buried woman while trying to steal her ring.[98] However, even when they were not obviously supernatural, resurrection stories often took on status as providences. If a prisoner revived after execution, it might be read as a divine judgement. A 1724 broadside recounted the story of an Edinburgh woman called Margaret Dickson, who was hanged for infanticide. Her body was cut down and given to her friends, but the men taking it away stopped at a village for a drink. While they were drinking, one of the men saw the lid of the coffin move. He opened it, and Margaret sat up in her coffin. After being bled she went on to make a full recovery. Her resurrection was taken as a suggestion of her innocence, with the broadside declaring: 'She still continued to deny that she had committed the crime. From her example, and the uncertainty of her guilt, it is to be hoped that juries will be cautious how they find a verdict where the case may appear doubtful.'[99]

97 Wodrow, *Analecta*, vol. 1, 97–8.

98 Jan Bondeson, *Buried Alive: The Terrifying History of Our Most Primal Fear* (New York, 2002), 31–50. In the Scottish version the woman was often said to be Margaret Halcro Erskine, originally from Orkney, who supposedly had an initial 'death' in 1670 or 1674 before finally dying in 1725. Another candidate was Marjory Elphinstone, second wife of Robert Drummond of Carnock, who lived near Inverurie and died in the early seventeenth century. James Tait, *Two Centuries of Border Church Life*, 2 vols (Kelso, 1889–91), vol. 2, 14–15.

99 *Margaret Dickson's Penetential Confession* ([Edinburgh], [1724]); see David Nash and Anne-Marie Kilday, *Cultures of Shame: Exploring Crime and Morality in Britain 1600–1900* (Basingstoke, 2010), ch. 3.

Wodrow preserved further wondrous resurrection stories, using them to make religious points just as he would with ghosts. In his accounts the resurrection was often temporary, with the corpse lying down dead again after delivering its message. A typical story was told to Wodrow by a Mr A. Simson, who heard it from the minister of Penpont in Dumfries and Galloway. Around the year 1676, the body of a recently-deceased child was found buried in a yard in Penpont. The minister ordered the child to be brought to the kirk, and the people to convene. After many others had passed by, a man approached the child, and the child raised its hand and pointed at him. This so struck the man's conscience that he immediately confessed to being the father of the child, to having 'begotten it in incest on his wife's sister', and to being privy to its murder.[100] Kirk sessions were keen to clamp down on immorality, and the story acted as a warning about the evils of illicit sexual relations and infanticide. Wodrow went on to explain that the guilty man 'was secured and delivered to the Shirrife, and I think the sentence of death was passed on him; but having means, he bribed the Shirrife and gote off'. Early modern judicial systems had their deficiencies, but God had not forgotten the man's sins.

People might also be revived to reveal the nature of the afterlife. *Analecta* records cases of a daughter who sat up on her father's prayers to reassure him that she was with Christ, and a woman who arose to declare that she was condemned to Hell for 'lying, backbeiting, and slandering of my nighbours'. Sinclair told a similar story, of a corpse rising to declare that it was condemned.[101] The best example, however, is another story from James Cowan. It concerned a Sussex lady 'of rare and eminent piety'.[102] After she died from an illness, her husband was inconsolable. He would not allow his friends to have the corpse removed, despite their chiding that he 'acted neither like a man nor a Christian'. Eventually God granted his wish, and his wife was resurrected. She described a visit to Heaven, a place that was 'all Glorious', filled with angels and 'glorified spirits'; in the midst of this 'glorious assembly' was a 'Glorious hy Throne and the Glorious Redeemer the Man Christ Jesus'. She was able to bask in this exuberance of glory for a short time only, before she was dragged back to Earth to 'undergo a Course of sufferings'. Her conception of Heaven was theologically unobjectionable. Renaissance thinkers had imagined a human, sensual Heaven, but Protestant scholars in the seventeenth and eighteenth centuries instead envisaged Heaven as theocratic, focused on the eternal worship of God.[103] This particular account also demonstrated the proper Christian attitude towards death: the lady was angry to have been dragged back by her husband's selfishness, and on seeing her body she 'had this Murnifull

100 Wodrow, *Analecta*, vol. 1, 86–7.
101 Ibid., vol. 4, 46; vol. 1, 117–18; Sinclair, *Satans Invisible World Discovered*, 156–7.
102 James Cowan to Robert Wodrow, [1707]: NLS, Wod.Fol.XXVIII 4846, fols 224–5.
103 Colleen McDannell and Bernhard Lang, *Heaven: A History*, 2nd edn (New Haven, 2001), 146–55.

and Melancholy reflection, Must I again reenter, that dead stinking Carcass wherein I have sinned and suffred so much'.

The ghosts recorded by Wodrow and Sinclair did not generally return in their own corpses. In one story told by Wodrow, the ghost explained that he had borrowed an 'aeriall body' for his visit.[104] The implication was that the soul returned while the body remained in its grave, maintaining the clean separation between body and soul after death that Sinclair advocated. Resurrections complicate this picture, but are not inconsistent. The Sussex lady's soul clearly left her body after death, and was forced to return there later. The corpses who rose to explain their fate after death were, it is implied, briefly allowed to do so by God before their souls departed their bodies once more. Alternatively, perhaps God himself manipulated the dead body. These stories do suggest that, with God's permission, the corpse might retain vitality. However, they represent a clear progression from the violent medieval revenants, which did not generally return with good Christian messages. Again, old traditions were revisited and depicted in a newly positive light.

Ghosts and an Intermediate State

While Wodrow and Sinclair used ghosts to defend Christianity in general, there were also cases of ghosts being employed towards more precise theological ends. Within Episcopalian culture, the eighteenth century saw growing interest in the doctrine of an intermediate state for souls between death and the Resurrection.[105] Calvin had allowed for a middle ground, Abraham's Bosom, where the elect rested before passing to Heaven at the Last Judgement.[106] Nevertheless, Presbyterian sermons and religious texts from the seventeenth and eighteenth centuries almost universally agreed that the soul faced an immediate judgement after death, and proceeded to Heaven (sometimes termed Abraham's Bosom) or Hell. The first Episcopalian to mount a serious challenge to this orthodoxy was the Aberdeen bishop Archibald Campbell (d. 1744). In 1721, he published a work called *The Doctrines of the Middle State between Death and the Resurrection*, a revised and expanded edition of a work he had first published anonymously in 1713. It asserted that there was a middle

[104] Wodrow, *Analecta*, vol. 1, 127.

[105] For a more in-depth discussion of this topic, see Martha McGill, 'A Protestant Purgatory? Visions of an Intermediate State in Eighteenth-Century Scotland', *Scottish Historical Review* 97 (2018), 153–86.

[106] John Calvin, *Calvin's Institutes: A New Compend*, ed. Hugh T. Kerr (Louisville, 1989), 123–4. See also John Calvin, *Psychopannychia*, in Thomas F. Torrance (ed.), *Tracts and Treatises in Defense of the Reformed Faith*, 3 vols (Grand Rapids, 1958), vol. 3, 413–90. There are useful discussions in Yosep Kim, *The Identity and the Life of the Church: John Calvin's Ecclesiology in the Perspective of His Anthropology* (Eugene, 2014), 78–81, and McKeever, 'Ghost in Early Modern Protestant Culture', 94–101.

state for souls, called Hades, with a variety of mansions. Some souls were inevitably damned, and were sent to the left. Those who repented on their deathbeds went to the lower mansions on the right, their fate uncertain. Those who repented earlier but did not have time to establish a fully virtuous life were carried by angels to the right, where they could progress, through a process of 'purgation and purification', to higher mansions. Pure souls travelled directly to the highest mansions, Paradise, to await their progression to Heaven at the Last Judgement. Campbell also argued that Christians should pray for the last three groups of souls.[107] Compared to the view that souls went directly to Heaven or Hell, Campbell's vision of the afterlife better allowed for ghosts, a point he noted:

> And by the way, I desire all those who believe that several *Dead* People have appeared again, to reconcile these *Apparitions* to the commonly received Doctrine of a *Soul's* going streight to the *Beatifick Vision*, or to *Gehenna* upon the *Death* of the *Body*, for it is not easy for me to conceive, that a *Wicked Soul* is *Released* from the proper *Hell* of *Torment*, once it is there, nor that a *Happy Soul* is turned out of *Heaven*, and banished from the *Beatifick Vision*, to appear upon Earth again upon any Occasion until the *Resurrection*.[108]

The Episcopalian bishop Thomas Rattray (1684–1743) also wrote a tract on the intermediate state. Like Campbell, he identified this middle state as Hades, and suggested that it contained a number of mansions for housing departed souls. He explained that 'the Remains of our evil Habits ... must be purged off after Death', and that there was consequently a 'Progressive Advancement, in the after state'. He also noted that 'haunting of Tombs' could be explained by the idea that dead souls remained attached to their old habits, and therefore desired to enter human bodies.[109]

Rattray's interest in this topic is probably what led him to preserve a ghost story. This story was reported to him on 30 December 1730, and concerned a man called William Souter from Middle Mause, Perthshire.[110] Over a two-year period from December 1728, Souter was haunted by a large grey dog. Ghost dogs were a common theme in English folklore, particularly in the south.

[107] Archibald Campbell, *The Doctrines of a Middle State between Death and the Resurrection* (London, 1721), for example xviii, xx, 57.

[108] Ibid., xvii.

[109] Thomas Rattray, letter on the intermediate state, n.d.: StA, MS Dep. 19/14/1, 44–5, 37. This manuscript was located by Douglas Kornahrens: Wallace Douglas Kornahrens, 'Eucharistic Doctrine in Scottish Episcopacy, 1620-1875' (University of St Andrews Ph.D. thesis, 2008), 111.

[110] Thomas Rattray, account of the Ghost Dog of Mause, 31 Dec. 1730: NRS, GD377/448. See also Maurice Fleming, *The Ghost o' Mause: And Other Tales and Traditions of East Perthshire* (Edinburgh, 1995). It was also told in the English *Gentleman's Magazine* in 1731, with the explanation that it had been published in Scotland. Handley, *Visions of an Unseen World*, 126–7.

In Scotland, apparitions of dogs were more usually emanations of the Devil.[111] The dog haunting Souter did seem rather diabolic; when it brushed against Souter's thigh it left him with a strange pain all night. However, when Souter conversed with it – after summoning it, in necromantic fashion, by drawing a circle about himself with a staff – the dog explained that he was Souter's uncle. He had killed a man thirty-five years ago. As he had committed the murder with a dog, he was compelled to appear as one. He had left his victim's bones under a bush at the roadside, and was unable to rest until he had seen them properly buried. After a couple of expeditions, Souter recovered the bones and arranged a burial. Thereafter, the haunting ceased. The idea that the dead should be buried in consecrated ground challenged the Calvinist belief that all of God's earth was equally sacred. Nevertheless, Rattray was impressed by the story. He wrote that it was 'as remarkable as perhaps anything you ever heard of', and 'leaves (I think) no ground of doubt to any man of sense'.

While the intermediate state was chiefly an Episcopalian interest, its most famous ghostly advocate sprang from the pen of a Presbyterian minister. This minister was William Ogilvie (c.1688–1729), who was admitted to Innerwick, East Lothian, in 1715.[112] The ghost was what remained of Thomas Maxwell, Laird of Coul. 'Coul' (also Cool, Cule or Cuil) was derived from the Gaelic cùil, meaning a corner or nook, and several Scottish estates bore the title. This particular Coul was a small estate in the parish of Buittle, in Galloway. Thomas Maxwell was laird of the estate from 1715, but had a 'tarnished reputation', having dealt dishonestly with his lands.[113] He died in January 1722, and the first accounts of his ghost appeared in February 1723. The initial iteration of the story was not Ogilvie's, but came from a man called William Sinclair, Maxwell's ex-servant. Sinclair had a few meetings with Coul's ghost. The first occurred when Sinclair was tending to his master's horses. Coul appeared, much to the terror of the horses, and declared that he could not rest until he had told Sinclair something. He was wearing his customary white coat and knotted wig. Sinclair refused, saying that he had nothing to do with anyone but God and his current master. The apparition then vanished.

On the second occasion, Coul accompanied Sinclair to the kirk, but lingered behind at the kirk stile. He waylaid Sinclair on the way back. Sinclair

111 On England see Theo Brown, 'The Black Dog', *Folklore* 69 (1958), 175–92. There are nine examples of the Devil appearing as a black dog in Julian Goodare et al., *The Survey of Scottish Witchcraft* (University of Edinburgh, 2003), http://www.shca.ed.ac.uk/witches, accessed 1 Feb. 2018. There are multiple more with the Devil merely as a dog. See also the black dog that appears in *A Full True and Particular Account of the Most Dreadful Apparrition: Of Robert Watt Wine-Merchant in Edinr, Who Appeared to James Macdonald Plaisterer in Lieth-Walk* ([Edinburgh?], [1794?]), and the brown dog that appears in the company of the ghost of Edward Avon in Sinclair, *Satans Invisible World Discovered*, 107.

112 Miller, 'Laird of Coul's Ghost', 259–60; Scott, *Fasti*, vol. 1, 140.

113 P. H. McKerlie, *History of the Lands and Their Owners in Galloway*, 5 vols (Edinburgh, 1870–9), vol. 3, 273.

saw a large, deranged-looking greyhound, which disappeared, and a man. He lost his senses, and presently found himself at the moat of Dumfries. There he saw a party of people, mostly women, with Coul among them. Coul began to entreat Sinclair to enter his service, displaying handfuls of gold. His debts, he explained, had not been properly discharged after his death; he wanted Sinclair to pass this on to his widow. Sinclair tried to leave, but people blocked his way, and some began to change shape, shifting into monstrously large toads. In one version of the story, Coul's skin colour was gradually darkening until he became black. Sinclair prayed, and eventually the party vanished. Not long afterwards, however, he was watering two horses when a great black horse with an unknown rider appeared, bearing down on him. One of the horses fell down dead on top of him, leaving him badly 'crushed and bruised'. The other horse died the next day. At this point, Sinclair reported the events to Robert Paton and Patrick Linn, ministers of Dumfries, and Thomas Mack, minister of Terregles. These ministers wrote the story down and, at least in Mack's case, passed it on.[114] The 1892 edition of Ogilvie's chapbook supplies the following supplement: 'At some subsequent appearance while the lad was about the same business, whether Coul had done him any real harm, or that the lad had fallen from his Horse thro' Fear & Confusion is uncertain; But so it was that the Lad was found Dead on the Road.'[115]

This story is a patchwork of different traditions. In part, it follows folkloric conventions for ghost stories. Animals shrinking away from the ghost was a common pattern, as was Coul's appearance in the clothes he wore during his lifetime. His need to rectify mistakes and sort out unfinished business before he could rest was in line with medieval tradition. However, the story also incorporates the Reformation picture of the ghost as a devil, and there are obvious crossovers with witchcraft discourses. The party was clearly influenced by stories of the Sabbat, the night-time gathering where witches paid homage to the Devil.[116] Coul took on the role of the Devil by offering Sinclair gold for his allegiance, another standard feature of witch stories. The letter that speaks of Coul's skin turning black is even more suggestive, as the Devil was frequently depicted as a black man.[117] However, elements of ghostliness remained; it is interesting that Coul resumed lamenting his debts even as people were turning into toads around him. By the 1720s the witch

[114] Account of the Laird of Coul's ghost, 12 Dec. 1723: NRS, CH12/12/755; Account of the Laird of Coul's ghost, 12 Feb. 1723: NRS, CH12/16/251; Thomas Mack to Robert Wodrow, 15 Feb. 1723: NLS, Wod.Lett.Qu.XIX, fols 283–4.

[115] William Ogilvie, *The Laird o' Coul's Ghost*, ed. J. F. S. Gordon (London, 1892), 20n1.

[116] For a basic overview see Jonathan L. Pearl, 'Sabbat', in Richard M. Golden (ed.), *Encyclopedia of Witchcraft: The Western Tradition*, 4 vols (Santa Barbara, 2006), vol. 4, 987–92.

[117] See Joyce Miller, 'Men in Black: Appearances of the Devil in Early Modern Scottish Witchcraft Discourse', in Julian Goodare, Lauren Martin and Joyce Miller (eds), *Witchcraft and Belief in Early Modern Scotland* (Basingstoke, 2008), 144–65.

trials were dying out. It is notable that this medley of ghost, Devil, witches and shapeshifters was taken seriously enough to be recorded and passed on.

However, it was Ogilvie's depiction that made Coul's ghost a famous figure. Ogilvie gave a slightly different version of Sinclair's account, explaining that on the first meeting the ghost noted Sinclair's confusion and arranged an appointment for the next day. Sinclair consulted the minister Robert Paton on whether he should keep the appointment, and was counselled against doing so. Not long afterwards he was riding with another young man when Coul attacked him with a mallet. His companion could see nothing, but Sinclair's horse fell down dead, and Sinclair explained that Coul had struck its forehead.[118] Ogilvie discussed this story with Robert Paton's son, one of his fellow ministers. He expressed his disapproval that Paton had dissuaded Sinclair from meeting with the ghost. He later informed some of his brethren that he had himself seen and conversed with the ghost. The matter lay quiet until Ogilvie died in 1729. Then a manuscript account of his dealings with the Laird of Coul's ghost was found in his desk, sealed and with the instruction that it should be opened after his death. It was kept by the family, but a copy was made by a printer in Edinburgh named Watkins – presumably Richard Watkins (d. 1747), recognised as one of His Majesty's Printers from 1741–4 and 1746–7. After Watkins's death the account fell into the hands of friends, who published it in Newcastle in 1750. The first Scottish edition was published in 1751, entitled *A Copy of Several Conferences and Meetings, &c. that Past betwixt the Reverend Mr. Ogilvie, Late Minister of the Gospel at Innerwick, and the Ghost of Mr. Maxwel Late Laird of Cool.*[119]

Ogilvie's encounters with Coul supposedly took place soon after Sinclair's, although there is a degree of confusion regarding the dating. Some versions of the chapbook give the date of Ogilvie's meetings as February 1722 – implausible, since Sinclair's encounters took place in February 1723. Other editions give a more probable date of 1724. Even 1744 appears.[120] The actual story, however, is identical in most editions.[121] On a February evening, Ogilvie was walking home when he heard somebody riding up behind him. Looking back, he saw a horse, and called: 'Who is there?' The answer came: 'The Laird of Coul, be not afraid.' Ogilvie thought that a friend was playing a trick on him, and threw his cane at the apparition, but it passed straight through him. He dismounted to pick it up, and 'had some Difficulty in mounting again, what by the ramping of my Horse, and what by Reason of a certain Kind of Trembling throughout

118 Frank Miller, 'The Laird of Coul's Ghost: A Galloway Chap-Book', *Transactions of the Dumfriesshire and Galloway Natural History & Antiquarian Society*, 3rd ser., 14 (1927), 261.
119 Miller, 'Laird of Coul's Ghost', 262–6.
120 See ibid., 266–72 for a bibliography of the various editions.
121 There are minor variations in spelling and sentence structure. Quotations are from the 1892 edition.

my whole Joints'.[122] Coul explained that he knew that Ogilvie had criticised the Dumfries ministers for telling William Sinclair to stay away from him, and hoped that Ogilvie would be willing to help instead. In response to Ogilvie's trepidation he assured him that 'you are as safe with me, and safer, if safer can be, than when I was alive'.[123] They reached a churchyard soon afterwards, and Ogilvie writes that Coul 'broke from me thro' the Churchyard with greater violence, than ever any man on horseback is capable of, and with such a singing and buzzing noise, as put me in greater Disorder, than I was all the Time I was with him'.[124] However, they soon met again, and Coul explained his affairs. He had cheated the relatives of deceased men by forging discharges of his debts to them, or forging bonds owing to him. He even owed Ogilvie himself 200 Scots pounds. The most pressing case was the injustice he had done to Homer Maxwell, having borrowed 2000 merks from him. He had stolen the bond upon Maxwell's death, and Maxwell's nine children were left starving. He wanted Ogilvie to explain these matters to his widow, noting that 'if that were done, I think I would be easie and happy'. Ogilvie objected that he would be thought 'brainsick and mad', while his fellow ministers would insist that the ghost was really the Devil.[125] He did, however, take the opportunity to question his ghostly visitor thoroughly regarding the estate of the dead. In defiance of traditional patterns for ghost stories, the chapbook ended without any resolution for the unhappy ghost.

Ogilvie's version of Coul was very different from Sinclair's. In Ogilvie's account, Coul explained that he was not returning in his own body, which was 'in the Grave rotting', but had borrowed 'such a Body as answers me in a Moment, for I can fly as fast as my Soul can do without it'. (His horse, in another echo of the 'ghost as an animal' theme, was his dead tenant Andrew Johnstoun.)[126] Sinclair's report, by contrast, highlighted Coul's similarity to his past self. In Ogilvie's account, Coul was no longer violent or diabolic, and there were no parties with women-cum-toads. Ogilvie was not really trying to tell a ghost story. He was using Coul as a vehicle through which to make theological arguments, and the presentation of the ghost was tailored accordingly. In his narrative, Coul refused to reveal whether he was in a state of happiness, but noted that he had not yet appeared before God or received any judgement from him. Ogilvie reminded him that it was generally believed that a private judgement took place immediately after death, before the Last Judgement. Coul, however, objected:

> No such Thing, no such Thing, no Tryal till the last Day: The Heaven which good Men enjoy immediately after Death, consists only in the Serenity of

[122] Ogilvie, *Laird o' Coul's Ghost*, 12–13.
[123] Ibid., 20–1.
[124] Ibid., 17–18.
[125] Ibid., 47–53, 63.
[126] Ibid., 24.

> their Thoughts, the Satisfaction of a good Conscience, and the certain Hope they have of an Eternity of Joy when that Day shall come. The Punishment or Hell of the wicked immediately after Death, consists in the dreadful Things of their awakened Conscience, and the Terror of facing the great Judge, and the sensible Apprehensions of eternal Torments ensuing; and this bears still a due Proportion to the Evils they have done, when they were living.[127]

He continued that those who were not truly wicked, but ill-educated and not mindful of 'the Concerns of Eternity', were in a different category from the worst sinners, and were 'not so much under the Load of the Divine Displeasure, as they are out of His Graces and Favours, for you know it is one Thing to be discourted, and quite another Thing to be persecuted with all the Power and Rage of an incensed earthly King'. He finished with the assertion that 'men's Faces in this World are not more various and different, than their Conditions are after Death'.[128] This was a more sympathetic vision than Calvin's binary division of the world into elect and reprobate. Ogilvie was dubious, noting that

> some Things you have advanced, seem to contradict the Scriptures, which I shall ever look upon as the infallible Truths of God; for I find by the Parable of Dives and Lazarus, that one was immediately carried up by the Angels to Abraham's Bosom, and the other thrust down to a Place of Torment.

Coul explained that this account was metaphorical, demonstrating that a man could be miserable during his life and happy thereafter, or vice versa.[129]

In taking an interest in the idea of an intermediate state, Ogilvie was deviating from the Presbyterian party line. It was a soundly Episcopalian doctrine, and was often associated with Catholic sympathies. The Church of Scotland minister John Willison lamented in 1744:

> Ah, how wofully have [the Episcopal clergy] degenerated from the Principles and Practice of their Fathers! ... being strongly attached to Jacobite Principles and a Popish Pretender, they were thereby induced to entertain favourable Thoughts of other Popish Superstitions and Errors, which at length many of them began to vent and stand up for; such as, A middle State for Souls after Death, and Prayers for the Dead.[130]

Ogilvie may not have known the Episcopalian writing on the topic, but since he specified that the account should be read only after his death, he was certainly aware that his eschatology might cause controversy. By putting his explanation in the mouth of a ghost, he could present himself as a respectable Presbyterian, objecting that Coul's views were unscriptural. Ghost stories

127 Ibid., 25–6.
128 Ibid., 29–30.
129 Ibid., 30–1.
130 McIntosh, *Church and Theology*, 32; John Willison, *A Fair and Impartial Testimony: Essayed in Name of a Number of Ministers, Elders, and Christian People of the Church of Scotland* (Edinburgh, 1744), 98.

could thus be used to promote a particular theological argument without having to espouse it officially. This was not, admittedly, a common approach. Ghosts remained uncomfortable territory for Presbyterians. The intermediate state was a contested topic among the Episcopalians, and Rattray's interest in hauntings was unusual. Nevertheless, the fact that ghosts might be used to advance theological arguments underlines how much more respectable they had become over the late seventeenth and early eighteenth centuries.

The Decline of the Evangelising Ghost?

In England, the rehabilitation of ghosts is associated primarily with the late seventeenth and early eighteenth centuries. As the eighteenth century progressed, the climate changed. Owen Davies writes that ghosts 'ceased to act as an ecumenical glue for factions within the Church of England' by the late 1730s. Ghost belief was increasingly associated with the Methodists, and as such 'became synonymous with pernicious religious enthusiasm'.[131] The Scottish religious scene was also fragmented, but ghost belief was not confessionalised in the same way. The impact of Methodism in Scotland was limited, and despite Rattray's interest in ghosts, they do not seem to have become particularly associated with Episcopalian culture. Nevertheless, the religious climate in late-eighteenth-century Scotland was not very amenable to ghosts. From about the 1760s, the Moderates were dominant within the kirk. The Moderates were closely associated with the Scottish Enlightenment, and tended to be critical of religious enthusiasm.[132] The Episcopalian church in the latter half of the eighteenth century was a beleaguered minority, suffering under harsh penal laws imposed in the wake of the 1745–6 Jacobite uprising.[133] The notion of an intermediate state drew more converts, including John Skinner, primus of the Episcopal Church from 1788 to 1816.[134] However, later eighteenth-century discussions of an intermediate state did not reference ghosts. The bishop George Innes (1717–81) wrote a manuscript tract asserting the reality of an intermediate state, but also argued that 'no mere man ever came from [after death] to give us information: none but Christ, who is both God and man'.[135]

131 Davies, *Haunted*, 122. Although see also Handley, *Visions of an Unseen World*, 140–76, which argues that ghost stories remained relevant across confessional divides.

132 See, for example, Sher, *Church and University*.

133 Rowan Strong, *Episcopalianism in Nineteenth-Century Scotland: Religious Responses to a Modernizing Society* (Oxford, 2002), 15–19.

134 For example, John Skinner, *A Course of Lectures, Delivered on the Six Sundays in Lent* (Aberdeen, 1786), 44–5.

135 George Innes, *The Primitive Doctrine: A Middle State of Happiness or Misery between Death and the Resurrection*, n.d.: NRS, CH12/21/10; George Innes, *Fourteen Discourses on Practical Subjects* (London, 1783), 10.

Proselytising ghosts did, however, linger at the fringes of religious culture. The Laird of Coul's ghost remained a point of interest throughout the eighteenth century. The founder of Methodism, John Wesley (1703–91), gave the story a broader circulation among educated audiences when he printed it in his *Arminian Magazine* in 1785.[136] Also in 1785, the story attracted the attention of Elizabeth Steuart of Coltness (d. 1803), 'Aunt Betty' to the Whig politician Henry Erskine.[137] Steuart's interest in spirits is indicated in a snippet from a young minister in reply to one of her letters: 'I should esteem it a favour to hear your sentiments more fully respecting those spirits which you say are common at this day. I am by no means disposed to call everything nervous, &c.'[138] She considered Ogilvie to be 'the most perfect man in his time', adding that 'The greatest men in every age have endeavoured to give the living world some account of the dead; but Mr. Ogilvie's relation of Coul's Ghost puts them all to shame: all other attempts are poor, mean, grovelling, and earthly'.[139] Steuart was attracted to the doctrine of the Swedish theologian Emanuel Swedenborg (1688–1772). Swedenborg emphasised the role of angels and spirits in everyday life. He also believed in an intermediate state, the World of Spirits, a half-way house between Heaven and Hell where men were judged after death. Steuart did not uphold Swedenborg's idea that a Last Judgement had already taken place in the World of Spirits, but she was a firm believer in a middle state for souls.[140] She wrote:

> It is long since I was convinced, that our seperated stat, first on our Death, is like the purgatory of the Roman Catholics; all who die goes down to the infancy of these Invisible Elements, that worked in our vessels, when alive, & produced, all our words & thought & action. In these Invisible Elements, we are taught, purified & Educated, & made fit, to act our part in the new heavens & the new Earth; & there we mount through the various stages of Government & be made angels & minestrating spirits, to Christ, who has under taken the redemption, of the world.[141]

Steuart wrote to Ogilvie's daughter Henrietta, arguing that the story of Coul's ghost should be republished, supplemented with her commentary. Henrietta refused. She explained that although she believed the story herself, she was

136 John Wesley, 'A Strange Account', *Arminian Magazine*, July–Aug. 1785, 378–81, 416–20.

137 Alexander Fergusson, *The Honourable Henry Erskine, Lord Advocate for Scotland* (Edinburgh, 1882), 369–87. Sometimes her name is given as Elizabeth Steuart-Barclay.

138 Ibid., 374–5.

139 William Ogilvie, *Narrative of Four Conferences between the Ghost of Mr. Maxwell, of Coul, and the Rev. Mr. Ogilvie, Minister of Innerwick*, ed. Elizabeth Steuart (London, 1808), 113, 22.

140 Fergusson, *Honourable Henry Erskine*, 383. On Swedenborg see Ernst Benz, *Emanuel Swedenborg: Visionary Savant in the Age of Reason*, trans. Nicholas Goodrick-Clarke (West Chester, 2002).

141 Elizabeth Steuart-Barclay, papers on the Laird of Coul's Ghost, 1788–1802: NLS, MS. 10786.

frightened that people would attack her father for his 'weakness and credulity'. Her friends also got involved: one destroyed Henrietta's papers on the affair, so that Henrietta would not have the power to mar her father's character and 'show [her] inthusiasm to the world'.[142] Steuart circulated her commentary privately instead, and her nephew published the work by her instructions in 1808, after both she and Henrietta had died.[143] The story of the Laird of Coul's ghost was subsequently retold by nineteenth-century spiritualists, who also tended to advocate for an intermediate state.[144]

The story was not only of interest to believers in an intermediate state, however. The introduction to the 1892 edition states that the chapbook was 'eagerly bought by all and sundry from the Flying Stationers who hawked it about the country'.[145] Frank Miller has identified nine editions from the eighteenth century and fifteen to seventeen from the nineteenth century.[146] No other ghost story seems to have been reprinted so frequently. This was almost certainly despite, rather than because of, the story's precise religious messages. In the 1770s, there was a debate in the *Edinburgh Weekly Magazine* about whether or not ghosts existed. One man, identified only by the initials C. G., declared:

> the story of Maxwell of Cule's re-appearance soon after death ... was a most nottour and flaming story not many years ago, and he continued to fright many for some time, till at last he found one Mr Ogilvie ... who had the courage to hold sundry conversations with his re-appearance, and to write down a number of particular facts and circumstances, which were printed, published, and sold in the streets of this, and sundry other market towns in Scotland, England, and Ireland.

C. G. argued that the story was factual, and that a 'good and instructive moral' could be drawn from it.[147] 'Fabricius' replied a month later, retorting that the Laird of Coul 'must have been the production of some shallow scribbler, with some small degree of sheer wit; for it represents a minister holding conferences with a ghost that are trifling and ridiculous'.[148] These men took little interest in the specific theological debates underpinning the story; they were mainly concerned with whether or not Coul proved the reality of ghosts. The interest of C. G., Wesley and Steuart demonstrates the resilience and flexibility of the evangelising ghost. Coul's apparition could be used to make specific theological arguments, but also to uphold more general religious doctrines. As in the case

142 Henrietta Hog to Elizabeth Steuart, 24 Mar. 1788: NLS, MS. 10785.

143 Fergusson, *Honourable Henry Erskine*, 379, 383–5; Ogilvie, *Narrative of Four Conferences*.

144 Johann Heinrich Jung-Stilling, *Theory of Pneumatology*, trans. Samuel Jackson (London, 1834), 453–60; 'The Rev. Mr. Ogilvy and the Laird of Cool', *Spiritual Magazine*, July 1866, 329–32.

145 J. F. S. Gordon, 'Introit', in William Ogilvie, *The Laird o' Coul's Ghost* (London, 1892), vi–vii.

146 Miller, 'Laird of Coul's Ghost', 266–72.

147 C. G. to the *Weekly Magazine, or Edinburgh Amusement*, 16 Apr. 1772, 74.

148 Fabricius to the *Weekly Magazine, or Edinburgh Amusement*, 7 May 1772, 167.

of Wodrow's and Sinclair's ghosts, inconveniently unorthodox points were simply ignored.

Satans Invisible World Discovered also became increasingly well known. When it was first published in 1685, it did not reach a large audience. Archibald Pitcairne's 1692 play *The Assembly* hints at its early readership. Pitcairne presents it as part of the library of a strict old Presbyterian lady. While the heroes of the play are disguised as Presbyterian ministers in an endeavour to woo the lady's nieces, she tells them of the books she has bought: 'Ther's Saml. Rutherford's Letters. Ther's Good News from Heavn. And ther's Satan's Invisible World. What think you, Mr John, of Satan's Invisible World?' 'Mr John', being in fact a young man 'not weall seen in divinity', has not heard of the work, and guesses wrongly when he replies that it is 'the best Sermon evr I heard'.[149] However, by the late eighteenth century the work had gone through multiple editions, and was said to be the 'second book in a peasant's library of two'.[150] The change in audience was reflected by the fact that later editions omitted Sinclair's anti-Cartesian preface, removing the work from the context of philosophical debate.[151] Supernatural stories were a popular genre, and the motivations behind the continued publication of *Satans Invisible World Discovered* were probably commercial as much as religious. Nevertheless, refuting atheists remained the overarching justification of the book.

This religious agenda also persisted in other works. In 1763, a Skye minister published *A Treatise on the Second Sight, Dreams and Apparitions: With Several Instances Sufficiently Attested*, under the pseudonym Theophilus Insulanus.[152] Insulanus primarily discussed second sight, but included some ghost stories. Most of his ghosts returned to confirm the reality of the afterlife. Insulanus approached his subject with all Sinclair's anxiety about the dangers of materialist worldviews. In the dedication to *Treatise on the Second Sight*, he noted that he was writing at a time when 'the pulpit resounds with repeated exclamations against the infidelity of the age, when vice reigns triumphant, and atheism, or at least deistical principles are openly avowed, and by too many much countenanced'.[153] In a curious turnaround from the general position in the wake of the Reformation, Insulanus argued that it was un-

149 Archibald Pitcairne, *The Phanaticks*, ed. John MacQueen (Woodbridge, 2012), act 5, scene 2, lines 44–8, p. 62; p. 5 (Dramatis Personae).

150 Christina Larner, *Enemies of God: The Witch-Hunt in Scotland* (London, 1981), 32; see Coleman O. Parsons, 'Introduction', in Coleman O. Parsons (ed.), *Satans Invisible World Discovered* (Gainesville, 1969), xxv.

151 For a list of editions see Parsons, 'Introduction', xxv–xxviii.

152 The identity of Theophilus Insulanus remains unclear. Most recent works give the name Donald MacLeod/McLeod; this is also the name given in John MacCulloch, *The Highlands and Western Isles of Scotland*, 4 vols (London, 1824), vol. 4, 63. Genealogies of the MacLeod family give, instead, William MacLeod. See Donald MacKinnon and Alick Morrison, *The MacLeods: The Genealogy of a Clan*, 5 vols (Edinburgh, 1968–76), vol. 2, 111.

153 Theophilus Insulanus, *A Treatise on the Second Sight, Dreams and Apparitions* (Edinburgh, 1763), dedication, iii.

Protestant to discourage the laity from taking an interest in apparitions: it was akin to the Catholic belief that the laity should not read the Bible themselves because they might misinterpret it.[154] He acknowledged that people of 'weak intellects' might become superstitious 'by a studious and too eager attention to revelation, by dreams, Second Sight, and other kinds of divination'. However, he thought it better that people should give way to superstition, as it would 'settle in the mind an awful sense of the essentials of religion', than that they should follow in the footsteps of deists and freethinkers.[155] He added that 'From the certainty of dreams, Second Sight, and apparitions, follows the plain and natural consequence of the existence of spirits, immateriality and immortality of the soul'.[156]

Similar considerations influenced the minister John Anderson's account of mysterious noises from a house in Stronsay, Orkney. The story featured in the Statistical Account of 1791–9.[157] It was accompanied by an unusually detailed justification, which is worth quoting in full:

> In this eminently enlightened age, when atheism and irreligion have been very active in bringing, not only superstition and enthusiasm, but religion itself to the Guillotine, it is highly probable, that the traits of character now exhibited will be held in derision, and the drawer therof exposed to infinite ridicule on account of the preceding narrative, by those who glory in being superior to vulgar prejudices. If this should be the case, he will not attempt to remonstrate, but only humbly propose the following queries. 1st, Are the inconsiderable remains of superstition and enthusiasm, which do affect the character only in small and unimportant matters; or scepticism, which gives a new and totally different direction to the understanding and the will, least dangerous to our happy establishment in church and state? And whereas the human mind is a fruitful field, in which wholesome herbs, or noxious weeds, will spring up and flourish, –2dly, Is it wiser to pluck up at once the whole existing crop, before we have duly considered the nature and tendency of the seed to be substituted in its place; or to continue to cultivate the seeds of revealed religion, (which system hath been held in high estimation by wise men in all ages of world,) and at the same time, gradually to check and eradicate pernicious errors and immoral practices? A candid examination of these queries may possibly furnish some apology, why the minister and people of this district are not very hasty to exchange old prejudice for new and strange doctrines, which eventually may be, and in a neighbouring nation have been subversive of the principles of religion natural and revealed.[158]

[154] Ibid., 119.

[155] Ibid., xvii–xviii.

[156] Ibid., 123, 44.

[157] On Anderson see Scott, *Fasti*, vol. 7, 274.

[158] John Anderson, 'United Parishes of Stronsay and Eday', in John Sinclair (ed.), *The Statistical Account of Scotland, 1791–1799*, electronic edn, 21 vols (University of Edinburgh, University of Glasgow, 1999), vol. 15, http://stataccscot.edina.ac.uk/link/osa-vol15-p387-parish-orkney-stronsay_and_eday, accessed 1 Feb. 2018, 432.

This explanation was, in part, a product of the contemporary climate. In declaring that religion had been 'brought to the Guillotine', Anderson was making a clear reference to the 1789 French Revolution. Although the political situation in Scotland did not escalate as it had in France, there was a wave of radicalism across the country in the early 1790s. Anderson was writing in 1794, when anti-French feeling was exacerbated by war and the excesses of the Reign of Terror.[159] It was therefore a time when clergymen were particularly keen to defend 'our happy establishment in church and state'. Ghosts were also used to this end in pamphlet literature, with dead revolutionaries returning to bemoan the evils of civil disobedience.[160] However, although Anderson's account reflected the contemporary political context, his basic message was nothing novel. Of course, he distanced himself from the 'old prejudice' he was defending, just as Insulanus hid behind a pseudonym. These authors were thus more cautious than Wodrow and Sinclair. Nevertheless, they reprised Wodrow and Sinclair's idea that atheism was a greater threat to the kirk than excessive credulity, and were prepared to take a (relatively) sympathetic view of apparition stories as a result. Although the evangelising ghost did not make its way into mainstream religious culture, it retained a place on the sidelines throughout the eighteenth century.

Conclusion

From the late seventeenth century, ghosts took on a more prominent role in Scottish society. The emergence of atheism as a comparable threat to enthusiasm and Catholicism resulted in some Protestants taking a new interest in the returning dead. Scotland's movement towards reclaiming ghosts was not on the same scale as England's. The religious context in the late seventeenth and early eighteenth centuries was too strained in Scotland; accusations of enthusiasm were a more acute threat than they were in England (at least prior to the rise of Methodism). However, Wodrow and Sinclair were respectable Presbyterians who collected stories from other educated people. Although they were not representative of the kirk as a whole, their interest indicates that ghosts had become marginally more acceptable. The growing fear of atheism is not the only explanation for this. Increased research into folkloric beliefs also slotted into a context of broadening geographical awareness, scientific

159 On radicalism see, for example, T. M. Devine, 'The Failure of Radical Reform in Scotland in the Late Eighteenth Century', in T. M. Devine (ed.), *Conflict and Stability in Scottish Society, 1700–1850* (Edinburgh, 1990), 51–64. The dating of Anderson's passage is from Anderson, 'United Parishes of Stronsay and Eday', 398.

160 See *Brissot's Ghost! Or, Intelligence from the Other World* (Edinburgh, 1794); *An Account of a Most Horrid, Bloody, and Terrible Apparition, Which Lately Appeared in the Parish of Shotts* (London, 1793). The ghosts of pamphlet literature are discussed on pp. 163–71.

investigation and nation-building.[161] Nevertheless, the primary function of the stories was to further a religious agenda. Ghosts were presented as having come from God, and demonstrated the reality of spirits and the afterlife. Beyond this, they showed significant theological flexibility. Stories were seemingly taken from popular culture, and were not completely purged of medieval elements. We see here a short-lived compromise between (part of the) Presbyterian establishment and unorthodox folk tradition.

Ghosts could also be harnessed to reflect on particular theological debates – becoming, for example, propagandists for an intermediate state. Admittedly, this was not always effectual. The popularity of the chapbook about the Laird of Coul's ghost probably owed little, if anything, to its religious teachings. A worthy moral message furnished a good excuse to print stories in the lucrative genre of the supernatural. Commercial considerations doubtless factored into the many editions of *Satans Invisible World Discovered*. However, as the eighteenth century progressed, there remained a strand of educated folk who used ghosts to make theological points, or who considered ghosts to be a valuable defence against atheism. By the nineteenth century, ghosts were still described as having a 'higher moral purpose'.[162] Although they remained unorthodox, ghosts became morally defensible. This cleared the way for the expansion of ghost stories and ghostlore more generally over the eighteenth century.

161 See pp. 147–8.

162 'The Voyages And Travels Of Columbus Secundus', *Blackwood's Edinburgh Magazine*, Nov. 1821, 399; see also Anne MacVicar Grant, *Essays on the Superstitions of the Highlanders of Scotland*, 2 vols (London, 1811), vol. 1, 114–15.

3

Scepticism and Debate

In a courtroom speech published in 1673, the lawyer George Mackenzie of Rosehaugh declared that he believed in witchcraft. Providence, he suggested, allowed witches to work their wiles on Earth, 'to the end that the being of Spirits may not be deny'd'. However, he went on to argue that society overstated the extent of the Devil's dominion, and objected that 'to kill one another, because we cannot comprehend the reason of what each other do, is the effect of a terrible distraction'.[1] Over the decades that followed, increasing numbers of lawyers and judges fell in with his way of thinking. Executions for witchcraft declined.[2] The last Scottish prosecution was in 1727, and witchcraft was decriminalised in 1736. After a period in which witchcraft was an ever-present menace for communities, magical forces were ebbing out of the sphere of everyday experience. Within philosophy, too, change was afoot; David Hume's 1748 *Enquiry Concerning Human Understanding* offered a commentary on miracles that threatened to overhaul traditional conceptions of the supernatural world. The eighteenth century is associated with the development of a newly sceptical outlook towards stories of the supernatural, at least within educated society. This extended to ghosts. Sightings of apparitions were increasingly explained away in natural terms, or mocked by satirists. However, ghosts retained a cultural presence, and outside of the spheres of high Enlightenment discourse, educated men were prepared to speak for them.

The Complexities of Scepticism

To understand eighteenth-century scepticism regarding the supernatural, it is necessary to first understand that the vast majority of thinkers operated within a Christian framework. There was rarely any question of rejecting the supernatural altogether. Debate instead focused on the precise types of spirits in existence, and the degree of supernatural intervention in everyday life.

1 George Mackenzie, *Pleadings in Some Remarkable Cases before the Supreme Courts of Scotland Since the Year 1661* (Edinburgh, 1673), 185–6.

2 See Brian P. Levack, *Witch-Hunting in Scotland: Law, Politics and Religion* (London, 2008), 131–44.

The end of the witch-hunts is an important signifier in the story of how Scots engaged with the supernatural, but doubt about witches did not necessarily imply doubt about other categories of the supernatural. To illustrate the complex relationship between belief and scepticism, we can consider the curious case of Archibald Pitcairne (1652–1713). Pitcairne was an Edinburgh physician and a Jacobite. His religious sentiments have been the subject of some scholarly speculation. In Edinburgh he was described as a deist, and 'by many alledged to be ane Atheist'.[3] Michael Hunter has uncovered an atheistical text that was found in Pitcairne's study after his death, possibly authored by Pitcairne himself.[4] Alasdair Raffe rejects the notion that Pitcairne was an atheist, but highlights Pitcairne's anti-clericalism and interest in natural religion, ultimately describing him as an 'authentically Scottish voice of religious heterodoxy'.[5] Whatever might have been his precise religious views, Pitcairne certainly doubted accounts of witchcraft.[6] He also mocked *Satans Invisible World Discovered* in his co-authored play *The Assembly*.[7]

However, sceptical though he was in some respects, Pitcairne apparently received visitations from a ghost. The details are recorded in manuscript keys to Pitcairne's poetry, one of which is in Pitcairne's own hand.[8] The manuscripts explained that while studying in Paris, Pitcairne made a pact with his friend Robert Lindsay that whoever died first should return to the other and describe his condition. Lindsay died in the winter of 1675–6, and on the night of his death Pitcairne dreamt that Lindsay appeared to him. Lindsay explained that 'they have buried my body in the Gray-Friars, I am tho alive and in a place the pleasures of which cannot be exprest in Scots, Greek or Latin. I have come with a well sayling small ship to Leith Road to carry yow thither'. Pitcairne agreed to go on condition that he could take leave of his father, mother and aunt. His friend objected: 'Archie, I have but the allowance of one tide, and yow shall not make your visits in so short a tyme. Farewell Archie, I'll come

3 Robert Wodrow, *Analecta: Or Materials for a History of Remarkable Providences Mostly Relating to Scotch Ministers and Christians*, ed. Matthew Leishman, 4 vols (Edinburgh, 1842–3), vol. 2, 255.

4 Michael Hunter, '*Pitcairneana*: An Atheist Text by Archibald Pitcairne', *Historical Journal* 59 (2016), 595–621.

5 Alasdair Raffe, 'Archibald Pitcairne and Scottish Heterodoxy, c.1688–1713', *Historical Journal* 60 (2017), 657.

6 See, for example, Lizanne Henderson, *Witchcraft and Folk Belief in the Age of Enlightenment: Scotland, 1670–1740* (Basingstoke, 2016), 119.

7 See p. 80.

8 Archibald Pitcairne, Account of Robert Lindsay's ghost, n.d.: BL, Sloane MS 3198, fols 15–16v. See John MacQueen and Winifred MacQueen, 'Introduction', in John MacQueen and Winifred MacQueen (eds), *Archibald Pitcairne: The Latin Poems* (Assen, 2009), 6, 45, 52; John MacQueen and Winifred MacQueen, 'Commentary' in the same volume, 301–3; John MacQueen, 'Introduction', in John MacQueen (ed.), *The Phanaticks* (Woodbridge, 2012), xxxii. For a printed version of Pitcairne's account see Samuel Hibbert, *Sketches of the Philosophy of Apparitions: Or, An Attempt to Trace Such Illusions to Their Physical Causes*, 2nd edn (Edinburgh, 1825), 211–12.

for yow at another tyme.' Pitcairne was said to dream of him every night since, and when he had an illness that seemed fatal, he never feared for himself, as his friend assured him that his time had not yet come.

The story was clearly in circulation in Edinburgh. Wodrow made several commentaries on it, each time apparently forgetting the previous one. In 1712, he wrote: 'The story of the apparition that Dr Pitcairn is ordinarly haunted with ... is generally belived at Edinburgh; and they tell me the name of the man that appears to him evry night is Lindsay, not Stevenson, as before.' In 1713, writing on Pitcairne's death, he noted: 'There goes a story of ane apparition he had frequently, which he ouned.' In 1723:

> I am told my Lord Grange tells a story, (enquire at him about it) of Dr Pitcairn, that he had an apparition before his death, which signifyed to him the precise day of his death, which came exactly to pass. This he told to some of his comrads a moneth before his death; but could not shake off the apprehension of it.[9]

Finally, in 1728, he gave a full story. He began:

> [Lord Grange] acquaints me that the Doctor [Pitcairne] has frequently told him of David (I think Lindsay is his name, if I remember) his constant appearing to him to that time, which was a litle before the Doctor's death. David was Clerk to the Council at Edinburgh, and had been intimat with the Doctor at the Colledge and Schools, and afterwards, and they used very frequently to be together.

In this version of the story, Pitcairne was in Paris when 'David' died in Edinburgh. His dream was as follows:

> Just about the time of David's death, as the Doctor afterwards came to knou, that same night the Doctor, at Paris, dreamed he was at Edinburgh, and heard of David's death, and did believe it, but afterwards he met him in the Land-market, and David desired he might go with him: That the Doctor said he was dead, and he would not go with him: That David said it was true his body was dead, and that they had caryed it to the Greyfriers Church-yeard, but he was still alive as much as before, and the Doctor behoved to go with him: That he went doun the street with him with reluctancy, and into severall houses wher they used to drink, but got not acces: That still he importuned the Doctor to go with him, and went doun Leith Wynd, and the Doctor went to Caltoun Craiges, and left him, and sau him go to a ship, and go out of his sight.[10]

Since then, David had appeared to Pitcairne every night. Wodrow noted that Pitcairne had confirmed the story, and even had a similar one about his sister.

9 Wodrow, *Analecta*, vol. 2, 379, 47–8.
10 Ibid., vol. 3, 520–2.

Since this apparition appeared only in dreams, no supernatural intervention was strictly necessary. It was strongly implied, however, and it is interesting that Pitcairne should have chosen to talk about the story. As detailed by John and Winifred MacQueen, Robert Lindsay's death had a significant impact on Pitcairne. He explored the theme of posthumous existence in his Latin poetry, and possibly wrote this account in the same vein.[11] However, it was not framed as fiction, and Pitcairne seems to have been content to have the story circulated as fact within Edinburgh. This case is an unusual one, but it encapsulates several significant themes. Firstly, it demonstrates that scepticism did not necessarily follow neat, predictable patterns. It was possible for educated folk to reject some popular supernatural beliefs as vulgar superstitions, but entertain others. Secondly, the difficulties in determining what the story meant to Pitcairne indicate some of the challenges involved in gauging society-wide levels of ghost belief. Thirdly, the story demonstrates the emotional import of ghosts. Pitcairne's account followed a common contemporary pattern, with the ghost returning to confirm the reality of the afterlife. However, it is also a story about the endurance of friendship, the significance of familial bonds, and the poignant pleasures of death. The latter two themes will be explored further in the next two chapters. The remainder of this chapter will further examine how scepticism about some supernatural forces could exist alongside belief in others. It is notable that Pitcairne discussed his ghostly visitor in relation to his Latin poetry, but not in his medical or theological works. Ghosts were cast out of certain spheres of debate, but remained relevant to other fields of educated discourse.

The Supernatural in Enlightenment Thinking

'What is to be thought of ghosts, witches, satyrs, furies and other spirits like that, which vulgar people believe in or fear?' Thus did regents address their students at King's College, Aberdeen, in standardised dictates that were recorded between 1694 and 1709. They were lecturing on pneumatology, or the study of minds and spirits, which was a branch of the metaphysics curriculum. The regents set about answering the question by explaining that

> Most of the things that are told about these [spirits] are nothing but old wives' tales, the inventions of poets, the phantasms of dreamers, the hallucinations of the waking, or the ridiculous fabrications of trifling monks, with which they try hard to make the confused and all too credulous common people believe in their fictitious purgatory.

11 MacQueen and MacQueen, 'Introduction', 6, 35.

The regents allowed that demons could sometimes appear in assumed bodies, 'to deceive credulous and unwary mortals and lead them to ruin', but added that divine benevolence rarely allowed these deceptions.[12]

The Aberdeen regents were, nevertheless, conscious of the looming spectre of materialism. The Marischal College regent George Peacock explained in 1697 that 'Among the monstrous fruits of the human mind can be found Hobbes's horrible and repulsive dogma, that no spirits exist'.[13] Pneumatology lectures, both from Aberdeen and elsewhere, stressed the reality of spirits. Regents taught that the existence of angels and demons was affirmed by Scripture, and upheld by the writing of ancient authorities, which mentioned apparitions, possessions and prophesying.[14] However, angels and demons were the only categories of spirit to be endorsed in this way. As the eighteenth century progressed, moreover, teaching on the world of spirits was increasingly supplanted by lectures on mechanics, physics, and the human mind. Adam Smith offered a justification for this when he criticised European universities for setting theology above philosophy, such that the 'doctrine of spirits, of which so little can be known, came to take up as much room as the doctrine of bodies, of which so much can be known'.[15] In 1766, Adam Ferguson explained that pneumatics had two branches, one concerned with the human mind, and one with the being and attributes of God. He outlined these two areas of focus, but made no mention of angels and demons, let alone other spirits, as a subject of interest.[16]

12 'De Lemuribus, Lamiis, Satyris, Furiis, aliisque ejusmodi quos vulgus credit, aut timet Spiritibus quid sit Sentiendum? Pleraque quae de iis narrantur nihil aliud sit nisi aniles fabulae poetarum figmenta, somniantium ludibria, vigilantium deliria, aut ridicula nugantium Monachorum commenta, quibus fictitii sui purgatorii fidem facere satagunt vesanae ac credulae nimis plebeculae; neque [tanquam?] diffiteor, quin Daemones aliquando fallacibus istiusmodi Speciebus mundanam possunt ingredi provinciam, ut credulos decipiant ac incautos in perniciem protrahunt mortales, licet id rarissime contingere permittet Divina erga homines Benignitas.' Alexander Stewart's lecture notes from George Skene and James Urquhart, 1708–9: AUL, MS 3922, 47; William Scot's lecture notes from William Black, c.1707: StA, MS 30314, 62; Alexander Irvine's lecture notes from [William Black?], 1694: NLS, Adv.MS.22.7.15, 258. I am grateful to Professor Thomas Ahnert for his assistance with this material.

13 'Inter monstrosos mentis humanae partûs, occurrit horrendum & aversandum illud *Hobesii* dogma, quod nulli extent spiritûs', George Peacock, *Theses Philosophicae* (Aberdeen, 1693), 5.

14 For example, John Macara's lecture notes from Thomas Taylor, 1707: StA, MS BC59. V8, sec. 'Appendix de Naturali Cognitione Angelorum', 1–2; lecture notes from John Law, 1704–5: GUL, MS Gen 873, sec. 'De Angelis'; James Craig's lecutre notes from John Loudon and John Law, 1699–1700: GUL, MS Murray 49, fols 88–88v. See Martha McGill, 'Angels, Devils, and Discernment in Early Modern Scotland', in Michelle D. Brock, Richard Raiswell and David Winter (eds), *Knowing Demons, Knowing Spirits* (Basingstoke, 2018), 242–3.

15 Quoted in Ian Simpson Ross, *The Life of Adam Smith*, 2nd edn (Oxford, 2010), 44.

16 Adam Ferguson, *Analysis of Pneumatics and Moral Philosophy* (Edinburgh, 1766), 7–28.

Of course, the centrality of God meant that the supernatural remained important to Ferguson's understanding of pneumatics. This is typical of Enlightenment culture. The field of debate became more narrow, but the supernatural was not cast out altogether. While collections of special providences lost their place within mainstream religious society, general providence remained a crucial concept for theologians and philosophers. God guided the universes envisaged by Francis Hutcheson, William Robertson, Adam Smith, and Adam Ferguson.[17] The greatest challenge to traditional Christian principles was posed by David Hume, in his critique of miracles. Having defined a miracle as 'a transgression of a law of nature by a particular volition of the Deity, or by the interposition of some invisible agent', Hume noted that the laws of nature were confirmed by long experience. When confronted with the story of a miracle, Hume explained, he would always ask himself whether it were more likely that these long-established laws should have been violated, or that the percipient of the miracle was a fool, a liar, or mistaken. Provocatively for the kirk, he took the example of a dead man returning to life, which 'has never been observed, in any age or country'.[18] He concluded that there was insufficient evidence to claim that any miracle had ever taken place, and that 'a miracle can never be proved, so as to be the foundation of a system of religion'.[19]

However, Hume's position was exceptional. Other authors rallied to the defence of miracles. George Campbell's 1762 *Dissertation on Miracles*, one of the best known rejoinders, argued that Hume's focus on testimony made it impossible for a human being to believe in anything that he or she had not directly experienced. Scripture-based arguments for miracles also emerged.[20] By the nineteenth century, miracles were still upheld as the primary proof of God's existence: in 1815 Sir Henry Moncrieff Wellwood asserted that 'if it were to be supposed that the general doctrine which asserts the existence of miracles is incredible or uncertain ... this would be in truth to suppose that the

[17] Francis Hutcheson, *A System of Moral Philosophy, in Three Books*, 2 vols (Glasgow, 1755), for example vol. 1, 131, 209–20; vol. 2, 377; on the other figures see Colin Kidd, 'The Scottish Enlightenment and the Supernatural', in Lizanne Henderson (ed.), *Fantastical Imaginations: The Supernatural in Scottish History and Culture* (Edinburgh, 2009), 106; Richard B. Sher, *Church and University in the Scottish Enlightenment: The Moderate Literati of Edinburgh* (Edinburgh, 1985), 102; Paul Oslington, 'Divine Action, Providence, and Adam Smith's Invisible Hand', in Paul Oslington (ed.), *Adam Smith as Theologian* (Abingdon, 2011), 61–74.

[18] David Hume, *An Enquiry Concerning Human Understanding*, in Mark C. Rooks (ed.), *The Complete Works and Correspondence of David Hume*, electronic edn (Charlottesville, 1995), http://pm.nlx.com/xtf/view?docId=hume/hume.05.xml;chunk.id=div.britphil.v37.5;toc.depth=1;toc.id=div.britphil.v37.5;brand=default, accessed 1 Feb. 2018, sec. 10, pt. 1, 114.

[19] Ibid., sec. 10, pt. 2, 127.

[20] M. A. Stewart, 'The Early British Reception of Hume's Writings', in Peter Jones (ed.), *The Reception of David Hume in Europe* (London, 2005), 30–42.

whole history of Christianity is false or questionable'.[21] Although Hume's work is rightly taken as a milestone in the development of Enlightenment thinking, the mainstream position remained that miracles had occurred, and could do so again by the grace of God.[22]

Also interesting are debates about the reality of the soul and afterlife. As the eighteenth century progressed, Cartesian notions of the body as an automaton lost their radicalism in the face of more extreme materialist frameworks, such as that of French physician Julien Offray de La Mettrie. Writing in 1748, La Mettrie presented man as a machine, and denied that any kind of soul existed independently of the body.[23] In response, philosophers leapt to the defence of the soul. The Scottish physicians Robert Whytt, George Cheyne and William Porterfield asserted that a separate soul was necessary for governing the action of the heart and other vital motions.[24] Moral arguments were also employed. If God was to be fair, it was necessary for there to be an afterlife where the soul could find recompense for the injustices of life on earth.[25] Supernatural revelation was also thought to confirm the reality of the soul and afterlife. The minister and rhetorician Hugh Blair explained in a published sermon that the belief in an afterlife, while common to all societies, 'sprung not from the refinements of science, or the speculations of philosophy; but from a deeper and stronger root, the natural sentiments of the human heart'.[26] However, John Henry argues that the response to La Mettrie was relatively insignificant both in scale and in the quality of the arguments produced. It was chiefly theologians who defended the soul; in the sphere of natural philosophy, the concept faded out of serious discussion. It was replaced, Henry suggests, by a new focus on the operations of the mind.[27] Notably, though, philosophers argued that the mind followed natural laws established by a divine power. Discourses about the mind remained focused on demonstrating the reality of God.

When divine intervention was accepted as a theoretical possibility, ghosts could conceivably be justified in philosophical terms. However, in practice

21 Quoted in Friedhelm Voges, 'Moderate and Evangelical Thinking in the Later Eighteenth Century: Differences and Shared Attitudes', *Records of the Scottish Church History Society* 22 (1985), 148–9.

22 See Stewart, 'Early British Reception', 30–42.

23 Julien Offray de La Mettrie, *Machine Man*, in Ann Thomson (ed.), *La Mettrie: Machine Man and Other Writings* (Cambridge, 1996), 1–40.

24 John P. Wright, 'Materialism and the Life Soul in Eighteenth-Century Scottish Physiology', in Paul Wood (ed.), *The Scottish Enlightenment: Essays in Reinterpretation* (Rochester [Vt.], 2000), 182, 184; John P. Wright, 'Metaphysics and Physiology: Mind, Body and the Animal Economy in Eighteenth-Century Scotland', in M. A. Stewart (ed.), *Studies in the Philosophy of the Scottish Enlightenment* (Oxford, 1990), 252, 268, 272, 281.

25 See Thomas Ahnert, 'The Soul, Moral Philosophy and Natural Religion in the Scottish Enlightenment', *Eighteenth Century Thought* 2 (2004), 235–6.

26 Ibid., 243.

27 John Henry, 'Psychology and the Laws of Nature: From Souls to the Powers of the Mind in the Scottish Enlightenment', in Andrew Cunningham and Ole Peter Grell (eds), *Medicine and Religion in Enlightenment Europe* (Aldershot, 2007), esp. 247–9.

there was no room for the returning dead in high Enlightenment theological and philosophical debate. Amidst challenges to the authority of Scripture, to the possibility of miracles, and to the existence of the soul, authors focused on developing philosophies that affirmed the reality of God without recourse to the evidence of phantoms. Writing in 1685, George Sinclair could use stories of ghosts to prove the reality of spirits, and frame the whole as a serious contribution to a philosophical debate. By the mid-eighteenth century, that was no longer a viable tactic. One author noted that biblical miracles were a very different kettle of fish from earlier accounts of prodigies, which he compared to ghost stories. Biblical miracles were 'with equal uniformity related by eye-witnesses, and confirmed by general testimony', while

> The prodigies of the Pagans we uniformly find introduced by, *it is said*, or *it is believed*, like some of our modern stories of ghosts, which are prefaced with *I saw a person, who said he saw another person who said he had heard of a third person who had seen a ghost.*[28]

In general terms, the supernatural was important to the religious debates of the Enlightenment. Ghosts were not.

Mental Disorders, Dreams, Enthusiasm and the 'Prejudices of Education'

Ghosts may have been absent from intellectual discourse about the reality of the world of spirits, but they nonetheless played a significant role in Enlightenment discussion. In the eighteenth century, particularly the latter half of it, there was a growing interest in the subject of mental disorders. Edinburgh Bedlam opened in 1743, and the 1750s saw surging numbers of people cognosced. Looking at Scottish records from the 1780s to 1810s, R. A. Houston has found three times as many tutories awarded on the basis that the subject was *incompos mentis*, compared to the average for the 1710s and 1720s.[29] Physicians increasingly conceptualised a separate mind, not governed by bodily processes.[30] Akihito Suzuki examines this change through a comparison of the work of Herman Boerhaave (1668–1738), a Leiden physician whose teachings were adopted in Edinburgh in the early eighteenth century, and William Cullen (1710–90), an Edinburgh physician working later in the eighteenth century. Boerhaave saw madness as a disease of the body. The body generated a false idea and the mind was tricked into believing it. Boerhaave explained:

[28] A. M., *Remarks on Revelation & Infidelity: Being the Substance of Several Speeches Lately Delivered in a Private Literary Society in Edinburgh* (Edinburgh, 1797), 213–14.

[29] R. A. Houston, *Madness and Society in Eighteenth-Century Scotland* (Oxford, 2000), 114.

[30] Akihito Suzuki, 'Dualism and the Transformation of Psychiatric Language in the Seventeenth and Eighteenth Centuries', *History of Science: An Annual Review of Literature, Research and Teaching* 33 (1995), 418.

> It is not the business of the physician to be acquainted with what the mind is, how it passes from one thought to another ... Though all these properties of the mind are real, yet is the knowledge of them of no use to the physician, so far as they have no relation to the body: for allowing him to be acquainted with all these particulars, and supposing that he endeavours to correct the inconsistent ideas of the madman by the most authentic reasoning ... yet with all his wisdom, he will be able to do nothing.[31]

For Cullen, however, madness was a disorder of the mind (although he also emphasised the role of the nervous system). He wrote:

> The doctrine which explains the condition of the body and of the mind necessary to life and health, is called physiology: I have added here a particular in my physiology that is not common – "and of the mind": ... I find that the conditions of the human mind must engage our attention more than they have done hitherto.[32]

In this context, there was a growing trend towards interpreting ghosts as a purely psychological phenomenon.[33] Psychological explanations for ghosts were not new to the eighteenth century. Ludwig Lavater's 1569 *De Spectris* suggested that hallucinations of ghosts stemmed from melancholy, fear, madness, drunkenness or weakness of the senses. In 1582, George Buchanan recounted that Kenneth III (Kenneth II by modern reckoning) murdered his son's rival in the late tenth century, and was subsequently admonished by a voice from Heaven. Buchanan explained that this voice was 'either a true one, as some think, or else such an one as his disquieted mind suggested (as it commonly happens to guilty consciences)'.[34] Robert Burton's *Anatomy of Melancholy* (1621) also argued that if people were very melancholic, 'dead mens bones, hobgoblins, ghosts, are ever in their minds', and in 1656, Hobbes wrote: 'For some men, as well sleeping as waking, but especially to guilty men ... Fear alone, helped a little with the stories of such Apparitions, hath raised in their minds terrible Phantasmes, which have been, and are still deceiptfully received for things really true.'[35] Stuart Clark has

31 Quoted in ibid., 425. On Boerhaave see Andrew Cunningham, 'Medicine to Calm the Mind: Boerhaave's Medical System, and Why It Was Adopted in Edinburgh', in Andrew Cunningham and Roger French (eds), *The Medical Enlightenment of the Eighteenth Century* (Cambridge, 1990), 40–66.

32 Quoted in Suzuki, 'Dualism', 433. See also Houston, *Madness and Society*, 270–1.

33 This shift has been well documented by scholars working on England. For example, Terry Castle, *The Female Thermometer: Eighteenth-Century Culture and the Invention of the Uncanny* (Oxford, 1995), ch. 10; Owen Davies, *The Haunted: A Social History of Ghosts* (New York, 2007), ch. 5; Shane McCorristine, *Spectres of the Self: Thinking About Ghosts and Ghost-Seeing in England, 1750–1920* (Cambridge, 2010), 31.

34 Ludwig Lavater, *Of Ghostes and Spirites Walking by Nyght*, trans. Robert Harrison (London, 1572, STC 15320), 113; George Buchanan, *Rerum Scoticarum Historia*, ed. Dana F. Sutton, electronic edn (University of Birmingham, 2009), http://www.philological.bham.ac.uk/boece, accessed 1 Feb. 2018, bk. vi, para. 35.

35 Robert Burton, *The Anatomy of Melancholy* (Oxford, 1621, STC 4159), 260; Hobbes quoted in Davies, *Haunted*, 142.

demonstrated that in the wake of the Reformation, and particularly over the course of the seventeenth century, the status of apparitions as genuine visual phenomena became less and less secure.[36]

However, psychological explanations for apparitions became significantly more common in the eighteenth century, particularly the second half of it. In Scotland, the minister William Cockburn linked hauntings and guilty consciences in a 1726 pamphlet, while in a 1766 trial from Aberdeen it was used as evidence against the accused that he was 'frighted with ghosts and apparitions'.[37] There was also extensive discussion of the powers of the imagination. In a piece published in the *Scots Magazine* in 1749, Thomas Melvill argued that apparitions were often figments of the imagination; the 'natural timorousness' of the human mind led it to pick out ghosts in the dark.[38] Henry Home, Lord Kames, similarly noted the disquieting effect of darkness:

> The object, which, in the dark, is seen but obscurely, leaves the heated imagination at full liberty, to bestow upon it the most dreadful appearance. This phantom of the imagination, conceived as a reality, unhinges the mind, and throws it into a fit of distraction. The imagination, now heated to the highest degree, multiplies the dreadful appearances to the utmost bounds of its conception. The object becomes a spectre, a devil, a hobgoblin, something more terrible than ever was seen or described.[39]

Adam Ferguson, for his part, underlined the importance of habits of thought:

> The person who habitually conceives that the church yard is haunted, or that goblins ply in the dark, trembles with fear, where another having no such conception is calm and undisturbed; and the mind, in either case, may be said to be the author of its own good, or its own harm.[40]

Within the medical profession, ghost-seeing became a symptom of some kind of disorder. In physicians' notebooks from the 1790s, one man's mind was said to have been so spoiled by alcoholism that when he could not drink he started 'imagining his house was haunted with spectres or devils'. An illiterate serving woman explained of her Glaswegian mistress Janet Brown: 'at times she is of high spirits and imagines her house is haunted

36 Stuart Clark, *Vanities of the Eye: Vision in Early Modern European Culture* (Oxford, 2007), 204–35, esp. 211.

37 William Cockburn, *The Being of God Proved from the Universal Voice of Conscience* (Edinburgh, 1726), 8; 'The Horrors and Torment of an Evil Conscience; and the Effects of a Disturbed Imagination', *Weekly Magazine, or Edinburgh Amusement*, 24 Oct. 1770, 100; 'The Abstract of the Trial of Helen Watt and William Keith, Continued', *Scots Magazine*, Dec. 1766, 625.

38 [Thomas Melvill] T. M., 'An Essay on Dreaming; Or, The State of the Mind in Sleep', *Scots Magazine*, Sept. 1749, 445.

39 Henry Home Kames, *Essays on the Principles of Morality and Natural Religion* (Edinburgh, 1751), pt. 2, 313.

40 Adam Ferguson, *Principles of Moral and Political Science*, 2 vols (Edinburgh, 1792), vol. 2, 101.

by spirits and threatened every person who were near her.'[41] In 1813, the physician John Ferriar (1761–1815) published *An Essay Towards a Theory of Apparitions*, which hypothesised about mental disorders through the vehicle of apparitions. Ferriar explained:

> It is well known, that in certain diseases of the brain, such as delirium and insanity, spectral delusions take place even during the space of many days. But it has not been generally observed, that a partial affection of the brain may exist, which renders the patient liable to such imaginary impressions, either of sight or sound, without disordering his judgment or memory. From this peculiar condition of the sensorium, I conceive that the best supported stories of apparitions may be completely accounted for.[42]

Samuel Hibbert's *Sketches of the Philosophy of Apparitions* (1824) took a similar approach, arguing that 'spectral illusions ought to be regarded as nothing more than recollected images of the mind, which have been rendered as intense as actual impressions'.[43] In 1832, the Scottish physicist David Brewster expanded on this theme, addressing his work to Walter Scott, who had himself explored physiological and psychological causes of apparitions in *Letters on Demonology and Witchcraft* (1830).[44] Brewster summarised Hibbert's 'admirable' work with the explanation that 'the pictures in the "mind's eye" are more vivid than the pictures in the body's eye'. He continued: 'I propose to go much farther, and to show that the "mind's eye" is actually the body's eye, and that the retina is the common tablet on which both classes of impressions are painted, and by means of which they receive their visual existence according to the same optical laws.'[45] When the pupil expands in the dark, he explained, it becomes impossible to see nearby objects distinctly. Nearby objects or living beings that reflect the light therefore become blurry white shapes, and easily appear supernatural, especially if 'coloured with all the vivid hues of the imagination'.[46] Similarly, changing light might cause figures to vanish. Brewster also explained apparitions as arising 'from a disordered state of the digestive organs' – an idea that would be memorably taken up in Charles Dickens's *A Christmas Carol* (1843), in which Scrooge informs Marley's ghost: 'You may be an undigested bit of beef, a blot of mustard, a crumb of cheese, a fragment of an underdone

41 Houston, *Madness and Society*, 308.
42 John Ferriar, *An Essay Towards a Theory of Apparitions* (London, 1813), 14–15.
43 Hibbert, *Sketches of the Philosophy of Apparitions*, 133.
44 See Michael Charlesworth, *Landscape and Vision in Nineteenth-Century Britain and France* (Aldershot, 2008), 40–4.
45 David Brewster, *Letters on Natural Magic, Addressed to Sir Walter Scott* (London, 1832), 48–9.
46 Ibid., 15–17.

potato. There's more of gravy than of grave about you, whatever you are!'[47] Ghost-seeing was not necessarily taken as a sign of insanity, but it was treated as a trick of the mind or body.

Just as discussion of psychological disorders and the power of the imagination flourished in the eighteenth and early nineteenth centuries, new discourses developed around the topic of dreaming. It was not uncommon for ghosts to appear in dreams. For many writers, this did not detract from their credibility. There were two main schools of thought regarding dreams in the eighteenth century. Some argued that they were a natural phenomenon caused by physiological processes; others believed that they were supernaturally inspired.[48] Robert Wodrow fell into the latter category. He told a story of a man who was so consumed by desire for a serving maid that 'he either dreamed, or, (if I mind,) the bed he lay in was burnt three times ... the fire within brought fire without; which was God contending with him, or the Devil permitted, in his agency'.[49] The possibility that the whole might have been only a dream made it no less notable to Wodrow, and no less an example of the workings of God (or the Devil). Andrew Baxter's 1733 *Enquiry into the Nature of the Human Soul* suggested that dreams were caused by spiritual beings who entered man's soul as he slept and took control of his senses. The Relief Church founder Thomas Gillespie (1708–74) theorised that dreams were usually 'the vain rovings of the imaginations', but believed that they might also be 'the effect of the agency of good or evil spirits'.[50]

However, as the eighteenth century progressed the physiological explanation of dreams became more popular.[51] Thomas Melvill and Dugald Stewart presented dreams as products of the imagination, and the 1797 *Encyclopaedia Britannica* rejected Andrew Baxter's invasive spirits as implausible, declaring instead that dreams were determined by health, habits and patterns of thought.[52] In his 1780 *Elementa Medicinae*, the physician John Brown argued that dreams were caused by the nerves responding involuntarily to outside impressions. In 1838, the surgeon Robert Macnish explained dreaming through phrenology, ascribing it to one or more organs of

47 Ibid., 47; Charles Dickens, *A Christmas Carol, In Prose: Being a Ghost Story of Christmas* (London, 1843), 27. For a fuller discussion of Ferriar, Hibbert, Brewster and Scott, see Srdjan Smajić, *Ghost-Seers, Detectives, and Spiritualists: Theories of Vision in Victorian Literature and Science* (Cambridge, 2010), ch. 2.

48 Jennifer Ford, *Coleridge on Dreaming: Romanticism, Dreams and the Medical Imagination* (Cambridge, 1997), 14; Sasha Handley, *Sleep in Early Modern England* (New Haven, 2016), 186–7.

49 Wodrow, *Analecta*, vol. 2, 315.

50 Ford, *Coleridge on Dreaming*, 18; Kenneth B. E. Roxburgh, *Thomas Gillespie and the Origins of the Relief Church in Eighteenth-Century Scotland* (Bern, 1999), 48.

51 Ford, *Coleridge on Dreaming*, 14.

52 [Melvill], 'Essay on Dreaming', 442, 446; Dugald Stewart, *Elements of the Philosophy of the Human Mind*, 3 vols (London, 1792–1827), vol. 1, 320–39; Ford, *Coleridge on Dreaming*, 22.

the brain remaining awake while the others slept.[53] By 1850, a book of dream interpretations published in Edinburgh with the title *The True Fortune Teller* contained the following disclaimer:

> The foregoing pages are published principally to show the superstitions which engrossed the mind of the population of Scotland during a past age, and which are happily disappearing before the progress of an enlightened civilisation. It is hoped, therefore, that the reader will not attach the slightest importance to the solutions of the dreams as rendered above, as dreams are generally the result of a disordered stomach, or an excited imagination.[54]

In this context, dreams were increasingly used as a means of explaining supernatural experiences, rather than an example thereof. Macnish argued that 'spectral illusions' were 'involuntary walking dreams' caused by inflammation of the brain. He continued: 'I allude to a large development of the organ of *Wonder*. Individuals with such a development are both strongly inclined to believe in the supernaturality of ghosts, and peculiarly liable to be visited by them.'[55] Physician and philosopher John Abercrombie also linked dreaming to spectral illusions, arguing in 1830 that 'A person, under the influence of some strong mental impression, drops asleep for a few seconds, – perhaps without being sensible of it: some scene or person connected with the impression appears in a dream, and he starts up under the conviction that it was a spectral appearance.'[56]

Amidst extensive discussion of the powers of the imagination, stark warnings were issued as to what would become of children whose minds were poisoned with ghost stories. The fourth edition of John Locke's *Essay Concerning Human Understanding* (1700) included his influential essay on the association of ideas, in which he complained about nursery maids indoctrinating children:

> The ideas of goblins and sprites have really no more to do with darkness than light: yet let but a foolish maid inculcate these often on the mind of a child, and raise them there together, possibly he shall never be able to separate them again so long as he lives, but darkness shall ever afterwards bring with it those frightful ideas, and they shall be so joined, that he can no more bear the one than the other.[57]

53 Ford, *Coleridge on Dreaming*, 28–9; Robert Macnish, *The Philosophy of Sleep*, 2nd edn (Glasgow, 1838), 41–111.

54 Quoted in Maureen Perkins, 'The Meaning of Dream Books', in Daniel Pick and Lyndal Roper (eds), *Dreams and History: The Interpretation of Dreams from Ancient Greece to Modern Psychoanalysis* (Hove, 2004), 127.

55 Macnish, *Philosophy of Sleep*, 246. See also George Combe, *A System of Phrenology*, 3rd edn (Edinburgh, 1830), 309–14; J. Mitchell and John Dickie, *The Philosophy of Witchcraft* (Paisley, 1839), 149.

56 John Abercrombie, *Inquiries Concerning the Intellectual Powers and the Investigation of Truth*, 2nd edn (Edinburgh, 1830), 369.

57 John Locke, *An Essay Concerning Humane Understanding*, 4th edn (London, 1700), bk. 3, ch. 33, para. 10, p. 223.

Writers often returned to this theme as the eighteenth century progressed. Writing in the 1790s, Elizabeth Mure of Caldwell commented that from about the mid-century there was a new cultural emphasis on the principle of liberty, broadly construed. When it came to educating girls, 'the outmost care was taken that fear of no kind should inslave the mind; nurses were turned off who would tell the young of Witches and Ghosts'.[58] Also in the 1790s, James Beattie criticised the practice of telling children ghost stories, while the poet Thomas Blacklock suggested that children should be told only of benevolent ghosts, not of 'vindictive ghosts, vindictive fiends, or avenging furies', which 'seize and pre-occupy every avenue of terror which is open in the soul'. Blacklock cautioned: 'Sooner should we hope to exorcise a ghost, or appease a fury, than to obliterate their images in a warm and susceptible imagination, where they have been habitually impressed, and where those feelings cannot be dissipated by external phaenomena'.[59]

This hints at another theme that featured frequently in writing on ghosts from this period: the gender and class-based nature of ghost belief. Eighteenth- and nineteenth-century discussions of ghosts often framed them as a vulgar superstition propagated by folk from the lower classes, especially women, whose minds had not received the benefits of a good education. Writing in 1763, the Skye minister Theophilus Insulanus paraphrased the views of a fellow minister, who objected to apparition stories on the grounds that they were 'apt to excite and lead us to superstition, to which severals of the unlearned, especially, are already disposed, and perhaps constitutionally inclined'.[60] Even people who believed in ghosts could mock the 'vulgar' for their credulity. Mrs McDonald, author of a 1797 novel called *Evening Amusements*, had a character explain that

> I have heard of wonderful apparitions, and visions, but I don't believe one word of them. That all old towers are haunted, is a common vulgar notion; the age and wasted gloomy figures of these old buildings, and their being at a distance from where the family inhabits, throws a sadness on the fancy, and a dread follows, which brings these ideal phantoms into the imagination, which is often the foundation of these foolish stories, seen and heard only by vapourish heads. That there is, and may be ghosts, I don't dispute; but never think a departed soul has so little employment as to return to earth to frighten old women and children, who never knew them nor their stories on earth.[61]

58 Elizabeth Mure, 'Some Remarks on the Change of Manners in My Own Time, 1700–1790', in William Mure (ed.), *Selections from the Family Papers Preserved at Caldwell*, 3 vols (Glasgow, 1854), vol. 1, 270.

59 James Beattie, *Elements of Moral Science*, 2 vols (Edinburgh, 1790–3), vol. 2, 142; Thomas Blacklock, *Poems by the Late Reverend Dr. Thomas Blacklock* (Edinburgh, 1793), xxiv. For a nineteenth-century example see Mitchell and Dickie, *Philosophy of Witchcraft*, 277, 171.

60 Theophilus Insulanus, *A Treatise on the Second Sight, Dreams and Apparitions* (Edinburgh, 1763), 112.

61 Mrs A. McDonald, *Evening Amusements, Or, What Happens in Life, a Novel*, 2 vols (Edinburgh, 1797), vol. 2, 3–4.

Associating ghost belief with 'old wives' from the lower classes was nothing new, and there was probably some truth in the idea that serving women told a disproportionate amount of ghost stories, in their capacity as nursemaids and nannies. Nevertheless, educated circles (particularly the literary world) also played a crucial role in developing and popularising conceptions of ghosts, even as they mocked common folk for believing in them.[62]

Belief in apparitions was also associated with certain religious groups. The Quakers and the Methodists were prime candidates, especially in England, but to a lesser extent in Scotland as well. In 1678, the minister John Brown offered a sardonic rebuttal to the writing of one Mr Cressy, who argued that 'God reveals himself to the soul by a supernatural species impressed in her, which revelations are either sensible, as apparitions, words &c. or intellectual, either immediatly, or by Angels'. Brown retorted: 'Our Quaker might have given us some such thing as a more likely ground of their quaking and trembling', adding that 'our Quakers way and worshipe hath been long ago in use among, & much applauded by the Fanatick Papists'.[63] During his tour of Scotland with Samuel Johnson, James Boswell made a remark to the Duchess of Argyll that implied a belief in second sight. In Boswell's words: 'The duchess said, "I fancy you will be a Methodist" – This was the only sentence her grace deigned to utter to me.'[64] More generally, belief in apparitions continued to be linked to religious enthusiasm. In a sermon probably given in the 1770s, the minister John Logan noted that a man who reported seeing a ghost would be considered 'a visionary enthusiast, disturbed in his imagination'.[65]

Class snobbery and psychological explanations were united in the rejection of ghosts that appears in the third edition of the *Encylopaedia Britannica*, produced in Edinburgh in 1797. The second edition (1778) had included an article on second sight, which reproduced a wholly sceptical assessment by James Beattie.[66] The 1797 edition was actually more sympathetic on this topic, retaining Beattie's evaluation but also offering the view of Samuel Johnson, who argued that reason could not disprove second sight and that it was therefore natural to 'yield to the force of testimony'.[67] However, articles on 'ghost' and 'spectre' were added to this edition, and were decidedly sceptical. The article on ghosts largely reproduced Francis Grose's 1787 summary of ghost traditions,

62 See chapter 4.

63 John Brown, *Quakerisme the Path-Way to Paganisme* (Edinburgh, 1678), 431. Cressy is quoted here.

64 Quoted in R. C. Finucane, *Ghosts: Appearances of the Dead and Cultural Transformation* (Amherst [N.Y.], 1996), 159.

65 John Logan, *Sermons by the Late Reverend John Logan*, 2 vols (Edinburgh, 1790–1), vol. 2, 51.

66 'Second-Sight', in *Encyclopaedia Britannica; Or, A Dictionary of Arts, Sciences, &c.*, 2nd edn, 10 vols (Edinburgh, 1778–83), vol. 10, 8071–2.

67 'Second Sight', in *Encyclopaedia Britannica; Or, A Dictionary of Arts, Sciences, and Miscellaneous Literature*, 3rd edn, 20 vols (Edinburgh, 1797), vol. 17, 236.

and referred the reader to the article on spectres for a philosophical discussion of apparitions.[68] This latter article addressed the subject at length. It began by defining a 'spectre' as 'an apparition, something made preternaturally visible to human sight, whether the ghosts of dead men or beings superior to man'. The belief in dead men returning, it noted, had been common for many centuries, and was known in 'rude and savage' nations. It continued:

> In Christian countries, too, notwithstanding the additional light which their religion has spread, and the great improvement in the sciences to which it has been subservient, the belief of ghosts and apparitions is very general, especially among the lower ranks. They believe that evil spirits sometimes make their appearance in order to terrify wicked men, especially those who have committed murder.– They suppose that the spirits of dead men assume a corporeal appearance, hover about churchyards and the houses of the deceased, or haunt the places where murders have been committed.[69]

The article then attacked belief in spectres. Death was too profound a change to be undone. Ghosts could serve a useful function by demonstrating the reality of the afterlife or enforcing moral codes, but Scripture already told man everything he needed to know on that front. The article complained that ghosts did not follow the rules of common sense; they never reported crimes to magistrates or judges, but rather divulged their information 'to some illiterate clown, who happens to live near the place where the crime was perpetrated; to some person who has no connection with the affair at all, and who in general is the most improper in the world for making the discovery'. In fact, ghosts never appeared before men 'of education and learning', but only to the 'ignorant' and 'credulous'.[70] The article went on to proffer explanations for ghost sightings, from 'the prejudices of the nursery' and the powers of imagination, to indistinct vision, dreams, opium, drunkenness, diseases such as 'the night-mare, the hypochondria, hysteric passion and madness', exaggerated rumours and the 'artifices of the waggish or self-interested'.[71]

Over the hundred years from the early eighteenth to the early nineteenth century, scepticism towards ghosts did not necessarily become more common; it merely changed. Ghost belief was mocked or pitied, associated with the ignorant and the insane. John Logan argued that a ghost-seer would be met with such universal scepticism that 'it is ten to one but he falls in with the opinion of the world, and believes the apparition to have been the phantom of his own fancy'.[72]

[68] 'Ghost', in *Encyclopaedia Britannica; Or, A Dictionary of Arts, Sciences, and Miscellaneous Literature*, 3rd edn, 20 vols (Edinburgh, 1797), vol. 7, 719–21; 'Spectre', in *Encyclopaedia Britannica; Or, A Dictionary of Arts, Sciences, and Miscellaneous Literature*, 3rd edn, 20 vols (Edinburgh, 1797), vol. 17, 677–84.

[69] 'Spectre', in *Encyclopaedia Britannica*, 3rd edn, vol. 17, 677.

[70] Ibid., vol. 17, 678–9, 680.

[71] Ibid.,vol. 17, 682–3.

[72] Logan, *Sermons*, 51.

However, it is worth remembering that ghost belief had not had a place in mainstream intellectual culture since at least the Reformation. At the beginning of the eighteenth century the primary way to dismiss ghosts was to redefine them as demons; by the end of the century the most common sceptical approach was to present ghosts as products of the mind. This meant that there was more freedom for folk to talk about ghosts without fear of being suspected of dealings with the Devil. Ghosts were also used by philosophers and physicians as a device through which to develop and discuss new theories regarding mental disorders, which offered them a place within the intellectual culture in the eighteenth century (particularly the latter half of it). As one work put it:

> Though these waking visions are the mere illusive creations of a diseased or over-excited imagination, they are not on that account the less worthy of the attention of the philosopher, as well as the physician: and instead of being regarded with the terror of the vulgar, or the disdain of the sceptic, they claim the calm and unprejudiced researches of philosophy, for the purpose of tracing their various phenomena to natural causes, and accurately ascertaining their relation to the state of the brain and the external senses.[73]

Ghost belief was still associated with folk culture (as it had been for centuries), but discussion about ghosts appeared much more frequently in the eighteenth century than it had in the seventeenth – in contrast to R. C. Finucane's assertion that apparitions 'no longer played an important part in the serious debates of the articulate'.[74] While there were newly popular ways to explain away ghosts, this does not mean that they were exorcised from society.

Ghosts and the Authorities

On the rare occasions when ghosts appeared before kirk or secular authorities in the eighteenth century, they were usually received sceptically. In June 1711, Bishop Alexander Rose wrote of a case of sweet music and voices heard emanating from an abbey by soldiers. He explained that this was so much talked about that the local advocate ordered a report from a baillie, which was then to be sent to court. However, the baillie clearly had a low opinion of the whole affair; he was careful to question the wrong people and ask the wrong questions, ensuring that there was nothing to report on.[75] In this case, both Rose and the advocate were ready to take the story seriously even if the baillie was not, but usually the records reveal a more uniform scepticism on the part of educated authorities. In 1730, the Edinburgh burgh court entered a servant

73 Mitchell and Dickie, *Philosophy of Witchcraft*, 146.
74 Finucane, *Ghosts*, 165.
75 Alexander Rose to Archibald Campbell, 28 June 1711: NRS, CH12/12/1823.

into the town's black book for spreading a rumour that her former employer's house was haunted.[76]

In October 1737, the minister Gilbert Gerard of Chapel of Garioch, Aberdeenshire, reported an interesting case to the kirk session.[77] He explained that he had been visited by a local young man, Geordie Watt. Watt lived at the farm of Bridgend, on the banks of the Urie, with four of his six brothers. Their widowed mother had died in the preceding February.[78] Watt reported that three or four weeks after his mother's death, a ghost had started appearing to him and his brothers. It had declared itself to be 'the very spirit of their glorified Mother', sent from Heaven to 'reveal several things to them for their temporal and Eternal good'. The ghost spoke in a 'shrill and heavenly Voice', wore a white veil, and was 'covered with white clean linnen, head and arms, down to the middle of the body before, and somewhat farther behind'. It gave them good advice, and told them 'the very secrets of their hearts', but its chief purpose was to instruct them 'that it was the will of the great God that Geordie Watt should marry Tibbie Mortimer ... because that Tibbie was now in a gracious State, and had been predestinated to Glory from All Eternity'. Tibbie (or Isabel) Mortimer was the only female servant in the family. When Watt protested about the unequal nature of the marriage, the ghost gathered the brothers together and insisted that 'unless Geordie Watt should marry Tibbie Mortimer, he and all his Brothers, and all things belonging to them should certainly be consumed with fire from heaven'.

It was then that Watt went to Gilbert Gerard with his story. The latter decided to pay a visit to the farm. One evening, he sat up with the brothers and waited. Sure enough, after some hours, a voice was heard outside a little window in Geordie Watt's bedroom. It pronounced 'with a very wild and vehement tone' that it had come to speak to them all in the name of the Trinity. The brothers were afraid, but Gerard leapt up and ran outside. He saw the shape of a woman, draped from head to toe in white linen. He charged over, and as the session coyly recorded, he 'made such a trial of the Apparition as he thought agreeable to the principles of the Christian Revelation and true Philosophy'; that is, he hit her with a stick, and thus discovered that she was no incorporeal spirit. Stripping away her veil, he revealed Tibbie Mortimer herself.

Gerard lectured her on the 'blasphemy, devilish tricks, and mischievous pranks', but Tibbie responded insolently, and only the pleas of the family kept her from being handed over to the civil magistrate. She was dismissed from her post. The kirk session branded her a 'vile, base, and impudent woman', and

[76] R. A. Houston, *Social Change in the Age of Enlightenment: Edinburgh, 1660–1760* (Oxford, 1994), 191.

[77] Chapel of Garioch kirk session minutes, 30 Oct. 1737: NRS, CH2/527/1/231–4. See the discussion in William Alexander, *Notes and Sketches Illustrative of Northern Rural Life in the Eighteenth Century* (Edinburgh, 1877), 203–7.

[78] See Chapel of Garioch kirk session minutes, 1 Feb. 1737: NRS, CH2/527/1/221.

accused her of having behaved 'in a course of horrid Blasphemy' and having 'prescribed charms and suspicious things'. It referred her to the presbytery for judgement. Some ten months later the presbytery convicted her of 'the sin & scandal of fornication with Geo. Watt in Bridgend as also of Acting the part of a Ghost and Blaspheming the Holy name of God'.[79] She was ordered to appear in sackcloth before the congregation. Tibbie was initially defiant, but eventually accepted her punishment, which lasted from December 1738 until April 1740.[80] Interestingly, Geordie was also involved. It is probable that there was a pregnancy in the case: the allusion that Tibbie was in a 'gracious state' implies as much. Geordie was suspected of being 'in less or more conscious of or having a hand in the abominable part that Isa. Mortimer acted', and was ordered to appear in sackcloth. He objected that 'he would never satisfy in saccloth for that which he knew nothing about', but did offer to make a penitential payment for fornication, which the session accepted.[81] When Geordie and Tibbie's affair began, and whether they had concocted the ghost plan together, cannot be known.

A further interesting story concerns a minister from Muckhart called David Wilson. Wilson was involved with (at least) two Presbyterian denominations: the Anti-Burghers and the Relief Synod. In 1733, the Secession had given rise to the Associate Presbytery, an alternative to the Church of Scotland. The Associate Presbytery had itself divided in 1747 over the question of the Burgher Oath. This was an oath to be sworn by a town burgess upon taking office, approving of the religion 'presently professed in this kingdom'. The Burghers and the Anti-Burghers had formed separate synods. The Relief Church was a Presbyterian denomination founded in 1761 by Thomas Gillespie after his deposition for opposing patronage. It had grown rapidly and had established its own synod in 1773.[82] Wilson joined the Relief Synod in May 1793, and began work in Pittenweem the next year.[83] Before joining the Relief Synod, he was apparently refused a licence by the Anti-Burghers for claiming that a ghost had appeared to him. This emerged in a pamphlet by an Aberdeenshire man called David Gellatly, who was ordained as the first Relief minister in Haddington in 1792, and deposed two years later on a charge of immorality. Wilson had formed one of the committee appointed to inspect the process against Gellatly. The pamphlet attacked Wilson, alongside other committee members. Gellatly wrote:

79 Chapel of Garioch kirk session minutes, 24 Sept. 1738: NRS, CH2/527/1/239.

80 Chapel of Garioch kirk session minutes, 3 Dec. 1738: NRS, CH2/527/1/241; Chapel of Garioch kirk session minutes, 20 Apr. 1740: NRS, CH2/527/1/261.

81 Chapel of Garioch kirk session minutes, 6 May 1739: NRS, CH2/527/1/249.

82 See, for example, Colin Kidd, 'Conditional Britons: The Scots Covenanting Tradition and the Eighteenth-Century British State', *English Historical Review* 117 (2002), 1158–9; Steve Bruce, *Scottish Gods: Religion in Modern Scotland, 1900–2012* (Oxford, 2014), 10; Roxburgh, *Thomas Gillespie*.

83 William Mackelvie, *Annals and Statistics of the United Presbyterian Church* (Edinburgh, 1873), 455.

> I must in justice to myself and to mankind observe, had it been true, as you maintain it is, that when you taught a private school near Alloa, a ghost appeared to you, and told you of some cruelty which others committed; this stranger would have deterred you from any act of injustice. Upon account of this story, I opposed your admission among the Relief; for I am firmly persuaded, like many others, that as Brissot's *ghost* was only two or three sheets of printed paper, so the ghost which you saw was a *fair folio* in sheets, which you polluted during night.[84] The Antiburghers refused you licence upon that account; at least they did not believe that you saw any ghost. The story which you told and fathered upon the ghost, concerning some respectable people in your then neighbourhood, was highly criminal, and for which they might have caused you severely suffer. Did the *real ghost* that you saw and *felt* with pleasure, father any thing upon you?[85]

Wilson's ghost apparently followed the traditional pattern of revealing a crime or injustice, but it was Wilson himself who came to be accused of 'highly criminal' behaviour. Although Wilson was accepted into the Relief Synod, the condemnation of Gellatly – and, if his account can be believed, of the Anti-Burghers – indicates that ministers were not supposed to be spreading ghost stories.

Other notable cases concern judicial authorities. In June 1754, Duncan Terig (alias Clerk) and Alexander Bain Macdonald of Aberdeenshire were tried for the murder of Arthur Davies, a sergeant in General Guise's Foot Regiment.[86] In 1749, Davies and others from his regiment were quartered in Braemar in Aberdeenshire. Davies went for a walk and was allegedly pursued, shot and robbed by Clerk and Macdonald. They were apprehended in 1753, and brought to trial the following year. A witness stated that he had been concealed in a hollow in the hill, and had seen Clerk and a companion shoot a man in blue and then handle the body. Testimony of several witnesses described seeing Macdonald, Clerk and the latter's wife in possession of various valuables once owned by Sergeant Davies. Macdonald and Clerk claimed that they had been out shooting deer, but their accounts were inconsistent.

Thus far, the weight of evidence was against Clerk and Macdonald. However, the prosecution offered a further testimony that may, if anything, have worked in the favour of the accused. A local man, Alexander Macpherson, attested that while he was in bed one night a blue-clad apparition had appeared to him. This apparition explained that he was Sergeant Davies, and gave the location of his murder, asking Macpherson to go and bury his bones. Macpherson asked him who his murderer was, but the apparition replied 'that if [Macpherson]

84 This referred to a well-known pamphlet, *Brissot's Ghost! Or, Intelligence from the Other World* (Edinburgh, 1794).

85 David Gellatly, *Relief Procedure Justly Exhibited* (Edinburgh, 1794), 80.

86 Reproduced in Walter Scott (ed.), *Trial of Duncan Terig Alias Clerk, and Alexander Bane Macdonald, for the Murder of Arthur Davis, Sergeant in General Guise's Regiment of Foot* (Edinburgh, 1831).

had not asked him, he might have told him, but as he had asked him, he said he either could not or would not'.[87] Macpherson did not go to bury the bones, and the vision reappeared, now naked, to appeal again. Macpherson repeated his question about the murderer, and this time the apparition replied that Clerk and Macdonald were the culprits. Macpherson then enlisted a friend's help; they found the bones in the spot described and buried them. In answer to a question from the defence advocate, Macpherson asserted that the ghost had spoken to him in Gaelic, not a language Davies had known. The advocate (probably not without a degree of class prejudice) mocked the idea that an English ghost would speak Gaelic, and it is clear that the court was reluctant to accept the evidence. Clerk and Macdonald were acquitted.

In 1779, the *Scots Magazine* published a story from Cheshire of a man who claimed to have been visited by a dead man's ghost in his sleep.[88] The ghost had revealed the location of his body and the name of his murderer. A search was conducted, and the body was found in the specified place. However, during the trial of the supposed murderer, the judge called the ghost to court. When the ghost failed to materialise, the judge had the dreamer arrested and convicted of the murder. A search of the dreamer's house discovered the dead man's belongings, vindicating the court's decision. This trial may not really have taken place, but even if it did not, the account further demonstrates the idea that ghosts had no place in a courtroom. There was an element of mockery in the judge's calling the ghost to court, just as there was in Macdonald and Clerk's advocate's scorn at the idea that an English ghost would speak Gaelic. Focus on these practicalities drove the mind away from traditional aspects of ghost stories – that ghosts could only appear at certain times and places and to certain people, or that ghosts had access to new spheres of knowledge – and forced ghosts to inhabit the everyday world, where their supernatural elements became fantastical.

However, there were also cases in which supernatural intervention was treated more sympathetically. In the spring of 1830, a pedlar was murdered in Assynt, Sutherland.[89] His body was recovered from a lake. Suspicion fell on a man called Hugh Macleod, as he had changed a ten pound note at the post office despite living in relative poverty. No further evidence was found to connect him with the crime, however, and he was on the verge of being released when a tailor called Kenneth Fraser came forward, avowing that he had dreamt about the murder. He had seen the cottage Macleod was living in, and a voice had explained (in Gaelic) that the pedlar's pack was hidden in a cairn of stones near the house. The articles were found as described, and

87 Ibid., 29.

88 'Discovery of a Murderer', *Scots Magazine*, Sept. 1779, 484.

89 *Brutal Assault and Murder!* ([Scotland?], 1830); 'Singular Ghost Story', *Aberdeen Magazine*, Feb. 1832, 94; Robert Chambers, *The Book of Days, A Miscellany of Popular Antiquities*, 2 vols (London, 1863–4), vol. 1, 394–5.

Macleod was later discovered to be in possession of a pair of stockings that had belonged to the pedlar. He was tried at the Circuit Court in Inverness, and Fraser gave evidence, explaining his dream. Macleod was found guilty and executed. Before his death he confessed the murder, and avowed: 'Kenneth Fraser, the dreamer, knew nothing of my transactions, or any thing that I have done. I now free him from the charge that has been brought against him; and I hope no person will say that he had any concern in the murder.'[90] There had evidently been doubts about Fraser's story, but his evidence nonetheless seems to have contributed to Macleod's conviction.

A final case was reported in 1848 by the English writer Catherine Crowe, who claimed to have heard it from Maurice Lothian, the pursuer's advocate. In 1835, a landlord called Mr Webster brought a case against his tenant, Captain Molesworth.[91] Molesworth had rented a house of his a few miles from Edinburgh. The family had lived there for about two months when they began to be troubled by strange noises. They heard footsteps, scratching, rustling; the walls trembled and sometimes the beds were lifted up. Their poltergeist would even answer questions through a system of knocks. Captain Molesworth's daughter Matilda had recently died, and his other daughter Jane was sickly and spent most of her time in bed. Webster accused Jane of making the noises, while many in the neighbourhood believed them to be caused by the ghost of Matilda, warning that her sister was soon to die as well. The unfortunate Jane was tied up as a test, but the noises continued. Molesworth lifted floorboards and made holes in the wall in an attempt to discover the source of the disturbances, but to no avail. Finally, he decided to leave the house. Webster brought the suit against him for damage done to the property, as well as for preventing other tenants from taking it by saying that it was haunted. Jane died soon after the removal, and the subsequent tenants had no problems. The case dragged out for two years, but apparently came to nothing. The fact that the case did not reach any swift resolution suggests that while there may have been doubts surrounding Molesworth's story, the matter was not clear cut.

These cases demonstrate scepticism, but they also indicate that ghost beliefs retained some credibility. Ghosts were taken seriously enough to end up in courtrooms, or to be employed for personal ends. The punishments for discussing dealings with ghosts did not amount to execution, the fate suffered by many of those accused of witchcraft, as well as by the Edinburgh student Thomas Aikenhead, who was convicted of blasphemy in 1696. However, Tibbie Mortimer's ghost impersonation earned her a punishment of several years' penance. Ghost belief was associated with the lower classes, and eighteenth-century authorities underlined the ridiculous aspects of ghost traditions.

90 'Singular Ghost Story', 94.

91 Catherine Crowe, *The Night Side of Nature, or Ghosts and Ghost Seers*, 2 vols (London, 1848), vol. 2, 292–5.

That they were forced to do so, however, demonstrates that ghosts still had some social standing.

Popular Print Culture: Debate

Scotland's periodical culture took off in the latter half of the eighteenth century, opening up a new venue for discussion and debate on ghosts. Periodicals were cheap publications, usually produced on a weekly or monthly basis. They discussed developments within the worlds of philosophy, theology, politics and the arts. One title is particularly useful when it comes to debates on ghosts: the *Edinburgh Weekly Magazine*, launched by Walter Ruddiman in July 1768.[92] It had some success, reaching a circulation of around 3,000 in the late 1770s.[93] Each issue began with readers' letters and essays, before moving on to poetry, reviews, and finally news. In the 1770s, the magazine printed a series of letters and essays discussing the question of whether ghosts existed. The debate was begun by an article by Philaretes, published in April 1771. (Unfortunately, the use of pseudonyms makes it impossible to identify the contributors, but it seems safe to assume that most were educated men.) Philaretes scorned the 'old woman in our breasts' which made so many people superstitious. His own grandmother knew *Satans Invisible World Discovered* by heart, and as a child he too was subject to the 'folly' of belief in apparitions. He was once greatly terrified when he mistook some dried fish for a ghost; another time he saw a spectre where there was only a goat. This 'preposterous education' had brought him only misery. As an adult he rejected completely the idea that the dead could leave Heaven or Hell. He did believe that spirits existed and served God – he allowed, for example, that people could have guardian angels – but he did not believe that these spirits could appear to humans. 'I am firmly persuaded', he declared, 'that no man ever did see an apparition, unless it was the product of his own fertile imagination'.[94]

Philaretes's article was promptly questioned, in May 1771, by Will Wiseman, who urged the case of the Witch of Endor.[95] In December 1771, a further retort was published by Palemon, arguing that the reality of apparitions had been proved by history and tradition. He gave biblical examples of visible spirits, and cited the 'famous' apparition of Provost Abraham Crichton of Sanquhar,

92 The periodical went through various titles, in part because it was restructured in 1779 to avoid stamp duty. From 1768–79 it was the *Weekly Magazine, or Edinburgh Amusement*; from 1779–82 it was the *Edinburgh Magazine, or, Literary Amusement*; and from 1782–4 it continued as the *Edinburgh Weekly Magazine*, although Ruddiman had died in 1781.

93 Bob Harris cited in Rhona Brown, *Robert Fergusson and the Scottish Periodical Press* (Aldershot, 2012), 6.

94 Philaretes to the *Weekly Magazine, or Edinburgh Amusement*, 11 Apr. 1771, 33–9 (quotations 33, 35, 38).

95 Will Wiseman to the *Weekly Magazine, or Edinburgh Amusement*, 9 May 1771, 165–6.

which 'may be depended on as an undoubted matter of fact'.[96] In response, Philaretes insisted that Palemon was thinking of angels, which did exist. He clarified that when he rejected apparitions he meant 'those non-entities of ghosts, fairies, hobgoblins and spectres, so much dreaded and implicitly believed in by the credulous vulgar'.[97] Soon afterwards, he was challenged again. In February 1772, M. told the story of a young man who mocked the existence of ghosts. The man accepted a challenge from friends to descend into a crypt at night and spend some time there alone. When he did so, he was seemingly attacked by some invisible assailant, and passed out in fear. He was recovered later by his friends, who found that he had merely slipped and pinioned his own tie into the floor. However, he thereafter became a believer in spirits, reasoning that the intensity of his terror was proof enough of supernatural influence. M. suggested that even sceptics might be swayed by this 'supernatural intelligence within'.[98] Philaretes responded scornfully:

> Mr M.'s lucubrations may do very well for a circle of women smoaking their pipes round the winter fire, but every man of inch-deep science will pity his forwardness and presumption to show himself in print, where, in point of sentiment, reasoning, judgement, and logical argumentation, he has shown that he is but a mere puking infant, not yet weaned from his mother's breast.[99]

In spite of this rebuke, several writers continued to defend ghosts. In April 1772, C. G. joined the argument. He agreed that no souls would leave Heaven, but argued determinedly for the possibility that the wicked might return. He highlighted the notoriety of the ghosts of the Laird of Coul and Provost Crichton. 'Whatever Philaretes or any other may think', he proclaimed, 'these are stubborn facts which cannot be denied'.[100] The next month brought a retort from a new contributor, Fabricius. He declared that stories of ghosts could not prove anything, and dismissed the Laird of Coul chapbook as 'trifiling' and 'ridiculous', penned by 'some shallow scribbler'.[101] As for Provost Crichton, his ghost was no more than a large bush. Fabricius explained that he believed in demonic spirits, but that it was ridiculous to imagine that the dead could return. Over the following years the debate acquired a host of additional participants. C. G. retorted with more stories; Palemon pointed out that learned men such as Joseph Addison had believed in ghosts; Toby Rattle called the non-believers 'perfect infidels', perhaps with undertones of sarcasm;

96 Palemon to the *Weekly Magazine, or Edinburgh Amusement*, 5 Dec. 1771, 296–7. On Crichton's ghost see p. 168.

97 Philaretes to the *Weekly Magazine, or Edinburgh Amusement*, 19 Dec. 1771, 355–7 (quotation 356).

98 M. to the *Weekly Magazine, or Edinburgh Amusement*, 6 Feb. 1772, 165–7 (quotation 165).

99 Philaretes to the *Weekly Magazine, or Edinburgh Amusement*, 27 Feb. 1772, 261–2 (quotation 262).

100 C. G. to the *Weekly Magazine, or Edinburgh Amusement*, 16 Apr. 1772, 74–5.

101 Fabricius to the *Weekly Magazine, or Edinburgh Amusement*, 7 May 1772, 167–8.

Neanias compared believers to old women, and so on.[102] For the most part the same arguments were simply recycled. One more original response, at least in form, was Sylvander's 1772 'Directions on Making a Modern Wit':

> In superficial trappings deck your mind,
> But let no deep reflection entrance find:
> ...
> With all the scorn of indignation curse
> The fab'lous stories of the doating nurse,
> Of ghosts, hobgoblins, apparitions, seen
> By ruin'd walls, or fairies on the green;
> Of witchcraft spells, or voices from the grave;
> The childish bugbears of a winter's eve.
> Then boldly doubt what cheating priests do tell
> Of sep'rate souls, future heav'n or hell;
> The paths of common sense and nature quit,
> You cannot fail to be a man of WIT.[103]

By the end of 1774, the argument had died down, although echoes of it continued to recur in following years, or in other periodicals. At the close of the decade, the *Edinburgh Eighth-Day Magazine* published a lengthy piece by J. McC in favour of ghosts. He noted that the ancient fathers of the church were 'as much persuaded of the reality of witches and apparitions, as of their own existence', and used biblical examples to demonstrate that dead souls could return: 'we read of Moses and Elias appearing to the disciples, at our Saviour's transfiguration; and, at his resurrection, we are told, that many bodies of saints, which slept in their graves, arose, went into Jerusalem, and appeared unto many.' McC argued that the contemporary trend of rejecting apparitions was borne of 'scepticism and irreligion'. He noted that ghosts were allowed to appear only for 'some important end and design', and for every true story there were a hundred fabrications. Nevertheless, ghosts performed a valuable function by proving the reality of a future state.[104] Clearly, no final consensus had been (or could be) reached, and familiar arguments might be recycled indefinitely. Periodical culture often reflected contemporary fashions, and Sylvander's derisive poem highlights the idea that scepticism was in vogue. However, it was not a universal outlook, even among the educated.

[102] C. G. to the *Weekly Magazine, or Edinburgh Amusement*, 23 July 1772, 97–9; Palemon to the *Weekly Magazine, or Edinburgh Amusement*, 9 July 1772, 45–6; Toby Rattle to the *Weekly Magazine, or Edinburgh Amusement*, 28 May 1772, 269; Neanias to the *Weekly Magazine, or Edinburgh Amusement*, 23 July 1772, 103–5.

[103] Sylvander, 'Directions for Making a Modern Wit', *Weekly Magazine, or Edinburgh Amusement*, 23 July 1772, 114.

[104] J. McC, 'Speech Delivered in the Pantheon', *Edinburgh Eighth-Day Magazine*, 13 Nov. 1779, 299–301.

Popular Print Culture: Satire

Sceptical views on ghosts were also showcased through the medium of satire. In 1792, a work called *An Account of Some Imaginary Apparitions: The Effects of Fear or Fraud* was printed in Dunbar. It presented a series of ghost stories. However, supernatural intervention was always ultimately disproved. When a tapping was heard at a hospital, the nurses (dryly referred to as 'sagacious ladies') refused to work any more.[105] The poltergeist finally proved to be a cat. Other ghosts turned out to be a burglar, an unprincipled friar and a tree-stump. The work mocked collections such as *Satans Invisible World Discovered*, and presented rational explanations for ghost-seeing: a guilty conscience, the power of established traditions.[106] Periodicals often parodied ghost stories in a similar fashion. A man spent a night in a haunted house, but the 'ghost' backed off sharply after he threatened it with a pistol; another thought he had been woken by a ghost and followed it, only to find that he was dreaming and sleep-walking.[107]

In April 1796, 'Felix Phantom' first printed the *Ghost*, which purportedly hailed from Fairyland (we see here the folkloric tradition that fairies lived in the land of the dead). It ran for forty-six issues over the course of that year. It chiefly contained literary criticism and satirical articles on a variety of topics, but the gimmick of the ghostly editor provoked some discussion of apparitions. In the first issue, Felix Phantom introduced himself. 'I am a departed Spirit', he began, and went on to explain that ghosts resided in 'fairy regions', and could assume any number of bodily shapes. All dead people went there, and free from the shackles of corporeality, all were 'enlightened and good friends'.[108] Indeed, Hume himself was there, and was profoundly sorry for his arguments against the supernatural. (A subsequent issue contained a letter from the ghost of Voltaire, apologising for having lured men into 'delusion' with his 'false doctrines'.)[109] Felix Phantom went on to explain that ghosts had long confused men and perpetuated superstition by causing miracles and prodigies, as well as inventing witchcraft. He was writing now to clear matters up and instruct mankind – not to provide amusement for 'old women of either sex'.[110]

Later in the same year the periodical gave an account of a dinner party, in which an array of characters represented a range of stances on ghosts. An old spinster, Miss Penelope Cobweb, believed wholeheartedly in ghosts, but was laughed down by the rest of the party. A gentleman suggested that, as Purgatory was a Catholic superstition, ghosts expiated their sins on earth

105 *An Account of Some Imaginary Apparitions, The Effects of Fear or Fraud* (Dunbar, [1792?]), 12.

106 Ibid., 9.

107 *The Edinburgh Medley of Entertainment*, 2 vols (Edinburgh, 1800), vol. 2, 21–4; 'Entertaining Story of a Sleep-Walker', *Edinburgh Magazine*, June 1761, 294–7.

108 Felix Phantom in the *Ghost*, 25 Apr. 1796, 1–2.

109 Ghost of Voltaire to the *Ghost*, 30 July 1796, 5–8 (quotations 5).

110 Phantom in the *Ghost*, 25 Apr. 1796, 4.

instead. A sceptic argued that ghosts were figments of the imagination. A clergyman insisted that ghosts were created by the Devil. A metaphysician cited the work of Emanuel Swedenborg, and suggested that apparitions appeared only in dreams, but were nonetheless real; only in that state (or in ecstasy, or madness, or when 'divested of carnal feelings') could spirits be perceived. Finally, a chieftain from the western isles noted his belief in second sight, and found that all of the ladies were instantly on his side.[111] The account of the dinner party suggests that the common templates for ghost believers and sceptics were well known. They were not treated kindly, however. Folkloric beliefs, such as second sight, or the dead passing to the land of the fairies, were toyed with; ghost belief was the preserve of old ladies. Miracles, prodigies and witchcraft were scorned. Even the process of debating ghosts, as shown in the dinner party, was ridiculed. The *Ghost* was frequently scathing, in its literary reviews as much as in its comments on ghost belief, and was not without enemies. The *Trifler* used a piece apparently by a fellow spectre to reveal 'the vain and absurd pretensions of the most despicable and insignificant of wretches', adding 'The Ghost was the work of some fools who had the happy talent of writing *nonsense* with equal facility and elegance'.[112] Regardless of its reception, however, the *Ghost* demonstrated a brand of brutally assured, mocking scepticism that had become common by the later eighteenth century.

However, these magazines served to keep ghost stories in circulation. Setting aside the publication of romantic and gothic stories and poems about ghosts, which shall be discussed in the next chapter, periodicals published accounts of ghosts as well as attacking them. The *Aberdeen Magazine* noted that 'a belief in spectres and apparitions has prevailed in all ages of the world, and many absurd fables have been propagated respecting those beings, which were probably invented to serve particular purposes, or had their origin in ignorance and superstition'. It nonetheless proceeded to offer a ghost story, explaining: 'Whether the following relation be of this kind or not, we shall not pretend to determine, but we are of the opinion that it merits some attention, on account of the noise which it made at the Court of France about the end of the last century.'[113]

Furthermore, satirical representations of ghosts contributed to the development of ghost stereotypes. Satirical works commonly exaggerated the more dramatic or fantastical elements of ghosts. This can be seen in the work of Tobias Smollett (1721–71), whose picaresque novels were popular in the mid-eighteenth century. Smollett presented more than a dozen cases of people

111 Felix Phantom in the *Ghost*, 18 May 1796, 29–32 (quotation 31).

112 Moropolemius to the *Trifler*, 4 July 1796, as given in the 1797 enlarged edn, 186–92; Richard Maw-Worm in the *Trifler*, 4 July 1796, as given in the 1797 enlarged edn, 192–3. The first edition included the same article but gave a different author and date. It did not include the editor's note. Feriatus to the *Trifler*, 21 May 1796, 199–206.

113 'Account of an Apparition in France', *Aberdeen Magazine*, 9 Apr. 1789, 194–5.

mistakenly believing that they had seen ghosts, often because of deliberate hoaxes. These hoaxes were elaborate affairs. In one case, 'Doctor Fillet having borrowed a couple of sheets from the landlady, dressed the misanthrope and Tom Clarke in ghostly apparel, which was reinforced by a few drops of liquid phosphorus, from Ferret's vial, rubbed on the fore-heads of the two adventurers'. The phosphorus 'exhibited a pale and lambent flame, extremely dismal and ghastly to the view'. Another man had a 'ghastly wound' painted on his forehead in order to imitate a ghost.[114] The most extravagant case of all appeared in *Peregrine Pickle* (1751):

> To the hide of a large ox, Pipes fitted a leathern vizor of a most terrible appearance, stretched on the jaws of a shark, which he had brought from sea, and accommodated with a couple of broad glasses instead of eyes. On the inside of these he placed two rushlights, and, with a composition of sulphur and saltpetre, made a pretty large fusee, which he fixed between two rows of the teeth. This equipage being finished, he, one dark night chosen for the purpose, put it on, and, following the commodore into a long passage, in which he was preceded by Perry with a light in his hand, kindled his firework with a match, and began to bellow like a bull.[115]

The end result resembled 'a hideous phantom vomiting blue flame'.[116]

Alexander Watson, a clerk from Port Glasgow, may not have shared Smollett's literary flair, but he similarly relished the dramatic potential of ghosts. In a 1794 poem mocking superstitious belief, he explained that apparitions

> Shew blood and wounds, as old wives prattle,
> Or heavy loads of ir'n chains rattle;
> The murder, by dumb signs, divulge,
> By whom, and how, and where, promulge;
> Enjoin revenge, or threats bestow.
> Nor, till reveng'd can rest below![117]

Watson proceeded to note that ghosts donned winding sheets and lurked in dark rooms, churchyards and lonely corners. They were afraid of daylight, and they cowered away at the crow of a cock. His ghosts were caricatures, only passingly similar to the apparitions that people actually reported to have met. Further exaggeration can be seen in *The Spectre Bridegroom*, a farce by the English dramatist William Thomas Moncrieff. It was based on Washington Irving's short story of the same name, and was first performed in London

[114] Tobias Smollett, *The Adventures of Sir Launcelot Greaves*, 2 vols (London, 1762), vol. 1, 141, 258.

[115] Tobias Smollett, *The Adventures of Peregrine Pickle*, 3 vols (Dublin, 1751), vol. 1, 100.

[116] Ibid.

[117] Alexander Watson, *The Anti-Jacobin, a Hudibrastic Poem in Twenty-One Cantos* (Edinburgh, 1794), 6.

in 1821. It appeared on the Scottish stage in the 1820s.[118] In Irving's story, a marriage is arranged without the parties having met. On the way to join the bride's family, the groom is killed. His friend goes to explain the situation, but falls in love with the proposed bride at a glance, and so conceals the truth and poses as the groom. When the news of his friend's death arrives, the family concludes that he must be a ghost. He plays this part until he has stolen the bride away and married her. In Moncrieff's version there is similarly no actual ghost, but the play is bursting with references to ghost traditions. Mr Nicodemus, a scholar of vampires, goes to inform a girl called Georgiana of the death of her fiancé, his cousin.[119] Upon arrival he is mistaken for the fiancé, and sent to dine by Georgiana's officious father Aldwink without managing to get a word in edgeways. When a servant then arrives who has seen the cousin's body, a typically farcical exchange results:

> Dick: Come – what! – ha' they brought his body here?
> Aldwink: No, he brought his body here himself.
> Dick: What! – in a hearse?
> Aldwink: No – on a horse; and you must go and wait on him.
> Dick: What – sit up all night wi' him?
> Aldwink: No; only till he's finished his supper.

Dick is left to wonder, not unreasonably, 'what be the good of turtle soup when a man be dead'.[120] Later the whole party, excepting Georgiana's level-headed cousin Lavinia, becomes convinced that their visitor is a ghost. He arrives at midnight and retires at cock-crow; he does not eat, does not speak until forced, and groans about the dreadful secret he has to reveal. Aldwink desires to exorcise him by stopping the key holes and banishing him to the Red Sea, to which Dick responds glumly: 'It would be o' no use, 'squire; he'd come down the chimney, dress'd all in white.'[121] A suitor of Georgiana's claims to have dispatched him:

> Firing was of no use; one might as well have shot at the air, for all the wounds it created; so I had at him with the Latin, Friar Bacon, Doctor Faustus, and Agrippa ... And, at length, I pressed him so hard, that he took himself off through the key-hole in a clap of thunder.[122]

118 *Playbills of the Theatre Royal Edinburgh* (NLS), http://digital.nls.uk/playbills, accessed 1 Feb. 2018.

119 The name implies that he will practise a deception: the Nicodemites, as described by Calvin in 1544, were those who hid their true religious beliefs. Jean Calvin, *L'Excuse à Messieurs les Nicodémites*, in *Traité des Reliques, Suivi de l'Excuse à Messieurs les Nicodémites* (Paris, 1921), 199–283.

120 William Thomas Moncrieff, *The Spectre Bridegroom: Or a Ghost in Spite of Himself* (London, 1821), act 1, scene 2, 12–13.

121 Ibid., act 1, scene 3, 16.

122 Ibid., act 2, scene 5, 31.

Lavinia alone retains her head, declaring: 'The reign of the invisible world has passed away with the ages of chivalry and ignorance; the establishment of Sunday schools ... has signed the death-warrant of all ghosts, past, present, and to come; so you will excuse me, if I remain incredulous.'[123] She finally receives the (rather dubious) reward of claiming the wealthy Nicodemus as her own husband. *The Spectre Bridegroom* delighted in the weird and wonderful traditions surrounding ghosts, and mocked the solemn, ornate world of gothic with its reference to Latin texts and claps of thunder.

A final example is furnished by the letter written by one Steven Widcumb to Lady Douglas of Bothwell Castle in 1799. Widcumb explained that he had played the ghost of Hamlet's father in Drury Lane, but was now out of a job. He proposed that as she was 'muche in wante of a Goste to hante your ruinated Cassle', he would be perfectly qualified. He asked for £15 yearly, and would furnish his own 'windin sheets, chock Lantern, spirit of wine, bludde and all the nessesary apareal for a complite goste, premishing that ife youre Ladishipe wishes at any time a partikulear Goste to friten a partikulear friend you will firnish the dresse'. He added: 'I expect to get my victuales from your owse. I ame in Persin fite for a Goste avin a megir persin, a ollow voice and can grone well when required. P.S. I cane cro like a cok ife requirde.'[124] What exactly Widcumb hoped to achieve by sending such an epistle is unclear, but the stereotype of the ghost emerges plainly. Literary critics have recognised the paradox of parody: parodic works attack their target texts, but simultaneously create and popularise new texts in their image. Parody, therefore, 'preserves in the moment that it destroys'.[125] Similarly, satirical depictions might have made ghosts less credible, but they promoted a vision of the ghost that could easily take root within the popular imagination.

Conclusion

Scepticism was an important element of the eighteenth-century approach to ghosts. There was no room for ghosts in high Enlightenment debates on miracles or the nature of the soul and afterlife. Robert Wodrow and George Sinclair were mainstream figures in late-seventeenth-century religious culture; a few decades later there were no comparably established philosophers or theologians arguing that ghosts could prove Christian tenets. Ghosts were explained in natural, rather than supernatural, terms, and with recourse to science before theology. This speaks to the impact of intellectual change during the Scientific Revolution and the Enlightenment.

123 Ibid., act 2, scene 2, 25.
124 Steven Widcumb to Lady Douglas, [1799]: NRS, GD24/5/122.
125 Simon Dentith, *Parody* (London, 2000), 189; see also Margaret A. Rose, *Parody//Meta-fiction* (London, 1979).

However, it does not follow that there was a decline in the cultural importance of ghosts. When ghosts were divorced from their demonic associations there was more freedom for stories to be circulated. Furthermore, as ghosts were a useful vehicle through which to explore new theories about psychological disorders, they became a fashionable subject. Satirical depictions of ghosts were often scathing, but helped to create and popularise a dramatic, memorable ghost archetype. Amidst the burgeoning print culture of the eighteenth century, ghosts featured more frequently in discussion and emerged as a more easily identifiable cultural trope.

The idea that ghosts were merely a vulgar superstition recurred frequently in eighteenth-century treatises. There was something self-congratulatory in this notion; it was used to signal social superiority. The Scottish class structure was diversifying over the course of the eighteenth century. In the latter half of the century in particular, a growing body of urban professionals came to constitute a new (or, at least, newly important) middle class.[126] Arguably, as old class divides based on noble lineage became less important, there was more value in drawing cultural distinctions. The 1707 Union with England also fostered a drive among fashionable Scotsmen to distance themselves from their nation's perceived backwardness.[127] However, the sceptics' clean divide between learned and unlearned was misleading. Ghosts retained enough credibility to appear before courts and kirk sessions, and educated people defended them in periodicals. As we shall see in the next chapter, moreover, ghosts had a command over the emotions. Rational argument might dampen their influence, but could not dispel them altogether.

126 See, for example, Stana Nenadic, 'The Rise of the Urban Middle Classes', in Tom M. Devine and Rosalind Mitchison (eds), *People and Society in Scotland, Vol. 1: 1760–1830* (Edinburgh, 1998), 109–26; David Allan, *Scotland in the Eighteenth Century: Union and Enlightenment* (Harlow, 2002), 108–18.

127 This theme is explored more fully in the next chapter.

4

Gothic and Romantic Ghosts

> Yea, when the cold blood shoots through every vein:
> When every hair's-pit on my shrunken skin
> A knotted knoll becomes, and to mine ears
> Strange inward sounds awake, and to mine eyes
> Rush stranger tears, there is a joy in fear.[1]

Thus speaks Joanna Baillie's Orra, a fourteenth-century noblewoman with a penchant for ghost stories. At her bidding, her ladies-in-waiting send her into transports of fear with their stories of 'things unearthly' that 'rise from the yawning tombs'.[2] One of these 'things unearthly' is the ghost of a noble knight, who went hunting in the Black Forest. The Count of Aldenbergh, a cruel ancestor of Orra's, tricked this knight into staying in his castle, and murdered him while he slept. Thereafter, local peasants reported sightings of spectral hunters and hounds, racing through the forest at midnight. The knight himself was said to sound a horn three times at the castle gate, before making his passage inside, seeking some descendant who could release his spirit. In due course, Orra is sequestered in this ill-omened castle, while a conniving villain attempts to prey upon her virtue. The ghost that subsequently appears is actually the hero come to save her, but Orra's weakened mind is driven to frenzy.

Written in 1812, the sorry story of Orra demonstrates an alternative trend in the presentation of ghosts. In the late eighteenth and early nineteenth centuries, the gothic and romantic movements placed new value on ghosts' emotive power. This chapter identifies two significant trends. By the first of these trends, ghosts became a shortcut into an uncanny world. They were used to reflect on universal themes, particularly madness, death, and the supernatural fear that Orra relishes. The second trend saw ghosts tied to a specifically Scottish present and past: they were employed to celebrate folk culture and to evoke the watchful presence of older generations. The ghosts of the first category usually featured in literary works in the gothic style. Those of the second category formed part of the romantic project of nation-building, and appeared in both works of fiction

1 Joanna Baillie, *Orra*, in *A Series of Plays, in Which It Is Attempted to Delineate the Stronger Passions of the Mind*, 3 vols (London, 1798–1812), vol. 3, act 2, scene 1, 29.

2 Ibid., vol. 3, act 2, scene 1, 28.

and folkloric studies. This is not to imply, however, that gothic and romanticism are clear-cut categories; the precise meaning of the terms is disputed, and there are plenty of areas of overlap. This chapter is concerned more with the ways in which ghosts were used than the labels that should be attached to them.

The Literary World

While I will not venture far into the scholarly debate on the definitions of gothic and romanticism, a brief survey may be useful. To begin with gothic, the current consensus is that there is no single, clearly identifiable essence. Instead gothic is viewed as a 'conglomeration of literary "kinds"', a 'discursive site', an 'atmosphere' or 'aesthetic'.[3] The recent trend has been to avoid even listing usual features of gothic, to guard against any implication that gothic has a 'static identity' or was produced in a formulaic fashion (as its eighteenth-century critics suggested).[4] Nevertheless, certain elements have been highlighted as common (although not universal or exclusive) components of the gothic aesthetic. These elements include an antiquarian taste for old ruins, castles, and monasteries; an interest in insanity and sadism; the use of supernatural themes; a 'preference for the style or affective state called sublimity'; and the condition of 'rupture, disjunction, fragmentation'.[5]

If the definition of gothic remains problematic, its historical trajectory is clearer. Horace Walpole's *The Castle of Otranto*, published in 1764, is generally credited with being the first gothic novel. Writing in 1811, Walter Scott praised Walpole for having helped to rehabilitate the term 'Gothic', which was 'used before his time to express whatever was in pointed and diametrical opposition to the rules of true taste'.[6] These negative associations never fully disappeared; gothic was often considered to have little true literary value, and was frequently described as a women's genre.[7] Even by 1824, one commentator felt the need

3 R. L. Platzner, quoted in Robert F. Geary, *The Supernatural in Gothic Fiction: Horror, Belief, and Literary Change* (Lewiston [N.Y.], 1992), 2; Robert Miles, *Gothic Writing, 1750–1820: A Genealogy*, 2nd edn (Manchester, 2002), 4; E. J. Clery, *The Rise of Supernatural Fiction, 1762–1800* (Cambridge, 1995), 90; Andrew Smith, *Gothic Literature* (Edinburgh, 2007), 4; Michael Gamer, *Romanticism and the Gothic: Genre, Reception, and Canon Formation* (Cambridge, 2000), 4.

4 Gamer, *Romanticism and the Gothic*, 9.

5 Smith, *Gothic Literature*, 4; Francis R. Hart, quoted in Geary, *Supernatural in Gothic Fiction*, 3; Miles, *Gothic Writing*, 3.

6 Walter Scott, 'Introduction', in Horace Walpole, *The Castle of Otranto: A Gothic Story* (Edinburgh, 1811), vi.

7 In Scott's 'Aunt Margaret's Mirror', Aunt Margaret recounts the symptoms of enjoyment of a good ghost story, but adds: 'I mean such are signs which indicate the crisis, when a female imagination is in due temperature to enjoy a ghost story. I do not pretend to describe those which express the same disposition in a gentleman.' Walter Scott, 'My Aunt Margaret's Mirror', in Frédéric Mansel Reynolds (ed.), *The Keepsake for 1829* (London, 1828), 11.

to emphasise that 'whatever small men, accustomed to move in one very small sphere of intellect, may say, the *horrible* is quite as legitimate a field of poetry and romance, as either the pathetic or the ludicrous'.[8] Nevertheless, gothic's blend of horror, romance and melodrama captured the popular imagination. The 1790s in particular were a heyday for the genre, seeing the publication of two vastly influential novels: Ann Radcliffe's *The Mysteries of Udolpho* (1794) and Matthew Lewis's *The Monk* (1796). Charles Maturin's *Melmoth the Wanderer* (1820) was another important work, but thereafter the genre declined, although gothic themes re-emerged in various Victorian sub-genres.[9] In the case of Scotland specifically, it is generally argued that gothic did not emerge until the nineteenth century, with the work of Walter Scott, James Hogg and the 'tales of terror' printed in *Blackwood's Edinburgh Magazine*.[10] However, as we shall see, motifs that would later be associated with gothic were appearing in Scottish literature from at least the mid-eighteenth century. The recent scholarly emphasis on the fluidity of gothic justifies a more liberal use of the term: my focus will be on gothic themes, rather than on gothic texts.

Gothic has often been presented as a subset of romantic fiction. However, Michael Gamer's detailed comparison rejects this reading, arguing that romanticism developed 'as a response to gothic's reception', and was framed as a form of 'high culture' in contrast to gothic's popularism.[11] In Scotland there was certainly a significant amount of overlap between gothic and romantic authors and works, but romanticism does not share gothic's association with themes of fear, displacement, madness and malevolence – or, to recall the more succinct phrasing of our 1824 commentator, 'the *horrible*'. It is, however, harder to say what Scottish romanticism was than what it was not. The European romantic movement is generally thought to have originated in Germany in the last decade of the eighteenth century.[12] Studies of Scottish romanticism tend to begin earlier, with the *Ossian* poetry in the 1760s or the work of Allan Ramsay in the early eighteenth century.[13] To talk of Scottish romanticism, therefore, is not necessarily to talk of Scotland within the romantic era, or at least not

8 'The Devil's Elixir', *Blackwood's Edinburgh Magazine*, July 1824, 55.

9 See Geary, *Supernatural in Gothic Fiction*, esp. 12.

10 Ian Duncan, 'Walter Scott, James Hogg and Scottish Gothic', in David Punter (ed.), *A New Companion to the Gothic* (Oxford, 2012), 123. See also David Punter, 'Scottish and Irish Gothic', in Jerrold E. Hogle (ed.), *The Cambridge Companion to Gothic Fiction* (Cambridge, 2002), 105–24.

11 Gamer, *Romanticism and the Gothic*, 4–5, 10.

12 See, for example, Marilyn Butler, 'Romanticism in England', in Roy Porter and Mikuláš Teich (eds), *Romanticism in National Context* (Cambridge, 1988), 38; Michael Ferber, 'Introduction', in Michael Ferber (ed.), *A Companion to European Romanticism* (Oxford, 2005), 1–9, as well as other essays in these volumes.

13 Fiona Stafford, 'Scottish Romanticism and Scotland in Romanticism', in Michael Ferber (ed.), *A Companion to European Romanticism* (Oxford, 2005), 4–69; Murray Pittock, *Scottish and Irish Romanticism* (Oxford, 2008), ch. 2. See Pittock's discussion of the dating of Scottish romanticism in this work, 1–3.

the romantic era as defined by historians working on England or Europe as a whole. To complicate the picture further, some critics have questioned whether a genuine Scottish romanticism existed at all. This viewpoint is summarised (and later challenged) by Ian Duncan, Leith Davis and Janet Sorensen:

> Scotland ... stands for an *inauthentic* Romanticism, defined by a mystified – purely ideological – commitment to history and folklore. Rather than be a site of Romantic production, Scotland's fate is to have become a Romantic object or commodity ... a series of kitsch, fake, more or less reactionary 'inventions of tradition', from Ossian and Scott to Flora MacLeod and *Brigadoon*.[14]

Furthermore, the influence of the Scottish Enlightenment is often emphasised at the expense of the romantic movement. As Murray Pittock outlines, the Enlightenment has been presented as the antithesis to romanticism, championing rationality and social progression while the romantics celebrated imagination and nostalgia for the primitive.[15]

Recent scholarship has challenged these ideas, highlighting the ways in which Enlightenment thought complemented romantic production.[16] In addition, there has been a tendency to move away from questions of authenticity. Katie Trumpener's 1997 *Bardic Nationalism* was the first in a line of works to take a more sympathetic view of Scottish romanticism. Instead of objecting that romantic authors did not accurately depict a Scottish past, recent historians have instead examined how the authors reimagined this past and used it to create new models of national identity, '[reconceiving] national history and literary history under the sign of the bard'. In this reading, anachronism becomes 'one of the constitutive tropes of a distinctive practice of Romantic historicism'.[17] One of the central features of Scottish romanticism, then, is the literary recreation of the nation's past.[18] As we shall see, ghosts had a part to play in this enterprise.

In understanding the spread of gothic and romantic conceptions of ghosts, it is important to consider the evolution of venues and production methods, which allowed literary works to reach a wider audience. The 1707

14 Ian Duncan, Leith Davis and Janet Sorensen, 'Introduction', in Leith Davis, Ian Duncan and Janet Sorensen (eds), *Scotland and the Borders of Romanticism* (Cambridge, 2004), 1.

15 Murray Pittock, 'Enlightenment, Romanticism and the Scottish Canon', in Gerard Carruthers and Liam McIlvanney (eds), *The Cambridge Companion to Scottish Literature* (Cambridge, 2012), 88.

16 Ibid., 88–101; Murray Pittock, 'Introduction: What Is Scottish Romanticism?', in Murray Pittock (ed.), *The Edinburgh Companion to Scottish Romanticism* (Edinburgh, 2011), 6–9; Duncan, Davis and Sorensen, 'Introduction', 1–19.

17 Katie Trumpener, *Bardic Nationalism: The Romantic Novel and the British Empire* (Princeton, 1997), xii; James Chandler, quoted in Duncan, Davis and Sorensen, 'Introduction', 10.

18 See Pittock, 'Introduction', 1–9, as well as the introduction to Pittock, *Scottish and Irish Romanticism*, for a much fuller consideration of the factors that constitute a national romanticism.

Union with England created more economic opportunities for Scottish booksellers. Enlightenment culture also boosted print production. In the latter half of the eighteenth century, there was a flourishing of shops, circulating libraries, publishing houses, literary periodicals and discussion groups.[19] Rapid development continued over the first three decades of the nineteenth century, a period that has been termed the 'golden age' of Scottish publishing.[20] Output was not limited to Enlightenment scholarship. Gerard Carruthers describes the 'invention of Scottish literature' in the long eighteenth century, and the early nineteenth century saw the emergence of the novel as an important art form, with Walter Scott as the trailblazer.[21] Regarding ghosts specifically, one particularly significant milestone is the founding of *Blackwood's Edinburgh Magazine* in 1817. Set up by the publisher William Blackwood as a Tory rival to the Whigs' *Edinburgh Review*, *Blackwood's* interested itself in antiquarianism, vernacular poetry and sensationalist fiction. It stood on the cutting edge of Scottish literary production, with James Hogg and Walter Scott among its frequent contributors, and it swiftly established a wide audience. Ghosts appeared frequently in the pages of *Blackwood's*, with the 'tale of terror' emerging as a sort of subset of gothic, which both embraced and subverted the conventions of the genre.[22]

Ghosts also made increasingly frequent appearances on Scottish stages from the late eighteenth century. The Reformation kirk has traditionally been accused of suppressing all kinds of dramatical production prior to this period. As several historians have shown, this is an over-simplification. Drama survived within folk culture and at court, religious plays were produced for some years, and plays were exported to Europe if not performed in

19 Richard B. Sher, *The Enlightenment and the Book: Scottish Authors and their Publishers in Eighteenth-Century Britain, Ireland, and America* (Chicago, 2007), 1–2, 608; Robert Crawford, *Scotland's Books* (London, 2007), 330; Bill Bell, 'The Scottish Book Trade at Home and Abroad, 1707–1918', in Ian Brown et al. (eds), *The Edinburgh History of Scottish Literature, Vol. 2: Enlightenment, Britain and Empire (1707–1918)* (Edinburgh, 2007), 221–2.

20 Crawford, *Scotland's Books*, 388; Bell, 'Scottish Book Trade', 223–4; Peter Garside, 'Publishing 1800–30', in Bill Bell (ed.), *The Edinburgh History of the Book in Scotland, Vol. 3: Ambition and Industry 1800–1880* (Edinburgh, 2007), 79–90.

21 Gerard Charles Carruthers, 'The Invention of Scottish Literature during the Long Eighteenth Century' (University of Glasgow Ph.D. thesis, 2001); Ian Duncan, *Scott's Shadow: The Novel in Romantic Edinburgh* (Princeton, 2007).

22 Robert Morrison and Daniel S. Roberts, '"A character so various, and yet so indisputably its own": A Passage to *Blackwood's Edinburgh Magazine*', in Robert Morrison and Daniel S. Roberts (eds), *Romanticism and* Blackwood's *Magazine: 'An Unprecedented Phenomenon'* (Basingstoke, 2013), 1–19, as well as other essays in this volume; Duncan, 'Walter Scott, James Hogg and Scottish Gothic', 132–3; Tim Killick, *British Short Fiction in the Early Nineteenth Century: The Rise of the Tale* (Aldershot, 2008), 24–6; Duncan, Davis and Sorensen, 'Introduction', 13.

Scotland.[23] Nevertheless, the kirk did place significant limitations on dramatic productions, and Scottish theatre also suffered from monarchical instability in the sixteenth century and the removal of the royal court in the seventeenth.[24] A turning point came in 1767, when a patent was granted for the Theatre Royal in Edinburgh, Scotland's first professional theatre. By 1800 there were nine permanent playhouses across Scotland.[25]

Shakespeare's use of ghosts ensured that they would never be strangers to the early modern stage. However, prior to the second half of the eighteenth century, Shakespeare was rarely seen in Scottish theatres. Only one edition of a Shakespeare work (*Venus and Adonis*) seems to have been published in Scotland before 1752. In the second half of the eighteenth century, Scottish editions of Shakespeare began to appear frequently, and early-nineteenth-century playbills reveal regular Shakespearean performances.[26] The Scottish stages were also visited by less illustrious ghosts. In 1762, a purported haunting at Cock Lane in London attracted widespread attention. Capitalising on the public interest, several theatres offered productions of Joseph Addison's 1715 *The Drummer: Or, The Haunted House*. The prologue to a Scottish production declared:

> If in this wise, this wonder-working age,
> We bring a Ghost upon the Scottish stage,
> No cynic sure, will treat with ill-tim'd passion
> The universal vogue, the reigning fashion![27]

Plays which featured ghosts (or, at least, supposed ghosts) seem to have been performed with reasonable frequency from the late eighteenth century.

23 See Ian Brown, *Scottish Theatre: Diversity, Language, Continuity* (Amsterdam, 2013), ch. 4; Sarah Carpenter, 'Scottish Drama until 1650', in Ian Brown (ed.), *The Edinburgh Companion to Scottish Drama* (Oxford, 2011), 6–21.

24 Bill Findlay, 'Beginnings to 1700', in Bill Findlay (ed.), *A History of Scottish Theatre* (Edinburgh, 1998), 15, 55, 60; Sarah Carpenter, 'Early Scottish Drama', in R. D. S. Jack (ed.), *The History of Scottish Literature, Vol. 1: Origins to 1600* (Aberdeen, 1988), 199, 210.

25 Adrienne Scullion, 'The Eighteenth Century', in Bill Findlay (ed.), *A History of Scottish Theatre* (Edinburgh, 1998), 80.

26 Andrew Murphy, 'Shakespeare Goes to Scotland: A Brief History of Scottish Editions', in Willy Maley and Andrew Murphy (eds), *Shakespeare and Scotland* (Manchester, 2004), 157–60; *Playbills of the Theatre Royal Edinburgh* (NLS), http://digital.nls.uk/playbills/index.html, accessed 1 Feb. 2018.

27 Quoted in John Jackson, *The History of the Scottish Stage, from Its First Establishment to the Present Time* (Edinburgh, 1793), appendix 5, 17. Clery, *Rise of Supernatural Fiction*, 16 gives the somewhat different Covent Lane version:
If in this credulous, believing age
We bring a harmless Ghost upon the Stage,
Some will perhaps conclude – in hope of gain,
We've lur'd the Knocking Spirit from Cock-lane.
Addison's play was about a famous English poltergeist, the Drummer of Tedworth. On this case see Michael Hunter, 'New Light on the "Drummer of Tedworth": Conflicting Narratives of Witchcraft in Restoration England', *Historical Research* 78 (2005), 311–53.

Allan Ramsay's 1725 *The Gentle Shepherd* (discussed further below) was very popular.[28] Playbills from the 1820s feature *Hamlet*, *Macbeth* and *Richard III* alongside titles such as *The Libertine, or, The Feast of the Spectre*; *Der Freischutz, or, The Spectre Huntsman of Bohemia*; *Banditti of Rosenwald, or, The Spectre of the Bleeding Nun*; and *The Spectre Bridegroom* (the latter being the satirical piece we encountered in the previous chapter).[29]

Ghosts were considered to be valuable dramatic devices. The prologue to *The Drummer: Or, The Haunted House* noted that ghosts contributed to the comedy of a play.[30] George MacLaurin's *Laura, or the Punishment of Perfidy* (published in 1812, ten years after the author's death) tells of a young woman, Laura, who is seduced by her guardian Lord Albert. The editor 'improved' the play (as he explained it) by inserting a rather incongruous scene at the beginning of the second act. While Albert sleeps, he is visited by the shrouded ghost of Laura's mother. She wields a dagger and explains that she had been deputed from above to chastise him with 'the cutting scourge of gnawing conscience'. She warns him to beware of both her dagger and her daughter, presaging the culmination of the play, which sees Albert stabbed by Laura.[31] Besides this dramatic foreshadowing, the ghost serves little function; Albert is already beset with guilt before her visit. The editor clearly considered a ghost to be a proper complement to a dramatic tragedy.

Little is recorded about how ghosts were actually presented on stage, but a few titbits survive. In England the actors often wore white sheets, and their faces were blanched with flour.[32] An exception was made for the ghost of Hamlet's father, who appeared in full armour. In the late 1790s, Stuart Moncrieff Threipland wrote to the editor of the *Scots Chronicle* about performances at the Theatre Royal, Edinburgh. He expressed his belief that it was a big improvement to have ghosts walking on and off the stage instead of using trapdoors.[33] Theatre manager John Jackson explained that when the ghost of Hamlet's father appeared, Hamlet's hat was engineered to fly off 'by the usual stage trick'. Sometimes lights would be made to appear blue, in

28 Scullion, 'Eighteenth Century', 93.

29 *Playbills of the Theatre Royal Edinburgh*. See pp. 112–14.

30 John Jackson, *History of the Scottish Stage*, 17–18.

31 George MacLaurin, *Laura, or, The Punishment of Perfidy*, in Colin MacLaurin and George MacLaurin, *The Poetical and Dramatic Works of Colin Maclaurin, Esq. Advocate, and of the Late George Maclaurin, Esq. Writer*, 2 vols (Edinburgh, 1812), vol. 1, act 2, scene 1, 101–2, and editor's note, 94.

32 Stanley Wells, 'Staging Shakespeare's Ghosts', in Murray Biggs (ed.), *The Arts of Performance in Elizabethan and Early Stuart Drama* (Edinburgh, 1991), 51; Michael Hattaway, *Elizabethan Popular Theatre: Plays in Performance* (London, 1982), 85. For a detailed analysis of sixteenth- and seventeenth-century theatrical ghosts in England, see Pierre Kapitaniak, *Spectres, Ombres et Fantômes: Discours et Représentations Dramatiques en Angleterre, 1576–1642* (Paris, 2008), esp. ch. 4 on ghosts' appearances.

33 Stuart Moncrieff Threipland, *Letters Respecting the Performances at the Theatre Royal, Edinburgh* (Edinburgh, 1800), 19.

keeping with the tradition that flames burned blue if a ghost was present.[34] These snippets suggest that ghosts had their own set of stage conventions. Both through print culture and the stage, the eighteenth and early nineteenth centuries saw ghosts marketed in new and alluring ways. As we shall see, they also took on new meanings.

'In grim Array the grizly Spectres rise'

As noted above, the development of Scottish gothic is generally associated with the early nineteenth century. However, Hamish Mathison has argued that gothic themes and techniques were used in Scotland from the early eighteenth century, with the work of Allan Ramsay marking the appearance of 'a "gothic" writing, where the gothic is understood as the realm within literature that imagines and utilises the supernatural as a constrained and contained terror'.[35] The example he gives is *The Gentle Shepherd* (1725), in which two country women devise a plot to scare the foolish farm-servant Bauldy. One woman plays the part of a witch and 'raises' the other, who is dressed 'like a dead Corse in Sheet as white as Milk'.[36] Bauldy is terrified, and gibbers to his master, who listens with contempt, and declares:

> What silly Notions crowd the clouded Mind,
> That is throw want of Education blind.[37]

While this ghost is certainly an object of terror to Bauldy, the audience is in on the joke throughout; the ghost is used for its comedic value, rather than to send shivers along the spines of readers or audience. The interest in genuine horror that would characterise gothic's engagement with the supernatural is not evident in Ramsay. These themes do, however, emerge in Scottish literature before the nineteenth century. In 1743, Robert Blair published a blank verse poem entitled 'The Grave'. It was one of the forerunners of the 'graveyard school' of poetry, which emerged around the middle of the eighteenth century, and fed into the development of gothic.[38] Casting his eye over a churchyard, Blair describes a lugubrious atmosphere, with ghosts drifting from the gloomy vaults:

[34] Jackson, *History of the Scottish Stage*, 339, 18.

[35] Hamish Mathison, 'Gothic Poetry in Scotland: The Ghaistly Eighteenth Century', *Gothic Studies* 14 (2012), 40.

[36] Allan Ramsay, *The Gentle Shepherd: A Scots Pastoral Comedy* (Edinburgh, 1725), act 5, scene 1, 73.

[37] Ibid., act 5, scene 1, 74.

[38] See Eric Parisot, *Graveyard Poetry: Religion, Aesthetics and the Mid-Eighteenth-Century Poetic Condition* (Farnham, 2013).

In grim Array the grizly Spectres rise,
Grin horrible, and, obstinately sullen
Pass and repass, hush'd as the Foot of Night.[39]

The ghosts he presents have no purposes, no ties to a pre-death mortal self, and little religious significance. They are primarily atmospheric figures. Blair's language emphasises their unsettling appearance above all: note the jarring alliteration and assonance of 'grim', 'grisly' and 'grin'. Blair was a Presbyterian minister, and 'The Grave' took an evangelistic tone, expounding the evils of the 'Foul Monster, *Sin!*', celebrating Christ as 'Th' illustrious Deliverer of mankind', and describing death as 'Our Bane turn'd to a Blessing!'[40] Nevertheless, his ghosts were not the Christian moralists favoured by Robert Wodrow or George Sinclair. 'The Grave' was hugely popular, and marks the beginning of a new trend in the presentation of ghosts.[41]

Blair's ghosts reflect a broader movement in eighteenth-century religious culture. Printed funeral sermons declined, and instead there was a rise of poetry dealing with death. Eric Parisot explains that poetry increasingly wrested authority from traditional religious texts, echoing a 'general trajectory during the early to mid-eighteenth century from the religious to the aesthetic'.[42] Scotland saw the introduction of toleration for Episcopalians in 1712, followed by the accession of the Moderates in the 1760s. This reduced the importance of precise theological disputes, and left more scope for alternative means of religious exploration.[43] Nevertheless, both the Evangelical and Moderate parties of the eighteenth-century church have been associated with 'anti-aesthetic instincts'. Crawford Gribben argues that Scottish Evangelicals were 'generally suspicious of creative writing across the genres' well into the nineteenth century.[44] These tensions are apparent in Blair's work. The earliest surviving draft of the poem contained the following lines:

39 Robert Blair, *The Grave: A Poem* (London, 1743), lines 40–2, p. 5.

40 Ibid., line 600, p. 31; line 668, p. 35; line 710, p. 37.

41 Gerard Carruthers, 'Blair, Robert (1699–1746)', *Oxford DNB* (Oxford University Press, 2004), http://www.oxforddnb.com/view/article/2570, accessed 1 Feb. 2018.

42 Parisot, *Graveyard Poetry*, 20.

43 David Allan, *Virtue, Learning and the Scottish Enlightenment: Ideas of Scholarship in Early Modern History* (Edinburgh, 1993), 8–9; David Allan, *Scotland in the Eighteenth Century: Union and Enlightenment* (Harlow, 2002), 63–7. More broadly see Thomas Ahnert, *The Moral Culture of the Scottish Enlightenment, 1690–1805* (New Haven, 2014); Richard B. Sher, *Church and University in the Scottish Enlightenment: The Moderate Literati of Edinburgh* (Edinburgh, 1985); John R. McIntosh, *Church and Theology in Enlightenment Scotland: The Popular Party, 1740–1800* (East Linton, 1997); Andrew Landale Drummond and James Bulloch, *The Scottish Church, 1688–1843: The Age of the Moderates* (Edinburgh, 1973).

44 Crawford Gribben, 'Religion and Scottish Romanticism', in Murray Pittock (ed.), *The Edinburgh Companion to Scottish Romanticism* (Edinburgh, 2011), 118, 119.

Where light-heel'd Ghosts, and visionary Shades
Unbody'd, thick, beneath the wan Cold Moon
Solemnly Stalking in her lone sojourn:
Glide by Each Other, in Imperiall Silence;

In the final, published version these lines were altered:

Where light-heel'd Ghosts, and visionary Shades,
Beneath the wan cold Moon (as Fame reports)
Embody'd, thick, perform their mystick Rounds.[45]

The insertion of 'as Fame reports' distanced Blair himself from ghost belief. Blair was working within a religious framework, and 'The Grave' grew out of a mid-century fashion for a dramatic, mournful style of piety that saw graveyard poetry used as an aid to private worship.[46] However, the poetic ghost could not be fully reconciled with religious orthodoxy. Looking at the picture in France, where there was a similar literary trend in the eighteenth century, John McManners suggests that the romanticised ghost could only really develop at the expense of religious interests: 'Perhaps, as religious themes ceased to be the staple subjects of artistic inspiration, a place was left which had not been available before, for the "gliding spectre and the groaning grave" and the harsh and haunting beauties of Nature.'[47]

Certainly, as gothic themes developed further in Scottish literature, religion was left by the wayside. Ghosts appeared without disclaimers like Blair's 'as Fame reports', and as in 'The Grave', their aesthetic features took centre stage. Ghosts were 'light of foot as any sprite', came 'upon the wings of night' and glided 'like a feeble beam of light'.[48] They had voices 'like thunder'.[49] Some ghosts had an ethereal beauty to them. The play *The Ghost of the Oratory* (1825) presents a 'ghost' who later proves to be a living woman. However, in contrast to Allan Ramsay's comical fake ghost, she is depicted with a poetic grandeur. She appears as a gliding figure with cold flesh, lifeless eyes, and a 'silky silent' step. Her 'light loose lawny vestement' is 'silver'd' with 'Heaven's gleam', and her young beholder, recounting the scene, remembers:

45 Blair, 'The Grave', lines 14–17 (first draft) and lines 24–6 (published version), quoted in J. A. Means, 'The Composition of *The Grave*', *Studies in Scottish Literature* 10 (1972), 4, 6; Parisot, *Graveyard Poetry*, 62.

46 Parisot, *Graveyard Poetry*, 4, 14.

47 John McManners, *Death and the Enlightenment: Changing Attitudes to Death Among Christians and Unbelievers in Eighteenth-Century France* (Oxford, 1981), 335.

48 'The Genius of Caledonia: A Poem on the Threatened French Invasion', *Edinburgh Magazine, or Literary Amusement*, June 1798, 464; Charles Kerr, 'Maria: An Irregular Ode', in *Juvenile Performances in Poetry* (Edinburgh, 1788), sec. 7, 66.

49 Patrick Gordon, *The Famous History of the Renown'd and Valiant Prince, Robert Sirnamed, the Bruce, King of Scotland, &c* (Edinburgh, 1718), bk. 1, 34.

> Fear's chill damp
> Impearl'd my brow,
> –but yet my quivering lip
> Burn'd with that queen-like ghost's so marvellous beauty.[50]

Other ghosts were more gruesome. James Beattie wrote of ghosts who 'glare[d] horrid from the sylvan gloom', while James Graeme's spectres flocked forth from their 'restless graves' at midnight and stalked 'in melancholy state', baring their gaping wounds.[51] Ghosts were 'lonely' figures, pale and shivering, fearful of light. They usually wore white, often white shrouds.[52] They generally haunted tombs and churchyards, but at night time could be expected anywhere lonely and solitary, with a particular penchant for old buildings such as castles. Tobias Smollett presented a typical elegy:

> I'll seek some lonely church, or dreary hall
> Where fancy paints the glimmering taper blue,
> Where damps hang mouldering on the ivy'd wall,
> And sheeted ghosts drink up the midnight dew;[53]

Ghosts of this sort appeared frequently in *Blackwood's* and other periodicals, as well as on the stage. One of the aforementioned playbills advertises *Banditti of Rosenwald; or, The Spectre of the Bleeding Nun*. This piece was described as a melodrama, and was based on the sub-plot of Matthew Gregory Lewis's *The Monk* (1796). *The Monk* tells the story of Raymond, Marquis de las Cisternas, who falls in love with Agnes, the niece of the Baroness of Lindenberg. Agnes is destined for a convent, however, and the two resolve to elope. As Agnes is under close guard, they plan to disguise her as the Bleeding Nun, a ghost who appears on 5 May every five years. However, Raymond ends up eloping with the actual ghost by mistake. He later learns that the ghost murdered her old lover, and was then killed herself. She haunts Raymond until he finds and buries her bones. This was a ghost from one of the archetypal gothic works, with a tragic back-story of doomed love and a ritualistic and dramatic mode of appearing. By the nineteenth century this romanticised vision of the ghost was common fictional fodder.

50 'The Ghost of the Oratory', *Blackwood's Edinburgh Magazine*, Oct. 1825, scene 4, 446–7.

51 James Beattie, 'Ode to Peace', in *Original Poems and Translations* (London, 1760), sec. 3:2, 7; James Graeme, 'Elegy 18' and 'Elegy 24', in *Poems on Several Occasions* (Edinburgh, 1773), 177, 189.

52 Gallovidiensis, 'Elegy to the Memory of Miss Dick', *Edinburgh Magazine, or Literary Miscellany*, Apr. 1796, 304; Tobias Smollett, 'Ode to Mirth', in *Plays and Poems Written by T. Smollett*, M. D. (London, 1777), 251; William Erskine, *Epistle from Lady Grange to Edward D-, Esq.* (London, 1798), 20; John Tait, 'The Vanity of Human Wishes, an Elegy, Occasioned by the Untimely Death of a Scots Poet', in Robert Fergusson, *Poems on Various Subjects, by Robert Fergusson, Part 2* (Edinburgh, 1779), 149.

53 Tobias Smollett, *The Adventures of Roderick Random*, 2 vols (London, 1748), vol. 2, 272.

While the ghost in the *Banditti of Rosenwald* had a central role in the plot, many ghosts followed the pattern seen in 'The Grave', appearing primarily as atmospheric devices. J. A. Means has suggested that this reflects the declining importance of the ghost: 'It is interesting to note that, as Englishmen ceased to believe in ghosts, the place of spirits in serious literature was reduced from that of agents (e.g., *Hamlet* and *Macbeth*) to that of a picturesque element in the background of the action, as in *The Grave* and late-eighteenth-century poetry generally.'[54] Setting aside the question of whether or not people were ceasing to believe in ghosts, there are two problems with this reading. Firstly, ghosts were still used as agents. Means might not have allowed *Banditti of Rosenwald* to be 'serious literature', but a more convincing argument can be made for the work of Joanna Baillie (1762–1851), which constitutes an important stepping stone in the development of Scottish gothic.[55] In Baillie's 1790 poem 'Night Scenes of Other Times', a woman called Margaret sets out on a stormy night to meet her beloved Edward. Edward, however, has been murdered, and Margaret is met by his ghost. She opts to join him in the tomb, and dies on the spot. Subsequently, Edward's ghost appears to his murderer, pale and bloody, a blade still in his heart, eyes 'dark and dreadful'. He does not speak, but makes such an impression that his murderer is haunted with 'gloomy fears' for the rest of his days.[56] Margaret herself bids a post-mortem goodbye to her grieving father through ghostly harp music. These ghosts are protagonists, rather than mere atmospheric devices.

Even when ghosts did remain in the background, they were more than a 'picturesque element'. Ghosts pervaded scenes with a sense of horror. This alone could influence – or even dictate – the action of a piece. Both Blair and Baillie wrote of figures (a schoolboy and a soldier, respectively) walking through churchyards only to be overtaken by fear. The atmosphere of the graveyard fills the characters with mounting dread, as both remember ghost stories they have been told. In the case of Baillie's soldier:

> Swift to his thoughts, unbidden, throng
> Full many a tale, forgotten long,
> Of ghosts, who at the dead of night
> Walk round their graves all wrapt in white,
> And o'er the church-yard dark and drear,
> Becken the traveller to draw near:[57]

[54] Means, 'Composition of *The Grave*', 6n11.

[55] See the essays in Thomas C. Crochunis (ed.), *Joanna Baillie, Romantic Dramatist: Critical Essays* (London, 2004).

[56] Joanna Baillie, 'Night Scenes of Other Times', in *Poems: Wherein It Is Attempted to Describe Certain Views of Nature and of Rustic Manners* (London, 1790), pt. 2, 46, 48.

[57] Joanna Baillie, 'To Fear', in *Poems: Wherein It Is Attempted to Describe Certain Views of Nature and of Rustic Manners* (London, 1790), 141.

The man, overcome with terror, collapses. Blair's schoolboy is similarly frightened, and flees, only to make new stories himself:

> Sudden! he starts, and hears, or thinks he hears
> The Sound of something purring at his Heels:
> Full fast he flies, and dares not look behind him,
> Till out of Breath he overtakes his Fellows;
> Who gather round, and wonder at the Tale
> Of horrid *Apparition*, tall and ghastly,[58]

Ghosts, therefore, could wield significant power without even having to make appearances. Psychological horror would become an important feature of gothic. The genre gradually placed more emphasis on inner turmoil, with caliginous landscapes coming to mirror the darkness of mental and emotional states.[59]

As we saw in the last chapter, in the latter half of the eighteenth century there was a move towards interpreting ghosts as the products of psychological disorders. Terry Castle has written insightfully of how this played into gothic fiction, encouraging the 'supernaturalizing of the mind itself'.[60] For writers, this offered an opportunity to explore the power of the supernatural without condoning it. Smollett provides an early example of this approach. In *The Adventures of Ferdinand Count Fathom* (1753) he plays with the power of the psychological ghost, torturing his hero with ominous scenes:

> The darkness of the night, the silence and solitude of the place, the indistinct images of the trees that appeared on every side, 'stretching their extravagant arms athwart the gloom,' conspired ... to disturb his fancy, and raise strange phantoms in his imagination. Although he was not naturally superstitious, his mind began to be invaded with an awful horror, that gradually prevailed over all the consolations of reason and philosophy.[61]

This theme is explored more fully in Joanna Baillie's aforementioned *Orra*, or in Alexander MacDonald's *Vimonda* (first performed 1787, first printed the following year). In *Vimonda*, the eponymous heroine is tormented by sightings of her father's ghost. The rational hero Melville, her lover, assures her that the ghost is no more than

58 Blair, *The Grave*, lines 63–8, p. 7.

59 Fred Botting, *Gothic: The New Critical Idiom*, 2nd edn (Abingdon, 2014), 83–4. See also Geary, *Supernatural in Gothic Fiction*.

60 Terry Castle, *The Female Thermometer: Eighteenth-Century Culture and the Invention of the Uncanny* (Oxford, 1995), 159–89 (quotation 161).

61 Tobias Smollett, *The Adventures of Ferdinand Count Fathom*, 2 vols (London, 1753), vol. 1, 113.

the creature of thy fancy,
Work'd up to phrenzy by sad thoughts and solitude.[62]

However, living in a continual state of fear shatters Vimonda's nerves. Even after the ghost proves to be her still-living father, Vimonda remains afraid of it.[63] When she subsequently believes (mistakenly) that Melville has been poisoned, she swiftly dies of a broken heart, betrayed again by her excessive sensibility.

The ghosts of the sixteenth and seventeenth centuries were frightening because they might be manifestations of the Devil. Gothic ghosts played on the terrors of insanity, with the mind itself becoming the site of supernatural intrusion. The tension between these two approaches – an external horror in the form of the Devil, and an internal psychologised horror – is most clearly exhibited in James Hogg's *The Private Memoirs and Confessions of a Justified Sinner* (1824). Robert Wringhim, the protagonist, grows up under the tutelage of the Reverend Wringhim. The reverend instructs him in antinomian principles, or the belief that the elect are destined for Heaven regardless of any sins committed in their lifetimes. Robert is subsequently approached by an enigmatic stranger. This young man, who calls himself only Gil-Martin, becomes Robert's constant companion, and encourages him in increasingly fanatical principles. Under Gil-Martin's supervision, Robert descends along a path of crime, culminating in suicide.

Gil-Martin is an ambiguous character, and has attracted extensive scholarly attention.[64] In some respects he is a typical manifestation of the Devil. Accused witches frequently reported that the Devil paid visits to them, offering them gold or other gifts, while spiritual diarists lamented his assiduous whisperings. Similarly, Gil-Martin courts Robert, beguiling him with promises of spiritual greatness, manipulating him into acts of evil. However, Hogg diverges from tradition when he blends the identities of Robert and Gil-Martin. According to early modern descriptions of diabolic temptation, the Devil could wage warfare internally as well as externally. Devils could manipulate the bodily humours, distort the vision, invade the blood and besiege the heart.[65] Hogg takes this

62 A. MacDonald, *Vimonda: A Tragedy* (Dublin, 1788), act 1, scene 5, 5.

63 Ibid., act 5, scene 2, 55.

64 Useful recent discussions include Ian Duncan, 'Fanaticism and Enlightenment in *Confessions of a Justified Sinner*', in Sharon Alker and Holly Faith Nelson (eds), *James Hogg and the Literary Marketplace: Scottish Romanticism and the Working-Class Author* (Farnham, 2009), 57–70; Penny Fielding, '*The Private Memoirs and Confessions of a Justified Sinner*: Approaches', in Ian Duncan and Douglas S. Mack (eds), *The Edinburgh Companion to James Hogg* (Edinburgh, 2012), 132–9; Michelle Faubert, 'John Ferriar's Psychology, James Hogg's *Justified Sinner*, and the Gay Science of Horror Writing', in Thomas H. Schmid and Michelle Faubert (eds), *Romanticism and Pleasure* (Basingstoke, 2010), 83–108.

65 See Michelle D. Brock, 'Internalizing the Demonic: Satan and the Self in Early Modern Scottish Piety', *Journal of British Studies* 54 (2015), 23–43.

interiority a step further. Gil-Martin has the power to appear in various guises, but takes on Robert's appearance when in his presence. Recalling their first meeting, Robert records 'What was my astonishment on perceiving that he was the same being as myself!' He later has the sense of being haunted by a 'second self'.[66] Gil-Martin can be read as a spectral extension of Robert, a personification of the sinful aspects of his character. There are echoes here of legends about doppelgängers. Nineteenth-century folklorists wrote that the apparitions seen by second sighted seers were spiritual doubles known as *taisch*, who perfectly resembled their earthly counterparts.[67] Hogg took up this theme of the fractured self, and turned the spectral double into something evil, a force that drew its power from the darkest recesses of the human mind. Gil-Martin is not a ghost, but he demonstrates the terrifying potential of apparitions in the late eighteenth and early nineteenth centuries. Enlightenment discourses urged that ghosts were all in the mind, and therefore need not be an object of fear. Gothic works and their forerunners acknowledged that ghosts might be all in the mind – and went on to show just how frightening that was.

There was another way in which gothic ghosts could be used to evoke fear: through their depiction of death. While once they had returned to discuss the joys of the afterlife, ghosts became reminders of the woes of death. Work on England has identified a reorientation in priorities during the Enlightenment: there was an increased focus on the departure from this world, rather than the ascension to a new one. Death did not become fully secularised, but there was a movement in that direction.[68] Furthermore, the mid-century mournful style of piety reflected a growing cultural emphasis on melancholy. Again considering the French case, McManners writes that 'sorrow was found to have a hypnotic attraction, and there were sophisticated delights to be discovered in melancholy'.[69] This pattern was also seen in Britain; a 1747 poem by Thomas Warton was titled 'The Pleasures of Melancholy'.[70] Drawing on this trend, poetic ghosts painted death in sorrowful hues. A poem from the 1780s began:

66 James Hogg, *The Private Memoirs and Confessions of a Justified Sinner*, ed. Adrian Hunter (Peterborough [Ont.], 2001), 131, 176.

67 See Elsa Richardson, *Second Sight in the Nineteenth Century: Prophecy, Imagination and Nationhood* (London, 2017), 41–3.

68 Julie Rugg, 'From Reason to Regulation: 1760–1850', in Peter C. Jupp and Clare Gittings (eds), *Death in England: An Illustrated History* (Manchester, 1999), 202–4, 227; Roy Porter, 'Death and the Doctors in Georgian England', in Ralph Houlbrooke (ed.), *Death, Ritual, and Bereavement* (London, 1989), 85. See also Houston, who cautions against accepting the secularisation narrative without qualification: R. A. Houston, *Punishing the Dead?: Suicide, Lordship, and Community in Britain, 1500–1830* (Oxford, 2010), ch. 6.

69 McManners, *Death and the Enlightenment*, 334.

70 See David B. Morris, 'A Poetry of Absence', in John Sitter (ed.), *The Cambridge Companion to Eighteenth-Century Poetry* (Cambridge, 2001), 234; Kenneth Simpson, *The Protean Scot: The Crisis of Identity in Eighteenth Century Scottish Literature* (Aberdeen, 1988), ch. 2.

Twas at the solemn midnight hour,
That hour when ghosts return,
O'er the dark grave the joys of life
For ever lost to mourn.[71]

Earlier ghosts, who most commonly returned in normal clothing and looked and talked as they had when alive, suggested that death was a mere translation to the afterlife. Romanticised ghosts presented death as a more profound transformation. Blair declared that it must be 'an awful Thing *to die*'.[72] He also underlined the universality of death in a way that was anything but reassuring:

the task be mine
To paint the gloomy horrors of the Tomb;
Th' appointed place of rendezvous, where all
These trav'llers meet.[73]

Joanna Baillie explored similar themes in her 1812 play *The Dream*, which followed a medieval general who struggled with his fear of impending execution. Baillie explained that she was endeavouring to rehabilitate the fear of death as a natural human impulse, although it was against 'the received rules of dramatic dignity, and common-place heroism'.[74]

Philippe Ariès has argued that death became more distant over the seventeenth and eighteenth centuries. Among theologians there was an attempt to 'soften [death's] intensity'.[75] Cemeteries were removed to the outskirts of cities, and there was less cultural focus on corpses and skeletons: 'it was the dark, disembodied shadow or the shrouded ghost, rather than the skeleton, that inspired fear after the seventeenth century.' He also notes a growing sense of nothingness; people took less solace in the hope of the beyond.[76] Nevertheless, the Enlightenment also saw the renewed threat of an untamed, 'savage' death. There was a surge of interest in melancholy and a fresh focus on the dead body, macabre eroticism, and violence in the natural world. Thereafter, the romantic movement of the nineteenth century emphasised the notion of the beautiful death.[77] Ariès's work is remarkable for its sweeping scope, and is necessarily general; it is unfair to expect his picture to apply on the micro as well as the macro level of history. Sasha Handley points out that Ariès's argument about the distancing of death is undermined by the 'dramatic physical representations

71 'Poetry', *Aberdeen Magazine, Literary Chronicle, and Review*, 31 Dec. 1789, 853–4.
72 Blair, *The Grave*, line 401, p. 22.
73 Ibid., lines 4–7, p. 3.
74 Joanna Baillie, 'To the Reader', in *A Series of Plays, in Which It Is Attempted to Delineate the Stronger Passions of the Mind*, 3 vols (London, 1798–1812), vol. 3, v–vi, viii.
75 Philippe Ariès, *The Hour of Our Death*, trans. Helen Weaver (Oxford, 1981), 314–15, 307.
76 Ibid., 328, 322, 342.
77 Ibid., 341, 353, ch. 10.

of death' furnished by ghost stories.[78] However, it is certainly fair to argue that there was a shift away from the cultural prominence of revenants and the medieval *Danse Macabre*, culminating in gothic ghosts. Although these ghosts might bear wounds and wear shrouds, they were also frequently ethereal. They emphasised the profound transformation that occurred with death, but they were mediated through romantic language and imagery. It is possible to fit this into Ariès's framework. Poetic ghosts did reflect a certain softening and distancing as compared to skeletons and walking corpses. They also had a sinister allure to them, foreshadowing the eroticism that (according to Ariès) became tied into notions of death later in the century, as well as the notions of the 'beautiful death' that would follow in the nineteenth.[79]

There are limits to how far this framework can be applied, however. Ariès links the softening of death to a growing mood of calm acceptance (although contrasts it with his notion of the resurgence of 'savage death').[80] This theme has been picked up by other historians. Looking at the English picture, Julie Rugg argues that as medical knowledge expanded and fear of eternal damnation receded, death lost much of its terror.[81] Roy Porter suggests that death 'ceased ... to be the ultimate enemy' and became instead a 'gentle friend', while Guenter B. Risse makes a similar argument with reference to the development of medicine during the Scottish Enlightenment.[82] This argument is less convincing in the light of the ghosts of gothic poetry. While they might represent death in a milder light than revenants or skeletons, they nonetheless emphasise horror and estrangement. As we have seen, gothic ghosts restored an aspect of terror to the Enlightenment's psychological interpretation of apparitions. Perhaps they can similarly be read as a reaction to the greater medicalisation of death. Physicians stripped death down to a 'natural bodily event', nullifying its element of supernatural horror.[83] Gothic ghosts remystified death, playing on the melancholic motif that was fashionable both in religious works and literary productions more broadly. They mark a shift away from the medieval fascination with the physical processes of death and decomposition, as well as a departure from that emphasis on the afterlife that we have seen in ghost stories from the late seventeenth and early eighteenth centuries. They

78 Sasha Handley, *Visions of an Unseen World: Ghost Beliefs and Ghost Stories in Eighteenth-Century England* (London, 2007), 15.

79 Ariès, *Hour of Our Death*, ch. 10. On the eroticisation of death in gothic literature see Jolene Zigarovich (ed.), *Sex and Death in Eighteenth-Century Literature* (Abingdon, 2013). Hamish Mathison's essay in this volume, '"Out of Tune": Sex, Death and Gothic Disharmony in Eighteenth-Century Scotland', 224–40, discusses the Scottish case. On Ariès, death and gothic more generally see Castle, *Female Thermometer*, ch. 8.

80 Ariès, *Hour of Our Death*, 307–15.

81 Rugg, 'From Reason to Regulation', 203.

82 Porter, 'Death and the Doctors', 85; Guenter B. Risse, *New Medical Challenges during the Scottish Enlightenment* (Amsterdam, 2005), 44.

83 Risse, *New Medical Challenges*, 44.

were used instead to depict a death that was tragic, frightening and picturesque in equal measure.

Ghosts in Vernacular Poetry

The remainder of this chapter will focus chiefly on how ghosts were used to explore national identity. This was primarily an eighteenth- and nineteenth-century development, but it built on established ideas. Scotland had long had the reputation of being a land of myth and magic. Hector Boece's 1527 *Scotorum Historiae* contained lengthy descriptions of the country's wondrous features. They included 'barnacle geese' – birds that grew on trees, or hatched from within fir cones. Boece also mentioned fish without fins, waves without wind and floating islands. These legends reappeared frequently in works about Scotland over the early modern period, reinforcing this reputation abroad.[84] In England, a perception emerged of Scotland (particularly the Highlands) as being overrun with superstitious beliefs.[85] When the Earl of Lauderdale sent supernatural stories to Richard Baxter in 1659, he requested that Baxter did not print them, as they would 'make the disaffected jeer Scotland, which is the object of Scorn enough already'.[86] In the eighteenth and early nineteenth centuries there was a shift towards celebrating this magical reputation, and intertwining it with romantic conceptions of the nation.

There were two primary ways in which romantic authors employed ghosts to reflect on national identity. Firstly, ghosts became representatives of a lively folk tradition. Instead of seeking to stamp out superstitious beliefs, romantic writers marketed them as a sign of Scottish cultural vibrancy. Secondly, ghosts were used as vehicles for social commentary. Ghosts were a symbol not just of the end of life, but also of the end of eras; their predilection for haunting old ruins reflected a desire to cling to times gone by. By their nature, they forced the past upon the present. They therefore became a useful tool through which to evaluate social development. Allan Ramsay (1686–1758), Robert Fergusson (1750–74) and Robert Burns (1759–96) emerged at the forefront of a poetic movement that embraced these trends, in part as a response to English

84 Martin Rackwitz, *Travels to Terra Incognita: The Scottish Highlands and Hebrides in Early Modern Travellers' Accounts, c.1600 to 1800* (Münster, 2007), 61–71.

85 Michael Hunter, 'Introduction', in Michael Hunter (ed.), *The Occult Laboratory: Magic, Science, and Second Sight in Late Seventeenth-Century Scotland* (Woodbridge, 2001), 1–4; Michael F. Graham, *The Blasphemies of Thomas Aikenhead: Boundaries of Belief on the Eve of the Enlightenment* (Edinburgh, 2008), 139; Lizanne Henderson and Edward J. Cowan, *Scottish Fairy Belief: A History* (East Linton, 2001), 27.

86 Richard Baxter, *The Certainty of the Worlds of Spirits, and Consequently, of the Immortality of Souls of the Malice and Misery of the Devils and the Damned* (London, 1691), 85–7.

cultural incursion.[87] The development of the printing press and the 1603 Union of Crowns had allowed for more interaction between England and Scotland. The flip-side was a growing perception that English language and culture were threatening to erode Scots and Scottish traditions. The 1707 Union only heightened these concerns. It became fashionable to spurn 'rustic' Scottish tastes and turns of phrase in favour of English equivalents, and collections of 'Scotticisms' were printed, advising Scots on words or phrases to avoid in refined company.[88] David Hume is often credited with producing the first list of this sort, as an accompaniment to his 1752 *Political Discourses*. Among other things, Hume cautioned readers to eschew the phrase 'butter and bread' in favour of 'bread and butter', replace 'simply impossible' with 'absolutely impossible', and say 'get an appetite' rather than 'get a stomach'.[89] Ramsay, Fergusson and Burns contested this cultural imperialism through vernacular explorations of Scottish tradition.

Allan Ramsay used ghosts to add colour to his depictions of the common folk of Scotland. However, his approach was frequently satirical; he associated ghost belief with ignorance and vulgarity. We have seen this at play in *The Gentle Shepherd*, in which the fearful Bauldy is humiliated for crediting a ghost hoax. In 'Elegy on John Cowper, Kirk-Treasurer's Man, Anno 1714' (first published 1718), Ramsay similarly described a returning ghost with the dry caution that his readers should

> tak good Tent ye dinna file
> Ye'r Breeks for Fear.[90]

87 See Rhona Brown, 'Allan Ramsay, Robert Fergusson and Robert Burns', in David Sergeant and Fiona J. Stafford (eds), *Burns and Other Poets* (Edinburgh, 2012), 23–38; Mathison, 'Gothic Poetry in Scotland', 34–46; Douglas Gifford, '"Nathaniel Gow's Toddy": The Supernatural in Lowland Scottish Literature from Burns and Scott to the Present Day', in Lizanne Henderson (ed.), *Fantastical Imaginations: The Supernatural in Scottish History and Culture* (Edinburgh, 2009), 110–40.

88 See, for example, M. A. Bald, 'The Anglicisation of Scottish Printing', *Scottish Historical Review* 23 (1926), 107–15; M. A. Bald, 'The Pioneers of Anglicised Speech in Scotland', *Scottish Historical Review* 24 (1927), 179–93; Christine Robinson and Roibeard Ó Maolalaigh, 'The Several Tongues of a Single Kingdom: The Languages of Scotland 1314–1707', in Ian Brown et al. (eds), *The Edinburgh History of Scottish Literature, Vol. 1: From Columba to the Union* (Edinburgh, 2007), 162–3; Charles Jones, 'Nationality and Standardisation in Eighteenth-Century Scotland', in Raymond Hickey (ed.), *Eighteenth-Century English: Ideology and Change* (Cambridge, 2010), 221–34; Joan Beal, 'Syntax and Morphology', in Charles Jones (ed.), *The Edinburgh History of the Scots Language* (Edinburgh, 1997), 336–8; Richard Bailey, 'Scots and Scotticisms: Language and Ideology', *Studies in Scottish Literature* 26 (1991), 65–77.

89 David Hume, 'Scotticisms', in *The Philosophical Works of David Hume*, 4 vols (Edinburgh, 1826), vol. 1, cxxvii, cxxix.

90 Allan Ramsay, *Elegies on Maggy Johnston, John Cowper, and Lucky Wood*, 2nd edn (Edinburgh, 1718), 14.

Ramsay began a literary trend, later continued by Smollett, of casting the supernatural in a humorous and farcical light. However, he also used ghosts as political messengers.[91] 'A Tale of Three Bonnets' (1722) tells of Duniwhistle, an old man on his deathbed, who calls his three sons to him and presents them each with a bonnet. These bonnets signify virtue, and the men are warned not to remove them. However, one son is seduced by Rosie, a beautiful heiress representing England. She attempts to destroy two of the bonnets. Duniwhistle returns as 'a stalwart Ghaist' with 'stern and angry Looks', and saves the bonnets. He upbraids the son who was seduced by Rosie's charms, but offers some hope for the future:

Be a' thy days an Ass,
And Hackney to this cunning *Lass*;
But for these BONNETS, I'll preserve them,
For *Bairns* unborn, that will deserve them.[92]

Similarly, Ramsay's 'The Vision' (1724), published under the name A. R. Scott and allegedly written around the year 1300, presents a figure from the past appearing in a dream and critiquing the Wars of Independence. As Douglas Gifford points out, the analysis might just as well be applied to the recent Jacobite engagements.[93] The apparition argues that trade is coming to a standstill and 'cunzie' (coin) is forsaking the land, and explains that Scotland will be renewed

Quhen *Scottish* Peirs slicht *Saxon* gold,
And turn trew heartit men;
Quhen Knaivry and Slaivrie,
Ar equally dispysd.[94]

These ghosts personify an idealised past Scotland, reproaching contemporary Scots for their submission to England. Ghosts were used similarly in other works after Ramsay's. A 1729 pamphlet by 'C. N.' described the ghostly return of John Hamilton, second Lord Belhaven, who died in 1708. Belhaven gave a speech against the Union in the year of his death. In the pamphlet he appears to reproach the 'sons of Caledon', and rants about the 'hottest Vengeance' and 'smoaking Sulphur' that awaits those who have

91 See also Hamish Mathison, 'Gothic Poetry in Scotland', 36–8.

92 Allan Ramsay, *A Tale of Three Bonnets* ([Edinburgh?], 1722), canto 4, 27. See Mathison, 'Gothic Poetry in Scotland', 36–8.

93 Gifford, 'Nathaniel Gow's Toddy', 115–16.

94 Allan Ramsay, 'The Vision', in Allan Ramsay (ed.), *The Ever Green, Being a Collection of Scots Poems*, 2 vols (Edinburgh, 1724), vol. 1, v. 13, p. 220.

Sold
Themselves to slavery, for betraying *Gold*:[95]

These themes re-emerged in Robert Fergusson's 'The Ghaists: A Kirk-Yard Eclogue' (1773). This poem describes a conversation between the ghosts of two Edinburgh men, George Heriot and George Watson, who meet in a graveyard to enjoy their 'nightly freedom' before the cock-crow sends them back to their tombs. They discuss the controversial Mortmain Bill, which was to compel Scottish trusts to buy government stock, and mourn the Union, foretelling Scotland's downfall:

Ah, Caledon! the land I yence held dear,
Sair mane mak I for thy destruction near;

They are themselves powerless to alter Scotland's course, but debate the possibility of engaging some ghost 'that trokes and conjures wi' Auld Nick' to cause meteorological chaos, 'Till Scotland's out o' reach o' England's pow'r'.[96] The implication is that truly patriotic Scots should stop at nothing to reclaim their national independence.

Robert Burns also offered critiques of Anglo-Scottish relations, most notably in 'Such a Parcel of Rogues in a Nation' (1791). However, he is better remembered for his depictions of the liveliness of Scottish folk belief. In 'Halloween' (1785), he annotated his Scots description of superstitious traditions with English explanations, underlining the indigenous nature of the folk culture he was exploring. Thereafter, 'Tam o' Shanter' (1790; first published 1791) presents a vision of this culture that is full of colour and vitality, delving into traditions of the witches' Sabbat with a mixture of bawdiness and genuine horror.[97] Neither of these poems included ghosts as such, but they celebrated a world of popular belief in which ghosts had a natural place. Burns also made use of ghostlike spirits to reflect on the changing nature of Scottish society, again with reference to English incursion. The power of the old Scottish aristocracy declined in the eighteenth century as the professional classes expanded. David Punter argues that a central theme of Scottish gothic was the replacement of a traditional, violent authority by 'the middling (and meddling) rule of law', which was perceived as destroying a national way of life.[98] Punter is writing about the work of Walter Scott, but his argument might also be applied to Burns's 'The Brigs of Ayr' (1787). This poem presents an argument between the spirits of two bridges. The Auld Brig symbolises a bygone generation:

95 C. N., *A Counsel of Criminal Ghosts to the Ghost of the Great Beilhaven* (Edinburgh, 1729), 3, 4.
96 Robert Fergusson, 'The Ghaists: A Kirk-Yard Eclogue', *Weekly Magazine, or Edinburgh Amusement*, 27 May 1773, 275–6. See Mathison, 'Gothic Poetry in Scotland', 41–2.
97 Duncan, 'Walter Scott, James Hogg and Scottish Gothic', 126.
98 Punter, 'Scottish and Irish Gothic', 110, 111–12.

Auld Brig appear'd of ancient Pictish race,
The vera wrinkles gothic in his face:

The New Brig represents a modern Scotland, clad in English finery:

New Brig was buskit in a braw, new coat,
That he, at *Lon'on*, frae ane *Adams* got;[99]

The New Brig mocks the Auld Brig as an 'ugly gothic hulk', and insults the 'gaunt, ghastly, ghaist-alluring edifices' of its architecture. The Auld Brig retorts: 'Conceited gowk! puff'd up wi' windy pride.'[100] It proceeds to criticise the 'staumrel, corky-headed, graceless Gentry' who had come to rule (and ruin) the country, and describes how the great folk of the past will

curse the time and place
When ye begat the base, degen'rate race![101]

Burns's approach is more even-handed than those of Ramsay and Fergusson. Both bridges are allowed their say, and their argument is ultimately overshadowed by the appearance of spirits of nature, benevolence, courage, learning and peace. Burns thus presents a way to move forward and reconcile the conflicting forces within Scottish society. Nevertheless, 'The Brigs of Ayr' continues along the path laid out by Ramsay and Fergusson, using ghostlike beings to explore the discord between Scotland's independent past and North British present.

Ossian and the Romanticisation of the Highlands

More obviously romanticised depictions of Scottish supernatural traditions also appeared, linked in particular to the Highlands. Perceptions of the Highlands changed significantly over the course of the eighteenth century. The region had traditionally been presented as a dangerous place, peopled by barbarians. In 1535, Peder Svave wrote that 'the wild Scots live in the manner of the Scythians, they are ignorant of the use of bread; when they are hungry they outstrip a stag in swiftness of foot, overtake it and kill it, and so sustain life: they eat the flesh raw, only squeezing out the blood'. The English antiquarian William Camden's 1586 *Britannia* described the Highlanders as wild, warlike,

99 Robert Burns, 'The Brigs of Ayr', in *Poems, Chiefly in the Scottish Dialect* (Edinburgh, 1787), 71. See Mathison, 'Gothic Poetry in Scotland', 35, 42–3.
100 Burns, 'The Brigs of Ayr', in *Poems*, 73, 76, 74.
101 Ibid., 79, 78.

cruel, hateful, and inclined to robbery and theft.[102] This stereotype was reinforced in eighteenth-century England by the Jacobite uprisings. However, after the 1745 uprising had been quelled, and the Highlanders had ceased to pose a genuine threat to British stability, their warlike qualities came to be perceived in a more positive light. A character of Smollett's explained:

> They greatly excel the Lowlanders in all the exercises that require agility; they are incredibly abstemious, and patient of hunger and fatigue; so steeled against the weather, that in travelling, even when the ground is covered with snow, they never look for a house, or any other shelter but their plaid, in which they wrap themselves up, and go to sleep under the cope of heaven. Such people, in quality of soldiers, must be invincible,[103]

From the start of the Seven Years' War in 1756 to the end of the Napoleonic Wars, more than 48,300 men were recruited from the Highlands and Islands to serve in regiments of the British army.[104] In 1766, William Pitt defended the recruitment of the 'hardy and intrepid race of men' from 'the mountains of the north'. The Highland soldier-hero became a recognised trope, enhanced by the emerging Enlightenment conception of the 'noble savage'.[105]

Furthermore, as roads were improved, tourism to the Highlands expanded. The 1780s and 1790s in particular saw burgeoning numbers of visitors, partly inspired by Samuel Johnson's account of his 1775 tour of the western isles.[106] There was a growing aesthetic appreciation for the region. Edmund Burt, visiting in the 1720s, was unimpressed by the landscape. It was all 'horrid Gloom', 'a dismal gloomy Brown, drawing upon a dirty Purple'; the mountains were 'monstrous Excrescencies'. The scenery, he asserted, was 'most of all disagreeable, when the Heath is in Bloom'.[107] Daniel Defoe, visiting Drumlanrig in the mid-1720s, called the mountains 'hideous'.[108] This was not limited to Englishmen: John Clerk of Penicuik toured northern Scotland in 1739, and wrote: 'From Dalwhinny, about 10 or 12 miles we came to Riven in Badenoch. By the way all along from the Blair to this place I cou'd see nothing but a barbarous tract of mountains on both hands and scarse a stalk of grass to be seen.'[109] However, by the later eighteenth century the landscape was commonly thought to be romantic and

102 Svave is quoted and Camden discussed in Rackwitz, *Travels to Terra Incognita*, 94, 52–4.

103 Tobias Smollett, *The Expedition of Humphry Clinker*, 2 vols (Dublin, 1771), vol. 2, 105.

104 Robert Clyde, *From Rebel to Hero: The Image of the Highlander, 1745–1830* (East Linton, 1995), 150.

105 Kenneth McNeil, *Scotland, Britain, Empire: Writing the Highlands, 1760–1860* (Columbus, 2007), 86, 27. See also Peter Womack, *Improvement and Romance: Constructing the Myth of the Highlands* (Basingstoke, 1988), ch. 2; Clyde, *From Rebel to Hero*, ch. 6.

106 Rackwitz, *Travels to Terra Incognita*, 146–248, esp. 192.

107 Edmund Burt, *Letters from a Gentleman in the North of Scotland*, 2 vols (London, 1754), vol. 2, letter 15, pp. 11, 10, 14.

108 Daniel Defoe, *A Tour Through the Whole Island of Great Britain*, ed. P. N. Furbank, W. R. Owens, and A. J. Coulson (New Haven, 1991), 323.

109 Quoted in Rackwitz, *Travels to Terra Incognita*, 235.

awe-inspiring. Thomas Pennant, travelling in 1769, declared that 'the pass into the *Highlands* is awefully magnificent', and described the mountains as a 'scene of horrible grandeur'.[110] Walter Scott is reported to have said that 'if I did not see the heather at least once a-year, *I think I should die!*'[111] This coincided with the development of landscape painting in Scotland, which resulted in the circulation of sublime Highland scenes.[112]

Literary works played an important role in developing these conceptions of the Highlands. One English figure is worth mentioning first of all. William Collins's *An Ode on the Popular Superstitions of the Highlands of Scotland* (written 1749–50, first published 1788) was an important forerunner in romantic depictions of the Highlands – or 'Fancy's land', to use Collins's terminology. The ghosts Collins presents are theatrical, poignant figures. The 'mournful sprite' of a drowned sailor returns to his wife while she sleeps, 'shiv'ring cold' and speaking in 'piteous accents'. He beseeches her to pursue her 'daily toils' as before, and think of him no more. Collins also describes how second sighted people see 'the gliding ghosts unbodied [trooping]' over the 'wat'ry strath or quaggy moss'.[113] Peter Womack points out that Collins drew his material from Martin Martin's account of Highland folklore, but dramatised it. Second sight apparitions were converted into ghosts, creating a 'Hebrides of melancholy and fear strikingly unlike Martin's'.[114] Collins's approach to the Highlands was unusual at the time he was writing, but just a few decades later (when the poem was published) his romanticised vision was in keeping with the popular view of the region.

This was largely because of the influence of the best known romantic work of eighteenth-century Scotland, James Macpherson's *Ossian* poetry. Macpherson (1736–96) composed and compiled this cycle of epic poetry with reference to Irish mythology and Scottish Gaelic ballads.[115] He claimed that the poems were the work of the ancient bard Ossian, translated from the Gaelic, and that they represented the rediscovery of a forgotten Celtic past. Publication began in 1760; a collected edition followed in 1765; and the world of Ossian became famous throughout Europe.[116] This world is an ethereal place, on the brink of dissolution. Ossian is a narrator in his old age, blind, and the last survivor of his race. Ghosts blend easily into the atmosphere, and

110 Thomas Pennant, *A Tour in Scotland 1769* (Chester, 1771), 74, 98.

111 From an 1817 letter by Washington Irving, given in John Gibson Lockhart, *Memoirs of the Life of Sir Walter Scott*, 2nd edn, 10 vols (Edinburgh, 1839), vol. 5, 249.

112 James L. Caw, *Scottish Painting Past and Present, 1620–1908* (Edinburgh, 1908), 136–62, esp. 138; Charles W. J. Withers, *Geography, Science and National Identity: Scotland Since 1520* (Cambridge, 2001), 153.

113 William Collins, *An Ode on the Popular Superstitions of the Highlands of Scotland* (London, 1788), v. 2, p. 10; v. 8, pp. 17–18; v. 4, p. 12.

114 Womack, *Improvement and Romance*, 91–2.

115 See Derick S. Thomson, *The Gaelic Sources of Macpherson's Ossian* (Edinburgh, 1952); Donald E. Meek, 'The Gaelic Ballads of Scotland: Creativity and Adaptation', in Howard Gaskill (ed.), *Ossian Revisited* (Edinburgh, 1991), 19–48.

116 Duncan, 'Walter Scott, James Hogg and Scottish Gothic', 72.

are featured frequently within the poetry. These ghosts follow classical Greek and Roman models, and are not terrifying or uncanny in the gothic fashion.[117] They are usually the ghosts of past heroes, a natural part of their world and venerated by their descendants. They come clad in armour and bearing the wounds of battle. Nevertheless, they tend to be incorporeal. One is seen with 'the stars dim-[twinkling] through his form'. Another explains: 'My ghost, O Connal, is on my native hills; but my corse is on the sands of Ullin.'[118] They are also poignant figures: pale and enfeebled, sorrowful, with weak voices and 'airy limbs'.[119] Their wounds and armour serve rather to accentuate their heroic, tragic elements than to tie them to their earthly selves. The chief of Erin, seeing an insubstantial ghost with a weak arm, cries: 'How art though changed, chief of Lara! ... Thou art not Calmar's ghost ... his arm was like the thunder of heaven.'[120]

Macpherson's ghosts are sometimes purely atmospheric figures; they 'fly on clouds and ride on winds'.[121] However, ghosts are also allowed an active role. They fight, foretell the future, and spur the living on to action. Fingal battles the spirit of Loda; his sword 'winds through the gloomy ghost', and 'the form [falls] shapeless into the air, like a column of smoke'.[122] In another work of Macpherson's a ghost returns to press his son into avenging his death:

> Before my eyes a ghastly vision stood;
> A mangled man, his bosom stain'd with blood!
> ...
> He hands my sword, emits a feeble groan,
> And weakly says, 'revenge me, O my son!'[123]

In a sense, this echoes the role of late-seventeenth- and early-eighteenth-century ghosts, who might similarly return to ensure that their murderers were brought

[117] On classical influences see Hugh Blair, *A Critical Dissertation on the Poems of Ossian* (London, 1763), 33–8; Jeremy M. Downes, *Recursive Desire: Rereading Epic Tradition* (Tuscaloosa, 2014), 140–1; Josef Bysveen, *Epic Tradition and Innovation in James Macpherson's Fingal* (Uppsala, 1982), 120–5; Fiona J. Stafford, *The Sublime Savage: James Macpherson and the Poems of Ossian* (Edinburgh, 1988), 138–9. For a slightly different viewpoint see Fiona J. Stafford, '"Dangerous Success": Ossian, Wordsworth, and English Romantic Literature', in Howard Gaskill (ed.), *Ossian Revisited* (Edinburgh, 1991), 63, which emphasises the frightening aspects of the Ossianic ghosts.

[118] James Macpherson, 'Fingal, an Ancient Epic Poem', in *The Works of Ossian, the Son of Fingal*, 2 vols (London, 1765), vol. 1, bk. 2, 33.

[119] Ibid., bk. 2, 34, bk. 4, 74; James Macpherson, 'The War of Caros: A Poem', in *The Works of Ossian, the Son of Fingal*, 2 vols (London, 1765), vol. 1, 144.

[120] James Macpherson, 'The Death of Cuchullin: A Poem', in *The Works of Ossian, the Son of Fingal*, 2 vols (London, 1765), vol. 1, 211–12.

[121] Macpherson, 'Fingal', in *Works of Ossian*, vol. 1, bk. 2, 35.

[122] James Macpherson, 'Carric-Thura, a Poem', in *The Works of Ossian, the Son of Fingal*, 2 vols (London, 1765), vol. 1, 279.

[123] James Macpherson, *The Highlander: A Poem* (Edinburgh, 1758), canto 5, 64–5.

to justice. Macpherson's ghosts did not operate within a religious framework, however, and could not be read as a tool of God's providential justice. Bonds of affection drew ghosts back to their kin, sentimentalising the scenes while also underlining the importance of clan networks within Highland society.[124] Given their great popularity, the poems of Ossian probably contributed more than any other Scottish work to the development of the notion of the ghost as a romantic literary device, divorced from religious significance.

As with the ghosts of Ramsay, Fergusson and Burns, Macpherson's ghosts can be read politically, in this case as a response to the Jacobite defeats. Macpherson was himself a Highlander, and his clan was involved in the 1745 uprising.[125] After the failure of the uprising, the government passed measures designed to subdue the Highlanders. Road building and mapping projects made the area more accessible, government garrisons were built, and more English-speaking schools were founded. The power of clan chiefs was limited, and traditional dress was banned.[126] The poems of Ossian hearken back to a romantic Celtic past (albeit a largely fabricated one), reinforcing Gaelic identity in the face of governmental suppression. Macpherson gave his work a patriotic message from the outset by dedicating it to John Stuart, Earl of Bute, the first Scottish prime minister. Stuart was regarded by some as a Highlander, despite having been born in Edinburgh and educated in England.[127] Furthermore, within Ossian's world there is a pervading sense that something beautiful has been left behind. Ossian is haunted by the past, by the memories of his dead kinsfolk.[128] The theme of degeneration reappears frequently, exemplified in the ghost who has eyes 'like two decaying flames'. Ghosts take an interest in the present; they are said to rest in caves together and talk of mortal men.[129] However, they stand above and apart from humans, the closest thing to the sublime that can be found in Ossian's world.[130] They represent a greater wisdom, the authority of age and of a venerable past, which is nevertheless

[124] Bysveen, *Epic Tradition*, 128.

[125] See Derick S. Thomson, 'Macpherson, James (1736–1796)', *Oxford DNB* (Oxford University Press, 2004), http://www.oxforddnb.com/view/article/17728, accessed 1 Feb. 2018; Stafford, *Sublime Savage*; Murray G. H. Pittock, *The Invention of Scotland: The Stuart Myth and the Scottish Identity, 1638 to the Present* (London, 1991), 73–9.

[126] Withers, *Geography, Science and National Identity*, 150; Bruce Lenman, *The Jacobite Risings in Britain, 1689–1746* (Dalkeith, 1980), 277–9; T. M. Devine, *Clanship to Crofter's War: The Social Transformation of the Scottish Highlands* (Manchester, 1994), 29, 113–14; Geoffrey Plank, *Rebellion and Savagery: The Jacobite Rising of 1745 and the British Empire* (Philadelphia, 2005), 106–7.

[127] J. A. Lovat-Fraser, *John Stuart, Earl of Bute* (Cambridge, 1912), 3; see Leith Davis, *Acts of Union: Scotland and the Literary Negotiation of the British Nation, 1707–1830* (Stanford, 1998), 75–81.

[128] Duncan, 'Walter Scott, James Hogg and Scottish Gothic', 125.

[129] Macpherson, 'Fingal', in *Works of Ossian*, bk. 2, 32, 35.

[130] See Bysveen, *Epic Tradition*, ch. 6; JoEllen M. DeLucia, '"Tales of Other Times": Scotland's Past and Women's Future in Eighteenth-Century British Writing' (Indiana University Ph.D. thesis, 2007), 75; Stafford, *Sublime Savage*, 156.

powerless to alter the sorry path of the future. The *Ossian* poetry draws on the melancholic themes we have seen in poetry such as Blair's, and diverts them into a mourning for the loss of a greater Scotland.

The Ghosts of Walter Scott and James Hogg

The Ossianic ghosts were majestic but chimerical, like the vision of Scottish history underlying the poetry. In the nineteenth century the revels ended, and Macpherson's spirits melted into air. With Scott at their forefront, early-nineteenth-century antiquarians moved to distance themselves from Macpherson's fabricated Celtic past – a process Colin Kidd has described as 'national demythologising'.[131] Nevertheless, there remained a drive to carve out a distinctive Scottish identity. War with France, agricultural and industrial revolutions and an increasingly integrated political culture brought Scotland and England closer together in the early nineteenth century, exacerbating fears that Scotland would be swallowed up altogether.[132] John Sinclair, compiler of the first Statistical Account of Scotland (1791–9), explained that the Scots 'have reason to be proud of the name of Britons', but nonetheless 'ought not to relinquish on that account, all remembrance of characteristic dress, language, music, or customs of their ancestors. If in these respects they become totally assimilated to the English, Scotland becomes completely confounded in England'.[133] While grand national myths were rejected, the romanticisation of folk belief and Highland traditions intensified. The latter was best exemplified by George IV's 1822 visit, masterminded by Sir Walter Scott, which saw Lowlanders – and George himself – donning kilts. In this context, ghosts remained significant: they could play the role of folkloric curiosities just as they could become ancient representatives of a great bygone Scotland. This was seen most clearly in the development of antiquarian studies. Before we move away from the realm of fiction, however, it is worth considering the ghosts of Walter Scott (1771–1832) and James Hogg (1770–1835). Hogg and Scott had different approaches to ghosts, but both demonstrate how the project of nation-building had changed by the nineteenth century.[134]

Scott's 'The Tapestried Chamber' (1829) has been described as the 'first modern British ghost story'.[135] It is an expanded version of a story that appeared

131 Colin Kidd, *Subverting Scotland's Past: Scottish Whig Historians and the Creation of an Anglo-British Identity, 1689–1830* (Cambridge, 1993), 257.

132 Michael Lynch, *Scotland: A New History* (London, 1992), 357–9; Womack, *Improvement and Romance*, 145; T. M. Devine, *The Scottish Nation, 1700–2007* (London, 2006), 244–5; Kidd, *Subverting Scotland's Past*, 273–5.

133 Quoted in McNeil, *Scotland, Britain, Empire*, 2.

134 See also Timothy C. Baker, 'The Ghost Story in Scotland', in Scott Brewster and Luke Thurston (eds), *The Routledge Handbook to the Ghost Story* (Abingdon, 2018), 186–90.

135 Roger Clarke, *A Natural History of Ghosts* (London, 2012), 308. See Susan Owens, *The Ghost: A Cultural History* (London, 2017), 173–4, for an interesting analysis.

in *Blackwood's* in 1818, attributed to 'A. B.'. A general stays in a room that was once witness to incest and 'unnatural murder'. He is disturbed in the night by a monstrous spectre: 'Upon a face which wore the fixed features of a corpse, were imprinted the traces of the vilest and most hideous passions which had animated her while she lived. The body of some atrocious criminal seemed to have been given up from the grave.'[136] This ghost is reminiscent of the medieval revenant. By contrast, the wraith of Alice in *The Bride of Lammermoor* (1819) is an ethereal figure, who leaves the grass untrodden as she passes.[137] The mysterious White Lady in *The Monastery* (1820) is similarly incorporeal, being able to melt into the air. She appears as a beautiful woman 'with a voice of ineffable sweetness'. Unlike the ghost in 'The Tapestried Chamber' or Alice's wraith, the White Lady is not identified as a dead person; Scott compares her to a brownie or fairy, and she explains that she is

> Something betwixt heaven and hell–
> Something that neither stood nor fell–[138]

Translucent and clad in white, however, the figure taps into ghost stereotypes. Scott's work demonstrates the interest in aesthetics that was characteristic of the romantic authors when it came to ghosts, but also hints at the diversity of ghost stereotypes in circulation.

While Scott presented two ends of a scale, Hogg went further, also offering everything in between. The ghost in *The Three Perils of Man* (1822) is a sorrowful, noble figure who appears as a gliding white-clad lady, resembling a 'flight o' white mist', a 'streamer o' light' or 'the reflection of a starn in the water'.[139] The ghost in 'The Mysterious Bride' (1830) looks like a normal young woman, clad in a white dress with a green bonnet and veil, and when her enamoured young laird meets her in a dream he finds her to be 'a being of real flesh and blood'. She behaves in a more sinister manner, luring the laird to his death.[140] Another of Hogg's ghosts is 'dressed in dead-clothes; that is, it was wrapt in a coarse white sheet, and had a napkin of the same colour round its head'.[141] Hogg also recognised revenant traditions. A supposed ghost has 'the appearance of a warrior sheathed in steel, but all encrusted in a sheet of blood. His mouth was wide open, and his jaws

136 Walter Scott, 'The Tapestried Chamber', in Frédéric Mansel Reynolds (ed.), *The Keepsake for 1829* (London, 1829), 142, 136. The *Blackwood's* story is [Walter Scott] A. B., 'Story of an Apparition', *Blackwood's Edinburgh Magazine*, Sept. 1818, 705–7.

137 Walter Scott, *The Bride of Lammermoor*, in *Tales of My Landlord*, 4 vols (Edinburgh, 1819), vol. 2, 218–20.

138 Walter Scott, *The Monastery: A Romance*, 3 vols (Edinburgh, 1820), vol. 1, 316.

139 James Hogg, *The Three Perils of Man: Or, War, Women, and Witchcraft*, 3 vols (London, 1822), vol. 1, 256–7. 'Starn' is 'star'.

140 James Hogg, 'The Mysterious Bride', *Blackwood's Edinburgh Magazine*, Dec. 1830, 943–50 (quotation 947).

141 James Hogg, 'The Adventures of Basil Lee', in Ian Duncan (ed.), *Winter Evening Tales* (Edinburgh, 2004), 56.

hanging down upon his breast, while his head seemed to be cleft asunder.'[142] Along similar lines, the ghost in 'Welldean Hall' (1820) returns in his dressing gown, but underneath his 'loins and limbs' are 'sheathed in red hot burning steel, while a corslet of the same glowing metal enclosed his breast and heart'. His face is filled with 'defiance, rage, and torment'.[143]

If Scott and Hogg were adventurous when it came to ghosts' appearances, they were more restrained with respect to broader messages. Their work does not pose the same challenge to Anglo-Scottish relations that can be seen in the poetry of Ramsay or Fergusson. Scott was pro-Union. He romanticised the Jacobite rebellions, but only because they were safely confined to the past. His aim was to furnish a distinctive Scottish identity without challenging the concept of Britishness, a unionist nationalist approach that would become more dominant as the nineteenth century progressed.[144] Like Burns, Scott took an interest in the supernatural primarily as the product of a distinctively Scottish folk tradition. Before introducing the wraith of Alice in *The Bride of Lammermoor*, he explained: 'We are bound to tell the tale as we have received it; and, considering the distance of the time, and propensity of those through whose mouths it has passed to the marvellous, this could not be called a Scottish story, unless it manifested a tinge of Scottish superstition.'[145] Similarly in *The Lay of the Last Minstrel* (1805), Scott consistently gave supernatural stories 'ethnographic validation', tying them back to local beliefs or traditions.[146]

The works of Hogg, meanwhile, lack the 'sense of national grievance' that is usually associated with the romantic national tale (to quote Graham Tulloch), and he was little concerned with contrasting divergent national cultures.[147] His approach to folklore was generally playful. He flirted with gothic themes, but subverted them, mingling the grotesque with the humorous. 'Welldean Hall' is brimming with gothic elements: a virtuous heroine, torn apart from her beloved and pursued by his lascivious brother; a hidden fortune; a ghost, clad in burning steel, terrorising the manor house he used to possess. However, Hogg's depictions of the locals' interactions with the ghost are sardonic, and contain no traces of genuine horror. There is plenty of humour in the butler's explanation of his encounter with the ghost, which ended with him in a

142 Hogg, *Three Perils of Man*, 308.

143 James Hogg, 'Welldean Hall', in Ian Duncan (ed.), *Winter Evening Tales* (Edinburgh, 2004), 453.

144 McNeil, *Scotland, Britain, Empire*, 51–2; Juliet Shields, *Sentimental Literature and Anglo-Scottish Identity, 1745–1820* (Cambridge, 2010), 5–6, ch. 5; Allan I. Macinnes, *Union and Empire: The Making of the United Kingdom in 1707* (Cambridge, 2007), 34–5; Graeme Morton, *Unionist-Nationalism: Governing Urban Scotland, 1830–1860* (East Linton, 1999).

145 Scott, *Bride of Lammermoor*, 217.

146 James Watt, *Contesting the Gothic: Fiction, Genre and Cultural Conflict, 1764–1832* (Cambridge, 1999), 133.

147 Graham Tulloch, 'Hogg and the Novel', in Ian Duncan (ed.), *The Edinburgh Companion to James Hogg* (Edinburgh, 2012), 125.

drunken stupor, such that 'If there had been fifty ghosts, it would have been the same to old Gibby'.[148]

For all his sportiveness, Hogg did not tend to mock his credulous characters. He allowed for subtlety within popular belief systems, having one of his characters explain that

> ye had need to tak care how ye dispute the existence of fairies, brownies, and apparitions ... ye may as weel dispute the gospel o' Sant Matthew. We dinna believe in a' the gomral fantastic bogles an' spirits that fley light headed fock up an down the country, but we believe in a' the apparitions that warn o' death, that save life, an' that discover guilt.[149]

Furthermore, Hogg did not consistently undermine the reality of his supernatural beings. The Brownie of Bodsbeck and the ghost in 'The Bridal of Polmood' both prove to be living men, and as we have seen, *The Private Memoirs and Confessions of a Justified Sinner* leaves scope for an alternative, psychological reading. However, Hogg also presented many stories with genuine supernatural creatures, 'Welldean Hall' included. Indeed, in 'The Mysterious Bride', Hogg complained about the tendency to undermine the reality of the supernatural:

> A great number of people nowadays are beginning broadly to insinuate that there are no such things as ghosts, or spiritual beings visible to mortal sight. Even Sir Walter Scott is turned renegade, and, with his stories made up of half-and-half, like Nathaniel Gow's toddy, is trying to throw cold water on the most certain, though most impalpable, phenomena of human nature. The bodies are daft. Heaven mend their wits.[150]

Hogg may not have had an overtly nationalist agenda, but his depiction of popular belief was laudatory. Compared to their seventeenth-century predecessors, the approaches of Scott and Hogg were depoliticised, but they bolstered ideas about the distinctiveness and importance of Scotland's folk culture.

Folkloric Studies

In the late seventeenth century, and again in the late eighteenth and early nineteenth centuries, there was a surge of interest in antiquarian pursuits. Individuals – usually educated men – collated folk stories, many with an element of supernatural intrigue. In theory, these early generations of

148 Hogg, 'Welldean Hall', 463–4.
149 James Hogg, 'The Wool-Gatherer', in *The Brownie of Bodsbeck, and Other Tales*, 2 vols (Edinburgh, 1818), vol. 2, 140.
150 Hogg, 'Mysterious Bride', 943. Nathaniel Gow was a well-known musician.

folklorists recorded what Linda Dégh has termed a legend – a tale that was believed to be rooted in truth.[151] This should have been a distinct genre from the inventions offered as fiction in magazines or other publications. In practice the barrier often fell down. John Mackay Wilson's *Tales of the Borders* (1834–40) is an example of a series that collected 'historical, traditionary and imaginative' stories, without generally distinguishing between the categories. Walter Scott and James Hogg wove traditional tales into their fictional writing, while the poems of Ossian were fiction masquerading as folklore. So far as possible, however, this section will focus on legends, and the ways in which they were employed.

We have seen that in the late seventeenth and early eighteenth centuries, men such as Robert Wodrow, George Sinclair and Robert Kirk collected supernatural stories for religious and scientific reasons. Another driving force was blossoming interest in geography. As Charles Withers notes, the last two decades or so of the seventeenth century saw a significant expansion of geographical knowledge in Scotland. The subject was increasingly taught in universities, and Sinclair himself was licensed to teach geography publicly in 1670. In 1682, the physician and antiquary Robert Sibbald was appointed Geographer Royal, and the mathematician John Adair was commissioned to prepare maps and chorography by an act of parliament passed in 1686.[152] Geographical knowledge was linked to national pride. In 1728, the schoolmaster and surveyor George Mark decried the inaccuracies in maps of the shires of Lothian, Tweeddale and Clydesdale, exclaiming:

> 'Tis truly strange why our Scottish Nobility and Gentry, who are so universally esteemed for their learning, Curiousity and Affection for their Country, should suffer an Omission of this Nature! Can they, whom their Neighbours as it were by way of Distinction call National, contentedly see themselves outdone by those Neighbours, in what so much concerns the Honour of their Nation?[153]

This interest in learning about the nation also drove folkloric research. It is no coincidence that it was around this time – in the 1690s – that Scotland made its most significant attempt to establish an overseas colony, with an ultimately disastrous expedition into the Isthmus of Panama (the Darien scheme). There was something imperialist about the investigation of Highland beliefs in particular; eighteenth-century movements to subdue the Highlands focused partly on exploring and describing the area. Furthermore, supernatural stories were tied to national pride, as they demonstrated God's interest in Scotland. We can recall that a key motivation for Wodrow in compiling *Analecta* was his

151 Linda Dégh, *Legend and Belief: Dialectics of a Folklore Genre* (Bloomington, 2001), ch. 2.
152 Withers, *Geography, Science and National Identity*, ch. 3; Christopher Fleet et al., *Scotland: Mapping the Nation* (Edinburgh, 2011), ch. 3.
153 Quoted in Withers, *Geography, Science and National Identity*, 149.

desire to show that 'in poor Scotland, the Lord, since the Reformation, hath manifested himself, and the secret of his covenant, to his servants and people, as much as any where since the primitive times'.[154]

Nevertheless, religion remained the primary motivator for most of the seventeenth- and early-eighteenth-century folklorists, and they recorded material selectively according to their theological goals. An exception was Martin Martin, who conducted his investigations in the 1690s and published his *Description of the Western Islands of Scotland* in 1703. Spurred on by the enquiries of the Royal Society in England, his primary intention was to record information about a little-known community, rather than to collect a specific subset of stories for theological purposes.[155] Martin's approach was unusual at the time, but as the eighteenth century progressed it became more common. Ballads and popular songs were an early area of interest. Allan Ramsay's *Tea-Table Miscellany* (1724–7) was an anthology that brought together 'A Collection of Choice Songs Scots and English'. From the 1760s, a large number of ballad collections were printed, and Walter Scott took up the baton with *Minstrelsy of the Scottish Border* (1802–3).[156] Thereafter, the first few decades of the nineteenth century saw a shift away from the exclusive focus on the ballad. Increasingly, the 'tale' came to be valued as a subject for antiquarian study. Tim Killick suggests that this was linked to Scott's shift from poetry to the novel. By the 1820s, it was also influenced by the short fiction popularised by *Blackwood's*. A strong market for book-length collections of short fiction had emerged by the 1820s, and supernatural stories were a common feature.[157] Local legends also began to draw fresh attention. The 1820s and 1830s in particular saw a great proliferation of works recording traditional stories and customs.[158]

By the nineteenth century there was little drive to use folk beliefs to make religious arguments. Ghosts still returned to seek revenge or right wrongs, and

154 Robert Wodrow, *The Correspondence of the Rev. Robert Wodrow*, ed. Thomas M'Crie, 3 vols (Edinburgh, 1842), vol. 2, 244.

155 See Withers, *Geography, Science and National Identity*, 87–94.

156 Killick, *British Short Fiction*, 122.

157 Ibid., 16, 33, 121–2.

158 For example, Allan Cunningham, *Traditional Tales of the English and Scottish Peasantry*, 2 vols (London, 1822); Robert Chambers, *Traditions of Edinburgh* (Edinburgh, 1824); Robert Chambers, *The Book of Days, A Miscellany of Popular Antiquities*, 2 vols (London, 1863–4); Robert Chambers, *The Picture of Scotland*, 2 vols (Edinburgh, 1827); William Grant Stewart, *The Popular Superstitions and Festive Amusements of the Highlanders of Scotland* (Edinburgh, 1823); Hugh Miller, *Scenes and Legends of the North of Scotland, or The Traditional History of Cromarty* (Edinburgh, 1835); John Graham Dalyell, *The Darker Superstitions of Scotland: Illustrated from History and Practice* (Edinburgh, 1834); John Wilson, *Lights and Shadows of Scottish Life* (Edinburgh, 1822); Andrew Picken, *Tales and Sketches of the West of Scotland* (Glasgow, 1824); James Denniston, *Legends of Galloway: Being a Series of Traditions, Illustrative of Its Ancient History, Customs, Manners, and Superstitions* (Edinburgh, 1825); John MacCulloch, *The Highlands and Western Isles of Scotland*, 4 vols (London, 1824).

several authors noted their value as moral safeguards when 'the devotional sentiment ... is either undeveloped or misdirected'.[159] However, there was no attempt on the part of the nineteenth-century folklorists to manipulate their readers into believing the ghosts' messages. The authors kept a sceptical distance, and there was a clear assumption that the reader would do the same. A more significant agenda was the project of nation-building. Despite the fact that the folkloric investigations of the late seventeenth and early eighteenth centuries corresponded with a surging interest in geography, it is notable that the nineteenth-century accounts conveyed a much stronger sense of place. Wodrow's and Sinclair's stories were presented as proof of supernatural phenomena rather than as reflections on the specific locales from which they originated, and their ghosts generally haunted people rather than places. The folklore of the early nineteenth century was much more likely to be associated with particular geographical locations. Even the ghosts themselves were often rooted to, and defined through, aspects of the scenery: Anne MacVicar Grant described the 'mountain ghosts', while Hugh Miller focused on the 'churchyard ghost'.[160] David Stewart of Garth noted how stories were tied to the Highland landscape, writing:

> we still meet with Highlanders who can give a connected, and minutely accurate detail of the history, genealogy, feuds, and battles of all the tribes and families in every district, or glen, for many miles round, and for a period of several hundred years; illustrating their details by a reference to every remarkable stone, cairn, tree, or stream, within the district; connecting with each some kindred story of a fairy or ghost, or the death of some person who perished in the snow, by any sudden disaster, or by some accidental rencounter;[161]

This process happened in part because gothic literature had popularised visions of haunted castles and churchyards (the former, in particular, do not seem to have been particularly common before the latter half of the eighteenth century). However, it is also evidence of how the practice of nation-building through culture and folklore had evolved. The result was that ghosts were associated more strongly both with their local communities, and with Scottish culture more broadly.

Geography also played an increasingly important role in shaping visions of ghosts. This is particularly evident in the case of the Highlands. Highland

[159] Hugh Miller, *Scenes and Legends of the North of Scotland; Or, The Traditional History of Cromarty*, 2nd edn (London, 1850), 353.

[160] Anne MacVicar Grant, *Essays on the Superstitions of the Highlanders of Scotland*, 2 vols (London, 1811), vol. 1, 224–5; Miller, *Scenes and Legends*, 2nd edn, 353.

[161] David Stewart, *Sketches of the Character, Manners, and Present State of the Highlanders of Scotland*, 2 vols (Edinburgh, 1822), vol. 1, 93. On the use of the supernatural in mnemomic mapping, see Karl Bell, *The Magical Imagination: Magic and Modernity in Urban England, 1780–1914* (Cambridge, 2012), ch. 6.

ghosts were presented as being ancient and warlike – or, at least, as having been so in the past. William Grant Stewart wrote: 'Unlike the present puny, green, worm-eaten effigies that now-a-days stalk about our premises, and, like the cameleon, feed upon the air, the ancient race of Highland ghosts were a set of stout, lusty, sociable ghosts.' They were usually corporeal. A ghost would 'do as much justice to a bicker of Highland crowdie as his earthly contemporaries', and was supposed to be 'material in its nature, quite susceptible of mortal pain, and liable to death or annihilation from the weapons of man'.[162] John MacCulloch presented a more complicated picture, but still insisted on elements of corporeality:

> Sometimes they seem pure spirit; at others, they have corporeal properties, or they unite the spiritual and the corporeal essences in one. They are formed of thin air, and disappear in smoke; on many more authorities than those of Ossian and Macpherson. If they are also immortal, as Ghosts ought to be, they sometimes die and are buried. They may also be killed. They are hard, because they pull a man's hair and box his ears; and heavy, because they must sometimes be lifted from the ground; when they resist, being tangible and ponderable.[163]

Although some ghosts were said to be 'moral, rational and prudent', most were 'ill-natured and cruel', and liked to pick fights with travellers:

> The warlike bogle of the last century carried about with him flails, cudgels, and such other pithy weapons as were suitable to the spirit of the times, and on his meeting with a human adventurer who had no objection to become his antagonist, his choice of weapons was left with the latter.[164]

These ghosts were similar to revenants, but while they had bodies and could eat, drink and fight, they were not usually depicted as actual corpses risen from graves. They also tended to appear over a long time-span, perhaps centuries. In contrast, revenants usually rose soon after death, when vital forces were thought to remain in the body, and rarely visited over an extended period of time. The influence of the *Ossian* poetry on this vision of the ghost is clear. As we shall see in the next chapter, it is questionable whether warlike Highland ghosts were part of Gaelic culture at all before Macpherson popularised the idea. Second sight apparitions seem to have been significantly more common than ghosts before authors began to transform the former into the latter. As with other aspects of the romanticisation of the Highlands, accurately reflecting tradition was not a great priority.

In a discussion of the invention of tradition, Hugh Trevor-Roper suggests that 'the whole history of Scotland has been coloured by myth', and that 'myth, in Scotland, is never driven out by reality, or by reason, but lingers on until

162 Stewart, *Popular Superstitions*, 5, 12.
163 MacCulloch, *Highlands and Western Isles*, vol. 4, 335.
164 Grant, *Essays on the Superstitions*, vol. 1, 225; Stewart, *Popular Superstitions*, 6, 22.

another myth has been discovered, or elaborated, to replace it'.[165] Certainly, Macpherson's vision of the Gaelic past was as mythical as his ghosts, and the nineteenth-century image of Highland culture was similarly idealised. For Colin Kidd, the rejection of the Ossianic origin stories ended the possibility of true Scottish Gaelic patriotism. The 'kitsch Gaelic identity' that emerged instead was 'a tame accessory of British unionism and imperialism, and did nothing to restore to Scots a powerful ethno-cultural identity'.[166] This argument is reinforced by the relative harmlessness of the ghost stories recorded by the early-nineteenth-century antiquarians. The ghosts were neither the subversive figures of eighteenth-century poetry, nor representatives of a noble Celtic past. Highland spectres were quaint, charming relics of the now-pacified region. The nineteenth-century romantic project, in the most unsympathetic reading, was no more than an imperialist process of cultural appropriation and rewriting that coincided with the genuine Highland way of life being brutally dismantled in the name of 'Improvement'.[167]

This criticism is both valid and important. Nevertheless, to dismiss the romantics' nation-building as either inconsequential, or as a purely destructive process, is to ignore the very real power of myth. An identity built on stories is not necessarily any less meaningful than an identity built on historical evidence and charts of lineage. Politically, the project of building Scottish identity ran aground in the early nineteenth century. When nationalism became a force in Scotland, it was within the context of union.[168] This period did, however, see the development of a specifically Scottish cultural identity. The legends created and relayed by bards were a valid way of maintaining national distinctiveness within an imperial framework, even when they were recognised to be largely fictional.[169] Ghosts were only one element of these legends, and most Scots probably associated them with local, rather than national, identity. Moreover, not all of the antiquarians were concerned with the Scottishness of the ghosts they discussed: MacCulloch declared that the Highlanders did not have 'any peculiar claims on their own tales and superstitions', but that similar beliefs could be found throughout Europe.[170] Nevertheless, Macpherson had popularised a vision of a misty, haunted Scottish landscape, and the nineteenth-century antiquarian movement tended to reinforce this reputation. Anne MacVicar Grant correlated the

165 Hugh Trevor-Roper, *The Invention of Scotland: Myth and History* (New Haven, 2008), xx.

166 Colin Kidd, 'Gaelic Antiquity and National Identity in Enlightenment Ireland and Scotland', *English Historical Review* 109 (1994), 1214.

167 Clyde, *From Rebel to Hero*, ch. 2; Devine, *Scottish Nation*, 244; Evan Gottlieb, *Feeling British: Sympathy and National Identity in Scottish and English Writing, 1707–1832* (Lewisburg [Pa.], 2007), 162; McNeil, *Scotland, Britain, Empire*, 14–15.

168 See Morton, *Unionist-Nationalism*.

169 Trumpener, *Bardic Nationalism*. See the preface for a summary of this argument.

170 MacCulloch, *Highlands and Western Isles*, vol. 4, 323.

supposed superstitious imaginations of the Highlanders with the wildness of the scenery.[171] William Grant Stewart opened his account of Highland ghosts by situating them within a national framework: 'ghosts have been, at all times, a plentiful commodity among the hills of Caledonia.'[172] MacCulloch, too, owned that 'All the world has heard of Highland Ghosts and Superstitions'.[173] Ghosts had become a detail in a poetic conception of Scotland, marketed both abroad and within the country itself.

Belief

What do gothic and romantic ghosts suggest about levels of belief? The most obvious conclusion is that ghosts were popular, but they were not generally taken to be objective realities. Gothic and romantic authors did not offer ghosts up as real specimens, but as a shorthand into a certain world, in which the reader was expected to suspend his or her disbelief. As we have seen, the psychologising of ghosts was common. There was discussion of dreams, trances, guilty consciences, the power of imagination and 'the glance of fancy's fearful eyes'.[174] Ghosts were acknowledged to be the preserve of the 'wrinkled Grandam' and 'ancient gossips', or the

> timorous school-boy, madly fear'd
> By many a rueful story often heard,[175]

When Alexander MacDonald's *Vimonda* was first performed in 1787, an epilogue was added that made the triumphant declaration:

> Now, thank our stars! the childish creed is lost,
> That gave such mighty influence to a ghost.[176]

The nineteenth-century folklorists also maintained a sceptical distance. Whereas Wodrow, Sinclair and Kirk had sympathy for the stories they recorded, and Martin was a believer in second sight, their nineteenth-century counterparts saw the stories as mere curiosities. William Grant Stewart drew clear lines between his storytellers and his readers:

[171] Grant, *Essays on the Superstitions*, vol. 1, 4, 256.
[172] Stewart, *Popular Superstitions*, 4.
[173] MacCulloch, *Highlands and Western Isles*, vol. 4, 320.
[174] John Copland, *Saint Andrews: Or, A Sentimental Evening Walk near the Ruins of That Ancient City* (Edinburgh, 1776), 38.
[175] Ibid., 39.
[176] Mr MacKenzie, 'Epilogue to Vimonda', *Universal Magazine*, Sept. 1787, 155.

> Nothing can appear more surprising to the refined reader, than that any human being, possessing the rational faculties of human nature, could for a moment entertain a notion so preposterous, as that a ghost, which conveys the idea of an immortal spirit, could be killed, or rather annihilated, by an arrow, dirk, or sixpence. It was, however, the opinion of the darker ages, that such an exploit as killing a ghost was perfectly practicable ... Such an opinion is repeatedly expressed in several passages of the Poems of Ossian, and in the doctrine of the *Seanachy*, down to the present day.[177]

By 1822, the poet and author Allan Cunningham had one of his characters complain that, whereas once tales and ballads of ghosts and other creatures 'would have been to one as food and raiment and white money', in modern times 'the wisdom of man so much abounds, that he is pleased with nought; he laughs at ancient beliefs, and calls for ocular proof, and testimony on oath, and the assurance of many witnesses, for all oral or recorded things'.[178] J. Mitchell and John Dickie similarly declared in 1839 that 'The superstition of the existence and re-appearance of ghosts ... [is] now being rapidly chased from the realities of existence, and the thousand miseries which flowed from a belief in unproved and unknown beings, like the mountain mists, are vanishing before the light of the sun of science'.[179]

This picture of scepticism should not be over-emphasised, however. Some of the romantics may have believed in ghosts. The poet James Thomson, who made occasional mentions of ghosts, was said to be afraid of them (a story would later circulate that his father was killed while trying to exorcise a ghost).[180] Scott adopted a sceptical stance in *Letters on Demonology and Witchcraft*, and wrote contemptuously of how he had heard Lord Chancellor Thomas Erskine 'tell a cock-and-a-bull story of having seen the ghost of his father's servant, John Burnet, with as much gravity as if he believed every word he was saying'.[181] Nevertheless, he described himself as 'an initiated Ghost-Seer' and 'ghost-raiser' in private correspondence.[182] One article in *Blackwood's* argued:

> It is possible that the greater part of [appearances from the world of spirits] may be merely the delusions of the senses, or unreal images, conjured up by an excited imagination; but the sceptical assertion of the non-existence and non-appearance of the spirits of the departed, is not confirmed by human experience, or by human history ... I think it neither unchristian nor unphilosophical, to entertain a qualified belief in the occasional appearance of beings from the invisible world.[183]

177 Stewart, *Popular Superstitions*, 12. A 'Seanachy' was an antiquarian or storyteller.

178 Cunningham, *Traditional Tales*, vol. 2, 45.

179 J. Mitchell and John Dickie, *The Philosophy of Witchcraft* (Paisley, 1839), 355.

180 James Sambrook, *James Thomson, 1700–1748: A Life* (Oxford, 1991), 10–11.

181 Quoted in Lockhart, *Memoirs of the Life of Sir Walter Scott*, vol. 9, 318.

182 Fiona Robertson, *Legitimate Histories: Scott, Gothic, and the Authorities of Fiction* (Oxford, 1994), 54; Michael Gamer, 'Gothic Fictions and Romantic Writing in Britain', in Jerrold E. Hogle (ed.), *The Cambridge Companion to Gothic Fiction* (Cambridge, 2002), 92.

183 'The Voyages and Travels of Columbus Secundus', *Blackwood's Edinburgh Magazine*, Nov. 1821, 398.

Another *Blackwood's* contributor noted that 'Ghosts … in spite of all that philosophy can do, have taken such a place in the imaginations, and, indeed, in the hearts of men, that their total banishment from thence must for ever remain an impossibility'.[184] Joanna Baillie similarly declared that the fear of ghosts 'is so universal and inherent in our nature, that it can never be eradicated from the mind, let the progress of reason or philosophy be what it may'.[185] Numerous authors insisted that everybody felt a shudder when walking through a dark graveyard. One writer explained that

> truly and emphatically may it be said, that the stout man who is so ingenious as to contrive stories of apparitions when sitting in a large company round the fireside, feels a little compunction, as well as palpitation, when he comes to reflect, in the glooms of solitude, on the sportability of his imagination.[186]

In notes made on his life, James Boswell (1740–95) recalls that as a young man he was 'terribly afraid of ghosts'. It was a fear he overcame 'not by reasoning about it', but 'by a habit of not thinking'.[187] When ghosts were such a well-established trope, they could cross the boundaries between fiction and reality, even for those inclined towards scepticism. Travelling through Scotland in 1784, the American architect William Thornton saw a vision of an old man with white hair in a floating white drapery, and promptly exclaimed: 'It is Ossian! ... It is that divine poet himself.'[188]

According to one common standpoint, it did not much matter whether or not ghosts existed, as they had a significant role in society regardless. Their value within literature and poetry was underlined: Scott noted that 'a supernatural tale is in most cases received as an agreeable mode of amusing society, and he would be rather accounted a sturdy moralist than an entertaining companion who should employ himself in assailing its credibility'.[189] The *Blackwood's* article on 'qualified belief' continued:

> But even allowing the existence and appearance of ghosts, spirits and fairies of every description to be questionable, their use in Poetry and Romance, and their higher moral purpose in deterring from crime those who are not to be restrained by other considerations, render a belief in their agency a desirable part of the code of faith among civilized nations.

[184] 'Devil's Elixir', 56.
[185] Baillie, 'To the Reader', in *Series of Plays*, vol. 3, iv.
[186] 'History of Mrs. Wells', in *The Asylum or Weekly Miscellany*, 3 vols (Glasgow, 1795–6), vol. 1, 204. See also Mitchell and Dickie, *Philosophy of Witchcraft*, 351.
[187] Quoted in Frederick A. Pottle, *James Boswell: The Earlier Years, 1740–1769* (New York, 1966), 16.
[188] Barthélemy Faujas de Saint-Fond, *A Journey through England and Scotland to the Hebrides in 1784*, ed. and trans. Archibald Geikie, 2 vols (Glasgow, 1907), vol. 1, 311. On this theme see Handley, *Visions of an Unseen World*, 181; Womack, *Improvement and Romance*, 110.
[189] Walter Scott, *Letters on Demonology and Witchcraft* (London, 1830), letter 10, 356.

It was said that there was no topic 'upon which, in all classes, talkers are so little apt to tire', whether or not these talkers actually believed in spectres.[190] One author wrote that he had, in effect, chosen to believe in ghosts. He owned that it might be a positive thing to feel no fear in a mysterious house or a graveyard. However, just as Orra found a joy in fear, this writer extolled the undertones of pleasure that accompanied supernatural terror, and 'the more exalted sense which a lurking tendency to superstitious apprehension adds to our relish of the sublime in poetry'.[191]

Although eighteenth-century intellectual culture celebrated the power of 'reason', there was also an emphasis on the importance of feelings. Moderate and orthodox clergymen were in agreement that human sentiments, or passions, were the fount of proper moral behaviour. David Hume declared that 'Reason is, and ought only to be the slave of the passions, and can never pretend to any other office than to serve and obey them'.[192] The 'cult of sensibility' was at its most influential in the latter half of the eighteenth century. This movement viewed intense emotional reactions as a mark of refinement.[193] In his 1763 *Critical Dissertation on the Poems of Ossian*, Hugh Blair praised Ossian's 'exquisite sensibility of heart'. Such was Ossian's emotional 'genius', there 'never were … finer pathetick situations, than what his works present … the heart when uttering its native language never fails, by powerful sympathy, to affect the heart'.[194] Elsewhere, Blair wrote that the man of feeling 'lives in a different sort of world from what the selfish man inhabits'.[195] Similarly, Henry Mackenzie's 1771 *The Man of Feeling* lauded the central character, Harley, whose compassionate nature led him into hardship, but who had 'a soul which did honour to humanity'.[196]

Although Blair and Mackenzie celebrated sensibility in men, the realm of the passions was particularly associated with women. Alexander Gerard, professor of moral philosophy in Aberdeen, explained in 1759: 'Great sensibility of taste is generally accompanied with lively passions. Women

[190] 'Voyages and Travels of Columbus Secundus', 399; 'A Chapter on Goblins', *Blackwood's Edinburgh Magazine*, Dec. 1823, 639.

[191] 'Phantasmagoriana', *Blackwood's Edinburgh Magazine*, Aug. 1818, 590.

[192] David Hume, *A Treatise of Human Nature*, in Mark C. Rooks (ed.), *The Complete Works and Correspondence of David Hume*, electronic edn (Charlottesville, 1995), http://pm.nlx.com/xtf/view?docId=hume/hume.02.xml;chunk.id=div.britphil.v34.1;toc.depth=1;toc.id=div.britphil.v34.1;brand=default, accessed 1 Feb. 2018, bk. 2, pt. 3, sec. 3, 414.

[193] See Janet Todd, *Sensibility: An Introduction* (London, 1986); G. J. Barker-Benfield, *The Culture of Sensibility: Sex and Society in Eighteenth-Century Britain* (Chicago, 1992); Markman Ellis, *The Politics of Sensibility: Race, Gender and Commerce in the Sentimental Novel* (Cambridge, 1996).

[194] Blair, *Critical Dissertation*, 15, 70–1.

[195] Hugh Blair, 'Sermon 32: On Sensibility', in *Sermons*, 5 vols (London, 1777–1801), vol. 3, 34.

[196] Henry Mackenzie, *The Man of Feeling* (London, 1771), 265.

have always been considered as possessing both in a more eminent degree than men.'[197] Within the periodical press, sensibility was described as 'the last finishing, and highest polish of the female character'.[198] As Clare Knowles has argued, sensibility became 'a costume' that fashionable ladies might assume at their convenience – a trend that was mocked in novels such as Charlotte Lennox's 1752 *The Female Quixote*, in which the romantically-minded heroine falls into swoons as a matter of propriety.[199] It was recognised that sensibility might incline people towards superstitious fearfulness. Introducing her *Plays on the Passions*, Baillie declared that 'those ... who possess strong imagination, quick fancy, and keen feeling, are most easily affected by [fear of ghosts]'.[200] Orra – like MacDonald's Vimonda – united delicacy, virtue and depth of feeling with a fear of apparitions. Mary, a heroine of Susan Ferrier's 1818 *Marriage*, is a woman of both sense and sensibility, who declares that 'I love to believe in things supernatural; it seems to connect us more with another world than when everything is seen to proceed in the mere ordinary course of nature'.[201] Just as the *Blackwood's* commentator chose to shiver at the supernatural in order to enjoy tales of terror, elegant ladies – and, to a lesser extent, sensitive gentlemen – might have considered it befitting to be afraid of ghosts.[202]

The question of belief, overall, is very difficult to unpick. The cultural trends in the latter half of the eighteenth century pushed in opposite directions simultaneously. It was a period when ghost believers were ridiculed and satirised as never before. Nevertheless, ghost stories were immensely popular, even among the satirists. There was perhaps an element here of trying to have your cake and eat it, and Anne MacVicar Grant's critique of gothic enthusiasts was scathing:

> These lovers of the awful and terrible, affected the highest contempt for the honest believers who trembled at ghosts they thought real; yet they were no otherwise superior to them, than the puppies who bark at the reflection of the moon in a pond, are to the dogs who, with more originality and better directed energy, bark at the moon herself.[203]

However, like other nineteenth-century folklorists, Grant was guilty of promoting and profiting from ghost stories, even while characterising them as the product of unsophisticated minds. Perhaps the most useful conclusion

[197] Alexander Gerard, *An Essay on Taste* (London, 1759), sec. 6, pt. 3, 200.
[198] 'A Conversation on Female Accomplishments', *Edinburgh Magazine, or Literary Miscellany*, May 1796, 365.
[199] Claire Knowles, *Sensibility and Female Poetic Tradition, 1780–1860: The Legacy of Charlotte Smith* (Farnham, 2009), 184; Charlotte Lennox, *The Female Quixote, or, The Adventures of Arabella*, 2 vols (London, 1752), for example vol. 2, bk. 7, 194.
[200] Baillie, 'To the Reader', in *Series of Plays*, vol. 3, v.
[201] Susan Ferrier, *Marriage: A Novel*, 3 vols (Edinburgh, 1818), vol. 2, 110.
[202] See also Handley, *Visions of an Unseen World*, 199; Owens, *Ghost*, 126.
[203] Grant, *Essays on the Superstitions*, vol. 1, 301.

that can be drawn is that the ontological status of ghosts was not of great importance. For believers and non-believers alike, they had become an established feature of the Scottish cultural landscape.

Conclusion

The development of fiction and folklore in the eighteenth and early nineteenth centuries gave ghosts a new lease of life. With the evolution of gothic themes in literature, ghosts became fashionable as atmospheric devices. Aesthetic features took on a new centrality: ghosts' appearances were explored in poetic terms, and the ghosts themselves were set in a dramatic light. This was further developed through the sublime, sorrowful phantoms of the *Ossian* poetry. By the nineteenth century, the romanticised ghost was a staple of the Scottish literary world, and could assume a rich variety of guises, as can be seen in the work of Scott and Hogg. For all the focus on aesthetics, however, ghosts were more than mere elements of the scenery. As they shed their demonic connotations and became more secularised (at least within the literary world), there was scope for ghosts to be used in new ways, employed on their own terms rather than as servants to God or the Devil. Gothic ghosts played on the natural human fear and fascination regarding death. The death they presented was not a happy passage to the afterlife, nor a natural medical process, but something grotesque and tragic – as well as oddly seductive. The second half of the eighteenth century emphasised psychological explanations for ghosts, but here too gothic writing reintroduced an element of terror, exploring the murky depths of mental illness. Ghosts were potent symbols, whether or not they were objective realities.

Ghosts also contributed to the romantic project of nation-building. They were used to explore the past in relation to the present, and to glorify and mourn a magical, bygone Scotland. The post-Union development of a backwards-looking nationalism, along with the growing importance of the romantic and gothic aesthetics, meant that ghosts were peculiarly well suited to the cultural context of the eighteenth and early nineteenth centuries. Antiquarians increasingly associated ghosts with local areas and features of the Scottish landscape, and a Highland ghost developed that played on the stereotypes of the region. Although not all ghosts were distinctly Scottish, the eighteenth century saw the development of the specifically Scottish ghost as a concept. These ghosts were part of a broader fantasy of a sublime Scotland – they haunted castles in the air. But while Scotland has been criticised as a mere 'romantic object or commodity', this was a process of self-fashioning that happened within the country, in a period when urbanisation and industrialisation were driving sentimental reflection on the past.[204] Ramsay, Smollett and other writers might satirise the ghost belief of the lower classes, and antiquarians might underline the divides between polite and vulgar, Lowland and Highland. Nevertheless, popular belief was valued as proof that Scotland maintained its own traditional culture. Evidence of Scottish distinctiveness could be called upon at will, whether in aid of a pro- or anti-unionist agenda. This was significant even if many of the emblems of Scottishness were mythical.

[204] See Richard J. Finlay, 'Caledonia or North Britain? Scottish Identity in the Eighteenth Century', in Dauvit Broun, Richard J. Finlay and Michael Lynch (eds), *Image and Identity: The Making and Re-Making of Scotland through the Ages* (Edinburgh, 1998), 153.

5

Ghosts in Popular Culture

Stories were told long before they were written down. The historian is always constrained by the limitations of written records, but this is particularly evident when it comes to looking at popular belief: it is difficult to determine the place of ghosts in Scottish culture when, for centuries, few considered ghost stories worth recording. Matters improve somewhat over the course of the eighteenth century. The end of the witch trials removes one body of sources, but this is outweighed by the development of print culture and antiquarian studies. This chapter uses ballads, cheap pamphlets and folklorists' accounts to assess popular perceptions of ghosts (although these three categories are not perfectly delineated: most obviously, ballads were often printed as broadsides). Within these sources, ghosts appeared in a multitude of forms. Corpses rose from their graves to return to their former sweethearts, flesh rotting and worm-infested; deceased villains bewailed their crimes, with eyes burst from their sockets, or genitalia leaking poison. Forsaken lovers drifted and lamented. There were stories of headless horses thronged in flames, of Highland spectres greedy for travellers' blood, of white ladies and fairy-ghosts and will o' the wisps. Ghosts were diverse, too, in their meanings: they sermonised about death or criminal behaviour, glorified love, subverted social hierarchies, upheld family or community traditions, and served as comedic figures.

It is important to note that all of these bodies of sources have drawbacks. Ballads offer the most direct window into folk culture, but they are difficult to trace and date. Cheap print culture is useful because it was targeted at a popular market, and could be read aloud, meaning that it was accessible to the illiterate. Adam Fox, Edward J. Cowan and Mike Paterson have demonstrated how cheap print can be used as a window into Scottish popular culture.[1] However, pamphlets were still composed by educated men, and it is difficult

1 Edward J. Cowan and Mike Paterson (eds), *Folk in Print: Scotland's Chapbook Heritage, 1750–1850* (Edinburgh, 2007); Adam Fox, 'The Emergence of the Scottish Broadside Ballad in the Late Seventeenth and Early Eighteenth Centuries', *Journal of Scottish Historical Studies* 31 (2011), 169–94; Adam Fox, '"Little Story Books" and "Small Pamphlets" in Edinburgh, 1680–1760: The Making of the Scottish Chapbook', *Scottish Historical Review* 92 (2013), 207–30; Adam Fox, 'Approaches to Ephemera: Scottish Broadsides, 1679–1746', in Kevin Murphy and Sally O'Driscoll (eds), *Studies in Ephemera: Text and Image in Eighteenth-Century Print* (Lanham, 2013), 117–41.

to judge how far they circulated. Finally, folklorists' accounts come diluted by the perceptions and preoccupations of their author. This chapter takes a broad view of popular culture: it includes stories that were produced by and for elites provided that they were demonstrably widespread in Scottish society. The aim of the chapter is not to avoid educated culture altogether, but to assess the ways in which ghosts were understood by the majority of the Scottish population.

Ballads

Ballads were an important feature of Scottish folk culture, and circulated in print as well as orally.[2] Ghosts were present, if not commonplace: Lizanne Henderson notes that fourteen of the 305 ballads collected by Francis James Child are concerned with ghosts or revenants, and a further four feature a magical corpse.[3] Few ballads can be accurately dated, but most of those recorded in the eighteenth and nineteenth centuries were probably significantly older. This is suggested, at least, by their presentation of ghosts. The ballad ghosts echo medieval traditions. They tend to be corporeal: they feel hunger, thirst, pain and sexual desire. In 'The Wife of Usher's Well' (Child 79), a mother knows that her dead sons will return, and prepares a feast and soft beds. When the sons appear, they claim to be in pain.[4] Furthermore, ghosts often arrive fresh from their graves. The ghost of Clerk Saunders (Child 69), on meeting his sweetheart Margaret, explains that he has come 'frae 'neath the darksome grund'. When Margaret wonders what has become of his 'bonnie arms', he declares:

> By worms they're eaten; in mools they're rotten;
> Behold, Margaret, and see;
> And mind, for a' your mickle pride,
> Sae will become o' thee![5]

Ballad ghosts might also be violent. 'Willie's Fatal Visit' (Child 255) tells of a young man who spends the night with his lover. The cock crows early and he mistakes the moonlight for daylight, leaving her house before sunrise. He meets a ghost who accuses him of sinful behaviour, and before dawn she has

2 Useful literature on this topic includes Hamish Henderson, 'The Ballad and Popular Tradition to 1660', in R. D. S. Jack (ed.), *The History of Scottish Literature, Vol. 1: Origins to 1600* (Aberdeen, 1988), 263–84; Emily Lyle (ed.), *Scottish Ballads* (Edinburgh, 1994); Edward J. Cowan (ed.), *The Ballad in Scottish History* (East Linton, 2000).

3 Lizanne Henderson, 'The Road to Elfland: Fairy Belief and the Child Ballads', in Edward J. Cowan (ed.), *The Ballad in Scottish History* (East Linton, 2000), 55.

4 Francis James Child, *The English and Scottish Popular Ballads*, 5 vols (Boston, 1882–98), vol. 2 pt. 1, 239.

5 Robert Chambers, *The Scottish Ballads* (Edinburgh, 1829), 241.

Riven him frae gair to gair,
And on ilka seat o' Mary's kirk
O' Willie she hang a share.[6]

'The Miller and the King's Daughter' (also known as 'The Twa Sisters'; Child 10) gives the story of two sisters. They are playing near some water when the elder pushes the younger in, killing her. A miller later comes across the dead body and crafts it into a violin. The breast bone is used as the body of the instrument, the fingers as pegs, the nose ridge as a bridge, and the veins as strings. When it is played, the violin speaks, and in traditional ghost fashion identifies herself and her murderer.[7] The dead body parts retain their identity, and are able to exert some degree of power. In addition, several ballads feature talking corpses. In 'Young Benjie' (Child 86) a young woman is killed, and her brothers resolve that to discover the perpetrator they must wait until midnight (ghosts usually appeared after dark, and often at the stroke of midnight). As the brothers expect, at 'the dead hour o the night' the corpse revives and identifies her murderer.[8] Another common theme was the idea that the dead body had such potency, it was actually poisonous to the living. In 'The Twa Brothers' (Child 49), when a woman requests a kiss of her dead love, she receives the following reply:

'My lips they are so bitter,' he says,
'My breath it is so strong,
If you get one kiss of my ruby lips,
Your days will not be long.'[9]

Identical or very similar lines appear in 'Sweet William's Ghost' (Child 77) and 'The Unquiet Grave' (Child 78). Ballads thus reinforced popular notions about the innate power of the dead body, and recalled medieval ideas of the corporeal revenant.

Some ballads did offer romanticised ghosts, that came 'gliding' and wore white shrouds, but it is likely that they were composed later.[10] One version of the traditional ballad 'Sweet William's Ghost' (Child 77) presents an incorporeal ghost, who claims to be a mere spirit and vanishes 'in a cloud of mist'.[11] However, these lines appeared in only one version, which likely dated from the nineteenth century. In another (probably earlier) version, the ghost actually walks to his

6 Peter Buchan, *Ancient Ballads and Songs of the North of Scotland*, 2 vols (Edinburgh, 1828), vol. 2, 261–2. 'Gair' is the opening of a garment.

7 Child, *English and Scottish Popular Ballads*, vol. 1 pt. 1, 118.

8 Ibid., vol. 2 pt. 2, 283.

9 Ibid., vol. 1 pt. 2, 439.

10 M., 'Robert and Margaret: A Ballad', *Weekly Magazine, or Edinburgh Amusement*, 1 Feb. 1776, 178.

11 Child, *English and Scottish Popular Ballads*, vol. 2 pt. 1, 228–9.

grave when his visit is over, and lies down therein.[12] Another romanticised ghost can be seen in the ballad 'William and Margaret', which was probably written by Scottish dramatist David Mallet around 1723.[13] The ballad presents the ghost of a woman returning to reproach her faithless lover:

'Twas at the silent Midnight-Hour,
When All were fast asleep;
In glided *Margaret's* grimly Ghost,
And stood at *William's* Feet.

Her Face was like an *April* Morn,
Clad in a wintry Cloud:
And Clay-cold was her Lilly Hand,
That held her sable Shroud.

Despite the romantic elements, Margaret implies that she had returned from the grave, noting 'The hungry *Worm* my *Sister* is'.[14] Furthermore, the 'clay cold' of her hand suggests a degree of corporeality. The sable shroud, incidentally, is an unusual feature – ghosts generally chose white over black – but it was perhaps chosen for poetic reasons, presenting a striking contrast with the 'lilly hand'.[15] Mallet presents a more picturesque ghost, but still acknowledges the ballad tradition of depicting ghosts as revenants. While in elite culture the revenant had largely fallen out of fashion, replaced first by the ghost as a servant of God and secondly by a more ethereal ghost, the ballads demonstrate the persistence of older folkloric themes.

Ballad ghosts occasionally came back to reveal their murderers or speak of the afterlife, but this was not the dominant pattern. More usually they returned simply to visit family members or lovers. They also reflected on the nature of death. David Buchan argues that the principle purpose of ballad ghosts was to caution against an improper degree of grieving.[16] In 'The Twa Brothers', a ghost pleads with his love:

O cease your weeping, my true-love,
And 'twill gie peace to me.[17]

12 Ibid., vol. 2 pt. 1, 230–1. See Lowry C. Wimberly, *Folklore in the English and Scottish Ballads* (Chicago, 1928), 228.
13 See David Atkinson, '"William and Margaret": An Eighteenth-Century Ballad', *Folk Music Journal* 10 (2014), 478.
14 David Mallet, *The Excursion: A Poem* (London, 1728), bk. 2, 75–80.
15 Francis Grose, *Superstitions* in *A Provincial Glossary: With a Collection of Local Proverbs* (London, 1787), 10.
16 David Buchan, 'Talerole Analysis and Child's Supernatural Ballads', in Joseph Harris (ed.), *The Ballad and Oral Literature* (Cambridge [Mass.], 1991), 75. See also Henderson, 'Road to Elfland', 68.
17 Child, *English and Scottish Popular Ballads*, vol. 1 pt. 2, 440.

These ghosts did, therefore, bear a broadly Christian message: death should be accepted with equanimity. However, they tended not to make mention of God, Heaven or Hell. Ghosts might have been useful as religious propagandists, political commentators or atmospheric devices, but the ballads serve as a reminder that they also survived for more straightforward reasons. With life expectancy hovering somewhere around thirty in the mid-eighteenth century, death was a familiar beast.[18] The ballad ghosts were a response to it. They underlined the inevitability of death, as we see with Clerk Saunders's reminder to Margaret that 'Sae will become o' thee'. Furthermore, in contrast to the rather prettified death frequently seen in Gothic poetry, ballads relished the goriness of rotting limbs, gluttonous worms and poisoned lips. There was more raw realism in this picture than in the kirk's sanitised version of the resurrection of the dead, which held that bodies would 'arise incorruptible'.[19] The ballads did not sentimentalise death, but presented it as a part of the natural order that should be borne with fortitude, positing that prolonged grieving would only disturb the dead. The argument that the dead could be affected beyond the grave by the grieving (or prayers) of the living was also out of line with Protestant doctrine, but it was a message that appealed on an emotional level, unlike the kirk's teaching that the living were completely cut off from the dead. The ghosts of ballads provided a way for communities to explore and contend with death, keeping roughly in line with Christian doctrine without being overly restricted by kirk directives.

Cheap Print Culture

The expansion of print culture in the eighteenth century opened up a new avenue for ghost stories. Broadsides and chapbooks were sold cheaply on the street, at markets and at fairs. As in the case of ballads, ghosts did not appear with great frequency, but they did feature from time to time. The National Library of Scotland's online collection of about 1,800 Scottish broadsides printed between 1650 and 1910 includes a dozen broadsides that contain apparitions, most from the eighteenth and early nineteenth centuries.[20] Another few dozen eighteenth-century pamphlets or chapbooks featuring ghosts have been preserved. Titles such as *The Laird of Coul's Ghost* and *Thrummy Cap and the Ghaist* became popular, as well as ghost stories from Scott, Hogg and other authors.[21] Some stories were told in prose, some in

18 R. A. Houston and I. D. Whyte, 'Introduction: Scottish Society in Perspective', in R. A. Houston and I. D. Whyte (eds), *Scottish Society, 1500–1800* (Cambridge, 1989), 4.

19 Arthur C. Cochrane (ed.), 'The Scottish Confession of Faith, 1560', in *Reformed Confessions of the Sixteenth Century* (Philadelphia, 1966), 184.

20 *The Word on the Street* (NLS, 2004), http://digital.nls.uk/broadsides, accessed 1 Feb. 2018.

21 Cowan and Paterson, *Folk in Print*, 30–1.

verse. Ghosts were often used as tragic or comical devices, but might also be presented as objective realities. A 1722 broadside declared: 'Whatever the World may think of Apparitions and Spectres, 'tis very certain, such has been before, and learned Divines still own the same Exist, and have appeared in the several past Ages.' There was no reason, it continued, that God should not 'make use of the Ministry of Spirits' to foretell extraordinary events, punish the guilty or manifest his will.[22] For the most part, however, pamphlets made little attempt to justify their ghosts: the central focus was on the story itself.

The presentation of ghosts varied. The revenant-like ghost of the ballads appeared with reasonable frequency, partly because popular ballads such as 'Sweet William's Ghost' were themselves printed. A broadside from around 1680 featured the speech of the ghost of a Fife laird, and depicted him walking from the grave:

> What accident, what strange mishap,
> Awakes me from my heavenly nap?
> What sprit? what God-head by the lave,
> Hath rais'd my Body from the Grave?[23]

Occasionally ghosts returned bearing wounds. One ghost was 'Streaming with blood, and pale as the sheeted inmates of the tomb'.[24] A couple of pamphlets even presented headless ghosts, reminiscent of the apparition of Fawdon, but otherwise not a typical pattern in Scottish ghost stories.[25] *MacKinnon's Ghost* offers a particularly colourful example of a wounded ghost. Mary MacKinnon was executed for murder in 1823. *MacKinnon's Ghost* gives her story in ballad form, with the stipulation that it should be sung to the tune of 'Margaret's Ghost' (another title for Mallet's aforementioned 'William and Margaret'). MacKinnon returns with her face cut by the anatomising knife, and her hand 'drench'd with native gore'. Her breast displays 'the scalpel's gash', and she speaks slowly in 'strangled accents'. Her face is said to be black and 'deformed with many a wound', and she declares to the friend she visits:

> Behold my tongue, half bitten through,
> That daily lied and curst-
> And mark mine eyes, lascivious blue,
> From forth their sockets burst.

22 *The St. James's Surprizing and Afrightful Apparition* ([Edinburgh?], 1722).

23 P. M., *The Speech of a Fyfe Laird, Newly Come from Grave* ([Scotland], [1680?]).

24 *The Vision of Dr Morris, or, The Spectral Warning* ([Edinburgh], 1821).

25 See, for example, *A Full True and Particular Account of the Most Dreadful Apparrition: Of Robert Watt Wine-Merchant in Edinr, Who Appeared to James Macdonald Plaisterer in Lieth-Walk* ([Edinburgh?], [1794?]). Scottish headless ghosts are briefly discussed in 'Sketches of Superstitions', *Chambers's Edinburgh Journal*, 10 Apr. 1841, 94. On the apparition of Fawdon see pp. 22–3.

Behold my carcass, hack'd and flay'd,
Which round and sleek should be-
And then bethink thee, careless jade,
The same may hap to thee![26]

The grotesque nature of the revenant is harnessed for dramatic effect, with MacKinnon's body serving as a canvas on which her sins are displayed. The depiction of the ghost reflects the horrors attached to the anatomy knife in the public imagination. Executed criminals were generally delivered to anatomists. Nevertheless, there was a shortage of corpses available for dissection, a deficiency that was addressed in part through a black market. Grave-robbing was a lucrative business, and in 1828 William Burke and William Hare ventured to greater depths of villainy by murdering sixteen people in order to sell their bodies.[27] The references to the 'hack'd and flay'd' corpse play on the provocative terror of dissection. The revenant was not as fashionable as the ethereal, gliding ghost, but the monstrous undead retained a place in the popular imagination, and could be employed to reflect on contemporary events and concerns.

The ghosts of pamphlet literature generally returned either in the clothes they had worn during their lifetimes, or in white. The ghosts of romantic literature frequently wore white, but the association between the dead and the colour white pre-dated this trend. White was a mourning colour, particularly for young women; Mary Queen of Scots was painted wearing a white veil when in mourning for her mother and father-in-law.[28] In the Book of Revelation, the souls of the dead are given white robes, and Calvin wrote that 'white robes and rest are given us' in Abraham's Bosom.[29] In addition, white winding sheets or death dresses were commonly used for the dead. One broadside featured a 'hideous spectre, with a visage as white as snow, his hair clotted with blood, and clad in a white winding-sheet, so thin, that it did not conceal his body, mangled and torn in many places'.[30] There was an element of the theatrical in the white-sheeted ghost, and this dramatic image was reinforced in other

26 *MacKinnon's Ghost* ([Edinburgh?], [1823?]). While the ballad itself is not dated, it is likely that it was produced reasonably soon after the execution, while the case remained topical, and it was collected by James Maidment along with other printed materials from 1823. NLS, Ry.II.c.26.

27 There is a useful passage on this in Gillian Bennett, *Bodies: Sex, Violence, Disease, and Death in Contemporary Legend* (Jackson [Miss.], 2009), 223–8, but for an in-depth analysis see Ruth Richardson, *Death, Dissection and the Destitute* (London, 1987).

28 Roy Strong, *Tudor and Jacobean Portraits*, 2 vols (London, 1969), vol. 1, 219; see Nigel Llewellyn, *Art of Death: Visual Culture in the English Death Ritual c.1500–c.1800* (London, 1991), 89.

29 Rev 6:11, King James Version; John Calvin, *Psychopannychia*, in Thomas F. Torrance (ed.), *Tracts and Treatises in Defense of the Reformed Faith*, 3 vols (Grand Rapids, 1958), vol. 3, 467.

30 *An Account of a Most Horrid, Bloody, and Terrible Apparition, Which Lately Appeared in the Parish of Shotts* (London, [1793?]).

ways. Ghosts might depart amid peals of thunder and lightning; one 'flew off in a flame of fire'.[31] Two pamphlets presented ghosts who smelled of sulphur; to reinforce the association with Hell, one of them was 'accompanied with a gloomy light, much resembling in colour the blaze of brimstone'.[32] The cheap print market explored a range of ghostly guises, but its depictions tended to be sensationalised.

Pamphlets and broadsides usually favoured moralising ghosts. One apparition came to reveal 'a most Horrid and Barbarous Murder and Robbery'; others warned of the torments of Hell, and one appeared to a friend to speak of the joys of Heaven.[33] Another pamphlet provided 'a dreadful example for wicked husbands', telling the story of a man who married a beautiful young lady against her friends' wishes. He spent their money in a 'riotous and debauched manner', was driven to despair, and hanged himself. His apparition was then seen and heard for a long time, 'making terrible noises to the great terror and disturbance of the neighbourhood'.[34] Again, there was an emphasis on drama and sensationalism. The upright moral message excused the pamphlets' spirited exploration of murder and debauchery. *An Abstract of the Bloody Massacre in Ireland*, published around 1700, offered a detailed and gory description of the killing of Protestants by Irish Catholics in 1641. In case the bias of the pamphleteer was not sufficiently evident, it went on to declare: 'Let us now consider, at least, some of God's Judgments upon the *Irish*, whereby he hath not left the Innocent blood of His Servants to be altogether unrevenged.' There followed several stories of apparitions:

> These bloody Hell-hounds, themselves confessed, That the Ghost of divers of the *Protestants*, which they had drowned at *Portadown Bridge*, were daily seen to walk upon the River, sometimes singing of Psalms, sometimes brandishing naked Swords, sometimes shreeking in a most hideous & fearful manner. So that many of the *Popish Irish* which dwelt thereabouts, being affrighted therewith were forced to remove their Habitations further off into the Country.[35]

In the medieval period there was a common notion that those who had died violently and prematurely would return to haunt the places of their deaths.

31 *Full True and Particular Account ... of Robert Watt.*

32 *The Historical Tragedy, of Young Beateman's Ghost, or The Perjured Maid, Justly Rewarded* ([Edinburgh], 1778); William Mann, *A Voice from the Dead, or, The Apparition of William Clarkson* (Paisley, 1826), 3, 7.

33 *An Account of a Most Horrid and Barbarous Murther and Robbery, Committed on the Body of Captain Brown* (Edinburgh, 1694); *Shaftsbury's Ghost to Doctor Oats: In a Vision, Concerning the Jesuits and Lords in the Tower* (Edinburgh, 1683); *The Second Letter, from the Ghost of Bailie Cuthbert* ([Edinburgh?], [1780?]); *An Account of the Apparition of the Late Lord Kilmarnock* (London, 1747).

34 *A Dreadful Example for Wicked Husbands: Or the Virtuous Wife in Distress* ([Edinburgh?], [1799?]).

35 *An Abstract of the Bloody Massacre in Ireland* ([Scotland?], [1700?]), 22.

An Abstract of the Bloody Massacre in Ireland appropriated the tradition, turning ghosts into tools of God's providential justice. This hybrid between folkloric ghosts and religious moralists was common within the cheap print market. One ghost returned to haunt the faithless lover who had driven her to suicide, but was consoled when he promised to pay for a proper burial for her.[36] Executed criminals also appeared (Mary MacKinnon included). Robert Johnston, probably the Robert Johnston who was executed for robbery in Edinburgh in 1818, returned in a pamphlet to tell other robbers to mend their ways, wailing:

> Plung'd in black Darkness and Eternal Night,
> For Crimes committed 'gainst Almighty Light,
> For Hell-bred Sins condemned I must be
> T' endure GOD's Wrath, in endless Misery.[37]

'Hare's dream' depicted William Hare languishing in his prison cell, tormented by the ghosts of those he had killed. One took the form of a groaning skeleton, another a shining angel. His deceased companion Burke also made an appearance, 'chain'd with the murderer's fetter', and counselled him to turn from his evil ways and bewail their sins. Hare concluded:

> O silent sleep,–I'll ne'er sleep again,
> To think on't makes me shiver;
> What tortures and what cruel pain,–
> Forget it shall I never.
> And whether in night's silent hour,
> Or in the sun shine day,
> Still will remain at my mind's door,
> Till I the debt of nature pay.[38]

There was a popular appetite for remorseful criminals: final speeches at the scaffold were a common subject for broadsides. Ghosts were similarly used to demonstrate that crimes never went unpunished, and to appease public outrage over notorious villains.

The same pattern could apply on a smaller scale, with local villains returning as ghosts. The Laird of Coul's Ghost is the best example; the chapbook detailing his story circulated widely and went through many editions. The

[36] *Captain Mulligan: Miss Bailey's Ghost* (Stirling, [1813–20?]).

[37] *Robert Johnston's Ghost, or, His Last Advice to the Gipsies, and Other Gangs of Robbers and Murderers in Scotland* ([Edinburgh?], [1720?]). On Johnston see, for example, V. A. C. Gatrell, *The Hanging Tree: Execution and the English People 1770–1868* (Oxford, 1996), 50.

[38] *Hare's Dream! Describing the Apparition of Burke and Others, Which Appeared to Him While in the Calton Jail* ([Edinburgh], [1829]).

chapbook about the Provost Abraham Crichton of Sanquhar may not have reached such lofty heights of celebrity, but it was also said to be well known.[39] According to a summary in the *Edinburgh Weekly Magazine* in the 1770s, the provost died in 1745, and thereafter was frequently spotted near his own grave, making strange grimaces. Eventually his son and a local minister (Mr Gibson) went to confront him, but the minister lost his nerve and the son met his father alone. The content of their meeting is not recorded, but the son subsequently removed a partition wall in his house, and sightings of the provost ceased.[40] Another article published the following month asserted that the minister was actually Mr Hunter, and he did not retreat.[41] Fuller versions appeared in the second half of the nineteenth century. James Brown declared that Provost Crichton had threatened to destroy a ruined kirk, declaring he would 'sune ding doon the Whigs' sanctuary'. Soon afterwards he fell from his horse and broke his neck. His ghost lingered behind, and upset young girls by grinning at them as they milked their cows. A chain was fixed to his grave to keep him down, without success. Finally, the reverend Mr Hunter of Penpont had 'personal dealings' with the ghost, and banished it forever.[42] Although it was devoid of complex theological arguments, this story bore notable similarities to that of the Laird of Coul. Both accounts featured a figure in a position of power, disliked by the local community. They were confirmed to be villains when they returned as ghosts. These stories carried a moral message, but also a notable element of social subversion: the unscrupulous rich were exposed and punished in the afterlife. This perhaps in part accounts for their success with a popular audience.[43]

Along similar lines, ghosts might be used to shame the villains of contemporary controversies. *Shaftsbury's Ghost to Doctor Oats* (1683) was a scathing attack on the English perjurer Titus Oates, who falsely claimed to have discovered a Catholic plot to kill Charles II. In the pamphlet Oates was visited from Hell by his recently-deceased ally the Earl of Shaftesbury. The ghost was described in colourful terms: 'He seem'd like the Emblem of Envy, his Hairs turned into Serpents, his Tap into a Pump, spouting with Sulphur and corroded

[39] I have not come across any surviving copies of the chapbook, and am relying on William Wilson's 1904 assertion that 'a full account of the wonderful doings of the resuscitated Provost was published in a chap-book, and, circulating over the length and breadth of the land, gave Abraham a notoriety that in life he could not have dreamed of'. William Wilson, *Folk Lore and Genealogies of Uppermost Nithsdale* (Dumfries, 1904), 33. On the Laird of Coul's ghost see pp. 000–000.

[40] C. G. to the *Weekly Magazine, or Edinburgh Amusement*, 16 Apr. 1772, 74.

[41] Fabricius to the *Weekly Magazine, or Edinburgh Amusement*, 7 May 1772, 167–8.

[42] James Brown, *The History of Sanquhar* (Dumfries, 1891), 16. For other versions see Robert Simpson, *History of Sanquhar* (Edinburgh, 1853), 86–8; Wilson, *Folk Lore and Genealogies*, 31–5.

[43] For an interesting discussion of social subversion in nineteenth-century English supernatural pamphlets, see Karl Bell, *The Magical Imagination: Magic and Modernity in Urban England, 1780–1914* (Cambridge, 2012), ch. 5.

Poison, with a long Veil of Hypocrisie Ermin'd and Spoted with Blood.'[44] This ghost was used to bring drama and humour to a political argument. A ghost was similarly employed to comment on a contemporary scandal in *The Vision of Dr Morris, or, The Spectral Warning* (1821). This broadside reflected on the Cockney Controversy of the early nineteenth century, when hostile reviews of English poets appeared in *Blackwood's Magazine*. John Scott, an editor who had published many of the poems, died in a duel related to the affair in 1821.[45] The pamphlet depicted the return of his ghost to Dr Morris, the pseudonym attached to the reviews (generally attributed to John Gibson Lockhart). Morris was termed the 'Scandal-Monger General', and was advised in ominous tones to mend his ways. While the ghost was victim rather than villain in this case, he was still used as a dramatic device: he returned with blood pouring from him, directed his 'lack lustre eye' to his 'cowardly enemy' and addressed him in 'hollow sepulchral tones'. Dramatic ghosts also appeared to make broader political commentary. *An Account of a Most Horrid, Bloody, and Terrible Apparition, which Lately Appeared in the Parish of Shotts* ([1793?]) featured the 'hideous spectre' with a 'mangled and torn body' mentioned above. Its arrival was heralded with a noise 'like the rolling of thunder', culminating in a 'loud and awful yell'. This broadside, like the longer *Brissot's Ghost!*, was a caution against rebellion: the ghost was a deceased Frenchman who appeared to a group of radicals, preaching on the horrors of the Revolution.[46]

Other works addressed more sentimental themes. In the last quarter of the eighteenth century, there was a surge in broadsides featuring tragic poems or ballads with moralising reflections on love. Most were imported from England, where they had been popular in the late seventeenth century. *The Kentshire Tragedy* told of a ship's captain who killed a man in a fight over a woman, only to be haunted at sea. He confessed his crime to his crew and was thrown overboard when a storm arose.[47] *The Leverpool Tragedy* and *The Gosford* (or *Gosport*) *Tragedy* described sailors who murdered their pregnant lovers, and were haunted by their ghosts.[48] *The Yarmouth Tragedy* and *Young Grigor's Ghost* cautioned cruel parents. Both told of parents who sent their daughter's lover away for being too poor. The lovers died and returned as ghosts, after which the daughters followed them into death, leaving the unhappy parents to

44 *Shaftsbury's Ghost*, 1.

45 See Leonidas M. Jones, 'The Scott-Christie Duel', *Texas Studies in Literature and Language* 12 (1971), 605–29; Kim Wheatley, 'The *Blackwood's* Attacks on Leigh Hunt', *Nineteenth-Century Literature* 47 (1992), 1–31; Mark Parker, *Literary Magazines and British Romanticism* (Cambridge, 2001), 20–7; Richard Cronin, *Paper Pellets: British Literary Culture after Waterloo* (Oxford, 2010), 1–6.

46 *Brissot's Ghost! Or, Intelligence from the Other World* (Edinburgh, 1794).

47 *The Kentshire Tragedy, or, The Constant Lovers Overthrow* ([Edinburgh?], 1794).

48 *The Leverpool Tragedy or The Perjur'd Sailor* ([Glasgow?], 1767); *The Gosford Tragedy: Or The Perjured Carpenter* ([Edinburgh?], 1775).

repent.[49] Finally, *The Historical Tragedy, of Young Beateman's Ghost* (which was unusually in prose rather than verse) presented a woman who broke a promise to her lover and married another man. She was subsequently stolen into death by the vengeful ghost of her forsaken lover, never to be seen again.[50] While pamphlets such as *Brissot's Ghost!* reinforced the social order, this type of story could subvert it, albeit subtly. The wealthy were presented as greedy and blind to true worth (similarly to Coul and Crichton); love and honour were exalted above all.

Some pamphlets were chiefly intended to entertain, and their ghosts were humorous or satirical. *Thrummy Cap and the Ghaist* was a popular chapbook by John Burness, cousin of Robert Burns. It told, in Scots, the story of the brave Thrummy Cap and his cowardly companion, who lodged in a haunted room. After a few farcical encounters with a ghost who looked exactly like him, Thrummy Cap helped to put right a fraud the ghost had committed during his lifetime.[51] *The Ghaist* or *Gibby and the Ghaist*, also told in Scots, similarly explained how a character called Gibby and his dog were forced to stay in a haunted room. They were visited overnight by the ghost of a murderer. The ghost bade Gibby to dig up his victim's bones and see them safely buried in holy ground. He took Gibby to the point where he had buried the bones, but Gibby could see nothing. He resolved to mark the spot by defecating on it, then return in the morning. Morning came, and he awakened:

> And something fand – *no sav'ry* – where he lay–
> –The bed was k-d, and the *ghaist* was flown![52]

Both *Thrummy Cap* and *Gibby and the Ghaist* parodied ghost traditions. Similarly, a broadside called *Ghosts, &c.!* began with the preamble that ghosts 'are evidently decreasing in number in these latter times'. It went on to describe how a mob gathered in Edinburgh

> to witness a spectre-like figure, arrayed in white, walking about a room in one of the houses. Unlike other ghosts, this one had a shadow, which being reflected upon a wall in the room, had a most dismal effect. The mob were so penetrated with horror that they contemplated the spectre in the profoundest silence, until it extinguished the candle it carried; and they withdrew.[53]

49 *The Yarmouth Tragedy: Shewing How by the Cruelty of Their Parents, Two Lovers Were Distroyed* ([Edinburgh?], 1775); *Young Grigor's Ghost* ([Edinburgh?], 1776).

50 *Young Beateman's Ghost.*

51 John Burness, 'Thrummy Cap', in *Plays, Poems, Tales and Other Pieces* (Montrose, 1819). There are numerous pamphlet versions. Thrummy Cap was an elf in Northumbrian folklore, but is not identified as such in Burness's work.

52 Robbin Faggot, *The Ghaist: A Poem* (Glasgow, 1810). The deleted word may be 'keiched' or similar.

53 *Ghosts, &c!* (Edinburgh, 1827).

Nothing more supernatural occurred in this story than an intimidating shadow, and the fear of 'the mob' was offered up as the chief talking point of the piece. The fact that the supposed ghost had a shadow was a hint that the mob might well have been mistaken, as was the candle: flames were supposed to blow out or burn blue in the presence of genuine ghosts.

Other publications went further still. Some pamphlets contained stories of ghost hoaxes as an 'antidote to superstition'.[54] One printer, George Miller, professed to regret having published a version of *The Laird of Coul's Ghost*, considering it immoral – a hint that ghost stories in the cheap press were perceived to be a form of bawdy entertainment, rather than edifying fables. To atone for it, he printed a work entitled *An Antidote to Superstition; Or a Cure for Those Weak Minds Which are Troubled with the Fear of Ghosts, Witches &c* around 1803.[55] It contained the same article by Philaretes that was printed in the *Edinburgh Weekly Magazine*, explaining 'the method he took to extricate himself from the fetters of superstition', and associating ghosts with the 'old woman' lurking in our breasts.[56] It also contained a section on how superstitions made people miserable, declaring: 'as it is the chief concern of the wise man to retrench the evils of life by the reasonings of philosophy; it is the employment of fools to multiply them by the sentiments of superstition.'[57] However, works of this sort were greatly outnumbered by those that took a more tolerant view of ghosts.

Overall, the print market revealed – and doubtless promoted – the wide variety of ghost stereotypes in circulation. Ghosts were used as vehicles for religious or political messages. They reflected on contemporary scandals, or on timeless themes such as death. They punished acts of depravity or crimes of love. They also appeared purely for entertainment purposes. In the late seventeenth century, the only printed material available on ghosts either dismissed them as demons, or (in the case of *Satans Invisible World Discovered*) presented them as religious propagandists. Over the course of the eighteenth century, ghosts' functions expanded rapidly. Oral culture probably remained the chief way in which ghost stories were transmitted, but the development of the print market boosted their potential, such that a figure like the Laird of Coul's ghost could become widely known. Pamphlets and broadsides may have been composed by educated folk, but they were democratising in a sense: they allowed ghost stories to be more easily shared between different social classes, and the stories themselves drew on both folklore and literary culture.

54 See p. 110.

55 Scott A. McLean, 'Cleansing the Hawker's Basket: Popular Literature and the Cheap Periodical Press in Scotland', *Studies in Scottish Literature* 32 (2001), 93–4.

56 See p. 107.

57 *An Antidote to Superstition: Or, A Cure for Those Weak Minds Which Are Troubled with the Fear of Ghosts, Witches &c.* (Dunbar, [1803?]), 1, 3, 17–18.

Folklorists' Accounts

Lastly, we come to folklorists' accounts. Within this body of sources there is plenty of anecdotal evidence for the general popularity of ghost stories. Robert Burns remembered with fondness an old woman who lived with his family, 'remarkable for her ignorance, credulity, and superstition'. She had a great collection of stories and songs about 'devils, ghosts, fairies, brownies, witches, warlocks, spunkies, kelpies, elf-candles, dead-lights, wraiths, apparitions, cantraips, giants, inchanted towers, dragons, and other trumpery'.[58] In 1777, John Brand noted that in Britain 'nothing is commoner in *Country Places*, than for a whole Family in a *Winter's Evening*, to sit round the Fire, and tell Stories of Apparitions and Ghosts'.[59] In the same decade, another writer described young people telling ghost stories together:

> When the lads and lasses for company join'd,
> In a crowd round the embers are met,
> Talk of fairies, and witches that ride on the wind,
> And of ghosts, till they're all in a sweat:[60]

Ghost stories also spread easily within a community. Robert Wodrow often received the same story from several different hands. The fact that some stories existed in different versions (as in the case of Provost Crichton's ghost, or the ghost that visited Archibald Pitcairne) demonstrates that they passed through multiple narrators.[61] The folklorists' appetite for ghosts may have been inspired by broader cultural trends (particularly the romantic movement), but this does not mean that ghost stories were not genuinely popular across different levels of society.

Folklorists' accounts, like cheap print culture, displayed a variety of ghosts. Familiar patterns appeared: ghosts returned to reveal their murderers, to reproach their loved ones for excessive grieving, or to resolve unfinished business. However, unlike other bodies of sources, folklorists' accounts presented a preponderance of ghosts without specific objectives. The ghosts of well-known villains stalked the streets without feeling the need to offer explicit moral lessons to the living (as they did in pamphlets). Various stories circulated about the ghost of the alleged warlock Major Thomas Weir (d. 1670). Weir was a staunch Presbyterian, well known in Edinburgh for his piety. As an elderly

[58] Quoted in Robert Crawford, *Scotland's Books* (London, 2007), 284.

[59] John Brand, *Observations on Popular Antiquities* (Newcastle, 1777), 102. See also the discussion in E. J. Clery, *The Rise of Supernatural Fiction, 1762–1800* (Cambridge, 1995), 2–5.

[60] 'The Wish: A Song', *Weekly Magazine, or Edinburgh Amusement*, 24 May 1770, 242; previously appeared as 'Winter', *Universal Magazine of Knowledge and Pleasure*, Jan. 1770, 43.

[61] On Pitcairne see pp. 86–8.

man he roused a scandal when he admitted to various sexual crimes, including adultery, incest and bestiality. His sister Jean confessed to having a sexual relationship with him, and also avowed that they were both in league with the Devil. The pair were executed, but their celebrity persisted. A 1720 letter noted that Major Weir's ghost was said to wander the Bowhead and argue with an old acquaintance. In the mid-eighteenth century, the spectres of the siblings were apparently an object of fear for a young James Boswell, and other Edinburgh schoolboys.[62] By the early nineteenth century, the stories in circulation were sensational: noises of dancing, howling and spinning were heard in the Weirs' former residence; the major galloped around on a headless horse, surrounded by a whirlwind of flame; and sometimes both siblings travelled in an infernal carriage, drawn by more headless horses, and driven by a hideous coachman with burning eyes. Their house was also said to be haunted by a headless calf.[63]

Other local villains were also suspected of post-mortem shenanigans. One was the aforementioned lawyer George Mackenzie of Rosehaugh (1636/8–1691), who was reviled for his harsh treatment of Covenanters.[64] His mausoleum was located in Greyfriars Kirkyard, Edinburgh, and Robert Chambers recorded that it was 'an object of horror to the good people of Edinburgh, as it was almost universally believed that the sprite of the persecutor could get no rest in its superb but gloomy tenement'.[65] 'Bluidy Mackenzie' remains a famed local poltergeist. Similarly, James Kirkton's (c.1620–99) *Secret and True History of the Church of Scotland from the Restoration to the Year 1678* records how James Baillie, Lord Forrester of Corstorphine, was stabbed and killed in 1679 by a woman called Christian Hamilton, with whom he had apparently had a romantic altercation. She was convicted of the murder and executed. Kirkton reported that the local village's inhabitants were greatly annoyed by the ghost of a woman who appeared on moonlit nights in the spot where the murder had happened, 'clothed all in white, with a bloody sword in her hand, wandering and wailing'.[66]

Those who had died prematurely, or who had not been buried properly, were also wont to rise again. In 1657–8, a mission of Jesuits in Scotland reported the case of the Baron of Hempisfield (or Amisfield), who persecuted Catholics during his lifetime. He drowned in a stream, and his body was swept away. His family were forced to bury a coffin containing only earth. Thereafter it was 'firmly believed' that the baron's ghost haunted his castle, 'calling upon his friends to

62 Colin Mackenzie to [the laird of Grant?], 21 July 1720: NRS, GD248/170/3; Frederick A. Pottle, *James Boswell: The Earlier Years, 1740–1769* (New York, 1966), 16–17.

63 Robert Chambers, 'Traditions of the Celebrated Major Weir', *Edinburgh Literary Journal*, 11 Apr. 1829, 307–8; George Sinclair, *Satans Invisible World Discovered* (Edinburgh, 1685), postscript, ¶–¶ ¶.

64 See p. 85.

65 Robert Chambers, *Traditions of Edinburgh*, revised edn (London, 1868), 245.

66 James Kirkton, *The Secret and True History of the Church of Scotland: From the Restoration to the Year 1678*, ed. Charles Kirkpatrick Sharpe (Edinburgh, 1817), 182–4.

help him with lamentable voice, but all in vain'.[67] About a century later, Thomas Pennant recorded a belief that tarans, or the spirits of unbaptised children, haunted areas of woodland – a notion that was also found in the Borders in the early nineteenth century.[68] In the Statistical Account of 1791–9, the entry for the county of Roxburgh noted that ghosts were thought to return when 'wilful or accidental death' had taken place. It gave the poignant example of a woman who died when she fell down a flight of stairs on her wedding day.[69] A man who drank himself to death in a bet was also said to linger, and Hugh Miller recorded the case of a murdered packman who wandered as a ghost until the hour arrived when he would have died naturally, had he not met with a violent end.[70]

Some popular stories drew on revenant traditions. Scott recorded one story that was 'frequently related by the peasants of Scotland'. A widow, alone with the corpse of her recently deceased husband, accidentally left the door ajar (in defiance of tradition). The corpse sat up and looked at her, 'frowning and grinning at her frightfully'. It did not lie down again until a Catholic priest arrived, put his finger in the corpse's mouth, and said the paternoster backwards. It then 'fell back on the bed, and behaved itself as a dead man ought to do'.[71] Another legend, said to be 'long current' in Glasgow, was recorded by Robert Chambers in 1827. A citizen 'threw the whole town into a state of inexpressible horror and consternation by giving out that, in passing at midnight through the kirk-yard, he saw a neighbour of his own, lately buried, rise out of his grave, and dance a jig with the devil', who played on the bagpipes. The authorities were said to be so horrified they sent the town drummer through the streets the next morning with the purpose of forbidding anyone to whistle, sing or play the 'infernal' tune the Devil had performed.[72]

Nevertheless, revenants were a relative rarity – perhaps surprisingly, since the ghosts of ballads tended to recall revenant beliefs. This was probably in part because romantic fiction had popularised the gliding, white-clad ghost at the expense of the walking corpse. It also reflects different haunting patterns. The dead body could only retain its vitality for a limited period. Revenants tended to return soon after death, and were then laid again by some means. Equally,

67 William Forbes-Leith (ed.), *Memoirs of Scottish Catholics during the Seventeenth and Eighteenth Centuries*, 2 vols (London, 1909), vol. 2, 72–3.

68 This appeared as an addition to the 1769 tour in Thomas Pennant, *A Tour in Scotland 1772, Part 2* (London, 1776), 13. On this belief in the Borders see E., 'Border Sketches No. II', *Edinburgh Magazine and Literary Miscellany*, Oct. 1817, 237.

69 Andrew Bell, 'Parish of Roxburgh', in John Sinclair (ed.), *The Statistical Account of Scotland, 1791–1799*, electronic edn, 21 vols (University of Edinburgh, University of Glasgow, 1999), vol. 19, http://stataccscot.edina.ac.uk/link/osa-vol19-p114-parish-roxburgh-roxburgh, accessed 1 Feb. 2018, 136.

70 Robert Chambers, *The Picture of Scotland*, 2 vols (Edinburgh, 1827), vol. 2, 338; Hugh Miller, *Scenes and Legends of the North of Scotland; Or, The Traditional History of Cromarty*, 2nd edn (London, 1850), 360–1.

71 Walter Scott, *Minstrelsy of the Scottish Border*, 3 vols (Edinburgh, 1802–3), vol. 3, 252–3.

72 Chambers, *Picture of Scotland*, vol. 1, 377.

purposeful ghosts tended to make one or two visits and rest in peace once their business was concluded. The ballads were an excellent medium through which to record and pass down the details of one-off events like this. Folklorists, however, were more likely to record stories of persistent long-term hauntings. While their more purposeful brethren haunted people, aimless ghosts who wandered indefinitely tended to haunt places, and thus more easily became intertwined with local identity. Persistent hauntings were regularly reinforced within the community memory, and there was an extra frisson of fear in telling the story of a ghost that might still raise its head. Attempts to convert the ghost into a religious messenger were undermined by this natural bias towards the ghost who could never find its peace.

A few ghost stories merit particular consideration because they recur in various sources, and thus seem to have been especially well known. In a story from Edinburgh, told as early as 1743 and popular in Walter Scott's childhood, a minister was blindfolded and taken at gunpoint to a bedroom.[73] He saw a beautiful young woman who had recently given birth, and was ordered to pray as he would for someone on the point of death. He objected, pointing out that she had delivered her child safely, but his protests fell on deaf ears. He said the prayers, the blindfold was restored, and he was ushered away. As he left the house he heard a shot. Once he was a good distance from the house he was given a pouch of money and threatened with death should he tell anybody of the adventure. Soon afterwards, the news spread that a house in the Canongate had burned down, killing the young woman who lived there. The minister was too afraid to tell anybody of his experience at the time, but years later he circulated it. Some time after his death a fire broke out where the house had formerly stood. Amidst the flames was seen the apparition of a beautiful woman in nightclothes, some fifty years old, who declared: '*Anes* burned, *twice* burned; the *third* time I'll scare you all!' In this case the ghost was tied not only to the house in which she had been murdered, but to the particular traumatic circumstances of the fire.

The story of Porteous was also widely discussed. It was told to Francis Grose in the late 1780s by a local woman. Slightly different versions were reported in the Statistical Account and by Charles Kirkpatrick Sharpe, and Robert Chambers later wrote a ballad about the affair.[74] It supposedly took place during the reign of

[73] From Scott's notes to the fifth canto of 'Rokeby', Walter Scott, *Rokeby: A Poem* (Edinburgh, 1813), civ–cviii.

[74] Francis Grose, *The Antiquities of Scotland*, 2 vols (London, 1789–91), vol. 1, 144; Charles Kirkpatrick Sharpe, 'Prefatory Notice', in Charles Kirkpatrick Sharpe (ed.), *Memorialls: Or the Memorable Things That Fell out Within This Island of Brittain from 1638 to 1684* (Edinburgh, 1818), lxxx–lxxxii; Thomas Marjoribanks, 'Parish of Lochmaben', in *The New Statistical Account of Scotland, 1834–45*, electronic edn, 15 vols (University of Edinburgh, University of Glasgow, 1999), vol. 4, http://stataccscot.edina.ac.uk/link/nsa-vol4-p377-parish-dumfries-lochmaben, accessed 1 Feb. 2018, 385; Robert Chambers, 'The Prisoner of Spedlins', *Chambers's Edinburgh Journal*, 15 Jan. 1853, 48.

Charles II (1660–85), and concerned the tower of Spedlins in Dumfries, owned at the time by Sir Alexander Jardine. A miller called Porteous was suspected of arson, and Jardine imprisoned him in the tower's dungeon. Soon afterwards Jardine was called away to Edinburgh and took the key to the dungeon with him, forgetting about his prisoner. He recollected after a few days and sent back a servant, but Porteous had starved. He had eaten one of his hands, and according to the version in the Statistical Account, one of his feet as well. His ghost proceeded to haunt the house. Jardine appealed for help. In Grose's version he called for a single minister, in the Statistical Account's he asked for 'a number', and in Sharpe's he summoned a 'whole army'. At the hands of the minister(s), the ghost was confined to the dungeon where he had died, although he could still be heard screaming therein. The minister(s) attached the spell to confine him to a bible and deposited it in a niche in the wall of the staircase. At one point it was removed to be rebound in Edinburgh, but the ghost then left its cell and caused such trouble that the bible was hastily restored.

Finally, there was the story of Pearlin Jean.[75] Charles Kirkpatrick Sharpe explained that when he was young, Pearlin Jean was 'the most remarkable ghost in Scotland'. Jean lived in Paris in the late seventeenth century, perhaps as a nun. There she met Robert Stuart, first baronet of the Borders estate of Allanbank, and they began a romance. However, he decided to return to Scotland without her. Jean came to him as he was stepping into his carriage to depart, and he ordered the postilion to drive on. She fell, and one of the wheels passed over her forehead, killing her. When Stuart drove up to the arched gateway at Allanbank he saw Pearlin Jean sitting on the top of it, head and shoulders covered in blood. Thereafter the house remained haunted for many years. Doors would open and slam shut again in the middle of the night, and noises such as the rustling of silk and pattering of high-heeled shoes were heard in bedrooms and passages. A servant saw the ghost in the orchard at night-time, dressed in large quantities of pearlin lace: this inspired her sobriquet. A group of seven ministers were called in to exorcise Pearlin Jean from the house, but their prayers had no effect. After a few years, the housekeeper tried a different tactic. Robert Stuart had by now married, and one wall was adorned with portraits of him and his wife. The housekeeper had a picture made of Jean, and hung it up in between the images of Robert and his wife. This seemed to pacify the ghost, and although she did not disappear completely, her behaviour became less troublesome. However, at length Robert's wife grew jealous and ordered the portrait to be removed. Thereafter, the ghost became worse natured than ever. Many years later, long after Robert's death, Jean was

[75] Account by Sharpe given in Catherine Crowe, *The Night Side of Nature, or Ghosts and Ghost Seers*, 2 vols (London, 1848), vol. 2, 189–92. For a version in verse sent to Sharpe in 1807, see John Marriott, 'Rev John Marriott to C. Kirkpatrick Sharpe, 1807', in Alexander Allardyce (ed.), *Letters from and to Charles Kirkpatrick Sharpe*, 2 vols (Edinburgh, 1888), vol. 1, 303–6.

still roaming the corridors of Allanbank. An eighteenth-century housekeeper reported seeing her frequently, and claimed she became so used to Jean's noise that it no longer alarmed her. Two ladies visiting in 1790 had heard nothing of Jean's story, but were disturbed throughout the night by something walking backwards and forwards in their bedchamber.

These three stories combined old and new patterns. The ghosts could not rest because they had died prematurely and unjustly, a common medieval pattern. Jean and Porteous still bore their wounds. None of the ghosts had a particular goal, and they did not appear to specific people, but were tied to the location of their deaths. The stories had moral messages, but religious points were vague at best. Ministers were powerless to contain Pearlin Jean, who could only be pacified through a reunion with her faithless lover. Using bibles to cast spells, as in the Porteous story, was certainly not orthodox Protestant behaviour. The stories were also tinged with romanticism. The settings – an old tower, a manor house, a burning building – had flavours of the gothic. The ghosts themselves were dramatic, poignant figures, innocent victims of gross injustices. During their lives they were underdogs, dependent on more powerful figures. They were let down, and their haunting was a form of revenge. As with some ghost pamphlets, there was also an element of social subversion, at least in the case of Jean and Porteous: higher-class figures were punished for mistreating their social inferiors. The woes of love, death and injustice were the primary themes of the stories, rather than the nature of the afterlife or the wiles of the Devil. Keith Thomas argues that ghosts progressively faded away from the late seventeenth century, when they ceased to perform valuable duties for society.[76] In fact, ghosts continued to be useful, but they did not need to be so in order to survive. It was enough for them to make good stories. The most enduring legends were those that had a strong element of human interest, and were tied to a particular location (rather than an individual), thus surviving over generations.

The Highlands

It is worth considering the case of the Highlands separately, because as discussed in the previous chapter, a distinctive Highland ghost became popular in the late eighteenth and early nineteenth centuries. As depicted in *Ossian* and by many of the nineteenth-century folklorists, the traditional Highland ghost was ancient, warlike, hearty and corporeal. It was similar to the ballad ghost, and also to revenants, but it was not depicted as a corpse risen from the grave, and it tended to appear repeatedly over an extended time-span. Possibly, however, this ghost was a mere regurgitation of Highland stereotypes, rather than an

[76] See p. 3.

authentic feature of Highland folklore. In Gaelic literature before *Ossian*, ghosts rarely appeared. Derick S. Thomson writes that there were many Gaelic songs on supernatural themes, but they were generally concerned with fairies, or occasionally shapeshifting.[77] There do not seem to have been ghosts of the Ossianic type in Macpherson's Gaelic sources. Thomson notes one case where Macpherson added a ghost to the typically 'unsentimental' Gaelic ballads. He also shows that while Macpherson presented the spirit of Loda as a 'gloomy ghost', in the source ballads this creature appeared as a 'monstrous hag'.[78] Macpherson borrowed heavily from Irish material, but warlike ghosts do not seem to have been an ancient Irish tradition either. Phyllis G. Jestice writes that 'Irish ghosts are usually benign', and that in folk culture, most ghost stories are 'postmedieval borrowings from other traditions'.[79] Peter Womack explains that Macpherson 'derided the spells and wizards he found in Fingalian material from Ireland'.[80] Just as William Collins decided that ghosts had more dramatic potential than second sight, Macpherson probably judged them a better complement to his romantic vision of Gaelic culture than the supernatural beings that actually appeared in his source material.

Writing in 1899, Alexander MacDonald noted that in the Highlands 'there are far more ghost stories based upon the wraith idea than upon that of the ghost'.[81] This is consistent with the accounts of folklorists prior to the mid-eighteenth century. Martin Martin's 1703 survey recorded a good deal on second sight, but very little on ghosts. He did describe people's sightings of 'spirits' in the shape of women, horses, swine, cats and fiery balls, and added that sometimes these spirits made noises and sang Irish songs. One mysterious voice 'resembled the voice of a woman who had died some time before, and the song related to her state in the other world'.[82] Martin also wrote of a rock mass called, in Gaelic, the 'Den of Ghosts', and described a valley that was said to be haunted by spirits termed 'the great men'. All those who entered the valley had to request the protection of the great men; otherwise they would leave the valley insane.[83] These examples do indicate a belief that the dead could linger, and the 'great men' of the valley have parallels with the ancient, menacing Highland ghosts of the nineteenth-century folklorists. These mentions from Martin are few and far between, however; he certainly does not depict ghost belief as an important facet of Highland culture. Martin also notes the belief in 'the great Giant Fin-Mac-Cowl', the warrior of Irish

77 Derick S. Thomson, *An Introduction to Gaelic Poetry*, 2nd edn (Edinburgh, 1989), 64.

78 Derick S. Thomson, *The Gaelic Sources of Macpherson's Ossian* (Edinburgh, 1952), 47, 52.

79 Phyllis G. Jestice, *Encyclopedia of Irish Spirituality* (Santa Barbara, 2000), 154–5.

80 Peter Womack, *Improvement and Romance: Constructing the Myth of the Highlands* (Basingstoke, 1988), 98.

81 Alexander MacDonald, 'Highland Ghosts', *Transactions of the Gaelic Society of Inverness* 14 (1899), 41.

82 Martin Martin, *A Description of the Western Isles of Scotland* (London, 1703), 334–5.

83 Ibid., 85–6.

mythology whose stories formed the basis for *Ossian*, but again there is no direct link to ghosts.[84] Similarly, Robert Kirk focused on second sight and fairies, referencing ghosts only through his explanation that some believed fairies to be the souls of the dead.[85] This was in part because Highland second sight was a relatively fashionable topic, having piqued the interest of Robert Boyle. However, Martin did discuss other superstitions, and it seems likely that he would have recorded more on ghost belief had it cropped up. Of course, there also might be geographical variation within the Gàidhealtachd; Martin's picture of the traditions of the western isles cannot necessarily be extended to the Highlands as a whole.

In the early-sixteenth-century *Flyting of Dumbar and Kennedie*, William Dunbar sneeringly referred to Walter Kennedy as a 'hungert heland gaist' (or a starving Highland ghost). He also wrote of how a noble (fictional) knight had

> cummered many Helland gaist,
> Amang thai dully glennis:[86]

While this suggests that there was some notion of Highland ghosts, Dunbar might have used the term for a monster (even a monstrous human).[87] Even if he were discussing ghosts, he did not draw a clear distinction between Highland and Lowland ghosts, besides in geographical terms. When ghosts from the Highlands were described in texts before *Ossian* – as, for example, in the trial over the murder of Sergeant Davies – they were not usually ancient warriors.[88] Instead they followed much the same patterns as Lowland ghosts. John Ramsay of Ochtertyre (1736–1814) was of this opinion, noting that Highland ghost beliefs 'are the same with those of the Lowlanders'.[89]

Accounts from the late eighteenth and early nineteenth centuries certainly stressed the warlike elements of Highland ghosts. The Statistical Account of 1791–9 declared that in Kirkmichael (in the county of Banff) the belief in the existence of ghosts was very prevalent. It identified the theme of the

84 Ibid., 152–3, 217, 219, 220.

85 Robert Kirk, 'Robert Kirk's *The Secret Commonwealth* and his "A Short Treatise of the Scotish-Irish Charms and Spells"', in Michael Hunter (ed.), *The Occult Laboratory: Magic, Science, and Second Sight in Late Seventeenth-Century Scotland* (Woodbridge, 2001), 83.

86 William Dunbar, 'Schir Johine the Ros, Ane Thing Thair Is Compild (The Flyting of Dumbar and Kennedie)', in Jacqueline Tasioulas (ed.), *The Makars: The Poems of Henryson, Dunbar and Douglas* (Edinburgh, 1999), v. 21, line 167, p. 347; William Dunbar, 'Of Sir Thomas Norray', in David Laing (ed.), *The Poems of William Dunbar*, 2 vols (Edinburgh, 1834), vol. 1, lines 13–14, p. 125. To 'cummer' is to harrass; 'dully' is gloomy.

87 See pp. 8–9.

88 On Sergeant Davies see pp. 104–5.

89 John Ramsay, *Scotland and Scotsmen in the Eighteenth Century*, ed. Alexander Allardyce, 2 vols (Edinburgh, 1888), vol. 2, 433.

combative ghost, and combined it with the traditional theme of ghosts seeking retribution, explaining:

> On the sequestered hill, and in the darksome valley, frequently does the benighted traveller behold the visionary semblance of his departed friend, perhaps of his enemy. The former addresses him in the language of affection; if danger is approaching, he is warned to prepare against it, or the means of avoiding it disclosed. By the latter, he is attacked with the vehemence of resentment. The inhabitants of this, and the visitant from the other world, engage in furious combat. For a while, the victory is in suspense. At length the ghost is overthrown, and his violence appeased: a few traits of his life upon earth are described. If he stole a ploughshare from his neighbour, the place where it lies concealed is pointed out. His antagonist is requested to restore it to the owner; and if he fails, punishment is threatened to follow the breach of promise; for, till restitution be made, so long must the miserable culprit be excluded from the regions of the happy.[90]

William Grant Stewart and John MacCulloch also wrote of corporeal, violent ghosts. Stewart noted that 'it is a common practice with the ghost of the present day to prowl about the country with the laudable intention of committing all the mischief in his power', and added that the ghost is 'perhaps, the best bruiser in the universe'.[91] Other stories reflected old folkloric themes of powerful corpses. The ghost of a man grabbed his widow's wrist, which was left blue and mortified, and she died in a week. Another breathed on a man and it 'seemed to freeze the blood in his veins'; he died in three days.[92] Nevertheless, while some folklorists were quick to characterise the 'ancient race' of 'stout, lusty, sociable ghosts', it is worth noting that a reasonably varied set of spectres was recorded.[93] Some ghosts appeared handsomely attired in Highland dress; others wore shrouds and had hideous, disturbing appearances; yet more were seen as merely 'numberless dusky and dim-seen forms rising above each other in the air, and muttering indistinct sounds'.[94] While some ghosts returned to cause mischief, ghosts also came back to condemn excessive grieving, because they had been murdered, to resolve unfinished business, to guard against body-snatching, or to help the living. Anne MacVicar Grant argued that Highland

90 John Grant, 'Parish of Kirkmichael', in John Sinclair (ed.), *The Statistical Account of Scotland, 1791–1799*, electronic edn, 21 vols (University of Edinburgh, University of Glasgow, 1999), vol. 12, http://stataccscot.edina.ac.uk/link/osa-vol12-p425-parish-banff-kirkmichael, accessed 1 Feb. 2018, 460.

91 William Grant Stewart, *The Popular Superstitions and Festive Amusements of the Highlanders of Scotland* (Edinburgh, 1823), 19, 20; John MacCulloch, *The Highlands and Western Isles of Scotland*, 4 vols (London, 1824), vol. 4, 338.

92 Anne MacVicar Grant, *Essays on the Superstitions of the Highlanders of Scotland*, 2 vols (London, 1811), vol. 1, 217–18, 230.

93 Stewart, *Popular Superstitions*, 5.

94 Hugh Miller, *Scenes and Legends of the North of Scotland, or The Traditional History of Cromarty* (Edinburgh, 1835), 369; Stewart, *Popular Superstitions*, 30; Grant, *Essays on the Superstitions*, vol. 1, 217–18, quotation 255.

ghosts were generally 'conjured up by affection', and appeared 'like "angels sent on errands full of love," to warn or soothe the survivors'.[95]

Specific Highland ghosts that became particularly well known, however, tended to follow more consistent patterns. Many were associated with certain families, a theme of ancestor protection that is relatively uncommon in western ghost stories. MacCulloch explained: 'Every Chief ... had his family spirit; a sort of Herald Mortuary, who forewarned him of death, as it had warned all his predecessors and was to warn his posterity for ever.'[96] Scott wrote of a female figure called May Moullach (discussed further below, as a figure commonly associated with brownies); she appeared to the Grant family to alert them to oncoming disasters.[97] There was the Glas Lich, a 'dreadful spectre' said to appear as a 'thin gigantic hag', or a 'tall, emaciated, gigantic female figure'. MacCulloch explained that she was 'the Angel of death to Barrisdale, or to Glengarry; for nobody seems very certain, and not many care'.[98] In *Waverley* Scott made use of the Bodach Glas, a grey-clad figure who appeared to foretell death. Robert Chambers explained that this could be traced to a legend in the Maclaine family: an ancestor who had been slain in battle would appear to the clan chief to notify him if somebody in the family were near death.[99] This ancestor always appeared on horseback. Both he and the horse were small; in particular, he had a small head, earning him the epithet Hugh of the Little Head. (The Gaelic was 'Eoghan', and in other sources Hugh was given as Ewen.) He appeared at night and would ride furiously around the house, making a noise like the rattling of chains. When observed he would gallop away. Chambers explained that Hugh himself had died according to a prophecy. On the eve of a battle he was told that if his wife voluntarily brought him breakfast the next morning the battle would go well; if he had to call for it he would be killed. His ungenerous wife failed this trial of love, and Hugh met his death as predicted.[100] A contemporary magazine explained that this spectre's 'mournful duty' was to attend his descendants at their deathbeds and escort their spirits to the afterlife.[101] MacCulloch also

95 Grant, *Essays on the Superstitions*, vol. 1, 113. 'Angels sent on errands full of love' is a quotation from Edward Young's 'Night Thoughts'. Edward Young, *Edward Young: Night Thoughts*, ed. Stephen Cornford (Cambridge, 1989), line 293, p. 80.

96 MacCulloch, *Highlands and Western Isles*, vol. 4, 337. See also Pennant, *Tour in Scotland 1772, Part 2*, 12–13.

97 Walter Scott, 'Notes to Canto Third', in *The Lady of the Lake: A Poem* (Edinburgh, 1810), 345.

98 MacCulloch, *Highlands and Western Isles*, vol. 4, 338; Thomas Pennant, *A Tour in Scotland 1772, Part 1* (Chester, 1774), 397; Scott, 'Notes to Canto Third', in *Lady of the Lake*, 345.

99 Robert Chambers, *Illustrations of the Author of Waverley: Being Notices and Anecdotes of Real Characters, Scenes, and Incidents, Supposed to Be Described in His Works*, 2nd edn (Edinburgh, 1825), 31.

100 Ibid., 31–2; see also 33–4.

101 'Traditions of the Western Highlands, No. III', *London Literary Gazette*, 20 Mar. 1824, 189.

described a Ewen of the Little Head who inhabited the mountains around Ben More, Mull. He was a giant, and lost his head in warfare, but another sprang up in its place. He appeared when a chief of Loch Buy was to die, and rode around the loch for three successive nights.[102]

There were stories of Hugh/Ewen getting into fights with his kinsmen or other locals, but the most violent spectre discussed by the early-nineteenth-century folklorists was Lham Dearg, the Ghost of the Bloody Hand.[103] He was said to haunt the woods of Glenmore and Rothiemurchus, dressed in armour. Scott stated that one of his hands was covered in blood, and he battled everyone he met. Scott presented Lham Dearg as an ancient tradition, explaining that 'the northern champions of old were accustomed peculiarly to search for, and delight in, encounters with such military spectres'.[104] In *Marmion*, Scott had the sixteenth-century poet David Lindsay present a story of

> A spectre fell, of fiendish might,
> In likeness of a Scottish knight,[105]

Scott also wrote of a combative Highland spectre he had seen described in a manuscript, which he estimated was about a century old.[106] Broadly speaking, this body of ghosts was in keeping with the Ossianic template of the Highland ghost. They were ancient and warlike. They also reflected the importance of clan society within the Highlands, remaining tied by kinship bonds long after their deaths. There was certainly a perception among Scott and his contemporaries that they were recording old traditions, and as there is little material on Highland beliefs before this period, the absence of earlier mentions of these ghosts is not sufficient evidence to the contrary. However, even if these ghosts were a feature of Highland folklore long before Macpherson came on to the scene, they do not seem to have been as widely discussed. The (admittedly limited) source material suggests that second sight was the primary way of interpreting and talking about Highland apparitions before the second half of the eighteenth century. Thereafter, ghosts moved into the spotlight. The stout, sturdy, combative ghost may have existed before, but it became significantly more popular, representing a fusion between traditional belief and the romantic vision of Highland society popularised by Macpherson.

102 MacCulloch, *Highlands and Western Isles*, vol. 4, 324–5. See also Scott, 'Notes to Canto Third', in *Lady of the Lake*, 347.

103 Stories about fights can be found in 'Traditions of the Western Highlands', 189; Chambers, *Illustrations of the Author of Waverley*, 33–4.

104 Walter Scott, 'Notes to Canto Third', in *Marmion: A Tale of Flodden Field* (Edinburgh, 1808), lxi, lxiv; Scott, 'Notes to Canto Third', in *Lady of the Lake*, 345. See also MacCulloch, *Highlands and Western Isles*, vol. 4, 338.

105 Scott, *Marmion*, canto 4, v. 22, p. 210.

106 Scott, 'Notes to Canto Third', in *Marmion*, lxii–lxiv.

It is also interesting to note that ghosts and second sight increasingly overlapped. When ghosts foreshadowed death they were taking on the role of second sight apparitions. Moreover, nineteenth-century folklorists sometimes conflated the two beliefs. MacCulloch drew a distinction between 'the Genius or Astral spirit of the Second Sight, and the true Ghost, or disembodied soul'. However, he also wrote:

> Every Highlander is born with an attached or rather a detached ghost, which accompanies him from the cradle to the grave ... The Genius, or ghost of our mountaineer, resembles, in every circumstance, even of dress, his principal: infantile at birth, and thus following him through life; undistinguishable from the reality, by those who possess the faculty of seeing the inhabitants of the invisible world; and changing his aspect, and even his dress, in an instant, and in exact conformity to the changes or caprices of the true man.[107]

Similarly, Stewart explained:

> Every native Highlander has allied to him, from his birth, one of those airy beings, in the character of an auxiliary or helpmate ... From the birth of the mortal to the eve of his death, the ghost, in point of similitude, is a perfect counterpart or representative of his earthly yoke-fellow ... A short time previous to the mortal's death, and when just on the eve of dissolution, the ghost undergoes a striking revolution in his appearance and habits ... he then becomes the awful emblem of death in all its similitudes. Attired in a shroud, and all the ensigns of the grave, the ghost nocturnally proceeds to the narrow house of his future residence, and there disappears ... The mortal resigns his breath, and is about to follow the course of the dead-candle to his new abode, when *Taish na Tialedh*, or the funeral foregoing, takes the road.[108]

Stewart clarified that the ghost was 'of course invisible to those not possessing the second-sight'.[109] He also noted that these ghosts would perform duties for their earthly counterparts after their deaths: 'In this respect, then, the peculiar advantage of the Highlander over his Lowland neighbour becomes perfectly apparent. Through the medium of a faithful ghost and a confidential friend, transactions, as intricate and ravelled as those of the Laird of Coul, can be easily simplified and assorted.'[110]

The ghostly double, the shrouded figure foreshadowing death, and the spectral funeral procession were all themes that appeared frequently in stories of second sight. However, this mode of explaining them, as the mortal's ghost journeying with him throughout life, did not commonly appear in the late-seventeenth- and early-eighteenth-century investigations into second sight.

[107] MacCulloch, *Highlands and Western Isles*, vol. 4, 335, 70.

[108] Stewart, *Popular Superstitions*, 4, 16, 28, 32. *Taish na Tialedh* is *taibhs' na tiodhlaig*, the apparition of the funeral. I am grateful to Dr Dòmhnall Uilleam Stiùbhart for his assistance here.

[109] Ibid., 17.

[110] Ibid., 38.

Martin explained: 'There is a way of foretelling Death by a Cry that they call *Taisk*, which some call a *Wrath* in the Low-land', and noted that second sight was called *Taish* in Irish.[111] MacCulloch wrote sneeringly: 'If Martin had understood his trade as he ought, he would have known that the Taisch was the Astral spirit of the individual.'[112] Robert Kirk came closer to this interpretation:

> Some men of that exalted sight (whither by airt or nature) have told me they have seen at those meetings [funeral banquets] a double-man, or the shape of the same man in two places, that is, a Superterranean and a Subterranean Inhabitant perfectly resembling one another in all points, who he notwithstanding could easily distinguish one from another by some secret tockens and operations.[113]

The connection with ghosts had become much clearer and more explicit by the nineteenth century, however. German stories of doppelgängers (or ghostly doubles) had become popular in the latter half of the eighteenth century, perhaps contributing to this interpretation of second sight.[114] It is possibly also a reflection of the growing importance of ghosts in Scottish culture: there was more general interest in charting their activities, and stories such as the Laird of Coul's came readily to mind as points of comparison. Again, although the evidence is far from conclusive, this may suggest that traditional second sight beliefs were being restyled by romantic folklorists. This phantasmal double was clearly a different category of spectre from the hearty, warlike Highland ghost. However, it was similarly used to underline the idea that the Highlands had their own ancient set of ghost traditions. This may have been the case, but it was only from the late eighteenth century that these supposed traditions were paraded as a point of cultural interest.

Fairies, Brownies, Will o' the Wisps and Banshees

In his *Letters on Demonology and Witchcraft* (1830), Walter Scott declared:

> [Banshees and brownies] ... are too limited, and too much obliterated from recollection, to call for special discussion ... but something remains to be said upon another species of superstition, so general that it may be called proper to mankind in every climate; so deeply rooted also in human belief, that it is found to survive in states of society during which all other fictions of the same order are entirely dismissed from influence. Mr. Crabbe, with his usual felicity, has called the belief in ghosts 'the last lingering fiction of the brain'.[115]

[111] Martin, *Description of the Western Isles*, 305, 300.
[112] MacCulloch, *Highlands and Western Isles*, vol. 4, 337.
[113] Kirk, 'Robert Kirk's *The Secret Commonwealth*', 80.
[114] See Crowe, *Night Side of Nature*, vol. 1, ch. 8.
[115] Walter Scott, *Letters on Demonology and Witchcraft* (London, 1830), letter 10, 354. The reference is to George Crabbe, *The Library: A Poem* (London, 1781), 28.

Similarly, in the second edition of his *Scenes and Legends* (1850), Hugh Miller asserted that 'Of all the wilder beliefs of our forefathers, there is none which so truly continues to exist as the belief in the churchyard spectre'.[116] These assertions, however, did not take into account how closely popular ghost beliefs were intertwined with beliefs about other supernatural beings. John MacCulloch complained of the Highlanders:

> Some of their Ghosts also are ordinary Elves and Goblins, confounded in the narrations: the Eating Ghost appears to be a corrupted Brownie; and, now and then, I believe he may be traced to the Vampires of Mycone. In other cases, the Ghost is plainly the Fire King, since he carries a light in his mouth; and, occasionally he is even confounded with Fairies and with ordinary Witches.[117]

Let us begin with the case of the fairies. The association between fairies and the dead was long standing. Fairyland was once linked with Hades, the land of the dead.[118] Robert Sempill wrote of 'nychtbouris sex or sewin' that the people 'belevit had bene in heawin' riding with the fairies.[119] Similarly, in the well-known Middle English poem *Sir Orfeo*, Orfeo saw in fairyland

> folk that were thider y-brought
> And thought dede, and nare nought.[120]

The witch trials offer further sixteenth- and seventeenth-century examples. Elspeth Reoch was visited by a dead kinsman who was also a fairy; Bessie Dunlop's ghostly visitor allowed her to maintain contact with the fairy realm; Andro Man met ghosts at a fairy gathering.[121] Robert Kirk reported the belief that 'Fairie-hills' were the dwelling-place of departed souls, or perhaps an intermediary location in which to await the Last Judgement.[122] James Garden explained to John Aubrey that a *Taishtar*, or second sighted person, was someone who 'converses with ghosts & spirits, or as they commonly call them,

116 Miller, *Scenes and Legends*, 2nd edn, 353.
117 MacCulloch, *Highlands and Western Isles*, vol. 4, 335–6.
118 See Lizanne Henderson and Edward J. Cowan, *Scottish Fairy Belief: A History* (East Linton, 2001), 19–20; K. M. Briggs, *The Anatomy of Puck: An Examination of Fairy Beliefs Among Shakespeare's Contemporaries and Successors* (London, 1959), ch. 9.
119 See p. 29.
120 Anne Laskaya and Eve Salisbury (eds), 'Sir Orfeo', in *The Middle English Breton Lays*, electronic edn (Medieval Institute Publications, 1995), http://d.lib.rochester.edu/teams/publication/laskaya-and-salisbury-middle-english-breton-lays, accessed 1 Feb. 2018, lines 388–9.
121 See the records of their cases at Julian Goodare et al., *The Survey of Scottish Witchcraft* (University of Edinburgh, 2003), http://www.shca.ed.ac.uk/witches, accessed 1 Feb. 2018.
122 Kirk, 'Robert Kirk's *The Secret Commonwealth*', 83, 85.

the fairies or fairie-folk'.[123] Touring Scotland in the 1760s, Thomas Pennant recorded an interesting story from Breadalbane. A man was working in a cabbage garden when he was swept into the air and carried into a field. There he found himself surrounded by a crowd of men and women, some of whom he knew had been dead for years. They spoke an unknown language, and their voices had a 'hollow sound'. They pushed him around, but when he said the name of God they all vanished but one. The one who remained made him promise to meet her in a week. He did so, but the spectre said she was in too much of a hurry to speak with him, and bade him leave again, promising that no harm would come to him.[124] This story recalls traditions of people being carried away to fairy realms, where groups partied together. Pennant noted that 'the friends and neighbours of the deceased, whom the old dreamer had named, were in the utmost anxiety at finding them in such bad company in the other world'.[125] The dead had clearly gone somewhere ungodly, yet were not burning in Hell. Fairyland stood as a third ground.

'White ladies' were a relatively common category of ghost in nineteenth-century folklore. However, they also had green-clad rivals. The colour green was linked to the natural world; perhaps ironically, this also tied it to the supernatural. When Robert Burns wrote about the apparition of a Scottish muse, he presented her as a beautiful woman in tartan, wearing a green mantle:

> Her *Mantle* large, of greenish hue,
> My gazing wonder chiefly drew;
> Deep *lights* and *shades*, bold-mingling, threw
> A lustre grand;
> And seem'd, to my astonish'd view,
> A *well-known* Land.[126]

Fairies and nature spirits were often said to wear green.[127] Occasionally ghosts imitated this pattern. A mansion in Blairgowrie, Perthshire, was haunted by a 'green lady'.[128] The 1834–45 Statistical Account recorded that in Leochel, County of Aberdeen, one area 'has the reputation of being haunted by the apparition of a lady in green or white; but the oldest living inhabitant not

123 James Garden, 'James Garden's Letters to John Aubrey', in Michael Hunter (ed.), *The Occult Laboratory: Magic, Science, and Second Sight in Late Seventeenth-Century Scotland* (Woodbridge, 2001), 150.

124 Thomas Pennant, *A Tour in Scotland 1769* (Chester, 1771), 89–90.

125 Ibid., 90.

126 Robert Burns, 'The Vision', in *Poems, Chiefly in the Scottish Dialect* (Kilmarnock, 1786), 90–1.

127 R. L. Tongue, 'Folk-Song and Folklore', *Folklore* 78 (1967), 298.

128 Robert McDonald, 'Parish of Blairgowrie', in *The New Statistical Account of Scotland, 1834–45*, electronic edn, 15 vols (University of Edinburgh, University of Glasgow, 1999), vol. 10, http://stataccscot.edina.ac.uk/link/ nsa-vol10-p897-parish-perth-blairgowrie, accessed 1 Feb. 2018, 915.

having had ocular demonstration, the colour of the dress remains doubtful.'[129] Writing in 1835, Hugh Miller discussed the Green Lady, terming her 'one of the old Scottish spectres, who flourished before the introduction of shrouds and dead linens'.[130] He gave several stories of these ladies. They were associated with death; some were explicitly the ghosts of dead people. One was apt to wander among cottages at night, bearing a goblin child in her arms. She would wash this child in the blood of the house's youngest inhabitant, who would then die. Another was 'Genius of the smallpox'.[131] In these stories, the green lady displayed characteristics of both ghosts and fairies. Fairies were often malevolent, and were known to play tricks on the households they visited. The mingling of fairy and ghost traditions created a purely folkloric creature, which did not appear in gothic literature or elite discussions of ghosts.

Then there was the case of brownies, a sub-category of fairies. Brownies served a particular household. They did chores, and occasionally played tricks on the inhabitants. They also might appear in second sight visions. The brownie was associated with the idea of a haunting spirit, and sometimes was depicted as an actual individual called Brownie. In 1606, William Birnie outlined the supposed connections between brownies and the dead in pagan eschatology, explaining that people who had lived good (but not perfect) lives had to spend some time serving mankind as Brunies.[132] James VI spoke of a spirit called Brownie who 'appeared in time of *Papistrie* and blindnesse, and haunted divers houses, without doing any evill, but doing as it were necessarie turnes up and down the house'.[133] In a 1701 account of Shetland, John Brand claimed that 'Not above 40 or 50 Years ago, almost every Family had a *Brouny*'.[134] Martin Martin similarly explained: 'A Spirit by the Countrey *People* call'd *Browny*, was frequently seen in all the most Considerable Families in the isles and North of *Scotland*, in the shape of a tall Man, but within these twenty or thirty years past, he is seen but rarely.' He also recorded a case of the figure Browny helping a man to win at cards.[135]

Brownies were by no means 'obliterated from recollection' by the nineteenth century, as James Hogg's *The Brownie of Bodsbeck* (1818) indicates. The overlap between brownies and ghosts is neatly demonstrated by two

[129] Alexander Taylor, 'Parish of Leochel and Cushnie', in *The New Statistical Account of Scotland, 1834–45*, electronic edn, 15 vols (University of Edinburgh, University of Glasgow, 1999), vol. 12, http://stataccscot.edina.ac.uk/link/nsa-vol12-p1102-parish-aberdeen-leochel, accessed 1 Feb. 2018, 1106.

[130] Miller, *Scenes and Legends*, 128.

[131] Ibid., 15.

[132] William Birnie, *The Blame of Kirk-Buriall, Tending to Perswade Cemiteriall Civilitie* (Edinburgh, 1606, STC 3089), ch. 12, C4v–D. See pp. 26–7.

[133] James VI, *Daemonologie, in Forme of Ane Dialogue*, in James Craigie and Alexander Law (eds), *Minor Prose Works of King James VI and I* (Edinburgh, 1982), bk. 3, ch. 2, 45.

[134] John Brand, *A Brief Description of Orkney, Zetland, Pightland-Firth & Caithness* (Edinburgh, 1701), 112.

[135] Martin, *Description of the Western Isles*, 334, 320.

nineteenth-century stories. *The Brownie o' Fearnden* appeared in a chapbook in 1832.[136] It described a brownie who served a family faithfully, and saved the goodwife's life by riding out for a midwife when she was in a difficult labour. *The Ghaist o' Fearnden* (1834) was by Peter Keith, who self-published a few ghost stories. It gave the same account of the family and the difficult labour, but it was a local ghost who rode for the midwife. In both versions the midwife rode with the brownie/ghost and commented on the broadness of his feet. *The Ghaist o' Fearnden* had an extra component: a passage in which the ghost admitted that he could not rest because he had stolen a pair of gloves during his lifetime, and gained absolution by revealing where he had hidden them.[137] This reinforced his identity as a returning dead person, but he was nonetheless a ghost who recalled brownie traditions.

In addition to Brownie there was a girl called Meg Mullach (or similar), who cropped up in a variety of different accounts, generally associated with the Highlands. She was usually said to look like a small, hairy creature in the shape of a young girl, with a particularly hairy left hand. James Garden explained in the 1690s that 'Megg Mullach, & Brownie ... are two ghosts, which (as it is constantly reported) of old haunted a family in Strathspey of the name of Grant'.[138] Meg was usually presented as a female; John MacCulloch described her as the 'female Brownie', and William Grant Stewart suggested that she and Brownie might have been man and wife.[139] However, she could also take a masculine form, and might even serve as a defender of men's rights. Walter Macfarlane's *Geographical Collections*, made in the mid-eighteenth century, recorded that the Grant family was haunted by

> a spirit called Meg Mulloch. It appeared like a little Boy, and in dark nights would hold a candle before the Goodman, and shew him the way home, and if the Goodwife would not come to bed, it would cast her in beyond him and if she refused to bring what he desired, it would cast it before him.[140]

Lachlan Shaw noted that the Tullochgorum family was haunted by '*Maag Moulach, i.e.* "One with the left hand all over hairy"', and that the synod had made enquiries into her appearances, but discovered little.[141] In the case of

136 *Thrummy Cap, a Tale; and The Brownie o' Fearnden, a Ballad* (Brechin, 1832). For another version see Alexander Laing, 'The Brownie of Fearnden', in Alexander Whitelaw (ed.), *The Book of Scottish Ballads: Collected and Illustrated with Historical and Critical Notices* (Glasgow, 1845), 502–3.

137 Peter Keith, *The Ghaist o' Fearnden; Auld Poumire; and Rob Man; Three Tales* ([Brechin?], 1834).

138 Garden, 'James Garden's Letters', 151.

139 MacCulloch, *Highlands and Western Isles*, vol. 4, 351; Stewart, *Popular Superstitions*, 142.

140 Walter MacFarlane, *Geographical Collections Relating to Scotland Made by Walter Macfarlane*, ed. Arthur Mitchell and James Toshach Clark, 3 vols (Edinburgh, 1906–8), vol. 3, 243.

141 Lachlan Shaw, *The History of the Province of Moray* (Edinburgh, 1775), 306. See also Pennant, *Tour in Scotland 1772, Part 2*, 13.

Meg we again see the confusion between ghosts and brownies or fairies. There was no suggestion that Meg was a returning dead person, but she was termed a 'ghost' or described as 'haunting' the families she attended. Both she and Brownie appear to have been well known, despite not being the kind of ghost that was popularised by gothic and romantic fiction.

Ghosts were also tied up with other popular beliefs surrounding death. Will o' the wisps – also known as dead lights, corpse candles or ignis fatuus – were lights that supposedly foreshadowed death. Martin Martin wrote that corpse candles were 'well known and attested', and described spirits appearing as 'fiery balls, which would follow men in the fields'.[142] Corpse candles were also mentioned by Thomas Pennant and by the Reverend John Beaton.[143] A 1782 text about Buckhaven in Fife, attributed to Dougal Graham, detailed the local belief in 'willie and the wisp', a fiery devil who led travellers to their death.[144] In the nineteenth century, the *Dumfries and Galloway Monthly Magazine* described the appearance of 'deid lichts' to a Dumfries lady in 1822, and Scott explained that the death of a Highland clan chief was 'sometimes supposed to be announced by a chain of lights of different colours'.[145] William Grant Stewart wrote of how, prior to a mortal's death, his ghostly counterpart would make a journey to his grave, attired in a shroud. He added: 'He is lighted on his way by a pale azure-coloured light of the size of that emitted by a *tallow* candle, which is of a flickering unsteady nature, sometimes vivid, and sometimes faint, as the mortal inhales and respires his breath.'[146]

In some cases, these lights were linked with actual dead souls. Anne MacVicar Grant told a suggestive story of six bright lights and a 'small greenish one', the souls of seven deceased children (the last born prematurely) who returned to their mother to comfort her nightly. In this case the lights did not foreshadow death, but this was unusual. Grant also wrote of a minister who saw a pair of small lights leaving a part of the churchyard where two children had been buried. They travelled to the nearby hamlet and returned accompanied by a larger light. Soon afterwards their father died.[147] The 1834 Statistical Account recorded that in Inverness, the 'luminous meteor' called Will o' the Wisp was seen every year since 1812. It was linked to a story of a woman who went at night to sand-banks to dig for some rue (Galium verum),

142 Martin, *Description of the Western Isles*, 313, 334.

143 Pennant, *Tour in Scotland 1769*, 160; J. L. Campbell and Derick Thomson, *Edward Lhuyd in the Scottish Highlands, 1699–1700* (Oxford, 1963), 53.

144 Merry Andrew, *The Antient and New History of Buck-Haven in Fife Shire* ([Edinburgh?], 1782), 22.

145 J. Maxwell Wood, *Witchcraft and Superstitious Record in Southwest Scotland* (Dumfries, 1911), 213; Scott, 'Notes to Canto Third', in *Lady of the Lake*, 346–7.

146 Stewart, *Popular Superstitions*, 28. See also MacCulloch, *Highlands and Western Isles*, vol. 4, 359; Jean Matthias D'Amour, *Memoirs of Mr. Matthias D'Amour*, ed. Paul Rodgers (London, 1836), 136; R. C. Maclagan, 'Ghost Lights of the West Highlands', *Folklore* 8 (1897), 203–56.

147 Grant, *Essays on the Superstitions*, vol. 1, 190–5, 258–61. See also 290.

a substance used as red dye. She went against her husband's will and in defiance of a prohibition by the local magistrates (the sand-banks, once excavated, were easily blown away). She never returned, and her body was never found. Shortly afterwards the meteor was first seen, giving rise to the theory that it was the ghost of 'the unfortunate and profane woman'.[148]

Certain noises also foreshadowed death. The crowing of a cock was a common example, and in the *Ossian* poetry, death could be heard on a harp.[149] Howling noises were also reported.[150] This recalled ideas about banshees, a feature of medieval folklore across Europe. Banshees screeched or wailed before death. They seem to have survived as a belief in Scotland. Pennant noted that 'in certain places, the death of people is supposed to be foretold by the cries and shrieks of *Benshi*', and although Scott claimed that banshees were largely 'obliterated from recollection' alongside brownies, he also reported that 'the Ben-Shie implies the female Fairy, whose lamentations were often supposed to precede the death of a chieftain of particular families'.[151] Banshees too might be intertwined with ghosts. James Macpherson wrote: 'It was long the opinion of the ancient Scots, that a ghost was heard shrieking near the place where a death was to happen soon after.'[152] The Statistical Account of 1791–9 recorded that in Applecross, in the county of Ross and Cromarty, 'The ghost of the dying, called tasks, are said to be heard, their cry being a repetition of the moans of the sick'.[153] Speaking of the Highlands, John Graham Dalyell noted: 'The ghosts of the dying are spoke of as in a separate state; and others were believed, not only to echo the moans of the sick, preceding dissolution, but after it to prove an audible guide to the place of sepulture.'[154]

These stories indicate how flexible and varied popular ghost beliefs could be. Although the late-seventeenth- and early-eighteenth-century focus on

148 Roderick MacLean, 'Parish of South Uist', in *The New Statistical Account of Scotland, 1834–45*, electronic edn, 15 vols (University of Edinburgh, University of Glasgow, 1999), vol. 14, http://stataccscot.edina.ac.uk/link/nsa-vol14-p182-parish-inverness-south_uist, accessed 1 Feb. 2018, 184.

149 Campbell and Thomson, *Edward Lhuyd in the Scottish Highlands*, 55.

150 Theophilus Insulanus, *A Treatise on the Second Sight, Dreams and Apparitions* (Edinburgh, 1763), 76, 113.

151 Pennant, *Tour in Scotland 1769*, 160; Scott, 'Notes to Canto Third', in *Lady of the Lake*, 346. At 345, Scott explains that domestic spirits such as Meg Mullach informed their families of approaching disaster by wailing. See also Scott's introduction to the Magnum Opus edition of *The Monastery*. Walter Scott, *Waverley Novels, Vol. 18: The Monastery* (Edinburgh, 1830), xv.

152 James Macpherson, 'Fingal, an Ancient Epic Poem', in *The Works of Ossian, the Son of Fingal*, 2 vols (London, 1765), vol. 1, bk. 1, 28.

153 John McQueen, 'Parish of Applecross', in John Sinclair (ed.), *The Statistical Account of Scotland, 1791–1799*, electronic edn, 21 vols (University of Edinburgh, University of Glasgow, 1999), vol. 3, http://stataccscot.edina.ac.uk/link/osa-vol3-p369-parish-ross_and_cromarty-applecross, accessed 1 Feb. 2018, 380.

154 John Graham Dalyell, *The Darker Superstitions of Scotland: Illustrated from History and Practice* (Edinburgh, 1834), 589.

combating atheism gave ghosts a new lease of life within elite texts, many popular ghost beliefs continued to operate outside of a Christian framework. The dead might become fairies, meteors, strange lights or noises. Gothic and romantic works popularised a more distinctive ghost stereotype, which would increasingly shape perceptions of ghosts in decades to come. However, in the early nineteenth century this process was still in its infancy. Folkloric ghosts remained diverse and entangled with other supernatural beings.

Belief

The fact that ghost stories were in circulation does not necessarily mean that people took them seriously. As we saw in the last chapter, there was a perception that ghost stories were valuable cultural relics regardless of whether or not they were credited. Unfortunately, there are few other ways to gauge levels of early modern belief. Educated men might complain about how ghost belief terrorised the 'unlearned', but they were not in the habit of conducting methodical surveys of belief.[155] Admittedly, when folklorists recorded stories it was often with the understanding – whether or not it was explicitly stated – that they were believed locally. Wodrow would often specify that his stories were generally believed, and when Francis Grose recorded the story of Porteous he noted that the woman who informed him seemed to believe 'every syllable'.[156] However, several folklorists rejected the idea of the credulous populace. Records from the Statistical Accounts of 1791–9 and 1834–45 hailed the demise of superstition, with one asserting that 'ghosts, gobblins, witches, and fairies have relinquished the land'.[157] Robert Chambers declared that in the late eighteenth century 'the shades of superstition began universally to give way in Scotland'.[158] Writing in the 1790s, Elizabeth Mure similarly consigned credulity to the realms of the past:

[155] Insulanus, *Treatise on the Second Sight*, 112.

[156] Grose, *Antiquities of Scotland*, vol. 1, 144.

[157] See, for example, John Tod, 'Parish of Mauchline', in *The New Statistical Account of Scotland, 1834–45*, electronic edn, 15 vols (University of Edinburgh, University of Glasgow, 1999), vol. 5, http://stataccscot.edina.ac.uk/link/nsa-vol5-p158-parish-ayrshire-mauchline, 167; A. Johnstone, 'Parish of Monquhitter: Additional Communications', in John Sinclair (ed.), *The Statistical Account of Scotland, 1791–1799*, electronic edn, 21 vols (University of Edinburgh, University of Glasgow, 1999), vol. 21, http://stataccscot.edina.ac.uk/link/osa-vol21-p138-appendix-aberdeen-monquhitter, 149. Quotation from William McRitchie, 'Parish of Clunie', in John Sinclair (ed.), *The Statistical Account of Scotland, 1791–1799*, electronic edn, 21 vols (University of Edinburgh, University of Glasgow, 1999), vol. 9, http://stataccscot.edina.ac.uk/link/osa-vol9-p225-parish-perth-clunie, 253. All accessed 1 Feb. 2018.

[158] Chambers, 'Traditions of the Celebrated Major Weir', 307.

> The fear of Hell and deceitful power of the Devil was at the bottom of all [the Scots'] religious sentiments. The established belief in witchcraft (for which many suffer'd) prevailed much at this time; Ghosts too and appearitions of various kinds were credit'd; few old houses was without a Ghost chamber that few people had Courage to sleep in. Omens and Dreams were much regarded even by people of the best Education. These were the manners of the last Century, and remained in part for 30 years in this.[159]

Hugh Miller even allowed for scepticism on the part of the man who told him ghost stories, explaining: 'He had, I suspect, a good deal of the skeptic in his composition, and regarded his ghost stories rather as the machinery of a sort of domestic poetry than as pieces of real history.'[160]

After touring Scotland in 1773, Samuel Johnson concluded that second sight belief had survived in the islands, although it was rejected by Lowlanders and ministers:

> It is the common talk of the Lowland *Scots*, that the notion of the *Second Sight* is wearing away with other superstitions; and that its reality is no longer supposed, but by the grossest people. How far its prevalence ever extended, or what ground it has lost, I know not. The Islanders of all degrees, whether of rank or understanding, universally admit it, except the Ministers, who universally deny it, and are suspected to deny it, in consequence of a system, against conviction.[161]

A discussion of Shetland from the 1834–45 Statistical Accounts declared that 'Witchcraft, charms, and apparitions, are firmly believed in', while the entry on Kilbride, Bute, similarly attested that 'the belief in ghosts, witches, and fairies, has still a firm hold of the minds of many'.[162] However, writing in 1824, MacCulloch proclaimed that the Highlanders were no more credulous on any topic than the Lowlanders. He noted that 'the real Ghosts or disembodied spirits of men, seem to have fled with the Second sight', adding that Macpherson probably borrowed his, perhaps from Norwegian mythology. He explained that Highlanders remembered ghosts because of their poetry, not because they featured in their belief system any more. He excepted only a few 'weak and credulous' people influenced by the dramatic landscape.[163] He also declared:

159 Elizabeth Mure, 'Some Remarks on the Change of Manners in My Own Time, 1700–1790', in William Mure (ed.), *Selections from the Family Papers Preserved at Caldwell*, 3 vols (Glasgow, 1854), vol. 1, 266.

160 Miller, *Scenes and Legends*, 2nd edn, 328–9.

161 Samuel Johnson, *A Journey to the Western Islands of Scotland* (London, 1775), 252.

162 Laurence Edmondaton, 'General Observations on the County of Shetland', in *The New Statistical Account of Scotland, 1834–45*, electronic edn, 15 vols (University of Edinburgh, University of Glasgow, 1999), vol. 15, http://stataccscot.edina.ac.uk/link/nsa-vol15-p145-general-shetland-county_general, 157; Allan McNaughton, 'Island of Arran: Parish of Kilbride', in *The New Statistical Account of Scotland, 1834–45*, electronic edn, 15 vols (University of Edinburgh, University of Glasgow, 1999), vol. 5, http://stataccscot.edina.ac.uk/link/nsa-vol5-p1-parish-bute-kilbride, 27. Both accessed 1 Feb. 2018.

163 MacCulloch, *Highlands and Western Isles*, vol. 4, 340–1.

> All the world has heard of Highland Ghosts and Superstitions, and we have been desired to believe that the people are as credulous as ever. This has been the consequence of repeating, as of to-day, things long past: it is, as I have often said, Romance attempting to pass for Truth. The Highlanders now believe just as much as their Pictish and Saxon neighbours.[164]

David Stewart of Garth similarly asserted that missionary work had caused people to lose 'a great portion of their belief in fairies, ghosts and the second sight'. Interestingly, he regretted the loss of these 'innocent, attractive and often sublime superstitions' which acted as a moral safeguard, adding 'the fear of a ghost is as honourable and legitimate a check as the fear of the gallows'.[165]

In short, there is no sure way to assess levels of belief. Whether or not they were credited, however, stories circulated. The development of print culture made accounts of ghosts accessible in a new format, and the fresh interest of folklorists may also have contributed to the wider dissemination of ghost stories. Again, even if they were not always taken to be objective realities, ghosts had value. This might stem from their religious messages, their reflections on death and social injustice, their significance as local celebrities, or simply the fact that they made good stories.

Conclusion

The ghosts of popular culture followed a variety of patterns. Revenants survived (particularly through the ballads), but the ethereal ghost also appeared, as did more or less everything in between. Ghosts were further diversified through being interwoven with beliefs about fairies, brownies, unusual lights and noises. Heavily romanticised ghosts seem to have appeared with more frequency as the eighteenth century progressed. As we saw in the last chapter, these ghosts were characterised by a focus on aesthetics. They might be of the white, gliding, occasionally resplendent variety; alternatively, they might be hearty, corporeal Highland spectres. They liked to haunt old castles and churchyards. While these ghosts owed much to literary trends, it is difficult to state that elite culture was simply imposing its own template on a divergent popular tradition. The white ghost was of long standing. Incorporeality could be traced to second sight or wraith apparitions, as much as to gothic poetry. The Highland ghost, while clearly in part inspired by stereotypes of the Highlanders and the *Ossian* poetry, also drew on popular traditions about revenants, giants and second sight apparitions. By emphasising some types of ghost at the expense of others, folklorists and fiction writers may have caused

164 Ibid., vol. 4, 320.

165 David Stewart, *Sketches of the Character, Manners, and Present State of the Highlanders of Scotland*, 2 vols (Edinburgh, 1822), vol. 1, 129.

certain traditions to attain a new dominance, but ghost stories nevertheless reflect a degree of reciprocity between popular and elite.

Despite the variety of popular ghosts, a few themes emerge with particular frequency. Ghosts generally signified that an established religious process had been violated – that process being the journey from death to the afterlife, and the grieving and burial practices surrounding it. Perhaps the death had been premature and/or violent; perhaps the living were mourning it too much; perhaps the ghost had left unfinished business. Stories of positive ghosts returning by divine permission to pass on messages about the afterlife were (unsurprisingly) much less common outside of evangelising texts. Ghosts did carry broad Christian messages, but they also represented a certain discomfort with the kirk's clean separation between the living and the dead. When ghosts returned to reproach their loved ones for grieving, they were supplanting the kirk as providers of pastoral care. Notable, too, is the Highland theme of ghosts appearing to their descendants to foreshadow oncoming deaths and escort the dead to the afterlife. Death was the domain of the ghost, and it was the ghost (rather than proper religious convictions) that secured safe passage to the world beyond. Ghosts also supplemented early modern judicial systems, revealing crimes or demonstrating that villains were thoroughly punished. They became a means of managing injustice, and some of the most popular stories of the period incorporated an element of social subversion; powerful figures were punished for mistreating their dependants. Ghosts survived in part because they patched up deficiencies in early modern systems of community support. The themes of death and social injustice also made for powerful and emotive stories, which were easily remembered and retold.

Ghosts often came to feed into community identity. They did this in part through tackling deviancy. The moralising nature of the stories meant that certain codes of behaviour were passed down over generations. A widow(er) grieving too heavily, or a lawyer behaving dishonestly, was not a private affair. It had the potential to affect the whole neighbourhood through causing a supernatural intrusion, and was condemned by the collective voices of the past. In this sense, ghosts were defenders of tradition. However, while ghostly visitations could be framed as punishments, they could also be objects of pride. The ghosts who haunted Highland families were presented as a distinction, despite the fact that they were usually harbingers of misfortune. Ghosts recorded by folklorists often made frequent reappearances in the same place and over a long period of time. These stories were reinforced by repeated sightings over the generations, and the ghosts became a local point of interest. While this was not necessarily a new pattern in the eighteenth century, it probably did become more widespread. As ghosts were gradually disassociated from demons they became better able to serve as community (or family) mascots. This was all the more significant in a period when clearances, industrialisation and urbanisation were creating a more mobile society, and breaking down traditional ties to the land. Ghost stories allowed people to retain a sense of connection to local environments. In addition, the expansion of print culture and the development of folklore as a discipline meant that stories were better preserved and better able to travel across the country. Whether or not this resulted in more people actually believing in ghosts is impossible to judge. Nevertheless, ghosts had an important place within Scottish folk culture. If some aspects of the Scottish Enlightenment threatened to undermine their importance, other developments in the period reinforced it.

Conclusion

The lingering dead are a timeless concept. There is a history to be written that traces ghostly manifestations across different cultures and periods, exploring the strands of continuity, and reflecting on what it means to be mortal. But ghosts also came in a wide variety of forms, and their evolutions tell a story as well. In the long eighteenth century, Scottish ghosts passed through several stages of development, and came to reflect on an increasingly wide range of contemporary concerns. By the end of the period, Scotland was marketed as a haunted nation. There is an irony in this, given that the Enlightenment is persistently associated with the rationalisation of Western culture. It is true that ghosts (and other supernatural beings) were re-evaluated in the light of the medical and philosophical developments of the period, but naturalised visions of ghosts constituted only one of multiple possible explanatory frameworks. Varied ways of thinking about ghosts reflect a range of complementary and competing cultural forces, and challenge overly simplistic models of social change.

Ghosts had an ambiguous place in medieval culture: they were sometimes interpreted as the returning dead, and sometimes as diabolic forces. After the Reformation and the demonological writing of James VI, the orthodox position became clearer. Apparitions were deceptions, whether conceived by drunkenness, melancholy or the wiles of the Devil. Some ghost stories remained in circulation, and the witch trials reinforced popular notions of the powerful dead. Nevertheless, this was a period when ghosts were sidelined; respectable ministers and theologians had little interest in discussing them. It is only with the work of George Sinclair and Robert Wodrow in the late seventeenth and early eighteenth centuries that we see a serious attempt to reinstate ghosts into the Protestant worldview. The approach never became mainstream, but it established a new template for ghosts. There were continued attempts to employ them as religious propagandists throughout the eighteenth century, whether in support of basic Christian tenets, or specific theological arguments.

Relatively few ghost stories emerged from about the 1730s to the 1760s. However, the late eighteenth and early nineteenth centuries were witness to a rapid expansion of printed ghost stories and discussion on ghosts. Periodicals opened up a new venue for debate, and there was a growth in scientific treatises dealing with apparitions. Gothic and romantic literature developed, theatre became more widespread, and a new antiquarian movement was born. Ghosts' functions broadened significantly. They could be humorous or satirical figures; they could be used to explore new conceptions of mental disorders, or visions of death; they could offer political, religious or moral commentary; they could be atmospheric devices; they could be displayed as a facet of local or national identity. There was no final consensus on how a ghost should look, behave or be interpreted, which meant that stories could be adapted to serve a variety of purposes.

These developments primarily took place in elite culture. Ghost stories as told in folk culture probably followed more stable patterns. Rural communities were not as susceptible to changes in fashion, and oral culture tended to preserve traditions. Peter Burke has famously argued that in the period from 1500 to 1800, educated society gradually distanced itself from the entertainments, interests and magical beliefs of the common folk. By 1800, the educated 'had ceased to participate spontaneously in popular culture, but they were in the process of rediscovering it as something exotic'.[1] Similarly, Lorraine Daston and Katharine Park describe the emergence of a 'cultural opposition between the enlightened and the vulgar, which turned on contrasting valuations of wonder and wonders', and Peter Maxwell-Stuart suggests that in eighteenth-century Scotland the lower classes ceased to talk to their superiors about witches or magic.[2] However, the degree of social polarisation should not be over-emphasised.[3] The story of the Laird of Coul's ghost provides a particularly clear example of how narratives could transcend social boundaries. Originally told by a servant, the story was later taken up and rewritten by a minister. It gained some degree of celebrity when published as a chapbook, and discussions in the periodical press suggest that it was known (and believed) across different social classes. Ghosts had been socially divisive after the Reformation, when they were marked as off-limits for respectable Protestants, but in the eighteenth century the balance shifted. It became more acceptable for educated folk to create, circulate and enjoy ghost stories without worrying about their theological implications. In this sense, the approaches of popular and elite culture were drawing closer, and there was more potential for stories to be shared between different classes.

1 Peter Burke, *Popular Culture in Early Modern Europe*, 3rd edn (Aldershot, 2009), 270–86 (quotation 286).

2 Lorraine Daston and Katharine Park, *Wonders and the Order of Nature, 1150–1750* (New York, 1998), 331; Peter Maxwell-Stuart, 'Witchcraft and Magic in Eighteenth-Century Scotland', in Owen Davies and Willem de Blécourt (eds), *Beyond the Witch Trials: Witchcraft and Magic in Enlightenment Europe* (Manchester, 2004), 94–5. See also Lizanne Henderson, *Witchcraft and Folk Belief in the Age of Enlightenment: Scotland, 1670–1740* (Basingstoke, 2016), 34.

3 See also Sasha Handley, *Visions of an Unseen World: Ghost Beliefs and Ghost Stories in Eighteenth-Century England* (London, 2007), 211–12.

Recent historiography has contested the idea that there was a widespread process of secularisation in the eighteenth century.[4] There was, however, a secularisation of magical forces. Focusing on Europe as a whole, Euan Cameron argues that religious intellectuals were ceasing to fear magic, and therefore abandoning the project of transforming popular belief systems.[5] The Scottish kirk was certainly still concerned with the proper education of parishioners, but there was a greater focus on moral conduct, rather than theological intricacies.[6] Ghosts in printed accounts showed less interest in evangelising. Interpretations of ghosts also became less reliant on the Christian framework. Ghosts were initially understood as demons; subsequently, some authors allowed that they might be the souls of the dead, permitted to return by God's providence. In the eighteenth century, they were more commonly explained as natural phenomena, or depicted as a sinister presence that was not obviously tied to divine or demonic forces. For Max Weber, disentangling magical beliefs and practices from orthodox religion was an important element of the process of disenchantment. Writing in 1904–5, Weber argued that the Reformation was a crucial milestone, as it encouraged the 'rationalization of the world' by downplaying the importance of sacramental magic as a means of attaining salvation.[7] In response, Robert Scribner has demonstrated that magical beliefs and practices remained central to religious experience in Protestant countries.[8] The eighteenth century did, however, see a more marked separation between religion and magic. It was a patchy process – there remained men and women who used ghosts as religious propagandists throughout the century – but a significant one nevertheless. Weber's disenchantment was a process of intellectualisation and rationalisation, correlated with the development of science and scientific technology, and centred around the idea the universe can be understood without reference to 'mysterious incalculable forces'.[9] This

4 See Callum G. Brown, *Religion and Society in Scotland since 1707* (Edinburgh, 1997), 8–11; Roger L. Emerson, 'The Religious, the Secular and the Worldly: Scotland 1680–1800', in James E. Crimmins (ed.), *Religion, Secularization and Political Thought: Thomas Hobbes to J. S. Mill* (London, 1989), 68–89; Alasdair Raffe, 'Presbyterianism, Secularization, and Scottish Politics after the Revolution of 1688–1690', *Historical Journal* 53 (2010), 317–37.

5 Euan Cameron, *Enchanted Europe: Superstition, Reason, and Religion, 1250–1750* (Oxford, 2010), 15.

6 See Thomas Ahnert, *The Moral Culture of the Scottish Enlightenment, 1690–1805* (New Haven, 2014).

7 Max Weber, *The Protestant Ethic and the Spirit of Capitalism*, trans. Talcott Parsons, electronic edn (Routledge, 2005), http://www.tandfebooks.com/action/showBook?doi=10.4324/9780203995808, accessed 1 Feb. 2018, 71.

8 Robert W. Scribner, 'The Reformation, Popular Magic, and the "Disenchantment of the World"', *Journal of Interdisciplinary History* 23 (1993), 475–94. See also Michael D. Bailey, 'The Disenchantment of Magic: Spells, Charms, and Superstition in Early European Witchcraft Literature', *American Historical Review* 111 (2006), 383–404, which demonstrates continuities between pre- and post-Reformation brands of scepticism.

9 Max Weber, 'Science as a Vocation', in H. H. Gerth and C. Wright Mills (eds), *From Max Weber: Essays in Sociology* (New York, 1946), 139.

was also ongoing in the eighteenth century, as demonstrated by the treatises explaining ghosts away in natural terms. However, this was only one of several strands of development.

Another pattern at play in the eighteenth century was the rise of ghosts as 'objects of aesthetic pleasure and fascination', particularly in literature and theatre.[10] Ghosts appeared as the spawn of afflicted minds, or as emblems of death. They were written to stir the imagination, and sometimes the boundaries between fact and fiction wavered. Gothic and romantic literature encouraged the (natural?) association between wild, lonely places and Weber's 'mysterious, incalculable forces'. Several authors noted that even the most convinced sceptic felt a shiver when walking through a dark churchyard. It was possible to have an instinctual, involuntary belief in ghosts despite not crediting them on an intellectual level. Historians have suggested that belief in magical forces did not disappear in the eighteenth century, but retreated from the public to the private sphere.[11] Gentlemen might openly declare themselves sceptics, but inwardly be less convinced (as has been argued in the case of Walter Scott).[12] It was also possible actively to choose a belief system in which sterile rationalism was downplayed in favour of intense emotional experience, and the sense of connection to a realm beyond the everyday. Ordinary folk had long believed in creatures such as ghosts without feeling the need to square this belief with kirk teachings. In the later eighteenth century, there was rising interest in sensibility – a model of virtue that placed more emphasis on depth of feeling than on piety. In this context, there was greater scope for fashionable men and women to entertain beliefs that did not accord with orthodox theology. While philosophical tracts emphasised naturalistic explanations of apparitions, and antiquarians painted them as the preserve of the vulgar, ghosts retained power within educated society.

Reworkings of Weber's disenchantment thesis are numerous. There are a cluster of works describing the alleged re-enchantment of modern society.[13] Allison P. Coudert has written compellingly of the re-enchantment of the eighteenth and nineteenth centuries, when 'enchantment escaped the confines of the church' and moved 'from outside of individuals into

[10] Alexandra Walsham, 'The Reformation and "The Disenchantment of the World" Reassessed', *Historical Journal* 51 (2008), 519.

[11] Handley, *Visions of an Unseen World*, 217; Walsham, 'Reformation and "The Disenchantment of the World"', 521; Jonathan Barry, *Witchcraft and Demonology in South-West England, 1640–1789* (Basingstoke, 2012), ch. 6.

[12] See p. 153.

[13] For example, Joshua Landy and Michael Saler (eds), *The Re-Enchantment of the World: Secular Magic in a Rational Age* (Stanford, 2009); Christopher Partridge, *The Re-Enchantment of the West: Alternative Spiritualities, Sacralization, Popular Culture and Occulture*, 2 vols (London, 2004–5); Gordon Graham, *The Re-Enchantment of the World: Art versus Religion* (Oxford, 2007); Morris Berman, *The Reenchantment of the World* (Ithaca [N.Y.], 1981). For a helpful survey, see Michael Saler, 'Modernity and Enchantment: A Historiographic Review', *American Historical Review* 111 (2006), 692–716.

the human imagination'.[14] Joshua Landy and Michael Saler argue that in the modern age 'there is a variety of secular and conscious strategies for re-enchantment, held together by their common aim of filling a God-shaped void'. These modes of enchantment offer an 'affirmation of existence' without relying on 'irrationalism'; modern enchantment 'delights but does not delude'.[15] These models recognise the significance of new ways of conceptualising the magical world, although in emphasising conscious imaginative strategies of re-enchantment, they perhaps underestimate the persistence of genuine belief. In a particularly ambitious recent study, Egil Asprem suggests that we should abandon the idea of disenchantment as a *process*, and instead consider disenchantment as a series of intellectual *problems* that were posed to historical actors, and that met with different responses according to cultural contexts. Reframing disenchantment as a 'conceptual map' or an 'analytical framework' certainly precludes further critiques, but if disenchantment becomes a set of questions rather than a proferred answer, we are left with a gap that must be filled by new, and doubtless similarly imperfect, explanatory models.[16]

Within the field of early modern history, an especially influential revisionist thesis is Alexandra Walsham's. Walsham suggests that instead of looking for a linear process of disenchantment, it might be more useful to think in terms of a 'perpetual spiral of desacralization and resacralization'. She defines desacralisation as 'the decline of belief in divine immanence'.[17] There are advantages to this more precise terminology. Categories of the supernatural were not always clearly demarcated, but it was nevertheless possible for certain beliefs to flourish as others declined. After the Reformation, many magical beliefs and rituals associated with Catholicism were branded superstitious, but witchcraft took on a new cultural prominence. With the Covenanting Revolution and the Wars of the Three Kingdoms there was a surging interest in special providences. The late seventeenth and early eighteenth centuries saw fresh interest in ghosts, fairies, angels and second sight, alongside continued interest in witchcraft and demonology. The 1736 decriminalisation of witchcraft meant that educated society spent less time worrying about the activities of the Devil. It also facilitated the spread of ghost stories, as there was less risk associated with talking about supernatural experiences. The framework of disenchantment does not easily allow for these nuances. Desacralisation,

14 Allison P. Coudert, 'Rethinking Max Weber's Theory of Disenchantment', in Albrecht Classen (ed.), *Magic and Magicians in the Middle Ages and the Early Modern Time: The Occult in Pre-Modern Sciences, Medicine, Literature, Religion, and Astrology* (Berlin, 2017), 707.

15 Joshua Landy and Michael Saler, 'Introduction', in Joshua Landy and Michael Saler (eds), *The Re-Enchantment of the World: Secular Magic in a Rational Age* (Stanford, 2009), 2, 3.

16 Egil Asprem, *The Problem of Disenchantment: Scientific Naturalism and Esoteric Discourse, 1900–1939* (Leiden, 2014), quotations 538, 534.

17 Walsham, 'Reformation and "The Disenchantment of the World"', 526, 504.

in contrast, conceptualises the simultaneous rise of witchcraft persecutions and declining belief in angelic messengers, charms, holy wells, and other expressions of divine presence. However, as magical forces become more secularised, 'desacralisation' and 'resacralisation' seem increasingly limited as descriptors of fluctuations in supernatural belief. 'Re-enchantment' implies little more than the developing influence of indeterminate mysterious forces, but the very imprecision of the Weberian terminology renders it suitable for the consideration of broad time-spans.[18]

Semantic quibbles aside, Walsham's cyclical pattern is worth considering further. She argues that there was a process of desacralisation following the Reformation. England in particular saw resacralisation in the late seventeenth and early eighteenth centuries, as evidenced by the work of figures such as Henry More and Joseph Glanvill. Further reactions against 'barren rationalism' include the development of folklore, the Methodist revival, the rise of romanticism and modern-day interest in the supernatural.[19] Considering Scottish ghosts specifically, there was certainly a cycle in terms of how many stories were recorded. As outlined above, there was a decline after the Reformation, an increase in the late seventeenth and early eighteenth centuries, a quiet spell from about the 1730s to the 1760s, and a surge in the late eighteenth and early nineteenth centuries. However, the late eighteenth and early nineteenth centuries also saw a much greater output of sceptical material on ghosts. Disenchantment and re-enchantment (or desacralisation and resacralisation) might happen simultaneously, rather than in alternating cycles. Wodrow and Sinclair's attempts to reclaim ghosts could be classed as re-enchantment, but were a reaction to what they perceived to be a contemporary society-wide disenchantment. Gothic and romantic depictions of ghosts, as well as arguments for their existence within periodicals, were in part a reaction to the medicalised visions that were also popular at the time. Fiction-writers and folklorists recorded and promoted ghost stories while also decrying them as vulgar.

It may be most useful to think in terms of a tug-of-war between the forces of disenchantment and re-enchantment. One side might gain an advantage for a time – as, for example, in the immediate wake of the Reformation – but in general, the stronger the tug of disenchantment, the stronger the reaction against it.[20] Thus, even as ghosts were described as figments of the imagination or the fantasies of the uneducated, stories proliferated, and ghostly uncanniness was explored and exploited at various levels of society. This re-enchantment

[18] For a fuller attempt at definition see Richard Jenkins, 'Enchantment and Re-Enchantment: Max Weber at the Millennium', *Max Weber Studies* 1 (2000), 29.

[19] Walsham, 'Reformation and "The Disenchantment of the World"', 526.

[20] For discussion of simultaneous enchantment and disenchantment, see Jason Ā Josephon-Storm, *The Myth of Disenchantment: Magic, Modernity, and the Birth of the Human Sciences* (Chicago, 2017), 21; Jenkins, 'Enchantment and Re-Enchantment', 13.

encompassed both continuity and change. The long eighteenth century saw revivals of older traditions, and new ways of conceptualising the presence and power of magical forces. Ghosts were invocations of the past, but also reformulated the past according to the interests of the present.

How typical were the Scottish patterns? An obvious first point of comparison is England. Handley offers a thorough survey of patterns of ghost belief over this period. Her findings suggest that the English developments were similar to those in Scotland, but generally began earlier, and were writ larger. The late-seventeenth- and early-eighteenth-century movement to reclaim ghosts happened on a much more significant scale in England, which had a larger population, a more developed print industry, a more significant Neoplatonist movement and a less volatile religious context.[21] The association between ghosts and demons also proved more persistent in Scotland, probably because of Scotland's proportionally greater engagement with witch-hunting. Discussion of ghosts in pamphlets and periodicals had its heyday in the late seventeenth and early eighteenth centuries in England, compared to the late eighteenth century in Scotland. The English theatre also flourished long before the art-form became securely established north of the border.[22] Psychological and physiological explanations for ghosts, as well as dramatised representations of them, circulated earlier and more widely in England.[23] Although Paul Kléber Monod argues that Scottish and English attitudes towards the occult diverged in the second half of the eighteenth century, their approaches to ghosts were broadly consistent.[24]

England was at the centre of the drive to reincorporate ghosts into Protestant theology in the late seventeenth and early eighteenth centuries, but there were echoes of the movement in other countries. Stories of ghosts returning with messages became more easily available in Lutheran countries from the late seventeenth century.[25] The German polymath Erasmus Francisci published stories 'proving' the reality of ghosts in the late seventeenth and early eighteenth centuries, while the Dutch minister Jacobus Koelman translated Glanvill's story of the Drummer of Tedworth.[26] As in Scotland and England, the intellectual

21 Handley, *Visions of an Unseen World*, ch. 1.

22 Ibid., chs 2, 4.

23 Ibid., 197–208, 113–14, 130–2. See also Owen Davies, *The Haunted: A Social History of Ghosts* (New York, 2007), chs 5, 8; Terry Castle, *The Female Thermometer: Eighteenth-Century Culture and the Invention of the Uncanny* (Oxford, 1995), ch. 10; Shane McCorristine, *Spectres of the Self: Thinking About Ghosts and Ghost-Seeing in England, 1750–1920* (Cambridge, 2010), ch. 1.

24 On Monod see p. 7.

25 Jürgen Beyer, 'On the Transformation of Apparition Stories in Scandinavia and Germany, c.1350–1700', *Folklore* 110 (1999), 45.

26 Sabine Doering-Manteuffel, 'The Dissemination of Magical Knowledge in Enlightenment Germany: The Supernatural and the Development of Print Culture', in Owen Davies and Willem de Blécourt (eds), *Beyond the Witch Trials: Witchcraft and Magic in Enlightenment Europe* (Manchester, 2004), 190; Cameron, *Enchanted Europe*, 281.

developments of the Enlightenment drove discussion of the supernatural.[27] In Germany in particular, leading philosophers engaged in a sustained analysis of ghosts. Immanuel Kant's 1766 *Dreams of a Spirit Seer*, written as a response to Emanuel Swedenborg, explored the idea that the human soul might constantly and unconsciously communicate with the 'immaterial natures of the spirit world'. Kant suggested that some particularly sensitive individuals might experience these communications as external forces, and mistakenly think that they were visited by spirits. He added that 'departed souls ... can never, it is true, be present to our outer senses ... but they may indeed act upon the spirit of man'. He also presented an alternative reading that dismissed ghosts as products of an over-active imagination, likening them to optical illusions.[28] However, even as ghosts were explained away, there was a burgeoning market for stories. Annekatrin Puhle has catalogued more than a thousand accounts of poltergeists and ghostly apparitions published in Germany between 1700 and 1900, as well as about a hundred titles from before that period.[29]

It is natural to assume that Protestants and Catholics would follow different patterns when it came to ghosts. However, contemporaries tended to overstate the differences. For all Keith Thomas's claims that ghosts became a shibboleth by which to distinguish Protestants and Catholics, English Catholics do not seem to have been more inclined to tell ghost stories than their Protestant counterparts in the period after the Reformation.[30] The Catholic Reformation sought to stamp out superstition just as had the Protestant Reformation. Pierre Le Loyer and Noel Taillepied were not as fervently opposed to ghost stories as Ludwig Lavater, but urged that they should be considered cautiously. Analysis of French and Spanish stories from the sixteenth and seventeenth centuries has revealed a significant degree of doubt among the authorities as to how apparitions should be interpreted.[31] This confusion persisted into the eighteenth century. Antoine Augustin Calmet's extensive work on apparitions and vampires (1746, revised 1751) allowed some ghost stories to be true, but depicted others as forgeries.[32]

27 See Cameron, *Enchanted Europe*, ch. 18.

28 Quoted in Stefan Andriopoulos, *Ghostly Apparitions: German Idealism, the Gothic Novel, and Optical Media* (Cambridge [Mass.], 2013), 26–9.

29 Annekatrin Puhle, 'Ghosts, Apparitions and Poltergeist Incidents in Germany between 1700 and 1900', *Journal of the Society for Psychical Research* 63 (1999), 292.

30 Keith Thomas, *Religion and the Decline of Magic: Studies in Popular Beliefs in Sixteenth and Seventeenth Century England* (London, 1971), 703; Francis Young, *English Catholics and the Supernatural, 1553–1829* (Farnham, 2013), ch. 3; Handley, *Visions of an Unseen World*, 172.

31 See Timothy Chesters, *Ghost Stories in Late Renaissance France: Walking by Night* (Oxford, 2011), ch. 2; William A. Christian, *Apparitions in Late Medieval and Renaissance Spain* (Princeton, 1981), ch. 3. On the Catholic approach see also Cameron, *Enchanted Europe*, 286–94.

32 See Fernando Vidal, 'Ghosts of the European Enlightenment', in Mu-chou Poo (ed.), *Rethinking Ghosts in World Religions* (Leiden, 2009), 163–82.

Scholars of folklore have identified a transformation in storytelling across Europe in the eighteenth century.[33] Fictional forms of writing evolved, the press became freer, and books became more easily available. In Germany and France as in Scotland and England, ghosts took central roles in gothic literature, and were used to explore a psychologised form of horror. Again, religious differences were of minimal importance: Daniel Hall argues that German gothic was more comfortable than French gothic with presenting genuine apparitions.[34] As in Scotland, interest in supernatural stories surged in the late eighteenth century especially. In Germany, there was an 'explosion in esoteric and occultist pamphlets, flyers, novels and treatises'.[35] H. C. Erik Midelfort identifies a period of 'increasing spiritualist enthusiasm' in Berlin in the 1780s, encouraged by William II's rise to the throne of Prussia. William 'supported ministers and courtiers devoted to religiously conservative, mystical, visionary, and anti-Enlightenment projects', with the result that 'ghosts and other spiritual bodies were suddenly back on the cultural agenda, and empirical evidence, at least, seemed to support their existence'.[36] In France, the popularity of mesmerism in the 1780s prompted renewed interest in apparitions as a topic, while England also saw a fresh boom of enthusiasm for occult matters from this decade.[37] The development of a romantic-nationalist programme of antiquarian studies in the nineteenth century can also be traced across Europe, and is often said to have originated with the work of the Brothers Grimm in Germany.[38]

Overall, discussion of ghosts seems to have followed similar patterns across the major Enlightenment centres. However, there is perhaps something more distinctive in the strand of literature and antiquarianism that tied ghosts to Scottish identity. The popularity of the *Ossian* poetry gave the Highlands a reputation for romantic wildness that was probably unparalleled. Gothic works established their castles on Highland moors, and folklorists sought out tales of Caledonian phantoms. There emerged a hearty Gaelic ghost, who duelled with unsuspecting travellers or watched over its descendants. The association between folk tradition and national identity was drawn in other countries as well, but with less emphasis on ghosts. Germany saw probably the most high-profile discussion of ghosts in the eighteenth and early nineteenth centuries,

33 Beyer, 'Transformation of Apparition Stories', 39.

34 Daniel Hall, *French and German Gothic Fiction in the Late Eighteenth Century* (Bern, 2005), 193.

35 Andriopoulos, *Ghostly Apparitions*, 80.

36 H. C. Erik Midelfort, *Exorcism and Enlightenment: Johann Joseph Gassner and the Demons of Eighteenth-Century Germany* (New Haven, 2005), 147.

37 Robert Darnton, *Mesmerism and the End of the Enlightenment in France* (Cambridge [Mass.], 1968); Paul Kléber Monod, *Solomon's Secret Arts: The Occult in the Age of Enlightenment* (New Haven, 2013), ch. 7.

38 See Jack Zipes, 'Introduction: The Golden Key to Folk and Fairy Tales: Unlocking Cultural Treasures', in Jack Zipes (ed.), *The Golden Age of Folk and Fairy Tales: From the Brothers Grimm to Andrew Lang* (Indianapolis, 2013), xvi–xviii, xxviii–xxxiii, esp. xxxii.

but ghosts were not particularly prominent in the tales of the Brothers Grimm, while other German folklorists went so far as to suppress 'mere ghost stories'.[39] In France, folklore played a relatively minor role in the formation of national identity.[40] In a study of England and Wales, Philip Schwyzer argues that literary ghosts participated in nation-building in the second half of the sixteenth century, serving as representatives of ancient Britain. However, he concludes that this project was consigned to oblivion after 1603.[41] Focusing on the long eighteenth century, Handley writes that ghosts were a significant component of 'individual, community and regional identities'.[42] Ghosts do not, however, seem to have been associated with a particular brand of Englishness.

As the weaker party in a union that much of the country had not wanted, Scotland had especial incentive to fashion a distinctive reputation. Its long-standing reputation for magic, combined with the grandeur of the Highland landscape, meant that supernatural figures of some sort were fitting mascots. Ghosts offered a way of recalling bygone eras, and so aligned well with the romantic agenda of building the present upon a sentimentalised past. For James Macpherson they were a majestic alternative to the wizards and hags of his source material. He was not the first to use ghosts to symbolise a romantic past Scotland, but he was responsible for the popularisation of the archetype. This image of Scottishness did not necessarily draw on genuine folkloric traditions, and the vision of a misty ghost-ridden nation probably would have been unfamiliar to many eighteenth-century Scots. However, it proved to be an enduring stereotype.

In the second half of the nineteenth century, there were continuities and evolutions in approaches to ghosts. There were no more grand narratives of spectral ancestors in the style of *Ossian*, but antiquarians continued to explore local legends. Robert Louis Stevenson's 'Thrawn Janet' (1881) kept alive the tradition of vernacular explorations of folklore. Modelled on George Sinclair's 1685 account of Isabel Heriot, the story presented a raised corpse 'wi' her grogram goon an' her black mutch, wi' the heid aye upon the shoother, an' the girn still upon the face o't'.[43] Margaret Oliphant also perpetuated gothic traditions; 'The Secret Chamber' (1876) burdened a picturesque Perthshire castle with the phantom of a wicked earl. The association between ghosts and Scottish identity persisted, and invited the kind of amiable mockery that is

39 Ines Köhler-Zülch, 'Heinrich Prohle: A Successor to the Brothers Grimm', in Donald Haase (ed.), *The Reception of Grimms' Fairy Tales: Responses, Reactions, Revisions* (Detroit, 1993), 47, 54n15, 54n17.

40 Anne Dymond, 'Displaying the Arlésienne: Museums, Folklife and Regional Identities in France', in Timothy Baycroft and David Hopkin (eds), *Folklore and Nationalism in Europe during the Long Nineteenth Century* (Leiden, 2012), 137.

41 Philip Schwyzer, *Literature, Nationalism and Memory in Early Modern England and Wales* (Cambridge, 2004), ch. 4.

42 Handley, *Visions of an Unseen World*, 186.

43 [Robert Louis Stevenson] R. L. S., 'Thrawn Janet', *Cornhill Magazine*, Oct 1881, 443.

commonly bestowed on national stereotypes. Writing in 1869, 'A Scoto-Celt' offered an exposé of the Scottish character. He declared that 'Every Scotchman believes in ghosts … The ghost steals on us from the mountain, the lake, the mist, the forest, the glen. Indeed, the ghost is the exclusive property of the Celtic race'. Being 'gaunt and bony', the Scotsman could '[hail] the ghost as a man and brother'. The English, for their part, were too fat for ghosts.[44]

The most important change in the later nineteenth century was the coming of the spiritualist movement. It reached Britain in the 1850s, and garnered a wide following in Scotland. The Glaswegian Daniel Dunglas Home was a celebrated medium not only locally, but across Europe.[45] Spiritualism gave humans new power over the supernatural realm. Ghosts returned not of their own accord or by divine or demonic agency, but in answer to the summons of a medium. This shift in power from the deity (or the Devil) to the human medium demonstrates how orthodox religion had lost its monopoly on ghost stories. Also notable is the 1882 foundation of the Society for Psychical Research (SPR), which aimed to give supernatural beliefs a scientific grounding.[46] The SPR was based in London, but its reach extended to Scotland, and Scotsmen Balfour Stewart and Andrew Lang were among its founders. It took a keen interest in psychological and physiological explanations for ghosts, refining eighteenth-century theories of hallucination.[47] However, the SPR also explored supernatural explanations for ghosts. Lang observed dryly that 'the ghosts have come forth again … We may all confess to a belief in ghosts, because we call them "phantasmogenetic agencies"'.[48]

The scientific supernaturalism of the SPR demonstrates the tug-of-war between disenchantment and re-enchantment. It is also significant that polls indicate a doubling in levels of British ghost belief since the Second World War, despite the fact that society has become progressively more secular.[49] If there were tentative hints, by the late eighteenth century, that it might be possible for educated people to believe in ghosts without reference to the Christian framework, nowadays that approach is securely established. Other eighteenth- and nineteenth-century patterns also persist. Ghosts remain the subject of psychological and parapsychological research.[50] They are wrapped up with romanticised readings of Scottish history, and marketed as a national

44 A Scoto-Celt, 'Scottish Characteristics: A Prelection', *Fraser's Magazine for Town and Country*, Apr. 1869, 456.

45 Janet Oppenheim, *The Other World: Spiritualism and Psychical Research in England, 1850–1914* (Cambridge, 1988), 10–17.

46 McCorristine, *Spectres of the Self*, 104.

47 Ibid., chs 3, 5 (quotation 105).

48 Andrew Lang, *Cock Lane and Common-Sense* (London, 1894), 303.

49 Paul Cowdell, 'Belief in Ghosts in Post-War England' (University of Hertfordshire Ph.D. thesis, 2011), 1–2.

50 See, for example, the work of the Koestler Parapsychology Unit, which is based in the Psychology Department at the University of Edinburgh.

attraction.[51] The horror genre keeps alive the conventions of gothic, and the romantics' white-sheeted ghost traipses the streets in diminutive hordes each Halloween. In various guises, ghosts continue to offer points of connection to the past, to the dead, to the world of the invisible or the illusory.

Ghosts cannot easily be contained within conceptual frameworks. In the long eighteenth century, ghosts obtained a foothold in respectable society because they were reinvented as religious propagandists. They prospered thereafter because they became progressively more secularised. Scientific explanations of ghosts as hallucinations flourished at the same time as visions of gloomy spectres stalking churchyards. Stereotypes of ghosts encompassed divine messengers, lovelorn maidens, monstrous tomb dwellers, Highland warriors, and snickering pranksters draped in bed linen. Ghosts have proved resilient because this flexibility allows them to serve a wide spectrum of social, cultural and religious agendas. Particular supernatural beings come in and out of fashion, and some – brownies, banshees, wraiths, water kelpies – are now generally seen as colourful folkloric oddities, or forgotten altogether. But the dead will always be familiar, and their lingering spirits have too much emotive power to be laid to rest.

[51] This can be seen in numerous collections of Scottish ghost stories. For a typical example see Dane Love, *Scottish Ghosts* (London, 1995).

Bibliography

MANUSCRIPT SOURCES

Aberdeen University Library

MS 3922	Alexander Stewart's lecture notes from George Skene and James Urquhart, 1708–9

British Library

Sloane MS 3198, fols 15–16v	Archibald Pitcairne, account of Robert Lindsay's ghost, n.d.

Glasgow University Library

MS Gen 873	Lecture notes from John Law, 1704–5
MS Murray 49	James Craig's lecture notes from John Loudon and John Law, 1699–1700

National Library of Scotland

Adv.MS.22.7.15	Alexander Irvine's lecture notes from [William Black?], 1694
MS 10785–6	Elizabeth Steuart-Barclay, papers on the Laird of Coul's Ghost, 1788–1802
Ry.II.c.26	Materials on Mary MacKinnon collected by James Maidment, 1823
Wod.Anal	Robert Wodrow's *Analecta*, 1701–34
Wod.Fol.XXVIII 4846, fols 222–5	James Cowan to Robert Wodrow, [1707]
Wod.Lett.Qu.II, fol. 143	James Cowan to Robert Wodrow, 26 Apr. 1710
Wod.Lett.Qu.XIX, fols 283–4	Thomas Mack to Robert Wodrow, 15 Feb. 1723

National Records of Scotland

CH2/527/1/221–61	Chapel of Garioch kirk session minutes, 1737–8
CH12/12/195	Ghost story from Westphalia, n.d.
CH12/12/224	Account of the Laird of Coul's ghost (William Ogilvie's version), n.d.
CH12/12/755	Account of the Laird of Coul's ghost (William Sinclair's version), 12 Dec. 1723
CH12/12/1823	Alexander Rose to Archibald Campbell, 28 June 1711
CH12/16/251	Account of the Laird of Coul's ghost (William Sinclair's version), 12 Feb. 1723
CH12/21/10	George Innes, *The Primitive Doctrine: A Middle State of Happiness or Misery between Death and the Resurrection*, n.d.
GD24/5/121	Wilfred Fazakerly to Lady Douglas, 1799
GD24/5/122	Steven Widcumb to Lady Douglas, [1799]
GD124/15/1181	Robert Barclay to Lord Grange, 28 Feb. 1718
GD124/15/1263	James Erskine, Lord Grange, *Account of the Highlanders and Highlands of Scotland*, 29 Dec. 1724 – 2 June 1725

GD248/170/3	Colin Mackenzie to [the laird of Grant?], 21 July 1720
GD377/448	Thomas Rattray, account of the Ghost Dog of Mause, 31 Dec. 1730
GD385/143	Assorted materials related to the Ghost Dog of Mause, n.d.

St Andrews University Library

MS 30315	William Scot's lecture notes from William Black, c.1707
MS BC59.V8	John Macara's lecture notes from Thomas Taylor, 1707
MS Dep. 19/14/1	Thomas Rattray, letter on the intermediate state, n.d.

NEWSPAPERS AND PERIODICALS

'The Abstract of the Trial of Helen Watt and William Keith, Continued', *Scots Magazine*, Dec. 1766, 625–7

'Account of a Ghost, from the Relation of a Clergyman to Whom it Appeared', *Edinburgh Magazine, or Literary Miscellany*, June 1786, 441–4

'Account of an Apparition in France', *Aberdeen Magazine*, 9 Apr. 1789, 194–5

Anon. to the *Weekly Magazine, or Edinburgh Amusement*, 10 Mar. 1774, 335–7

Blair, A. to the *Weekly Magazine, or Edinburgh Amusement*, 4 Feb. 1773, 169–71

C. G. to the *Weekly Magazine, or Edinburgh Amusement*, 16 Apr. 1772, 74–5

—— to the *Weekly Magazine, or Edinburgh Amusement*, 23 July 1772, 97–9

Chambers, Robert, 'Traditions of the Celebrated Major Weir', *Edinburgh Literary Journal*, 11 Apr. 1829, 307–8

Cham-pi-pi the Son in the *Ghost*, 19 June 1796, 77–80

'A Chapter on Goblins', *Blackwood's Edinburgh Magazine*, Dec. 1823, 639–46

'A Conversation on Female Accomplishments', *Edinburgh Magazine, or Literary Miscellany*, May 1796, 360–5

'Curious Observations on the Sepulchral Lamps of the Romans', *Edinburgh Magazine*, Dec. 1759, 635–8

'The Devil's Elixir', *Blackwood's Edinburgh Magazine*, July 1824, 55–67

'Discovery of a Murderer', *Scots Magazine*, Sept. 1779, 484

'A Dream', *Scots Magazine*, Dec. 1779, 650

E., 'Border Sketches No. II', *Edinburgh Magazine and Literary Miscellany*, Oct. 1817, 236–9

'Entertaining Story of a Sleep-Walker', *Edinburgh Magazine*, June 1761, 294–7

Fabricius to the *Weekly Magazine, or Edinburgh Amusement*, 7 May 1772, 167–8

Fanaticus, 'A Terrible Apparition', *Weekly Magazine, or Edinburgh Amusement*, 8 Sept. 1774, 330

Fergusson, Robert, 'The Ghaists: A Kirk-Yard Eclogue', *Weekly Magazine, or Edinburgh Amusement*, 27 May 1773, 275–6

Feriatus to the *Trifler*, 21 May 1796, 199–206

'From Mist's Weekly Journal, Sept. 3', *Caledonian Mercury*, 12 Sept. 1726, 6111–12

Gallovidiensis, 'Elegy to the Memory of Miss Dick', *Edinburgh Magazine, or Literary Miscellany*, Apr. 1796, 303–4

'The Genius of Caledonia: A Poem on the Threatened French Invasion', *Edinburgh Magazine, or Literary Amusement*, June 1798, 464–5

'The Ghost of the Oratory', *Blackwood's Edinburgh Magazine*, Oct. 1825, 433–58

Ghost of Voltaire to the *Ghost*, 30 July 1796, 5–8

Hogg, James, 'The Bogle', *Edinburgh Literary Journal*, Mar. 1831, 171–2

——, 'The Mysterious Bride', *Blackwood's Edinburgh Magazine*, Dec. 1830, 943–50

'The Horrors and Torment of an Evil Conscience; and the Effects of a Disturbed Imagination', *Weekly Magazine, or Edinburgh Amusement*, 24 Oct. 1770, 97–102
M., 'Robert and Margaret: A Ballad', *Weekly Magazine, or Edinburgh Amusement*, 1 Feb. 1776, 178
M. to the *Weekly Magazine, or Edinburgh Amusement*, 6 Feb. 1772, 165–7
M. to the *Weekly Magazine, or Edinburgh Amusement*, 24 Mar. 1774, 391–2
MacKenzie, Mr, 'Epilogue to Vimonda', *Universal Magazine*, Sept. 1787, 155
Maw-Worm, Richard in the *Trifler*, 4 July 1796, 1797 enlarged edn, 192–3
McC, J., 'Speech Delivered in the Pantheon', *Edinburgh Eighth-Day Magazine*, 13 Nov. 1779, 299–301
[Melvill, Thomas] T. M., 'An Essay on Dreaming; Or, The State of the Mind in Sleep', *Scots Magazine*, Sept. 1749, 442–6
Moropolemius to the *Trifler*, 4 July 1796, 1797 enlarged edn, 186–92
N. A. to the *Weekly Magazine, or Edinburgh Amusement*, 27 Feb. 1772, 262–4
Neanias to the *Weekly Magazine, or Edinburgh Amusement*, 23 July 1772, 103–5
'Observations on Gothic Superstition', *Edinburgh Magazine, or Literary Miscellany*, Feb. 1799, 115–18
'Observations on the Frenzy of Tasso, Collins, and Chatterton', *Edinburgh Magazine, or Literary Miscellany*, Feb. 1799, 108–12
Oliphant, Margaret, 'The Secret Chamber', *Blackwood's Edinburgh Magazine*, Dec. 1876, 709–29
'On the Ancient and Modern Use of Ghosts', *Edinburgh Magazine, or Literary Miscellany*, Feb. 1800, 108–11
Palemon to the *Weekly Magazine, or Edinburgh Amusement*, 5 Dec. 1771, 296–7
—— to the *Weekly Magazine, or Edinburgh Amusement*, 9 July 1772, 45–6
'Phantasmagoriana', *Blackwood's Edinburgh Magazine*, Aug. 1818, 589–96
Phantom, Felix in the *Ghost*, 25 Apr. 1796, 1–4
—— in the *Ghost*, 2 May 1796, 9–12
—— in the *Ghost*, 18 May 1796, 29–32
—— in the *Ghost*, 27 Aug. 1796, 37–40
Philanthropist to the *Weekly Magazine, or Edinburgh Amusement*, 7 July 1774, 40–2
Philaretes to the *Weekly Magazine, or Edinburgh Amusement*, 11 Apr. 1771, 33–9
—— to the *Weekly Magazine, or Edinburgh Amusement*, 19 Dec. 1771, 355–7
—— to the *Weekly Magazine, or Edinburgh Amusement*, 27 Feb. 1772, 261–2
'Poetry', *Aberdeen Magazine, Literary Chronicle, and Review*, 31 Dec. 1789, 853–4
Rattle, Toby to the *Weekly Magazine, or Edinburgh Amusement*, 28 May 1772, 269
'Remarks on an Argument in Favour of the Reality of Spectral Appearances', *Edinburgh Magazine, or Literary Miscellany*, Nov. 1794, 367–70
Rentfree, Thomas to the *Edinburgh Magazine, or Literary Miscellany*, May 1786, 292–6
'The Rev. Mr. Ogilvy and the Laird of Cool', *Spiritual Magazine*, July 1866, 329–32
Scoto-Celt, A, 'Scottish Characteristics: A Prelection', *Fraser's Magazine for Town and Country*, Apr. 1869, 451–465
[Scott, Walter] A. B., 'Story of an Apparition', *Blackwood's Edinburgh Magazine*, Sept. 1818, 705–7
Sincerus to the *Weekly Magazine, or Edinburgh Amusement*, 8 Sept. 1774, 327–9
'Singular Ghost Story', *Aberdeen Magazine*, Feb. 1832, 89–94
'Sketches of Superstitions', *Chambers's Edinburgh Journal*, 10 Apr. 1841, 94–5
'A Sketch of Scotch Diablerie in General', *Fraser's Magazine for Town and Country*, Mar. 1842, 317–31

[Stevenson, Robert Louis] R. L. S., 'Thrawn Janet', *Cornhill Magazine*, Oct. 1881, 436–43.

Sylvander, 'Directions for Making a Modern Wit', *Weekly Magazine, or Edinburgh Amusement*, 23 July 1772, 113–14

'Traditions of the Western Highlands, No. III', *London Literary Gazette*, 20 Mar. 1824, 189–90

'The Voyages and Travels of Columbus Secundus', *Blackwood's Edinburgh Magazine*, Nov. 1821, 389–405

Wesley, John, 'A Strange Account', *Arminian Magazine*, July–Aug. 1785, 378–81, 416–20

'Winter', *Universal Magazine of Knowledge and Pleasure*, Jan. 1770, 43

Wiseman, Will to the *Weekly Magazine, or Edinburgh Amusement*, 9 May 1771, 165–6

'The Wish: A Song', *Weekly Magazine, or Edinburgh Amusement*, 24 May 1770, 242

Z., 'Concluding Particulars of the Life of James Hogg, the Ettrick Shepherd', *Scots Magazine and Edinburgh Literary Miscellany*, Nov. 1805, 820–3

PRINTED PRIMARY SOURCES

Abercrombie, John, *Inquiries Concerning the Intellectual Powers and the Investigation of Truth*, 2nd edn (Edinburgh, 1830)

An Abstract of the Bloody Massacre in Ireland ([Scotland?], [1700?])

An Account of a Most Horrid and Barbarous Murther and Robbery, Committed on the Body of Captain Brown (Edinburgh, 1694)

An Account of a Most Horrid, Bloody, and Terrible Apparition, Which Lately Appeared in the Parish of Shotts (London, [1793?])

An Account of a Wonderful Prodigy Seen in the Air ([Edinburgh?], 1722)

An Account of Some Imaginary Apparitions, The Effects of Fear or Fraud (Dunbar, [1792?])

An Account of Some Strange Apparitions Had by a Godly Man in Kintyre, Who Hath Been Blind Six Years ([Edinburgh?], 1734)

An Account of Terrible Apparitions and Prodigies (Glasgow, 1721)

An Account of the Apparition of the Late Lord Kilmarnock (London, 1747)

Allardyce, Alexander (ed.), *Letters from and to Charles Kirkpatrick Sharpe*, 2 vols (Edinburgh, 1888)

A. M., *Remarks on Revelation and Infidelity: Being the Substance of Several Speeches Lately Delivered in a Private Literary Society in Edinburgh* (Edinburgh, 1797)

Amour, Jean Matthias D', *Memoirs of Mr. Matthias D'Amour*, ed. Paul Rodgers (London, 1836)

Anderson, John, 'United Parishes of Stronsay and Eday', in John Sinclair (ed.), *The Statistical Account of Scotland, 1791–1799*, electronic edn, 21 vols (University of Edinburgh, University of Glasgow, 1999), vol. 15, http://stataccscot.edina.ac.uk/link/osa-vol15-p387-parish-orkney-stronsay_and_eday, accessed 1 Feb. 2018

Annand, William, *Pater Noster, Our Father, or, The Lord's Prayer Explained the Sense Thereof and Duties Therein from Scripture, History, and Fathers* (Edinburgh, 1670)

An Antidote to Superstition: Or, A Cure for Those Weak Minds Which Are Troubled with the Fear of Ghosts, Witches &c. (Dunbar, [1803?])

The Antiquated Usages, Which Have Made so Great a Noise amongst Us, Briefly Examined, and Found Insufficient (Edinburgh, 1728)

The Apparition (Edinburgh, 1727)

Aquinas, Thomas, *Summa Theologica*, trans. Fathers of the English Dominican Province, 3 vols (New York, 1947–8)

Aubrey, John, *Miscellanies* (London, 1696)

Baillie, Joanna, *Poems: Wherein It Is Attempted to Describe Certain Views of Nature and of Rustic Manners* (London, 1790)
——, *A Series of Plays, in Which It Is Attempted to Delineate the Stronger Passions of the Mind*, 3 vols (London, 1798–1812)
Baillie, Robert, *Letters and Journals of Robert Baillie, A. M.*, ed. David Laing, 3 vols (Edinburgh, 1841–2)
Bannatyne, George, *The Bannatyne Manuscript*, ed. W. Tod Ritchie (Edinburgh, 1928–34)
Bannatyne, Richard, *Memorials of Transactions in Scotland, 1569–1573*, ed. Robert Pitcairn (Edinburgh, 1836)
Baxter, Richard, *The Certainty of the Worlds of Spirits, and Consequently, of the Immortality of Souls of the Malice and Misery of the Devils and the Damned* (London, 1691)
Beattie, James, *Elements of Moral Science*, 2 vols (Edinburgh, 1790–3)
——, *Original Poems and Translations* (London, 1760)
Bell, Andrew, 'Parish of Roxburgh', in John Sinclair (ed.), *The Statistical Account of Scotland, 1791–1799*, electronic edn, 21 vols (University of Edinburgh, University of Glasgow, 1999), vol. 19, http://stataccscot.edina.ac.uk/link/osa-vol19-p114-parish-roxburgh-roxburgh, accessed 1 Feb. 2018
Bell, Thomas, *Grapes in the Wilderness: Or, A Discourse of the Dispensations of God towards His People* (Glasgow, 1705)
——, *Nehemiah the Tirshatha, or, The Character of a Good Commissioner to Which Is Added Grapes in the Wilderness* (Edinburgh, 1692)
B. G., *The Relation of a Strange Apparition in the Air, on the 19 Day of August, 1653* ([Edinburgh?], 1654)
Birnie, William, *The Blame of Kirk-Buriall, Tending to Perswade Cemiteriall Civilitie* (Edinburgh, 1606, STC 3089)
Blacklock, Thomas, *Poems by the Late Reverend Dr. Thomas Blacklock* (Edinburgh, 1793)
Blair, Hugh, *A Critical Dissertation on the Poems of Ossian* (London, 1763)
——, *Sermons*, 5 vols (London, 1777–1801)
Blair, Robert, *The Grave: A Poem* (London, 1743)
Blair, Robert, *The Life of Mr. Robert Blair*, ed. T. M'Crie (Edinburgh, 1848)
Boethius, Hector, *Scotorum Historia*, ed. Dana F. Sutton, electronic edn (University of Birmingham, 2010), http://www.philological.bham.ac.uk/boece, accessed 1 Feb. 2018
Bonny Jean: To Which Are Added, Tweedside, Although My Meg's Gi'en Me the Bag, Samuel Macaree's Ghaist (Stirling, 1824)
Bovet, Richard, *Pandaemonium, or the Devil's Cloyster, Being a Further Blow to Modern Sadduceism* (London, 1684)
Boyd, Zacharie, *The Last Battell of the Soule in Death* (Edinburgh, 1628, STC 3446a.5)
Brand, John, *A Brief Description of Orkney, Zetland, Pightland-Firth & Caithness* (Edinburgh, 1701)
Brand, John, *Observations on Popular Antiquities* (Newcastle, 1777)
Brewster, David, *Letters on Natural Magic, Addressed to Sir Walter Scott* (London, 1832)
Brissot's Ghost! Or, Intelligence from the Other World (Edinburgh, 1794)
Brown, John, *Quakerisme the Path-Way to Paganisme* (Edinburgh, 1678)
Brown, William, *Impiety and Superstition Expos'd: A Poetical Essay* (Edinburgh, 1710)
Brutal Assault and Murder! ([Scotland?], 1830)
Buchanan, George, *Rerum Scoticarum Historia*, ed. Dana F. Sutton, electronic edn (University of Birmingham, 2009), http://www.philological.bham.ac.uk/scothist, accessed 1 Feb. 2018
Buchan, Peter, *Ancient Ballads and Songs of the North of Scotland*, 2 vols (Edinburgh, 1828)

Burness, John, 'Thrummy Cap', in *Plays, Poems, Tales and Other Pieces* (Montrose, 1819), 190–201
Burns, Robert, *Poems, Chiefly in the Scottish Dialect* (Kilmarnock, 1786)
——, *Poems, Chiefly in the Scottish Dialect* (Edinburgh, 1787)
Burt, Edmund, *Letters from a Gentleman in the North of Scotland*, 2 vols (London, 1754)
Burton, Robert, *The Anatomy of Melancholy* (Oxford, 1621, STC 4159)
Calvin, John, *Calvin: Commentaries*, ed. Joseph Haroutunian (London, 1958)
——, *Calvin's Institutes: A New Compend*, ed. Hugh T. Kerr (Louisville, 1989)
——, *L'Excuse à Messieurs les Nicodémites*, in *Traité des Reliques, Suivi de l'Excuse à Messieurs les Nicodémites* (Paris, 1921), 199–283
——, *Psychopannychia*, in Thomas F. Torrance (ed.), *Tracts and Treatises in Defense of the Reformed Faith*, 3 vols (Grand Rapids, 1958), vol. 3, 413–90.
Campbell, Archibald, *A Discourse Proving That the Apostles Were No Enthusiasts* (London, 1730)
Campbell, Archibald, *The Doctrines of a Middle State between Death and the Resurrection* (London, 1721)
Campbell, Daniel, *Meditations on Eternity* (Glasgow, 1721)
Campbell, George, *A Dissertation on Miracles* (Edinburgh, 1762)
Campbell, Ninian, *A Treatise upon Death* (Edinburgh, 1635, STC 4533)
Captain Mulligan: Miss Bailey's Ghost (Stirling, [1813–20?])
Chambers, Robert, *The Book of Days, A Miscellany of Popular Antiquities*, 2 vols (London, 1863–4)
——, *Illustrations of the Author of Waverley: Being Notices and Anecdotes of Real Characters, Scenes, and Incidents, Supposed to Be Described in His Works*, 2nd edn (Edinburgh, 1825)
——, *The Picture of Scotland*, 2 vols (Edinburgh, 1827)
——, *The Scottish Ballads* (Edinburgh, 1829)
——, *Traditions of Edinburgh* (Edinburgh, 1824)
——, *Traditions of Edinburgh*, revised edn (London, 1868)
Cheyn, William, *The Great Danger and Vanity or Folly of Atheism Discovered in a Dialogue between an Atheist and a Believer* (Edinburgh, 1720)
Child, Francis James, *The English and Scottish Popular Ballads*, 5 vols (Boston, 1882–98)
C. N., *A Counsel of Criminal Ghosts to the Ghost of the Great Beilhaven* (Edinburgh, 1729)
Cochrane, Arthur C. (ed.), 'The Scottish Confession of Faith, 1560', in *Reformed Confessions of the Sixteenth Century* (Philadelphia, 1966), 159–84
Cockburn, William, *The Being of God Proved from the Universal Voice of Conscience* (Edinburgh, 1726)
Collins, William, *An Ode on the Popular Superstitions of the Highlands of Scotland* (London, 1788)
Combe, George, *A System of Phrenology*, 3rd edn (Edinburgh, 1830)
The Compleat Wizzard: Being a Collection of Authentic and Entertaining Narratives of the Real Existence and Appearance of Ghosts, Demons, and Spectres (London, 1770)
Copland, John, *Saint Andrews: Or, A Sentimental Evening Walk near the Ruins of That Ancient City* (Edinburgh, 1776)
Crabbe, George, *The Library: A Poem* (London, 1781)
Crawford, William, *The Works of the Truly Pious and Learned Mr. William Crawford Late Minister of the Gospel at Wilton*, 2 vols (Edinburgh, 1748)
——, *Zion's Traveller: Or, The Soul's Progress to Heaven*, 2nd edn (Edinburgh, 1743)
Crowe, Catherine, *The Night Side of Nature, or Ghosts and Ghost Seers*, 2 vols (London, 1848)

Cunningham, Allan, *Traditional Tales of the English and Scottish Peasantry*, 2 vols (London, 1822)
Dalyell, John Graham, *The Darker Superstitions of Scotland: Illustrated from History and Practice* (Edinburgh, 1834)
Davies, Owen (ed.), *Ghosts: A Social History*, 5 vols (London, 2010)
Defoe, Daniel, *An Essay on the History and Reality of Apparitions* (London, 1728)
——, *A Tour Through the Whole Island of Great Britain*, ed. P. N. Furbank, W. R. Owens, and A. J. Coulson (New Haven, 1991)
Denniston, James, *Legends of Galloway: Being a Series of Traditions, Illustrative of Its Ancient History, Customs, Manners, and Superstitions* (Edinburgh, 1825)
Dickens, Charles, *A Christmas Carol, In Prose: Being a Ghost Story of Christmas* (London, 1843)
Douglas, Gavin, *The Aeneid (1513)*, ed. Gordon Kendal (London, 2011)
A Dreadful Example for Wicked Husbands: Or the Virtuous Wife in Distress ([Edinburgh?], [1799?])
Drummond, William, *Flowres of Sion* ([Edinburgh], 1623, STC 7247)
——, *Poems: By William Drummond, of Hawthorne-Denne* (Edinburgh, 1616, STC 7255)
Duff, William, *An Essay on Original Genius; and Its Various Modes of Exertion in Philosophy and the Fine Arts, Particularly in Poetry* (London, 1767)
Dunbar, William, 'Apon the Midsummer Evin, Mirriest of Nichtis (The Tretis Of The Twa Mariit Wemen and the Wedo)', in Jacqueline Tasioulas (ed.), *The Makars: The Poems of Henryson, Dunbar and Douglas* (Edinburgh, 1999), 545–68
——, 'Of Sir Thomas Norray', in David Laing (ed.), *The Poems of William Dunbar*, 2 vols (Edinburgh, 1834), vol. 1, 125–7
——, 'Schir Johine the Ros, Ane Thing Thair Is Compild (The Flyting of Dumbar and Kennedie)', in Jacqueline Tasioulas (ed.), *The Makars: The Poems of Henryson, Dunbar and Douglas* (Edinburgh, 1999), 338–51
Dundass, James, *An Impartial Enquiry into the Rise and Progress of the Ancient Usage of Prayers for the Dead* (Edinburgh, 1743)
Durham, James, *The Blessedness of the Death of Those That Die in the Lord* ([Glasgow?], 1681)
——, *A Commentarie upon the Book of the Revelation* (Edinburgh, 1658)
The Edinburgh Medley of Entertainment, 2 vols (Edinburgh, 1800)
Edmondaton, Laurence, 'General Observations on the County of Shetland', in *The New Statistical Account of Scotland, 1834–45*, electronic edn, 15 vols (University of Edinburgh, University of Glasgow, 1999), vol. 15, http://stataccscot.edina.ac.uk /link/nsa-vol15-p145-general-shetland-county_general, accessed 1 Feb. 2018
Encyclopaedia Britannica; Or, A Dictionary of Arts, Sciences, &c., 2nd edn, 10 vols (Edinburgh, 1778–83)
Encyclopaedia Britannica; Or, A Dictionary of Arts, Sciences, and Miscellaneous Literature, 3rd edn, 20 vols (Edinburgh, 1797)
Erskine, Ralph, *The Happy Congregation: Or, The Great Gathering of the People to Shiloh* (Edinburgh, 1726)
Erskine, William, *Epistle from Lady Grange to Edward D-, Esq.* (London, 1798)
Faggot, Robbin, *The Ghaist: A Poem* (Glasgow, 1810)
Ferguson, Adam, *Analysis of Pneumatics and Moral Philosophy* (Edinburgh 1766)
——, *Principles of Moral and Political Science*, 2 vols (Edinburgh, 1792)
Fergusson, Alexander, *The Honourable Henry Erskine, Lord Advocate for Scotland* (Edinburgh, 1882)
Ferriar, John, *An Essay Towards a Theory of Apparitions* (London, 1813)

Ferrier, Susan, *Marriage: A Novel*, 3 vols (Edinburgh, 1818)

Fleming, Robert, *The Fulfilling of the Scripture, in Three Parts*, reprint of 1681 3rd edn, 2 vols (Glasgow, 1801)

Forbes-Leith, William (ed.), *Memoirs of Scottish Catholics during the Seventeenth and Eighteenth Centuries*, 2 vols (London, 1909)

Fordyce, James, *A Collection of Hymns and Sacred Poems* (Aberdeen, 1787)

Fraser, John, 'John Fraser's *Deuteroskopia*', in Michael Hunter (ed.), *The Occult Laboratory: Magic, Science, and Second Sight in Late Seventeenth-Century Scotland* (Woodbridge, 2001), 187–204

A Full True and Particular Account of the Most Dreadful Apparrition: Of Robert Watt Wine-Merchant in Edinr, Who Appeared to James Macdonald Plaisterer in Lieth-Walk ([Edinburgh?], [1794?])

Garden, James, 'James Garden's Letters to John Aubrey', in Michael Hunter (ed.), *The Occult Laboratory: Magic, Science, and Second Sight in Late Seventeenth-Century Scotland* (Woodbridge, 2001), 118–59

Gellatly, David, *Relief Procedure Justly Exhibited* (Edinburgh, 1794)

Gentlemen of the Seagate Congregation, *A True Narrative of the Case between the Episcopal Congregation of the Seagate of Dundee, on the One Part; and Bishop Raitt with the Reverend Mr. William Robertson, on the Other* (Edinburgh, 1745)

Gerard, Alexander, *An Essay on Taste* (London, 1759)

Ghosts, &c! (Edinburgh, 1827)

Glanvill, Joseph, *Saducismus Triumphatus* (London, 1681)

The Glasgow Miscellany, or, Amusing Companion, 2 vols (Glasgow, 1800)

Glas, John, *A View of the Heresy of Aerius* (Edinburgh, 1745)

Gordon, Patrick, *The Famous History of the Renown'd and Valiant Prince, Robert Sirnamed, the Bruce, King of Scotland, &c* (Edinburgh, 1718)

The Gosford Tragedy: Or the Perjured Carpenter ([Edinburgh?], 1775)

Graeme, James, *Poems on Several Occasions* (Edinburgh, 1773)

Grant, Anne MacVicar, *Essays on the Superstitions of the Highlanders of Scotland*, 2 vols (London, 1811)

Grant, John, 'Parish of Kirkmichael', in John Sinclair (ed.), *The Statistical Account of Scotland, 1791–1799*, electronic edn, 21 vols (University of Edinburgh, University of Glasgow, 1999), vol. 12, http://stataccscot.edina.ac.uk/link/osa-vol12-p425-parish-banff-kirkmichael, accessed 1 Feb. 2018

Gregor, Walter, *Notes on the Folk-Lore of the North-East of Scotland* (London, 1881)

Grose, Francis, *The Antiquities of Scotland*, 2 vols (London, 1789–91)

——, *A Provincial Glossary: With a Collection of Local Proverbs* (London, 1787)

Guild, William, *An Answer to a Popish Pamphlet Called The Touch-Stone of the Reformed Gospell* (Aberdeen, 1656)

——, *Anti-Christ Pointed and Painted Out in His True Colours* (Aberdeen, 1655)

Halyburton, Thomas, *Natural Religion Insufficient, and Reveal'd Necessary to Man's Happiness in His Present State* (Edinburgh, 1714)

Hare's Dream! Describing the Apparition of Burke and Others, Which Appeared to Him While in the Calton Jail ([Edinburgh], [1829])

Hary, *The Wallace: Selections*, ed. Anne McKim, electronic edn (Medieval Institute Publications, 2003), http://d.lib.rochester.edu/teams/publication/mckim-the-wallace-selections, accessed 1 Feb. 2018

Hibbert, Samuel, *Sketches of the Philosophy of Apparitions: Or, An Attempt to Trace Such Illusions to Their Physical Causes*, 2nd edn (Edinburgh, 1825)

The Historical Tragedy, of Young Beateman's Ghost, or The Perjured Maid, Justly Rewarded ([Edinburgh], [1778?])

'History of Mrs. Wells', in *The Asylum or Weekly Miscellany*, 3 vols (Glasgow, 1795–6), vol. 1, 202–5

The History of Witches, Ghosts, and Highland Seers (Berwick, [1775?])

Hogg, James, *The Brownie of Bodsbeck, and Other Tales*, 2 vols (Edinburgh, 1818)

——, *The Private Memoirs and Confessions of a Justified Sinner*, ed. Adrian Hunter (Peterborough [Ont.], 2001)

——, *The Three Perils of Man: Or, War, Women, and Witchcraft*, 3 vols (London, 1822)

——, *Winter Evening Tales*, ed. Ian Duncan (Edinburgh, 2004)

Howell, Thomas Jones, and William Cobbett, *A Complete Collection of State Trials and Proceedings for High Treason and Other Crimes and Misdemeanors from the Earliest Period to the Year 1783, with Notes and Other Illustrations*, 21 vols (London, 1816)

Hume, David, *An Enquiry Concerning Human Understanding*, in Mark C. Rooks (ed.), *The Complete Works and Correspondence of David Hume*, electronic edn (Charlottesville, 1995), http://pm.nlx.com/xtf/view?docId=hume/hume.05.xml;chunk.id=div. britphil. v37.5;toc.depth=1;toc.id=div.britphil.v37.5;brand=default, accessed 1 Feb. 2018

——, 'Scotticisms', in *The Philosophical Works of David Hume*, 4 vols (Edinburgh, 1826), vol. 1, cxxv–cxxix

——, *A Treatise of Human Nature*, in Mark C. Rooks (ed.), *The Complete Works and Correspondence of David Hume*, electronic edn (Charlottesville, 1995), http:// pm.nlx.com/xtf/view?docId=hume/hume.02.xml;chunk.id=div.britphil. v34.1;toc. depth=1;toc.id=div.britphil.v34.1;brand=default, accessed 1 Feb. 2018

Hutcheson, Francis, *A System of Moral Philosophy, in Three Books*, 2 vols (Glasgow, 1755)

Innes, George, *Fourteen Discourses on Practical Subjects* (London, 1783)

Insulanus, Theophilus, *A Treatise on the Second Sight, Dreams and Apparitions* (Edinburgh, 1763)

Irvine, Christopher, *Medicina Magnetica: Or, The Rare and Wonderful Art of Curing by Sympathy* ([Edinburgh], 1656)

Jackson, John, *The History of the Scottish Stage, from Its First Establishment to the Present Time* (Edinburgh, 1793)

James VI, *Daemonologie, in Forme of Ane Dialogue*, in James Craigie and Alexander Law (eds), *Minor Prose Works of King James VI and I* (Edinburgh, 1982), 1–58

Johnson, Samuel, *A Journey to the Western Islands of Scotland* (London, 1775)

Johnstone, A., 'Parish of Monquhitter: Additional Communications', in John Sinclair (ed.), *The Statistical Account of Scotland, 1791–1799*, electronic edn, 21 vols (University of Edinburgh, University of Glasgow, 1999), vol. 21, http://stataccscot.edina.ac.uk /link/ osa-vol21-p138-appendix-aberdeen-monquhitter, accessed 1 Feb. 2018

Joynes, Andrew (ed.), *Medieval Ghost Stories: An Anthology of Miracles, Marvels, and Prodigies* (Woodbridge, 2001)

Jung-Stilling, Johann Heinrich, *Theory of Pneumatology*, trans. Samuel Jackson (London, 1834)

Kames, Henry Home, *Essays on the Principles of Morality and Natural Religion* (Edinburgh, 1751)

Keith, Peter, *The Ghaist o' Fearnden; Auld Poumire; and Rob Man; Three Tales* ([Brechin?], 1834)

The Kentshire Tragedy, or, The Constant Lovers Overthrow ([Edinburgh?], 1794)

Kerr, Charles, *Juvenile Performances in Poetry* (Edinburgh, 1788)

Kirk, Robert, 'Robert Kirk's *The Secret Commonwealth* and his "A Short Treatise of the Scotish-Irish Charms and Spells"', in Michael Hunter (ed.), *The Occult Laboratory: Magic, Science, and Second Sight in Late Seventeenth-Century Scotland* (Woodbridge, 2001), 77–117

Kirkton, James, *The Secret and True History of the Church of Scotland: From the Restoration to the Year 1678*, ed. Charles Kirkpatrick Sharpe (Edinburgh, 1817)

Knox, John, *The History of the Reformation of the Church of Scotland* (London, 1644)

Laing, Alexander, 'The Brownie of Fearnden', in Alexander Whitelaw (ed.), *The Book of Scottish Ballads: Collected and Illustrated with Historical and Critical Notices* (Glasgow, 1845), 502–3

Lang, Andrew, *Cock Lane and Common-Sense* (London, 1894)

Laskaya, Anne and Eve Salisbury (eds), 'Sir Orfeo', in *The Middle English Breton Lays*, electronic edn (Medieval Institute Publications, 1995), http://d.lib.rochester.edu/teams/publication/laskaya-and-salisbury-middle-english-breton-lays, accessed 1 Feb. 2018

Lauder, John (ed.), *The Decisions of the Lords of Council and Session, from June 6th, 1678, to July 30th, 1712*, 2 vols (Edinburgh, 1759–61)

Lavater, Ludwig, *Of Ghostes and Spirites Walking by Nyght*, trans. Robert Harrison (London, 1572, STC 15320)

Law, Robert, *Memorialls: Or the Memorable Things That Fell out Within This Island of Brittain from 1638 to 1684*, ed. Charles Kirkpatrick Sharpe (Edinburgh, 1818)

Lennox, Charlotte, *The Female Quixote, or, The Adventures of Arabella*, 2 vols (London, 1752)

The Leverpool Tragedy or the Perjur'd Sailor ([Glasgow?], 1767)

Lewis, Gregory, *The Monk: A Romance*, 3 vols (Waterford, 1796)

Lindsay, David, *The Poetical Works of Sir David Lyndsay*, ed. David Laing, 3 vols (Edinburgh, 1879)

Lindsay, Robert, *The History of Scotland: From 21 February, 1436 to March, 1565* (Edinburgh, 1728)

Livingstone, John, *Memorable Characteristics, and Remarkable Passages of Divine Providence*, in W. K. Tweedie (ed.), *Select Biographies*, 2 vols (Edinburgh, 1845), vol. 1, 293–348

Locke, John, *An Essay Concerning Humane Understanding*, 4th edn (London, 1700)

Lockhart, John Gibson, *Memoirs of the Life of Sir Walter Scott*, 2nd edn, 10 vols (Edinburgh, 1839)

Logan, John, *Sermons by the Late Reverend John Logan*, 2 vols (Edinburgh, 1790–1)

Loudon, John, *Theses Philosophicae* (Edinburgh, 1697)

Le Loyer, Pierre, *A Treatise of Specters or Straunge Sights, Visions and Apparitions Appearing Sensibly unto Men* (London, 1605, STC 15448)

MacCulloch, John, *The Highlands and Western Isles of Scotland*, 4 vols (London, 1824)

MacDonald, Alexander, *Vimonda: A Tragedy* (Dublin, 1788)

MacFarlane, Walter, *Geographical Collections Relating to Scotland Made by Walter Macfarlane*, ed. Arthur Mitchell and James Toshach Clark, 3 vols (Edinburgh, 1906–8)

Mackail, Hugh, *The Last Publick Sermon, Being a Faithful and Free One, Preached by Mr. Hugh Mackaile* (Edinburgh, 1749)

Mackay, Charles, *Memoirs of Extraordinary Popular Delusions*, 2 vols (London, 1841)

Mackenzie, George, *The Laws and Customes of Scotland, in Matters Criminal* (Edinburgh, 1678)

——, *Pleadings in Some Remarkable Cases before the Supreme Courts of Scotland Since the Year 1661* (Edinburgh, 1673)

Mackenzie, George, *Synopsis Apocalyptica: Or, A Short Plain Explication and Application of Daniel's Prophecy and of St. John's Revelation* (Edinburgh, 1708)

Mackenzie, Henry, *The Man of Feeling* (London, 1771)

MacKinnon's Ghost ([Edinburgh?], [1823?])

MacLaurin, George, *Laura, or, The Punishment of Perfidy*, in Colin MacLaurin and George MacLaurin, *The Poetical and Dramatic Works of Colin Maclaurin, Esq. Advocate, and of the Late George Maclaurin, Esq. Writer*, 2 vols (Edinburgh, 1812), vol. 1, 63–207

MacLean, Roderick, 'Parish of South Uist', in *The New Statistical Account of Scotland, 1834–45*, electronic edn, 15 vols (University of Edinburgh, University of Glasgow, 1999), vol. 14, http://stataccscot.edina.ac.uk/link/nsa-vol14-p182-parish-inverness-south_uist, accessed 1 Feb. 2018

Macleod, Malcolm, *History of Witches &c* (London, 1793)

Macnish, Robert, *The Philosophy of Sleep*, 2nd edn (Glasgow, 1838)

Macpherson, James, *The Works of Ossian, the Son of Fingal*, 2 vols (London, 1765)

——, *The Highlander: A Poem* (Edinburgh, 1758)

Mallet, David, *The Excursion: A Poem* (London, 1728)

Mann, William, *A Voice from the Dead, or, The Apparition of William Clarkson* (Paisley, 1826)

Margaret Dickson's Penetential Confession ([Edinburgh], [1724])

Marjoribanks, Thomas, 'Parish of Lochmaben', in *The New Statistical Account of Scotland, 1834–45*, electronic edn, 15 vols (University of Edinburgh, University of Glasgow, 1999), vol. 4, http://stataccscot.edina.ac.uk/link/nsa-vol4-p377-parish-dumfries-lochmaben, accessed 1 Feb. 2018

Martin, Martin, *A Description of the Western Isles of Scotland* (London, 1703)

Maxwell, Herbert (ed. and trans.), *The Chronicle of Lanercost, 1272–1346* (Glasgow, 1913)

McDonald, Mrs A., *Evening Amusements, or, What Happens in Life, a Novel*, 2 vols (Edinburgh, 1797)

McDonald, Robert, 'Parish of Blairgowrie', in *The New Statistical Account of Scotland, 1834–45*, electronic edn, 15 vols (University of Edinburgh, University of Glasgow, 1999), vol. 10, http://stataccscot.edina.ac.uk/link/nsa-vol10-p897-parish-perth-blairgowrie, accessed 1 Feb. 2018

McNaughton, Allan, 'Island of Arran: Parish of Kilbride', in *The New Statistical Account of Scotland, 1834–45*, electronic edn, 15 vols (University of Edinburgh, University of Glasgow, 1999), vol. 5, http://stataccscot.edina.ac.uk/link/nsa-vol5-p1-parish-bute-kilbride, accessed 1 Feb. 2018

McQueen, John, 'Parish of Applecross', in John Sinclair (ed.), *The Statistical Account of Scotland, 1791–1799*, electronic edn, 21 vols (University of Edinburgh, University of Glasgow, 1999), vol. 3, http://stataccscot.edina.ac.uk/link/osa-vol3-p369-parish-ross_and_cromarty-applecross, accessed 1 Feb. 2018

McRitchie, William, 'Parish of Clunie', in John Sinclair (ed.), *The Statistical Account of Scotland, 1791–1799*, electronic edn, 21 vols (University of Edinburgh, University of Glasgow, 1999), vol. 9, http://stataccscot.edina.ac.uk/link/osa-vol9-p225-parish-perth-clunie, accessed 1 Feb. 2018

Merry, Andrew, *The Antient and New History of Buck-Haven in Fife Shire* ([Edinburgh?], 1782)

La Mettrie, Julien Offray de, *Machine Man*, in Ann Thomson (ed.), *La Mettrie: Machine Man and Other Writings* (Cambridge, 1996), 1–40

Miller, Hugh, *Scenes and Legends of the North of Scotland, or The Traditional History of Cromarty* (Edinburgh, 1835)

——, *Scenes and Legends of the North of Scotland; Or, The Traditional History of Cromarty*, 2nd edn (London, 1850)

Mitchell, James, *Memoirs of the Life of James Mitchell of Dykes, in the Parish of Ardrossan* (Glasgow, 1759)

Mitchell, J., and John Dickie, *The Philosophy of Witchcraft* (Paisley, 1839)

Moncrieff, William Thomas, *The Spectre Bridegroom: Or a Ghost in Spite of Himself* (London, 1821)

Montgomerie, Alexander, and Patrick Hume, 'The Flyting betwixt Montgomery and Polwart', in James Cranstoun (ed.), *The Poems of Alexander Montgomerie* (Edinburgh, 1887), 55–86

More, Henry, *An Antidote against Atheism* (London, 1653)

Mure, Elizabeth, 'Some Remarks on the Change of Manners in My Own Time, 1700–1790', in William Mure (ed.), *Selections from the Family Papers Preserved at Caldwell*, 3 vols (Glasgow, 1854), vol. 1, 259–72

A New Vocabulary English and Latin, for the Use of Schools, 5th edn (Edinburgh, 1720)

Ogilvie, William, *A Copy of Several Conferences and Meetings, &c. that Past betwixt the Reverend Mr. Ogilvie, Late Minister of the Gospel at Innerwick, and the Ghost of Mr. Maxwel Late Laird of Cool* ([Edinburgh?], 1751)

——, *Copy of Several Conferences and Meetings, Giving an Account of what Past betwixt the Reverend Mr. Ogilvie, Late Minister of the Gospel at Innerwick, and the Ghost of Mr. Maxwel, Late Laird of Cool* ([Edinburgh?], [1790?])

——, *The Laird o' Coul's Ghost*, ed. J. F. S. Gordon (London, 1892)

——, *The Laird of Cools Ghost, Being a Copy of Several Conferences and Meetings That Passed between the Reverend Mr. Ogilvie, Late Minister of the Gospel at Innerwick, in East Lothian, and the Late Laird of Cool's Ghost* (Edinburgh, [1800?])

——, *The Laird of Cool's Ghost, Being, a Wonderful and True Account of Several Conferences betwixt the Revd. Mr Ogilvie, Late Minister of the Gospel at Innerwick, and the Ghost of the Deceast Mr Maxwell, Late Laird of Cool* (Dumfries, 1786)

——, *Narrative of Four Conferences between the Ghost of Mr. Maxwell, of Coul, and the Rev. Mr. Ogilvie, Minister of Innerwick*, ed. Elizabeth Steuart (London, 1808)

Peacock, George, *Theses Philosophicae* (Aberdeen: Marischal College, 1693)

Pennant, Thomas, *A Tour in Scotland 1769* (Chester, 1771)

——, *A Tour in Scotland 1772, Part 1* (Chester, 1774)

——, *A Tour in Scotland 1772, Part 2* (London, 1776)

Person, David, *Varieties: Or, A Surveigh of Rare and Excellent Matters Necessary and Delectable for All Sorts of Persons* (London, 1635, STC 19781)

Picken, Andrew, *Tales and Sketches of the West of Scotland* (Glasgow, 1824)

Pitcairne, Archibald, *Archibald Pitcairne: The Latin Poems*, ed. John MacQueen and Winifred MacQueen (Assen, 2009)

——, *The Phanaticks*, ed. John MacQueen (Woodbridge, 2012)

Pitcairn, Robert (ed.), *Criminal Trials in Scotland, 1488–1624*, 4 vols (Edinburgh, 1833)

P. M., *The Speech of a Fyfe Laird, Newly Come from Grave* ([Scotland], [1680?])

Pope, Walter, *The Life of the Right Reverend Father in God, Seth, Lord Bishop of Salisbury* (London, 1697)

Pye, John, *A True and Perfect Account of a Strange and Dreadful Apparition Which Lately Infested and Sunk a Ship Bound for New-Castle* (Edinburgh, 1672)

Raitt, James, *An Instructed Historical Account of the Settlement in the Episcopal Congregation of Dundee in 1727* ([Edinburgh?], 1744)

Ramsay, Allan, *Elegies on Maggy Johnston, John Cowper, and Lucky Wood*, 2nd edn (Edinburgh, 1718)

—— (ed.), *The Ever Green, Being a Collection of Scots Poems*, 2 vols (Edinburgh, 1724)

——, *The Gentle Shepherd: A Scots Pastoral Comedy* (Edinburgh, 1725)

——, *A Tale of Three Bonnets* ([Edinburgh?], 1722)
——, *The Tea-Table Miscellany: Or, A Collection of Choice Songs*, 3 vols (Edinburgh, 1724–7)
Ramsay, John, *Scotland and Scotsmen in the Eighteenth Century*, ed. Alexander Allardyce, 2 vols (Edinburgh, 1888)
Rattray, Thomas, *The Ancient Liturgy of the Church of Jerusalem* (London, 1744)
Robert Johnston's Ghost, or, His Last Advice to the Gipsies, and Other Gangs of Robbers and Murderers in Scotland ([Edinburgh?], [1720?])
Robertson, David (ed.), *South Leith Records, Compiled from the Parish Registers for the Years 1588 to 1700* (Edinburgh, 1911)
Robertson, John, *Rusticus Ad Clericum, or, The Plow-Man Rebuking the Priest in Answer to Verus Patroclus* ([Aberdeen?], 1694)
Saint-Fond, Barthélemy Faujas de, *A Journey through England and Scotland to the Hebrides in 1784*, ed. and trans. Archibald Geikie, 2 vols (Glasgow, 1907)
Scott, Walter, *The Bride of Lammermoor*, in *Tales of My Landlord*, 4 vols (Edinburgh, 1819), vol. 2, 3–324, vol. 3, 3–131
——, 'Introduction', in Horace Walpole, *The Castle of Otranto: A Gothic Story* (Edinburgh, 1811), iii–xliii
——, *The Lady of the Lake: A Poem* (Edinburgh, 1810)
——, *Letters on Demonology and Witchcraft* (London, 1830)
——, *Marmion: A Tale of Flodden Field* (Edinburgh, 1808)
——, *Minstrelsy of the Scottish Border*, 3 vols (Edinburgh, 1802–3)
——, *The Monastery: A Romance*, 3 vols (Edinburgh, 1820)
——, 'My Aunt Margaret's Mirror', in Frédéric Mansel Reynolds (ed.), *The Keepsake for 1829* (London, 1828), 1–44
——, *The Poetical Works of Sir Walter Scott, Bart.*, ed. J. G. Lockhart, 12 vols (Edinburgh, 1833–4)
——, *Rokeby: A Poem* (Edinburgh, 1813)
——, 'The Tapestried Chamber', in Frédéric Mansel Reynolds (ed.), *The Keepsake for 1829* (London, 1829), 123–42
—— (ed.), *Trial of Duncan Terig Alias Clerk, and Alexander Bane Macdonald, for the Murder of Arthur Davis, Sergeant in General Guise's Regiment of Foot* (Edinburgh, 1831)
——, *Waverley Novels, Vol. 18: The Monastery* (Edinburgh, 1830)
——, *Waverley Novels, Vol. 34: Redgauntlet* (Edinburgh, 1832)
The Second Letter, from the Ghost of Bailie Cuthbert ([Edinburgh?], [1780?])
Shaftsbury's Ghost to Doctor Oats: In a Vision, Concerning the Jesuits and Lords in the Tower (Edinburgh, 1683)
Sharpe, Charles Kirkpatrick, 'Prefatory Notice', in Charles Kirkpatrick Sharpe (ed.), *Memorialls: Or the Memorable Things That Fell out Within This Island of Brittain from 1638 to 1684* (Edinburgh, 1818), vii–cxiv
Shaw, Lachlan, *The History of the Province of Moray* (Edinburgh, 1775)
Simson, Patrick, *A Short Compend of the Historie of the First Ten Persecutions Moved against Christians Divided into III. Centuries* (Edinburgh, 1613–16, STC 23601)
Sinclair, George, *The Hydrostaticks, or, The Weight, Force, and Pressure of Fluid Bodies, Made Evident by Physical, and Sensible Experiments* (Edinburgh, 1672)
——, *Satans Invisible World Discovered* (Edinburgh, 1685)
Skinner, John, *A Course of Lectures, Delivered on the Six Sundays in Lent* (Aberdeen, 1786)
Smollett, Tobias, *The Adventures of Ferdinand Count Fathom*, 2 vols (London, 1753)
——, *The Adventures of Peregrine Pickle*, 3 vols (Dublin, 1751)
——, *The Adventures of Roderick Random*, 2 vols (London, 1748)
——, *The Adventures of Sir Launcelot Greaves*, 2 vols (London, 1762)

——, *The Expedition of Humphry Clinker*, 2 vols (Dublin, 1771)
——, 'Ode to Mirth', in *Plays and Poems Written by T. Smollett, M. D.* (London, 1777), 250–2
Some Predictions or Prophesies ... Likewise, an Account of an Apparition in the Castle of Edinburgh, in the Year 1651 or 1652 (Edinburgh, 1739)
Stewart, Dugald, *Elements of the Philosophy of the Human Mind*, 3 vols (London, 1792–1827)
Stewart, William Grant, *The Popular Superstitions and Festive Amusements of the Highlanders of Scotland* (Edinburgh, 1823)
The St. James's Surprizing and Afrightful Apparition ([Edinburgh?], 1722)
Strange and Wonderfull Apparitions That Was Seen in the Air ([Edinburgh?], 1719)
Stuart, John (ed.), *Extracts from the Presbytery Book of Strathbogie, A.D. 1631–1654* (Aberdeen, 1843)
—— (ed.), *Selections from the Records of the Kirk Session, Presbytery, and Synod of Aberdeen* (Aberdeen, 1846)
Taillepied, Noel, *Psichologie, ou Traité de l'Apparition des Esprits* (Rouen, 1588)
Tait, John, 'The Vanity of Human Wishes, an Elegy, Occasioned by the Untimely Death of a Scots Poet', in Robert Fergusson, *Poems on Various Subjects, by Robert Fergusson, Part 2* (Edinburgh, 1779), 149–51
Taylor, Alexander, 'Parish of Leochel and Cushnie', in *The New Statistical Account of Scotland, 1834–45*, electronic edn, 15 vols (University of Edinburgh, University of Glasgow, 1999), vol. 12, http://stataccscot.edina.ac.uk/link/nsa-vol12-p1102-parish-aberdeen-leochel, accessed 1 Feb. 2018
Telfair, Alexander, *A True Relation of an Apparition, Expressions and Actings, of a Spirit* (Edinburgh, 1696)
Thomson, Derick S. (ed.), *Gaelic Poetry in the Eighteenth Century: A Bilingual Anthology* (Aberdeen, 1993)
Thomson, Thomas, *A Diurnal of Remarkable Occurrents That Have Passed within the Country of Scotland* (Edinburgh, 1833)
Threipland, Stuart Moncrieff, *Letters Respecting the Performances at the Theatre Royal, Edinburgh* (Edinburgh, 1800)
Thrummy Cap, a Tale; and The Brownie o' Fearnden, a Ballad (Brechin, 1832)
Tod, John, 'Parish of Mauchline', in *The New Statistical Account of Scotland, 1834–45*, electronic edn, 15 vols (University of Edinburgh, University of Glasgow, 1999), vol. 5, http://stataccscot.edina.ac.uk/link/nsa-vol5-p158-parish-ayrshire-mauchline, accessed 1 Feb. 2018
A True and Impartial Relation of a Wonderful Apparition That Happen'd in the Royal Camp in Flanders (Edinburgh, 1692)
The Vision of Dr Morris, or, The Spectral Warning ([Edinburgh], 1821)
Visits from the World of Spirits, or, Interesting Anecdotes of the Dead (London, 1791)
Walker, Patrick, *Six Saints of the Covenant*, ed. David Hay Fleming, 2 vols (London, 1901)
Watson, Alexander, *The Anti-Jacobin, a Hudibrastic Poem in Twenty-One Cantos* (Edinburgh, 1794)
Webster, James, *Select Sermons Preach'd on Several Texts* (Edinburgh, 1723)
Webster, John, *The Displaying of Supposed Witchcraft* (London, 1677)
Wedderburn, Alexander, *Heaven upon Earth, or, The History of the Transfiguration of Jesus Chirst Opened* (Edinburgh, 1703)
Willison, John, *A Fair and Impartial Testimony: Essayed in Name of a Number of Ministers, Elders, and Christian People of the Church of Scotland* (Edinburgh, 1744)
——, *A Treatise Concerning the Sanctifying of the Lord's Day* (Edinburgh, 1716)
Wilson, John, *Lights and Shadows of Scottish Life* (Edinburgh, 1822)

Wilson, John Mackay, *Wilson's Tales of the Borders: A Selection*, ed. T. Henderson (Edinburgh, 1934)
Wodrow, Robert, *Analecta: Or Materials for a History of Remarkable Providences Mostly Relating to Scotch Ministers and Christians*, ed. Matthew Leishman, 4 vols (Edinburgh, 1842–3)
——, *The Correspondence of the Rev. Robert Wodrow*, ed. Thomas M'Crie, 3 vols (Edinburgh, 1842)
——, *Early Letters of Robert Wodrow, 1698–1709*, ed. L. W. Sharp (Edinburgh, 1937)
——, *The History of the Sufferings of the Church of Scotland*, 2 vols (Edinburgh, 1721–2)
The Yarmouth Tragedy: Shewing How by the Cruelty of Their Parents, Two Lovers Were Distroyed ([Edinburgh?], 1775)
Young, Edward, *Edward Young: Night Thoughts*, ed. Stephen Cornford (Cambridge, 1989)
Young Grigor's Ghost ([Edinburgh?], 1776)

PUBLISHED SECONDARY SOURCES

Ahnert, Thomas, *The Moral Culture of the Scottish Enlightenment, 1690–1805* (New Haven, 2014)
——, 'The Soul, Moral Philosophy and Natural Religion in the Scottish Enlightenment', *Eighteenth Century Thought* 2 (2004), 233–53
Alexander, William, *Notes and Sketches Illustrative of Northern Rural Life in the Eighteenth Century* (Edinburgh, 1877)
Allan, David, 'Enlightenment (1660–1843): General (Including Philosophy)', in Michael Lynch (ed.), *Oxford Companion to Scottish History*, electronic edn (University of Oxford, 2007), http://www.oxfordreference.com/view/10.1093/acref/ 9780199234820.001.0001/ acref-9780199234820-e-74?rskey=qoL62n&result=1#acref-9780199234820-eSub-0040, accessed 1 Feb. 2018
——, *Scotland in the Eighteenth Century: Union and Enlightenment* (Harlow, 2002)
——, *Virtue, Learning and the Scottish Enlightenment: Ideas of Scholarship in Early Modern History* (Edinburgh, 1993)
Anderson, John, 'Sinclair, George (d. 1696?)', *Oxford DNB* (Oxford University Press, 2009), http://www.oxforddnb.com/view/article/25615, accessed 1 Feb. 2018
Andriopoulos, Stefan, *Ghostly Apparitions: German Idealism, the Gothic Novel, and Optical Media* (Cambridge [Mass.], 2013)
Ariès, Philippe, *The Hour of Our Death*, trans. Helen Weaver (Oxford, 1981)
Asprem, Egil, *The Problem of Disenchantment: Scientific Naturalism and Esoteric Discourse, 1900–1939* (Leiden, 2014)
Atkinson, David, '"William and Margaret": An Eighteenth-Century Ballad', *Folk Music Journal* 10 (2014), 478–511
Bailey, Michael D., 'The Disenchantment of Magic: Spells, Charms, and Superstition in Early European Witchcraft Literature', *American Historical Review* 111 (2006), 383–404
Bailey, Richard, 'Scots and Scotticisms: Language and Ideology', *Studies in Scottish Literature* 26 (1991), 65–77
Baker, Ian S., '"Do Ghosts Exist?": A Summary of Parapsychological Research into Apparitional Experiences', in John Newton and Jo Bath (eds), *Early Modern Ghosts* (Durham, 2002), 109–25
Baker, Timothy C., *Contemporary Scottish Gothic: Mourning, Authenticity, and Tradition* (Basingstoke, 2014)
——, 'The Ghost Story in Scotland', in Scott Brewster and Luke Thurston (eds), *The Routledge Handbook to the Ghost Story* (Abingdon, 2018), 188–96
Balaban, John, 'Blind Harry and "The Wallace"', *Chaucer Review* 8 (1974), 241–51

Bald, M. A., 'The Anglicisation of Scottish Printing', *Scottish Historical Review* 23 (1926), 107–15

——, 'The Pioneers of Anglicised Speech in Scotland', *Scottish Historical Review* 24 (1927), 179–93

Barber, Paul, *Vampires, Burial, and Death: Folklore and Reality* (New Haven, 1988)

Barker-Benfield, G. J., *The Culture of Sensibility: Sex and Society in Eighteenth-Century Britain* (Chicago, 1992)

Barnett, S. J., *The Enlightenment and Religion: The Myths of Modernity* (Manchester, 2003)

Barry, Jonathan, *Raising Spirits: How a Conjuror's Tale was Transmitted across the Enlightenment* (Basingstoke, 2013)

——, *Witchcraft and Demonology in South-West England, 1640–1789* (Basingstoke, 2012)

Bath, Jo, and John Newton, '"Sensible Proof of Spirits": Ghost Belief during the Later Seventeenth Century', *Folklore* 117 (2006), 1–14

Beal, Joan, 'Syntax and Morphology', in Charles Jones (ed.), *The Edinburgh History of the Scots Language* (Edinburgh, 1997)

Beik, William, 'The Dilemma of Popular History', *Past & Present* 141 (1993), 207–15

Bell, Bill, 'The Scottish Book Trade at Home and Abroad, 1707–1918', in Ian Brown et al. (eds), *The Edinburgh History of Scottish Literature, Vol. 2: Enlightenment, Britain and Empire (1707–1918)* (Edinburgh, 2007), 221–7

Bell, Karl, *The Magical Imagination: Magic and Modernity in Urban England, 1780–1914* (Cambridge, 2012)

Bennett, Gillian, *Alas, Poor Ghost!: Traditions of Belief in Story and Discourse* (Logan [Utah], 1999)

——, *Bodies: Sex, Violence, Disease, and Death in Contemporary Legend* (Jackson [Miss.], 2009)

——, 'Ghost and Witch in the Sixteenth and Seventeenth Centuries', *Folklore* 97 (1986), 3–14

——, *Traditions of Belief: Women and the Supernatural* (London, 1987)

Bentinck, Charles Donald, *Dornoch Cathedral and Parish* (Inverness, 1926)

Benz, Ernst, *Emanuel Swedenborg: Visionary Savant in the Age of Reason*, trans. Nicholas Goodrick-Clarke (West Chester, 2002)

Berman, Morris, *The Reenchantment of the World* (Ithaca [N.Y.], 1981)

Bertie, David M., *Scottish Episcopal Clergy, 1689–2000* (Edinburgh, 2000)

Beyer, Jürgen, 'On the Transformation of Apparition Stories in Scandinavia and Germany, c.1350–1700', *Folklore* 110 (1999), 39–47

Black, G. F., *County Folklore III: Examples of Printed Folklore Concerning the Orkney and Shetland Islands*, ed. Northcote W. Thomas (London, 1903)

Black, Winston, 'Animated Corpses and Bodies with Power in the Scholastic Age', in Joëlle Rollo-Koster (ed.), *Death in Medieval Europe: Death Scripted and Death Choreographed* (Abingdon, 2017), 71–92

BMG Research, 'British Public Reveal their Beliefs in New Survey', May 2017 (Bostock Marketing Group), http://www.bmgresearch.co.uk/british-public-reveal-beliefs-new-survey, accessed 1 Feb. 2018

Bondeson, Jan, *Buried Alive: The Terrifying History of Our Most Primal Fear* (New York, 2002)

Bostridge, Ian, 'Witchcraft Repealed', in Jonathan Barry, Marianne Hester and Gary Roberts (eds), *Witchcraft in Early Modern Europe: Studies in Culture and Belief* (Cambridge, 1996), 309–34

Botting, Fred, *Gothic: The New Critical Idiom*, 2nd edn (Abingdon, 2014)

Bowie, Karin, *Scottish Public Opinion and the Anglo-Scottish Union, 1699-1707* (Woodbridge, 2007)

Bowyer, R. A., 'The Role of the Ghost-Story in Mediaeval Christianity', in Helen Parish (ed.), *Superstition and Magic in Early Modern Europe: A Reader* (London, 2015), 177–92

Briggs, K. M., *The Anatomy of Puck: An Examination of Fairy Beliefs Among Shakespeare's Contemporaries and Successors* (London, 1959)

Briggs, Robin, *Witches and Neighbours: The Social and Cultural Context of European Witchcraft*, 2nd edn (Oxford, 2002)

Broadie, Alexander, 'The Rise (and Fall?) of the Scottish Enlightenment', in T. M. Devine and Jenny Wormald (eds), *The Oxford Handbook of Modern Scottish History* (Oxford, 2012), 370–85

Brock, Michelle D., 'Internalizing the Demonic: Satan and the Self in Early Modern Scottish Piety', *Journal of British Studies* 54 (2015), 23–43

——, *Satan and the Scots: The Devil in Post-Reformation Scotland, c.1560–1700* (Abingdon, 2016)

Brown, Callum G., *Religion and Society in Scotland since 1707* (Edinburgh, 1997)

Brown, Deborah, 'The Sixth Meditation: Descartes and the Embodied Self', in David Cunning (ed.), *The Cambridge Companion to Descartes'* Meditations (Cambridge, 2014), 240–57

Brown, Ian, *Scottish Theatre: Diversity, Language, Continuity* (Amsterdam, 2013)

Brown, James, *The History of Sanquhar* (Dumfries, 1891)

Brown, Keith M., *Noble Society in Scotland: Wealth, Family, and Culture from the Reformation to the Revolution* (Edinburgh, 2000)

Brown, Rhona, 'Allan Ramsay, Robert Fergusson and Robert Burns', in David Sergeant and Fiona J. Stafford (eds), *Burns and Other Poets* (Edinburgh, 2012), 23–38

——, *Robert Fergusson and the Scottish Periodical Press* (Aldershot, 2012)

Brown, Stewart J., 'Religion and Society to c.1900', in T. M. Devine and Jenny Wormald (eds), *The Oxford Handbook of Modern Scottish History* (Oxford, 2012), 78–98

Brown, Theo, 'The Black Dog', *Folklore* 69 (1958), 175–92

——, *The Fate of the Dead: A Study in Folk-Eschatology in the West Country After the Reformation* (Cambridge, 1979)

Bruce, Steve, *Scottish Gods: Religion in Modern Scotland, 1900–2012* (Oxford, 2014)

Buchan, David, 'Talerole Analysis and Child's Supernatural Ballads', in Joseph Harris (ed.), *The Ballad and Oral Literature* (Cambridge [Mass.], 1991), 60–77

Buchan, David, and Edward D. Ives, 'Tale Roles and Revenants: A Morphology of Ghosts', *Western Folklore* 45 (1986), 143–60

Burke, Peter, *Popular Culture in Early Modern Europe*, 3rd edn (Aldershot, 2009)

Burns, R. M., *The Great Debate on Miracles: From Joseph Glanvill to David Hume* (London, 1981)

Burns, William E., *An Age of Wonders: Prodigies, Politics, and Providence in England, 1657–1727* (Manchester, 2002)

Buse, Peter, and Andrew Stott, 'Introduction: A Future for Haunting', in Peter Buse and Andrew Stott (eds), *Ghosts: Deconstruction, Psychoanalysis, History* (Basingstoke, 1999), 1–21

Butler, Marilyn, 'Romanticism in England', in Roy Porter and Mikuláš Teich (eds), *Romanticism in National Context* (Cambridge, 1988), 37–67

Bysveen, Josef, *Epic Tradition and Innovation in James MacPherson's Fingal* (Uppsala, 1982)

Caciola, Nancy, *Afterlives: The Return of the Dead in the Middle Ages* (Ithaca [N.Y.], 2016)

——, *Discerning Spirits: Divine and Demonic Possession in the Middle Ages* (Ithaca [N.Y.], 2003)

——, 'Wraiths, Revenants, and Ritual in Medieval Culture', *Past & Present* 152 (1996), 3–45
Cameron, Euan, *Enchanted Europe: Superstition, Reason, and Religion, 1250–1750* (Oxford, 2010)
Campbell, John Gregorson, *The Gaelic Otherworld: Superstitions of the Highlands and the Islands*, ed. Ronald Black (Edinburgh, 2005)
Campbell, J. L., and Derick Thomson, *Edward Lhuyd in the Scottish Highlands, 1699–1700* (Oxford, 1963)
Campbell, R. H., and Andrew S. Skinner (eds), *The Origins and Nature of the Scottish Enlightenment* (Edinburgh, 1982)
Capp, Bernard, *Astrology and the Popular Press: English Almanacs 1500–1800* (London, 1979)
Carlson, Julie A., 'Baillie's Orra: Shrinking in Fear', in Thomas C. Crochunis (ed.), *Joanna Baillie, Romantic Dramatist: Critical Essays* (London, 2004), 206–20
Carpenter, Sarah, 'Early Scottish Drama', in R. D. S. Jack (ed.), *The History of Scottish Literature, Vol. 1: Origins to 1600* (Aberdeen, 1988), 199–211
——, 'Scottish Drama until 1650', in Ian Brown (ed.), *The Edinburgh Companion to Scottish Drama* (Oxford, 2011), 6–21
Carruthers, Gerard, 'Blair, Robert (1699–1746)', *Oxford DNB* (Oxford University Press, 2004), http://www.oxforddnb.com/view/article/2570, accessed 1 Feb. 2018
Castle, Terry, *The Female Thermometer: Eighteenth-Century Culture and the Invention of the Uncanny* (Oxford, 1995)
Caw, James L., *Scottish Painting Past and Present, 1620–1908* (Edinburgh, 1908)
Chadwick, N. K., 'Norse Ghosts (A Study in the *Draugr* and the *Haugbúi*)', *Folklore* 57 (1946), 50–65
Chapman, Malcolm, *The Gaelic Vision in Scottish Culture* (London, 1978)
Charlesworth, Michael, *Landscape and Vision in Nineteenth-Century Britain and France* (Aldershot, 2008)
Chesters, Timothy, *Ghost Stories in Late Renaissance France: Walking by Night* (Oxford, 2011)
Christian, William A., *Apparitions in Late Medieval and Renaissance Spain* (Princeton, 1981)
Clarke, Roger, *A Natural History of Ghosts* (London, 2012)
Clark, J. C. D., 'Providence, Predestination and Progress: Or, Did the Enlightenment Fail?', *Albion* 35 (2003), 559–89
Clark, Stuart, *Thinking with Demons: The Idea of Witchcraft in Early Modern Europe* (Oxford, 1997)
——, *Vanities of the Eye: Vision in Early Modern European Culture* (Oxford, 2007)
Clery, E. J., *The Rise of Supernatural Fiction, 1762–1800* (Cambridge, 1995)
Clyde, Robert, *From Rebel to Hero: The Image of the Highlander, 1745–1830* (East Linton, 1995)
Collins, Kenneth J., *The Theology of John Wesley: Holy Love and the Shape of Grace* (Nashville, 2007)
Copeland, Clare, and Jan Machielsen (eds), *Angels of Light? Sanctity and the Discernment of Spirits in the Early Modern Period* (Leiden, 2013)
Coudert, Allison P., 'Rethinking Max Weber's Theory of Disenchantment', in Albrecht Classen (ed.), *Magic and Magicians in the Middle Ages and the Early Modern Time: The Occult in Pre-Modern Sciences, Medicine, Literature, Religion, and Astrology* (Berlin, 2017), 705–39
Cowan, Edward J. (ed.), *The Ballad in Scottish History* (East Linton, 2000)
——, 'The Discovery of the Future: Prophecy and Second Sight in Scottish History', in Lizanne Henderson (ed.), *Fantastical Imaginations: The Supernatural in Scottish History and Culture* (Edinburgh, 2009), 1–28

——, 'Witch Persecution and Folk Belief in Lowland Scotland: The Devil's Decade', in Julian Goodare, Lauren Martin and Joyce Miller (eds), *Witchcraft and Belief in Early Modern Scotland* (Basingstoke, 2008), 71–94

Cowan, Edward J., and Mike Paterson (eds), *Folk in Print: Scotland's Chapbook Heritage, 1750–1850* (Edinburgh, 2007)

Craven, J. B., *Church Life in South Ronaldshay and Burray in the Seventeenth Century* (Kirkwall, 1911)

Crawford, Julie, *Marvelous Protestantism: Monstrous Births in Post-Reformation England* (Baltimore, 2005)

Crawford, Robert, *Scotland's Books* (London, 2007)

Crochunis, Thomas C. (ed.), *Joanna Baillie, Romantic Dramatist: Critical Essays* (London, 2004)

Cronin, Richard, *Paper Pellets: British Literary Culture after Waterloo* (Oxford, 2010)

Cunningham, Andrew, 'Medicine to Calm the Mind: Boerhaave's Medical System, and Why It Was Adopted in Edinburgh', in Andrew Cunningham and Roger French (eds), *The Medical Enlightenment of the Eighteenth Century* (Cambridge, 1990), 40–66

Curry, Patrick, *Prophecy and Power: Astrology in Early Modern England* (Cambridge, 1989)

Darnton, Robert, *Mesmerism and the End of the Enlightenment in France* (Cambridge [Mass.], 1968)

Daston, Lorraine, 'Marvelous Facts and Miraculous Evidence in Early Modern Europe', *Critical Inquiry* 18 (1991), 93–124

Daston, Lorraine, and Katharine Park, *Wonders and the Order of Nature, 1150–1750* (New York, 1998)

Davidson, H. R. E., and W. M. S. Russell (eds), *The Folklore of Ghosts* (Cambridge, 1981)

Davidson, Jane P., *Early Modern Supernatural: The Dark Side of European Culture, 1400–1700* (Santa Barbara, 2012)

Davies, Owen, 'Ghosts', in Christopher Moreman (ed.), *The Routledge Companion to Death and Dying* (Abingdon, 2017), 343–51

——, *The Haunted: A Social History of Ghosts* (New York, 2007)

——, 'Introduction', in Owen Davies (ed.), *Ghosts: A Social History*, 5 vols (London, 2010), vol. 1, ix-xlix

——, *Witchcraft, Magic and Culture, 1736–1951* (Manchester, 1999)

Davies, Owen, and Francesca Matteoni, *Executing Magic in the Modern Era: Criminal Bodies and the Gallows in Popular Medicine*, electronic edn (Palgrave Macmillan, 2017), https://doi.org/10.1007/978-3-319-59519-1, accessed 1 Feb. 2018

Davies, Owen, and Willem de Blécourt (eds), *Beyond the Witch Trials: Witchcraft and Magic in Enlightenment Europe* (Manchester, 2004)

Davis, Colin, 'État Présent: Hauntology, Spectres and Phantoms', *French Studies* 59 (2005), 373–9

Davis, Leith, *Acts of Union: Scotland and the Literary Negotiation of the British Nation, 1707–1830* (Stanford, 1998)

Davis, Matthew M., '"Ask for the Old Paths": Johnson and the Nonjurors', in J. C. D. Clark and Howard Erskine-Hill (eds), *The Politics of Samuel Johnson* (Basingstoke, 2012), 112–67

Dawson, Jane E. A., *Scotland Re-Formed, 1488–1587* (Edinburgh, 2007)

Dégh, Linda, *Legend and Belief: Dialectics of a Folklore Genre* (Bloomington, 2001)

Dentith, Simon, *Parody* (London, 2000)

Derrida, Jacques, *Specters of Marx: The State of the Debt, the Work of Mourning, and the New International*, trans. Peggy Kamuf (New York, 1994)

Devine, T. M., *Clanship to Crofter's War: The Social Transformation of the Scottish Highlands* (Manchester, 1994)

——, 'The Failure of Radical Reform in Scotland in the Late Eighteenth Century', in T. M. Devine (ed.), *Conflict and Stability in Scottish Society, 1700–1850* (Edinburgh, 1990), 51–64

——, *The Scottish Nation, 1700–2007* (London, 2006)

Devine, T. M., and J. R. Young (eds), *Eighteenth Century Scotland: New Perspectives* (East Linton, 1999)

Doering-Manteuffel, Sabine, 'The Dissemination of Magical Knowledge in Enlightenment Germany: The Supernatural and the Development of Print Culture', in Owen Davies and Willem de Blécourt (eds), *Beyond the Witch Trials: Witchcraft and Magic in Enlightenment Europe* (Manchester, 2004), 187–206

Donagan, Barbara, 'Providence, Chance and Explanation: Some Paradoxical Aspects of Puritan Views of Causation', *Journal of Religious History* 11 (1981), 385–403

Donaldson, Gordon, *The Faith of the Scots* (London, 1990)

Downes, Jeremy M., *Recursive Desire: Rereading Epic Tradition* (Tuscaloosa, 2014)

Drummond, Andrew Landale, and James Bulloch, *The Scottish Church, 1688–1843: The Age of the Moderates* (Edinburgh, 1973)

Duncan, Ian, 'Fanaticism and Enlightenment in *Confessions of a Justified Sinner*', in Sharon Alker and Holly Faith Nelson (eds), *James Hogg and the Literary Marketplace: Scottish Romanticism and the Working-Class Author* (Farnham, 2009), 57–70

——, *Scott's Shadow: The Novel in Romantic Edinburgh* (Princeton, 2007)

——, 'Walter Scott, James Hogg and Scottish Gothic', in David Punter (ed.), *A New Companion to the Gothic* (Oxford, 2012), 123–34

Duncan, Ian, Leith Davis and Janet Sorensen, 'Introduction', in Leith Davis, Ian Duncan and Janet Sorensen (eds), *Scotland and the Borders of Romanticism* (Cambridge, 2004), 1–19

Dymond, Anne, 'Displaying the Arlésienne: Museums, Folklife and Regional Identities in France', in Timothy Baycroft and David Hopkin (eds), *Folklore and Nationalism in Europe during the Long Nineteenth Century* (Leiden, 2012), 137–60

Edgar, Andrew, *Old Church Life in Scotland: Lectures on Kirk-Session and Presbytery Records* (Paisley, 1886)

Edwards, Kathryn A. (ed.), *Everyday Magic in Early Modern Europe* (Farnham, 2015)

——, 'The History of Ghosts in Early Modern Europe: Recent Research and Future Trajectories', *History Compass* 10 (2012), 353–66

——, (ed.), *Werewolves, Witches, and Wandering Spirits: Traditional Belief and Folklore in Early Modern Europe* (Kirksville, 2002)

Ellis, Markman, *The Politics of Sensibility: Race, Gender and Commerce in the Sentimental Novel* (Cambridge, 1996)

Emerson, Roger, 'The Contexts of the Scottish Enlightenment', in Alexander Broadie (ed.), *The Cambridge Companion to the Scottish Enlightenment* (Cambridge, 2003), 9–30

——, 'Did the Scottish Enlightenment Emerge in an English Cultural Province?', *Lumen: Selected Proceedings from the Canadian Society for Eighteenth-Century Studies* 14 (1995), 1–24

——, *Essays on David Hume, Medical Men and the Scottish Enlightenment: 'Industry, Knowledge and Humanity'* (Farnham, 2009)

——, 'The Religious, the Secular and the Worldly: Scotland 1680–1800', in James E. Crimmins (ed.), *Religion, Secularization and Political Thought: Thomas Hobbes to J. S. Mill* (London, 1989), 68–89

Faubert, Michelle, 'John Ferriar's Psychology, James Hogg's *Justified Sinner*, and the Gay Science of Horror Writing', in Thomas H. Schmid and Michelle Faubert (eds), *Romanticism and Pleasure* (Basingstoke, 2010), 83–108

Ferber, Michael, 'Introduction', in Michael Ferber (ed.), *A Companion to European Romanticism* (Oxford, 2005), 1–9

Fielding, Penny, '*The Private Memoirs and Confessions of a Justified Sinner*: Approaches', in Ian Duncan and Douglas S. Mack (eds), *The Edinburgh Companion to James Hogg* (Edinburgh, 2012), 132–9

Findlay, Bill, 'Beginnings to 1700', in Bill Findlay (ed.), *A History of Scottish Theatre* (Edinburgh, 1998), 1–79

Finlay, Richard J., 'Caledonia or North Britain? Scottish Identity in the Eighteenth Century', in Dauvit Broun, Richard J. Finlay and Michael Lynch (eds), *Image and Identity: The Making and Re-Making of Scotland through the Ages* (Edinburgh, 1998), 143–56

Finucane, R. C., *Ghosts: Appearances of the Dead and Cultural Transformation* (Amherst [N.Y.], 1996)

Fisher, Keely, 'The Crying of Ane Play: Robin Hood and Maying in Sixteenth-Century Scotland', in John Pitcher (ed.), *Medieval and Renaissance Drama in England, Vol. 12* (Cranbury, 1999), 19–58

Fleming, Maurice, *The Ghost o' Mause: And Other Tales and Traditions of East Perthshire* (Edinburgh, 1995)

Ford, Jennifer, *Coleridge on Dreaming: Romanticism, Dreams and the Medical Imagination* (Cambridge, 1997)

Fox, Adam, 'Approaches to Ephemera: Scottish Broadsides, 1679–1746', in Kevin Murphy and Sally O'Driscoll (eds), *Studies in Ephemera: Text and Image in Eighteenth-Century Print* (Lanham, 2013), 117–41

——, 'The Emergence of the Scottish Broadside Ballad in the Late Seventeenth and Early Eighteenth Centuries', *Journal of Scottish Historical Studies* 31 (2011), 169–94

——, '"Little Story Books" and "Small Pamphlets" in Edinburgh, 1680–1760: The Making of the Scottish Chapbook', *Scottish Historical Review* 92 (2013), 207–30

——, *Oral and Literate Culture in England, 1500–1700* (Oxford, 2000)

Foyster, Elizabeth A., and Christopher A. Whatley (eds), *A History of Everyday Life in Scotland, 1600 to 1800* (Edinburgh, 2010)

Frace, Ryan K., 'Religious Toleration in the Wake of Revolution: Scotland on the Eve of Enlightenment (1688–1710s)', *History* 93 (2008), 355–75

Fraser, William, *The Earls of Cromartie, Their Kindred, Country and Correspondence*, 2 vols (Edinburgh, 1876)

Gamer, Michael, 'Gothic Fictions and Romantic Writing in Britain', in Jerrold E. Hogle (ed.), *The Cambridge Companion to Gothic Fiction* (Cambridge, 2002), 85–104

——, *Romanticism and the Gothic: Genre, Reception, and Canon Formation* (Cambridge, 2000)

Garside, Peter, 'Publishing 1800–30', in Bill Bell (ed.), *The Edinburgh History of the Book in Scotland, Vol. 3: Ambition and Industry 1800–1880* (Edinburgh, 2007), 79–90

Gaskill, Malcolm, *Crime and Mentalities in Early Modern England* (Cambridge, 2000)

——, 'The Displacement of Providence: Policing and Prosecution in Seventeenth- and Eighteenth-Century England', *Continuity and Change* 11 (1996), 341–74

Gatrell, V. A. C., *The Hanging Tree: Execution and the English People 1770–1868* (Oxford, 1996)

Gaukroger, Stephen, *Descartes: An Intellectual Biography* (Oxford, 1997)

Gay, Peter, *The Enlightenment: An Interpretation* (New York, 1966)

Geary, Robert F., *The Supernatural in Gothic Fiction: Horror, Belief, and Literary Change* (Lewiston [N.Y.], 1992)

Gellera, Giovanni, 'The Philosophy of Robert Forbes: A Scottish Scholastic Response to Cartesianism', *Journal of Scottish Philosophy* 11 (2013), 191–211

Gent, Jacqueline Van, *Magic, Body and the Self in Eighteenth-Century Sweden* (Leiden, 2009)

Gifford, Douglas, '"Nathaniel Gow's Toddy": The Supernatural in Lowland Scottish Literature from Burns and Scott to the Present Day', in Lizanne Henderson (ed.), *Fantastical Imaginations: The Supernatural in Scottish History and Culture* (Edinburgh, 2009), 110–40

Glouberman, M., *Descartes: The Probable and the Certain* (Amsterdam, 1986)

Le Goff, Jacques, *The Birth of Purgatory*, trans. Arthur Goldhammer (Chicago, 1986)

Goodare, Julian, 'Between Humans and Angels: Scientific Uses for Fairies in Early Modern Scotland', in Michael Ostling (ed.), *Fairies, Demons and Nature Spirits: 'Small Gods' at the Margins of Christendom* (London, 2018), 169–90

——, 'The Cult of the Seely Wights in Scotland', *Folklore* 123 (2012), 198–219

——, 'Scotland', in Bob Scribner, Roy Porter and Mikuláš Teich (eds), *The Reformation in National Context* (Cambridge, 1994), 95–110

——, 'Scottish Witchcraft in Its European Context', in Julian Goodare, Lauren Martin and Joyce Miller (eds), *Witchcraft and Belief in Early Modern Scotland* (Basingstoke, 2008), 26–50

——, 'The Scottish Witchcraft Panic of 1597', in Julian Goodare (ed.), *The Scottish Witch-Hunt in Context* (Manchester, 2002), 51–72

——, (ed.), *Scottish Witches and Witch-Hunters* (Basingstoke, 2013)

——, (ed.), *The Scottish Witch-Hunt in Context* (Manchester, 2002)

——, 'Witchcraft in Scotland', in Brian P. Levack (ed.), *The Oxford Handbook of Witchcraft in Early Modern Europe and Colonial America* (Oxford, 2013), 300–17

——, 'Women and the Witch-Hunt in Scotland', *Social History* 23 (1998), 288–308

Goodare, Julian et al., 'Introduction to Scottish Witchcraft', *The Survey of Scottish Witchcraft* (University of Edinburgh, 2003), http://www.shca.ed.ac.uk/research/witches/introduction.html, accessed 1 Feb. 2018

Goodare, Julian, Lauren Martin and Joyce Miller (eds), *Witchcraft and Belief in Early Modern Scotland* (Basingstoke, 2008)

Gordon, Anne, *Candie for the Foundling* (Edinburgh, 1992)

Gordon, Avery, *Ghostly Matters: Haunting and the Sociological Imagination*, 2nd edn (Minneapolis, 2008)

Gordon, Bruce, 'Malevolent Ghosts and Ministering Angels: Apparitions and Pastoral Care in the Swiss Reformation', in Bruce Gordon and Peter Marshall (eds), *The Place of the Dead: Death and Remembrance in Late Medieval and Early Modern Europe* (Cambridge, 2000), 87–109

Gordon, J. F. S., 'Introit', in William Ogilvie, *The Laird o' Coul's Ghost* (London, 1892), v–x

Göttler, Christine, and Wolfgang Neuber (eds), *Spirits Unseen: The Representation of Subtle Bodies in Early Modern European Culture* (Leiden, 2008)

Gottlieb, Evan, *Feeling British: Sympathy and National Identity in Scottish and English Writing, 1707–1832* (Lewisburg [Pa.], 2007)

Gowing, Laura, 'The Haunting of Susan Lay: Servants and Mistresses in Seventeenth-Century England', *Gender & History* 14 (2002), 183–201

Graham, Gordon, *The Re-Enchantment of the World: Art versus Religion* (Oxford, 2007)

Graham, Michael F., *The Blasphemies of Thomas Aikenhead: Boundaries of Belief on the Eve of the Enlightenment* (Edinburgh, 2008)

Greenblatt, Stephen, *Hamlet in Purgatory* (Princeton, 2001)
Gribben, Crawford, 'Religion and Scottish Romanticism', in Murray Pittock (ed.), *The Edinburgh Companion to Scottish Romanticism* (Edinburgh, 2011)
Hall, Daniel, *French and German Gothic Fiction in the Late Eighteenth Century* (Bern, 2005)
Handley, Sasha, 'Apparitions and Anglicanism in 1750s Warwickshire', in Peter Clarke and Tony Claydon (eds), *The Church, the Afterlife and the Fate of the Soul* (Woodbridge, 2009), 311–22
——, 'Reclaiming Ghosts in 1690s England', in Kate Cooper and Jeremy Gregory (eds), *Signs, Wonders, Miracles: Representations of Divine Power in the Life of the Church* (Woodbridge, 2005), 345–55
——, *Sleep in Early Modern England* (New Haven, 2016)
——, *Visions of an Unseen World: Ghost Beliefs and Ghost Stories in Eighteenth-Century England* (London, 2007)
Hanegraaff, Wouter J., 'How Magic Survived the Disenchantment of the World', *Religion* 33 (2003), 357–80
Hattaway, Michael, *Elizabethan Popular Theatre: Plays in Performance* (London, 1982)
Hefling, Charles, 'Scotland: Episcopalians and Nonjurors', in Charles Hefling and Cynthia Shattuck (eds), *The Oxford Guide to The Book of Common Prayer: A Worldwide Survey* (Oxford, 2006), 166–75
Heiland, Donna, *Gothic and Gender: An Introduction* (Oxford, 2004)
Helt, J. S. W., 'The "dead who walk": Materiality, Liminality and the Supernatural World in Francois Richard's "Of false revenants"', *Mortality* 5 (2010), 7–17
Henderson, Hamish, 'The Ballad and Popular Tradition to 1660', in R. D. S. Jack (ed.), *The History of Scottish Literature, Vol. 1: Origins to 1600* (Aberdeen, 1988), 263–84
Henderson, Lizanne, 'The Road to Elfland: Fairy Belief and the Child Ballads', in Edward J. Cowan (ed.), *The Ballad in Scottish History* (East Linton, 2000), 54–72
——, 'The (Super)natural Worlds of Robert Kirk: Fairies, Beasts, Landscapes and Lychnobious Liminalities', *Bottle Imp* 20 (2006), 1–4.
——, 'The Survival of Witchcraft Prosecutions and Witch Belief in South-West Scotland', *Scottish Historical Review* 85 (2006), 52–74
Henderson, Lizanne, and Edward J. Cowan, *Scottish Fairy Belief: A History* (East Linton, 2001)
Henry, John, 'Psychology and the Laws of Nature: From Souls to the Powers of the Mind in the Scottish Enlightenment', in Andrew Cunningham and Ole Peter Grell (eds), *Medicine and Religion in Enlightenment Europe* (Aldershot, 2007), 243–58
Heyd, Michael, *Be Sober and Reasonable: The Critique of Enthusiasm in the Seventeenth and Early Eighteenth Centuries* (Leiden, 1995)
Hoffman, Paul, *Essays on Descartes* (New York, 2009)
Holland, Richard, *Haunted Wales* (Stroud, 2011)
Houran, James, and Rense Lange (eds), *Hauntings and Poltergeists: Multidisciplinary Perspectives* (Jefferson [N.C.], 2001)
Houston, R. A., *Madness and Society in Eighteenth-Century Scotland* (Oxford, 2000)
——, *Punishing the Dead?: Suicide, Lordship, and Community in Britain, 1500–1830* (Oxford, 2010)
——, *Scottish Literacy and the Scottish Identity: Illiteracy and Society in Scotland and Northern England, 1600–1800* (Cambridge, 2002)
——, *Social Change in the Age of Enlightenment: Edinburgh, 1660–1760* (Oxford, 1994)
——, 'Women in the Economy and Society of Scotland, 1500–1800', in R. A. Houston and I. D. Whyte (eds), *Scottish Society, 1500–1800* (Cambridge, 1989), 118–47

Houston, R. A., and I. D. Whyte, 'Introduction: Scottish Society in Perspective', in R. A. Houston and I. D. Whyte (eds), *Scottish Society, 1500–1800* (Cambridge, 1989), 1–36

Hunter, Michael, 'Introduction', in Michael Hunter (ed.), *The Occult Laboratory: Magic, Science, and Second Sight in Late Seventeenth-Century Scotland* (Woodbridge, 2001), 1–33

——, 'New Light on the "Drummer of Tedworth": Conflicting Narratives of Witchcraft in Restoration England', *Historical Research* 78 (2005), 311–53

——, '*Pitcairneana*: An Atheist Text by Archibald Pitcairne', *Historical Journal* 59 (2016), 595–621

——, 'The Problem of "Atheism" in Early Modern England', *Transactions of the Royal Historical Society* 35 (1985), 135–57

——, *Robert Boyle, 1627–91: Scrupulosity and Science* (Woodbridge, 2000)

Hunter, Michael and David Wootton, 'Introduction', in Michael Hunter and David Wootton (eds), *Atheism from the Reformation to the Enlightenment* (Oxford, 1992), 1–12

Hutton, Ronald, *The Stations of the Sun: A History of the Ritual Year in Britain* (Oxford, 1996)

Israel, Jonathan I., *Democratic Enlightenment: Philosophy, Revolution, and Human Rights 1750–1790* (Oxford, 2011)

——, *Radical Enlightenment: Philosophy and the Making of Modernity, 1650–1750* (Oxford, 2001)

Jakobsson, Ármann, 'The Fearless Vampire Killers: A Note about the Icelandic *Draugr* and Demonic Contamination in *Grettis Saga*', *Folklore* 120 (2009), 307–16

Jenkins, Richard, 'Enchantment and Re-Enchantment: Max Weber at the Millennium', *Max Weber Studies* 1 (2000), 11–32

Jestice, Phyllis G., *Encyclopedia of Irish Spirituality* (Santa Barbara, 2000)

Jones, Charles, 'Nationality and Standardisation in Eighteenth-Century Scotland', in Raymond Hickey (ed.), *Eighteenth-Century English: Ideology and Change* (Cambridge, 2010), 221–34

Jones, Leonidas M., 'The Scott-Christie Duel', *Texas Studies in Literature and Language* 12 (1971), 605–29

Josephon-Storm, Jason Ā, *The Myth of Disenchantment: Magic, Modernity, and the Birth of the Human Sciences* (Chicago, 2017)

Kanerva, Kirsi, 'From Powerful Agents to Subordinate Objects? The Restless Dead in Thirteenth- and Fourteenth-Century Iceland', in Joëlle Rollo-Koster (ed.), *Death in Medieval Europe: Death Scripted and Death Choreographed* (Abingdon, 2017), 40–70

Kapitaniak, Pierre, *Spectres, Ombres et Fantômes: Discours et Représentations Dramatiques en Angleterre, 1576–1642* (Paris, 2008)

Kaplan, Barbara Beigun, 'Turberville, Daubeney (1612–1696)', *Oxford DNB* (Oxford University Press, 2004), http://www.oxforddnb.com/view/article/27823, accessed 1 Feb. 2018

Kennedy, David J., *Eucharistic Sacramentality in an Ecumenical Context* (Farnham, 2013)

Keyworth, David, *Troublesome Corpses: Vampires and Revenants from Antiquity to the Present* (Southend-on-Sea, 2007)

——, 'Was the Vampire of the Eighteenth Century a Unique Type of Undead-Corpse?', *Folklore* 117 (2006), 241–60

Kidd, Colin, 'Conditional Britons: The Scots Covenanting Tradition and the Eighteenth-Century British State', *English Historical Review* 117 (2002), 1147–76

——, 'Gaelic Antiquity and National Identity in Enlightenment Ireland and Scotland', *English Historical Review* 109 (1994), 1197–1214

——, 'The Scottish Enlightenment and the Supernatural', in Lizanne Henderson (ed.), *Fantastical Imaginations: The Supernatural in Scottish History and Culture* (Edinburgh, 2009), 91–109

——, *Subverting Scotland's Past: Scottish Whig Historians and the Creation of an Anglo-British Identity, 1689–1830* (Cambridge, 1993)

Killick, Tim, *British Short Fiction in the Early Nineteenth Century: The Rise of the Tale* (Aldershot, 2008)

Kim, Yosep, *The Identity and the Life of the Church: John Calvin's Ecclesiology in the Perspective of His Anthropology* (Eugene, 2014)

King, Charles W., 'The Roman Manes: The Dead as Gods', in Mu-chou Poo (ed.), *Rethinking Ghosts in World Religions* (Leiden, 2009), 95–114

Knowles, Claire, *Sensibility and Female Poetic Tradition, 1780–1860: The Legacy of Charlotte Smith* (Farnham, 2009)

Köhler-Zülch, Ines, 'Heinrich Prohle: A Successor to the Brothers Grimm', in Donald Haase (ed.), *The Reception of Grimms' Fairy Tales: Responses, Reactions, Revisions* (Detroit, 1993), 41–58

Kornahrens, Douglas, 'Praying for the Christian Departed: A Brief View of the Doctrine and Practice in Scottish Episcopacy', *Theology in Scotland* 18 (2011), 47–79

Kyle, Richard, 'John Knox's Concept of Divine Providence and Its Influence on His Thought', *Albion* 18 (1986), 395–410

Landy, Joshua and Michael Saler, 'Introduction', in Joshua Landy and Michael Saler (eds), *The Re-Enchantment of the World: Secular Magic in a Rational Age* (Stanford, 2009), 1–15

——, (eds), *The Re-Enchantment of the World: Secular Magic in a Rational Age* (Stanford, 2009)

Lang, Andrew, *Cock Lane and Common-Sense* (London, 1894)

Larner, Christina, *Enemies of God: The Witch-Hunt in Scotland* (London, 1981)

Lecouteux, Claude, *Return of the Dead: Ghosts, Ancestors, and the Transparent Veil of the Pagan Mind*, trans. John E. Graham (Rochester [Vt.], 2009)

Lenman, Bruce, *The Jacobite Risings in Britain, 1689–1746* (Dalkeith, 1980)

Levack, Brian P., *The Devil Within: Possession and Exorcism in the Christian West* (New Haven: Yale University Press, 2013)

——, *Witch-Hunting in Scotland: Law, Politics and Religion* (London, 2008)

Lewis, Belinda, 'Protestantism, Pragmatism and Popular Religion: A Case Study of Early Modern Ghosts', in John Newton and Jo Bath (eds), *Early Modern Ghosts* (Durham, 2002), 79–92

Llewellyn, Nigel, *Art of Death: Visual Culture in the English Death Ritual c.1500–c.1800* (London, 1991)

Lovat-Fraser, J. A., *John Stuart, Earl of Bute* (Cambridge, 1912)

Love, Dane, *Scottish Ghosts* (London, 1995)

Lyle, Emily (ed.), *Scottish Ballads* (Edinburgh, 1994)

Lynch, Michael, 'Preaching to the Converted? Perspectives on the Scottish Reformation', in A. A. MacDonald, M. Lynch and I. B. Cowan (eds), *The Renaissance in Scotland: Studies in Literature, Religion, History and Culture* (Leiden, 1994), 301–43

——, *Scotland: A New History* (London, 1992)

MacDonald, Alexander, 'Highland Ghosts', *Transactions of the Gaelic Society of Inverness* 14 (1899), 40–9

Macdougall, Norman, *James IV: The Stewart Dynasty in Scotland* (Edinburgh, 2006)

Macfarlane, Alan, *Witchcraft in Tudor and Stuart England: A Regional and Comparative Study* (London, 1970)

Macinnes, Allan I., *Union and Empire: The Making of the United Kingdom in 1707* (Cambridge, 2007)

Mackelvie, William, *Annals and Statistics of the United Presbyterian Church* (Edinburgh, 1873)

Mackie, R. L., *King James IV of Scotland: A Brief Survey of His Life and Times* (London, 1976)

MacKinnon, Donald and Alick Morrison, *The MacLeods: The Genealogy of a Clan*, 5 vols (Edinburgh, 1968–76)

Maclagan, R. C., 'Ghost Lights of the West Highlands', *Folklore* 8 (1897), 203–56

MacQueen, John, 'Introduction', in John MacQueen (ed.), *The Phanaticks* (Woodbridge, 2012)

MacQueen, John and Winifred MacQueen, 'Commentary', in John MacQueen and Winifred MacQueen (eds), *Archibald Pitcairne: The Latin Poems* (Assen, 2009), 301–458

——, 'Introduction', in John MacQueen and Winifred MacQueen (eds), *Archibald Pitcairne: The Latin Poems* (Assen, 2009), 1–64

Maggi, Armando, *In the Company of Demons: Unnatural Beings, Love, and Identity in the Italian Renaissance* (Chicago, 2006)

Maple, Eric, *The Realm of Ghosts* (London, 1964)

Marshall, Peter, *Beliefs and the Dead in Reformation England* (Oxford, 2002)

——, 'Deceptive Appearances: Ghosts and Reformers in Elizabethan and Jacobean England', in Helen Parish and William G. Naphy (eds), *Religion and Superstition in Reformation Europe* (Manchester, 2002), 188–208

——, 'The Guardian Angel in Protestant England', in Joad Raymond (ed.), *Conversations with Angels: Essays Towards a History of Spiritual Communication, 1100–1700* (Basingstoke, 2011), 295–316

——, '"The Map of God's Word": Geographies of the Afterlife in Tudor and Early Stuart England', in Bruce Gordon and Peter Marshall (eds), *The Place of the Dead: Death and Remembrance in Late Medieval and Early Modern Europe* (Cambridge, 2000), 110–30

——, *Mother Leakey and the Bishop: A Ghost Story* (Oxford, 2007)

Marshall, Peter and Alexandra Walsham (eds), *Angels in the Early Modern World* (Cambridge, 2006)

Mason, Roger (ed.), *John Knox and the British Reformations* (Aldershot, 1998)

Mathison, Hamish, 'Gothic Poetry in Scotland: The Ghaistly Eighteenth Century', *Gothic Studies* 14 (2012), 34–46

——, '"Out of Tune": Sex, Death and Gothic Disharmony in Eighteenth-Century Scotland', in Jolene Zigarovich (ed.), *Sex and Death in Eighteenth-Century Literature* (Abingdon, 2013), 224–40

Maxwell-Stuart, P. G., *Ghosts: A History of Phantoms, Ghouls and Other Spirits of the Dead* (Stroud, 2006)

——, *Poltergeists: A History of Violent Ghostly Phenomena* (Stroud, 2011)

——, 'Witchcraft and Magic in Eighteenth-Century Scotland', in Owen Davies and Willem de Blécourt (eds), *Beyond the Witch Trials: Witchcraft and Magic in Enlightenment Europe* (Manchester, 2004), 81–99

McCallum, John, *Reforming the Scottish Parish: The Reformation in Fife, 1560–1640* (Aldershot, 2010)

McCorristine, Shane, *Spectres of the Self: Thinking About Ghosts and Ghost-Seeing in England, 1750–1920* (Cambridge, 2010)

McDannell, Colleen and Bernhard Lang, *Heaven: A History*, 2nd edn (New Haven, 2001)

McGill, Martha, 'Angels, Devils, and Discernment in Early Modern Scotland', in Michelle D. Brock, Richard Raiswell and David Winter (eds), *Knowing Demons, Knowing Spirits* (Basingstoke, 2018), 239–63

——, 'A Protestant Purgatory? Visions of an Intermediate State in Eighteenth-Century Scotland', *Scottish Historical Review* 97 (2018), 153–86.

McIntosh, John R., *Church and Theology in Enlightenment Scotland: The Popular Party, 1740–1800* (East Linton, 1997)

McKerlie, P. H., *History of the Lands and Their Owners in Galloway*, 5 vols (Edinburgh, 1870–9)

McLean, Scott A., 'Cleansing the Hawker's Basket: Popular Literature and the Cheap Periodical Press in Scotland', *Studies in Scottish Literature* 32 (2001), 88–100

McManners, John, *Death and the Enlightenment: Changing Attitudes to Death Among Christians and Unbelievers in Eighteenth-Century France* (Oxford, 1981)

McNeil, Kenneth, *Scotland, Britain, Empire: Writing the Highlands, 1760–1860* (Columbus, 2007)

Means, J. A., 'The Composition of *The Grave*', *Studies in Scottish Literature* 10 (1972), 3–9

Meek, Donald E., 'The Gaelic Ballads of Scotland: Creativity and Adaptation', in Howard Gaskill (ed.), *Ossian Revisited* (Edinburgh, 1991), 19–48

Menn, Stephen, *Descartes and Augustine* (Cambridge, 2002)

Midelfort, H. C. Erik, *Exorcism and Enlightenment: Johann Joseph Gassner and the Demons of Eighteenth-Century Germany* (New Haven, 2005)

——, 'Madness and Civilization in Early Modern Europe: A Reappraisal of Michel Foucault', in Barbara C. Malament (ed.), *After the Reformation: Essays in Honor of J. H. Hexter* (Manchester, 1980), 247–66

Miles, Robert, *Gothic Writing, 1750–1820: A Genealogy*, 2nd edn (Manchester, 2002)

Miller, Frank, 'The Laird of Coul's Ghost: A Galloway Chap-Book', *Transactions of the Dumfriesshire and Galloway Natural History & Antiquarian Society*, 3rd ser., 14 (1927), 259–72

Miller, Joyce, 'Men in Black: Appearances of the Devil in Early Modern Scottish Witchcraft Discourse', in Julian Goodare, Lauren Martin and Joyce Miller (eds), *Witchcraft and Belief in Early Modern Scotland* (Basingstoke, 2008), 144–65

Monod, Paul Kléber, *Solomon's Secret Arts: The Occult in the Age of Enlightenment* (New Haven, 2013)

Morris, David B., 'A Poetry of Absence', in John Sitter (ed.), *The Cambridge Companion to Eighteenth-Century Poetry* (Cambridge, 2001), 225–48

Morrison, Robert and Daniel S. Roberts, '"A character so various, and yet so indisputably its own": A Passage to *Blackwood's Edinburgh Magazine*', in Robert Morrison and Daniel S. Roberts (eds), *Romanticism and* Blackwood's *Magazine: 'An Unprecedented Phenomenon'* (Basingstoke, 2013), 1–19

Morton, Graeme, *Unionist-Nationalism: Governing Urban Scotland, 1830–1860* (East Linton, 1999)

Mullan, David George, *Narratives of the Religious Self in Early-Modern Scotland* (Aldershot, 2010)

Murphy, Andrew, 'Shakespeare Goes to Scotland: A Brief History of Scottish Editions', in Willy Maley and Andrew Murphy (eds), *Shakespeare and Scotland* (Manchester, 2004), 157–71

Murray, Alexander, *Suicide in the Middle Ages, Vol. 2: The Curse on Self-Murder* (Oxford, 2000)

Nash, David and Anne-Marie Kilday, *Cultures of Shame: Exploring Crime and Morality in Britain 1600–1900* (Basingstoke, 2010)

Nenadic, Stana, 'The Rise of the Urban Middle Classes', in Tom M. Devine and Rosalind Mitchison (eds), *People and Society in Scotland, Vol. 1: 1760–1830* (Edinburgh, 1998), 109–26

Newton, Michael, *A Handbook of the Scottish Gaelic World* (Dublin, 2000)

Oldridge, Darren, *Strange Histories: The Trial of the Pig, the Walking Dead, and Other Matters of Fact from the Medieval and Renaissance Worlds*, 2nd edn (Abingdon, 2018)

Oppenheim, Janet, *The Other World: Spiritualism and Psychical Research in England, 1850–1914* (Cambridge, 1988)

Oslington, Paul, 'Divine Action, Providence, and Adam Smith's Invisible Hand', in Paul Oslington (ed.), *Adam Smith as Theologian* (Abingdon, 2011), 61–74

Owens, Susan, *The Ghost: A Cultural History* (London, 2017)

Parisot, Eric, *Graveyard Poetry: Religion, Aesthetics and the Mid-Eighteenth-Century Poetic Condition* (Farnham, 2013)

Parker, Geoffrey, 'Success and Failure during the First Century of the Reformation', *Past & Present* 136 (1992), 43–82

Parker, Holt N., 'Toward a Definition of Popular Culture', *History & Theory* 50 (2011), 147–70

Parker, Mark, *Literary Magazines and British Romanticism* (Cambridge, 2001)

Parkinson, David J., '"The Legend of the Bischop of St. Androis Lyfe" and the Survival of Scottish Poetry', *Early Modern Literary Studies* 9 (2003), 51–24

Parsons, Coleman O., 'Introduction', in Coleman O. Parsons (ed.), *Satans Invisible World Discovered* (Gainesville, 1969), v-xxviii

Partridge, Christopher, *The Re-Enchantment of the West: Alternative Spiritualities, Sacralization, Popular Culture and Occulture*, 2 vols (London, 2004–5)

Pearl, Jonathan L., 'Sabbat', in Richard M. Golden (ed.), *Encyclopedia of Witchcraft: The Western Tradition*, 4 vols (Santa Barbara, 2006), vol. 4, 987–92

Pearson, Jacqueline, '"Then she asked it, what were its Sisters names?": Reading between the Lines in Seventeenth-Century Pamphlets of the Supernatural', *Seventeenth Century* 28 (2013), 63–78

Perkins, Maureen, 'The Meaning of Dream Books', in Daniel Pick and Lyndal Roper (eds), *Dreams and History: The Interpretation of Dreams from Ancient Greece to Modern Psychoanalysis* (Hove, 2004), 123–56

Pittock, Murray, 'Enlightenment, Romanticism and the Scottish Canon', in Gerard Carruthers and Liam McIlvanney (eds), *The Cambridge Companion to Scottish Literature* (Cambridge, 2012), 86–102

——, 'Introduction: What Is Scottish Romanticism?', in Murray Pittock (ed.), *The Edinburgh Companion to Scottish Romanticism* (Edinburgh, 2011), 1–9

——, *The Invention of Scotland: The Stuart Myth and the Scottish Identity, 1638 to the Present* (London, 1991)

——, *Scottish and Irish Romanticism* (Oxford, 2008)

Plank, Geoffrey, *Rebellion and Savagery: The Jacobite Rising of 1745 and the British Empire* (Philadelphia, 2005)

Pócs, Éva, *Between the Living and the Dead: A Perspective on Witches and Seers in the Early Modern Age* (Budapest, 1999)

Porter, Roy, 'Death and the Doctors in Georgian England', in Ralph Houlbrooke (ed.), *Death, Ritual, and Bereavement* (London, 1989), 77–94

——, *Enlightenment: Britain and the Creation of the Modern World* (London, 2000)

Pottle, Frederick A., *James Boswell: The Earlier Years, 1740–1769* (New York, 1966)

Puhle, Annekatrin, 'Ghosts, Apparitions and Poltergeist Incidents in Germany between 1700 and 1900', *Journal of the Society for Psychical Research* 63 (1999), 292–305

Punter, David, 'Scottish and Irish Gothic', in Jerrold E. Hogle (ed.), *The Cambridge Companion to Gothic Fiction* (Cambridge, 2002), 105–24
Purkiss, Diane, *Troublesome Things: A History of Fairies and Fairy Stories* (London, 2000)
Rackwitz, Martin, *Travels to Terra Incognita: The Scottish Highlands and Hebrides in Early Modern Travellers' Accounts, c.1600 to 1800* (Münster, 2007)
Raffe, Alasdair, 'Archibald Pitcairne and Scottish Heterodoxy, c.1688–1713', *Historical Journal* 60 (2017), 633–57
——, *The Culture of Controversy: Religious Arguments in Scotland, 1660–1714* (Woodbridge, 2012)
——, 'Intellectual Change before the Enlightenment: Scotland, the Netherlands and the Reception of Cartesian Thought, 1650–1700', *Scottish Historical Review* 94 (2015), 24–47
——, 'Presbyterianism, Secularization, and Scottish Politics after the Revolution of 1688–1690', *Historical Journal* 53 (2010), 317–37
——, 'Presbyterians and Episcopalians: The Formation of Confessional Cultures in Scotland, 1660–1715', *English Historical Review* 125 (2010), 570–98
Redwood, John, *Reason, Ridicule, and Religion: The Age of Enlightenment in England, 1660–1750* (Cambridge [Mass.], 1976)
Richardson, Ruth, *Death, Dissection and the Destitute* (London, 1987)
Risse, Guenter B., *New Medical Challenges during the Scottish Enlightenment* (Amsterdam, 2005)
Robertson, Fiona, *Legitimate Histories: Scott, Gothic, and the Authorities of Fiction* (Oxford, 1994)
Robinson, Christine and Roibeard Ó Maolalaigh, 'The Several Tongues of a Single Kingdom: The Languages of Scotland 1314–1707', in Ian Brown et al. (eds), *The Edinburgh History of Scottish Literature, Vol. 1: From Columba to the Union (until 1707)* (Edinburgh, 2007), 153–63
Roper, Lyndal, 'Witchcraft and Fantasy in Early Modern Germany', *History Workshop* 32 (1991), 19–43
Rose, Margaret A., *Parody//Meta-fiction* (London, 1979)
Ross, Ian Simpson, *The Life of Adam Smith*, 2nd edn (Oxford, 2010)
Roxburgh, Kenneth B. E., *Thomas Gillespie and the Origins of the Relief Church in 18th Century Scotland* (Bern, 1999)
Royan, Nicola and Dauvit Broun, 'Versions of Scottish Nationhood, c.850–1707', in Ian Brown et al. (eds), *The Edinburgh History of Scottish Literature, Vol. 1: From Columba to the Union (until 1707)* (Edinburgh, 2007), 168–83
Rugg, Julie, 'From Reason to Regulation: 1760–1850', in Peter C. Jupp and Clare Gittings (eds), *Death in England: An Illustrated History* (Manchester, 1999), 202–29
Saler, Michael, 'Modernity and Enchantment: A Historiographic Review', *American Historical Review* 111 (2006), 692–716
Sambrook, James, *James Thomson, 1700–1748: A Life* (Oxford, 1991)
Schmitt, Jean-Claude, *Ghosts in the Middle Ages: The Living and the Dead in Medieval Society*, trans. Teresa Lavender Fagan (Chicago, 1998)
Schofield, William Henry, *Mythical Bards and The Life of William Wallace* (Cambridge [Mass.], 1920)
Schwyzer, Philip, *Literature, Nationalism and Memory in Early Modern England and Wales* (Cambridge, 2004)
Scott, Hew, *Fasti Ecclesiae Scoticanae*, new edn, 7 vols (Edinburgh, 1915–28)
Scott, W. W., 'Lindsay, Robert, of Pitscottie (c.1532–c.1586)', *Oxford DNB* (Oxford University Press, 2004), http://www.oxforddnb.com/view/article/16715, accessed 1 Feb. 2018

Scribner, Bob, 'Is a History of Popular Culture Possible?', *History of European Ideas* 10 (1989), 175–91

——, 'The Reformation, Popular Magic, and the "Disenchantment of the World"', *Journal of Interdisciplinary History* 23 (1993), 475–94

Scullion, Adrienne, 'The Eighteenth Century', in Bill Findlay (ed.), *A History of Scottish Theatre* (Edinburgh, 1998), 80–136

Sharpe, James, *Instruments of Darkness: Witchcraft in Early Modern England* (London, 1996)

——, 'Witch-Hunting and Witch Historiography: Some Anglo-Scottish Comparisons', in Julian Goodare (ed.), *The Scottish Witch-Hunt in Context* (Manchester, 2002), 182–97

Sharp, L. W., 'Introduction', in L. W. Sharp (ed.), *Early Letters of Robert Wodrow* (Edinburgh, 1937), xv–l

Shaw, Jane, *Miracles in Enlightenment England* (New Haven, 2006)

Sher, Richard B., *Church and University in the Scottish Enlightenment: The Moderate Literati of Edinburgh* (Edinburgh, 1985)

——, *The Enlightenment and the Book: Scottish Authors and their Publishers in Eighteenth-Century Britain, Ireland, and America* (Chicago, 2007)

Shields, Juliet, *Sentimental Literature and Anglo-Scottish Identity, 1745–1820* (Cambridge, 2010)

Simpson, Jacqueline, *Icelandic Folktales and Legends* (Berkeley [Calif.], 1972)

——, 'Repentant Soul or Walking Corpse? Debatable Apparitions in Medieval England', *Folklore* 114 (2003), 389–402

——, '"The Weird Sisters Wandering": Burlesque Witchery in Montgomerie's Flyting', *Folklore* 106 (1995), 9–20

Simpson, Kenneth, *The Protean Scot: The Crisis of Identity in Eighteenth Century Scottish Literature* (Aberdeen, 1988)

Simpson, Robert, *History of Sanquhar* (Edinburgh, 1853)

Skoczylas, Anne, *Mr Simson's Knotty Case: Divinity, Politics, and Due Process in Early Eighteenth-Century Scotland* (Montreal, 2001)

Smajić, Srdjan, *Ghost-Seers, Detectives, and Spiritualists: Theories of Vision in Victorian Literature and Science* (Cambridge, 2010)

Smith, Andrew, *Gothic Literature* (Edinburgh, 2007)

Smith, Nigel, 'The Charge of Atheism and the Language of Radical Speculation, 1640–1660', in Michael Hunter and David Wootton (eds), *Atheism from the Reformation to the Enlightenment* (Oxford, 1992), 131–58

Soergel, Philip M., 'Miracle, Magic, and Disenchantment in Early Modern Germany', in Peter Schäfer and Hans G. Kippenberg (eds), *Envisioning Magic: A Princeton Seminar and Symposium* (Leiden, 1997), 215–34

——, *Miracles and the Protestant Imagination: The Evangelical Wonder Book in Reformation Germany* (New York, 2012)

Spicer, Andrew, '"Defyle Not Christ's Kirk with Your Carrion": Burial and the Development of Burial Aisles in Post-Reformation Scotland', in Bruce Gordon and Peter Marshall (eds), *The Place of the Dead: Death and Remembrance in Late Medieval and Early Modern Europe* (Cambridge, 2000), 149–69

Spinks, Bryan D., *Liturgy in the Age of Reason: Worship and Sacraments in England and Scotland 1662–c.1800* (Farnham, 2008)

Springborg, Patricia, 'Hobbes on Religion', in Tom Sorell (ed.), *The Cambridge Companion to Hobbes* (Cambridge, 1996), 346–80

Sprinker, Michael (ed.), *Ghostly Demarcations: A Symposium on Jacques Derrida's* Spectres of Marx (London, 1999)

Stafford, Fiona J., '"Dangerous Success": Ossian, Wordsworth, and English Romantic Literature', in Howard Gaskill (ed.), *Ossian Revisited* (Edinburgh, 1991), 49–72

——, 'Scottish Romanticism and Scotland in Romanticism', in Michael Ferber (ed.), *A Companion to European Romanticism* (Oxford, 2005), 49–66

——, *The Sublime Savage: James Macpherson and the Poems of Ossian* (Edinburgh, 1988)

Stephen, Jeffrey, *Scottish Presbyterians and the Act of Union 1707* (Edinburgh, 2007)

Stevenson, David, 'Blair, Robert (1593–1666)', *Oxford DNB* (Oxford University Press, 2004), http://www.oxforddnb.com/view/article/2569, accessed 1 Feb. 2018

Stewart, David, *Sketches of the Character, Manners, and Present State of the Highlanders of Scotland*, 2 vols (Edinburgh, 1822)

Stewart, M. A., 'The Early British Reception of Hume's Writings', in Peter Jones (ed.), *The Reception of David Hume in Europe* (London, 2005), 30–42

——, 'Religion and Rational Theology', in Alexander Broadie (ed.), *The Cambridge Companion to the Scottish Enlightenment* (Cambridge, 2003), 31–59

Strauss, Gerald, 'The Dilemma of Popular History', *Past & Present* 132 (1991), 130–49

——, 'The Dilemma of Popular History: Reply', *Past & Present* 141 (1993), 215–19

Strong, Rowan, *Episcopalianism in Nineteenth-Century Scotland: Religious Responses to a Modernizing Society* (Oxford, 2002)

Strong, Roy, *Tudor and Jacobean Portraits*, 2 vols (London, 1969)

Sugg, Richard, *Mummies, Cannibals, and Vampires: The History of Corpse Medicine from the Renaissance to the Victorians* (Abingdon, 2011)

Sutherland, Alex, *The Brahan Seer: The Making of a Legend* (Bern, 2009)

Suzuki, Akihito, 'Dualism and the Transformation of Psychiatric Language in the Seventeenth and Eighteenth Centuries', *History of Science: An Annual Review of Literature, Research and Teaching* 33 (1995), 417–47

Sveinsson, Einar Ólafur, *The Folk-Stories of Iceland* (London, 2003)

Tait, James, *Two Centuries of Border Church Life*, 2 vols (Kelso, 1889–91)

Tarlow, Sarah, *Ritual, Belief and the Dead in Early Modern Britain and Ireland* (Cambridge, 2011)

Thomas, Keith, *Religion and the Decline of Magic: Studies in Popular Beliefs in Sixteenth and Seventeenth Century England* (London, 1971)

Thompson, E. P., 'History from Below', *The Times Literary Supplement* 3345 (1996), 279

Thomson, Derick S., *The Gaelic Sources of Macpherson's Ossian* (Edinburgh, 1952)

——, *An Introduction to Gaelic Poetry*, 2nd edn (Edinburgh, 1989)

——, 'Macpherson, James (1736–1796)', *Oxford DNB* (Oxford University Press, 2004), http://www.oxforddnb.com/view/article/17728, accessed 1 Feb. 2018

Throness, Laurie, *A Protestant Purgatory: Theological Origins of the Penitentiary Act, 1779* (Aldershot, 2008)

Todd, Janet, *Sensibility: An Introduction* (London, 1986)

Todd, Margo, *The Culture of Protestantism in Early Modern Scotland* (New Haven, 2002)

Tongue, R. L., 'Folk-Song and Folklore', *Folklore* 78 (1967), 293–303

Trevor-Roper, Hugh, *The Invention of Scotland: Myth and History* (New Haven, 2008)

Trumpener, Katie, *Bardic Nationalism: The Romantic Novel and the British Empire* (Princeton, 1997)

Tulloch, Graham, 'Hogg and the Novel', in Ian Duncan (ed.), *The Edinburgh Companion to James Hogg* (Edinburgh, 2012), 122–31

Tyson, R. E., 'Population Patterns to 1770', in Michael Lynch (ed.), *Oxford Companion to Scottish History*, electronic edn (University of Oxford, 2007), http://www.oxfordreference.com/view/10.1093/acref/9780199234820.001.0001/acref-9780199234820-e-238?rskey=I3vw3P&result=1#acref-9780199234820-eSub-0180, accessed 1 Feb. 2018

Valletta, Frederick, *Witchcraft, Magic and Superstition in England, 1640–1670* (Aldershot, 2004)

VanderMolen, Ronald J., 'Providence as Mystery, Providence as Revelation: Puritan and Anglican Modifications of John Calvin's Doctrine of Providence', *Church History* 47 (1978), 27–47

Vidal, Fernando, 'Ghosts of the European Enlightenment', in Mu-chou Poo (ed.), *Rethinking Ghosts in World Religions* (Leiden, 2009), 163–82

Voges, Friedhelm, 'Moderate and Evangelical Thinking in the Later Eighteenth Century: Differences and Shared Attitudes', *Records of the Scottish Church History Society* 22 (1985), 141–57

Walker, D. P., 'The Cessation of Miracles', in Ingrid Merkel and Allen G. Debus (eds), *Hermeticism and the Renaissance: Intellectual History and the Occult in Early Modern Europe* (Washington, 1988), 111–24

Walsham, Alexandra, 'Invisible Helpers: Angelic Intervention in Post-Reformation England', *Past & Present* 208 (2010), 77–130

——, 'Miracles in Post-Reformation England', in Kate Cooper and Jeremy Gregory (eds), *Signs, Wonders, Miracles: Representations of Divine Power in the Life of the Church* (Woodbridge, 2005), 273–306

——, *Providence in Early Modern England* (Oxford, 1999)

——, 'The Reformation and "The Disenchantment of the World" Reassessed', *Historical Journal* 51 (2008), 497–528

——, *The Reformation of the Landscape: Religion, Identity, and Memory in Early Modern Britain and Ireland* (Oxford, 2011)

Wasser, Michael, 'The Mechanical World-View and the Decline of Witch-Beliefs in Scotland', in Julian Goodare, Lauren Martin and Joyce Miller (eds), *Witchcraft and Belief in Early Modern Scotland* (Basingstoke, 2008), 206–26

Watt, James, *Contesting the Gothic: Fiction, Genre and Cultural Conflict, 1764–1832* (Cambridge, 1999)

Weber, Max, *The Protestant Ethic and the Spirit of Capitalism*, trans. Talcott Parsons, electronic edn (Routledge, 2005), http://www.tandfebooks.com/action/showBook?doi=104324/9780203995808, accessed 1 Feb. 2018

——, 'Science as a Vocation', in H. H. Gerth and C. Wright Mills (eds), *From Max Weber: Essays in Sociology* (New York, 1946), 129–56

Wells, Stanley, 'Staging Shakespeare's Ghosts', in Murray Biggs (ed.), *The Arts of Performance in Elizabethan and Early Stuart Drama* (Edinburgh, 1991), 50–69

Wells, Vaughan T., 'Law, Robert (d. c.1686)', *Oxford DNB* (Oxford University Press, 2004), http://www.oxforddnb.com/view/article/16152, accessed 1 Feb. 2018

Westwood, Jennifer, and Sophia Kingshill, *The Lore of Scotland: A Guide to Scottish Legends* (London, 2009)

Whaley, Joachim (ed.), *Mirrors of Mortality: Studies in the Social History of Death* (Abingdon, 2011)

Whatley, Christopher A., *The Industrial Revolution in Scotland* (Cambridge, 1997)

Wheatley, Kim, 'The *Blackwood's* Attacks on Leigh Hunt', *Nineteenth-Century Literature* 47 (1992), 1–31

White, Allan, 'Gordon, George, Fourth Earl of Huntly (1513–1562)', *Oxford DNB* (Oxford University Press, 2004), http://www.oxforddnb.com/view/article/11034, accessed 1 Feb. 2018

Wigelsworth, Jeffrey R., *Deism in Enlightenment England: Theology, Politics, and Newtonian Public Science* (Manchester, 2009)

Wilby, Emma, *Cunning Folk and Familiar Spirits: Shamanistic Visionary Traditions in Early Modern British Witchcraft and Magic* (Brighton, 2005)

Wilson, Stephen, *The Magical Universe: Everyday Ritual and Magic in Pre-Modern Europe* (London, 2000)

Wilson, William, *Folk Lore and Genealogies of Uppermost Nithsdale* (Dumfries, 1904)

Wimberly, Lowry C., *Folklore in the English and Scottish Ballads* (Chicago, 1928)

Withers, Charles W. J., *Geography, Science and National Identity: Scotland Since 1520* (Cambridge, 2001)

Wolterstorff, Nicholas, 'Locke's Philosophy of Religion', in Vere Chappell (ed.), *The Cambridge Companion to Locke* (Cambridge, 1994), 172–98

Womack, Peter, *Improvement and Romance: Constructing the Myth of the Highlands* (Basingstoke, 1988)

Wood, J. Maxwell, *Witchcraft and Superstitious Record in Southwest Scotland* (Dumfries, 1911)

Wootton, David, 'New Histories of Atheism', in Michael Hunter and David Wootton (eds), *Atheism from the Reformation to the Enlightenment* (Oxford, 1992), 13–54

Wormald, Jenny, *Court, Kirk, and Community: Scotland, 1470–1625* (Edinburgh, 1991)

Wright, John P., 'Materialism and the Life Soul in Eighteenth-Century Scottish Physiology', in Paul Wood (ed.), *The Scottish Enlightenment: Essays in Reinterpretation* (Rochester [Vt.], 2000), 177–97

——, 'Metaphysics and Physiology: Mind, Body and the Animal Economy in Eighteenth-Century Scotland', in M. A. Stewart (ed.), *Studies in the Philosophy of the Scottish Enlightenment* (Oxford, 1990), 251–301

Wunderli, Richard, and Gerald Broce, 'The Final Moment before Death in Early Modern England', *Sixteenth Century Journal* 20 (1989), 259–75

Yeoman, Louise, '"Away with the Fairies"', in Lizanne Henderson (ed.), *Fantastical Imaginations: The Supernatural in Scottish History and Culture* (Edinburgh, 2009), 29–46

——, 'Wodrow, Robert (1679–1734)', *Oxford DNB* (Oxford University Press, 2004), http://www.oxforddnb.com/view/article/29819, accessed 1 Feb. 2018

Young, Francis, *English Catholics and the Supernatural, 1553–1829* (Farnham, 2013)

Zigarovich, Jolene (ed.), *Sex and Death in Eighteenth-Century Literature* (Abingdon, 2013)

Zipes, Jack, 'Introduction: The Golden Key to Folk and Fairy Tales: Unlocking Cultural Treasures', in Jack Zipes (ed.), *The Golden Age of Folk and Fairy Tales: From the Brothers Grimm to Andrew Lang* (Indianapolis, 2013), xvi–xxxvii

THESES

Carruthers, Gerard Charles, 'The Invention of Scottish Literature during the Long Eighteenth Century' (University of Glasgow Ph.D. thesis, 2001)

Cowdell, Paul, 'Belief in Ghosts in Post-War England' (University of Hertfordshire Ph.D. thesis, 2011)

DeLucia, JoEllen M., '"Tales of Other Times": Scotland's Past and Women's Future in Eighteenth-Century British Writing' (Indiana University Ph.D. thesis, 2007)

German, Kieran, 'Aberdeen, Aberdeenshire and Jacobitism in the North-East of Scotland, 1688-1750' (University of Aberdeen Ph.D. thesis, 2010)

Henderson, Lizanne, 'Supernatural Traditions and Folk Beliefs in an Age of Transition: Witchcraft and Charming in Scotland, c.1670–1740' (University of Strathclyde Ph.D. thesis, 2004)

Kornahrens, Wallace Douglas, 'Eucharistic Doctrine in Scottish Episcopacy, 1620-1875' (University of St. Andrews Ph.D. thesis, 2008)
McKeever, Amanda Jane, 'The Ghost in Early Modern Protestant Culture: Shifting Perceptions of the Afterlife, 1450–1700' (University of Sussex D.Phil. thesis, 2010)
Newton, John Geoffrey, 'An Examination of Interpretations of Ghosts from the Reformation to the Close of the Seventeenth Century' (Durham University Ph.D. thesis, 2003)
Raeburn, Gordon, 'The Long Reformation of the Dead in Scotland' (Durham University Ph.D. thesis, 2012)
Ridder-Patrick, Jane, 'Astrology in Early Modern Scotland, ca.1560–1726' (University of Edinburgh Ph.D. thesis, 2012)
Shepherd, Christine M., 'Philosophy and Science in the Arts Curriculum of the Scottish Universities in the 17th Century' (University of Edinburgh Ph.D. thesis, 1975)
Shepherd, Deirdre A. M., 'Walter Scott, James Hogg and Uncanny Testimony: Questions of Evidence and Authority' (University of Edinburgh Ph.D. thesis, 2009)

DATABASES

British Periodicals (ProQuest), http://bp.chadwyck.com
Dictionary of the Scots Language (Scottish Language Dictionaries), http://www.dsl.ac.uk
Early English Books Online (ProQuest), http://eebo.chadwyck.com/home
Eighteenth Century Collections Online (Gale), http://galenet.galegroup.com/servlet/ECCO
Eighteenth Century Journals (Adam Matthew), http://www.18thcjournals.amdigital.co.uk
English Short Title Catalogue (British Library), http://estc.bl.uk
Goodare, Julian et al., *The Survey of Scottish Witchcraft* (University of Edinburgh, 2003), http://www.shca.ed.ac.uk/witches
Oxford Dictionary of National Biography (Oxford University Press), http://oxforddnb.com
Oxford English Dictionary Online (Oxford University Press), http://www.oed.com
Playbills of the Theatre Royal Edinburgh (National Library of Scotland), http://digital.nls.uk/playbills
The Statistical Accounts of Scotland, 1791–1845 (University of Glasgow, University of Edinburgh), http://stataccscot.edina.ac.uk
The Word on the Street (National Library of Scotland, 2004), http://digital.nls.uk/broadsides
All last accessed 1 Feb. 2018.

Index